Illustrated History
of
Landscape Design

ELIZABETH BOULTS
and
CHIP SULLIVAN

WILEY

John Wiley & Sons, Inc.

Copyright © 2010 by John Wiley & Sons, Inc. All rights reserved

Published by John Wiley & Sons, Inc., Hoboken, New Jersey

Published simultaneously in Canada

For general information about our other products and services, please contact our Customer Care Department within the United States at (800) 762-2974, outside the United States at (317) 572-3993 or fax (317) 572-4002.

Wiley also publishes its books in a variety of electronic formats. Some content that appears in print may not be available in electronic books. For more information about Wiley products, visit our web site at www.wiley.com.

Library of Congress Cataloging-in-Publication Data:

Boults, Elizabeth, 1949-
   Illustrated history of landscape design / by Elizabeth Boults and Chip Sullivan.
      p. cm.
   Includes index.
   ISBN 978-0-470-28933-4 (cloth)
   1. Landscape design—History. I. Sullivan, Chip. II. Title.
   SB472.45.B68 2009
   712.09—dc22

                              2009041794

Printed in the United States of America

10 9 8 7 6 5 4 3 2 1

To our parents,
George and Florence Boults,
and
Mary Catherine Sullivan,
and the memory of Charles Harvey Sullivan.

Contents

Introduction... xi

PREHISTORY–6th CENTURY 1

Cosmological Landscapes   2

Ancient Gardens   4

Landscape and Architecture   6

Genius Loci   8

6th–15th CENTURIES.................................... 15

Western Europe: Walled Minds, Walled Gardens   20

Moorish Spain: An Indelible Influence   28

China: Nature's Splendor in a Garden   38

Japan: In the Spirit of Nature   46

15th CENTURY 57

Japan: Muromachi Era   61

China: Ming Dynasty   65

Central Asia: Timurid Garden Cities   66

Italy: Curious Minds, Broadened Vistas   68

16th CENTURY 75

Italy: The Rebirth of Rome   79

Renaissance Gardens in France and England   93

The Early Botanic Garden: An Encyclopedia of Plants   99

Early Mughal Gardens: Persian Art Forms Travel East   100

Japan: The Momoyama Era   101

17th CENTURY 107

Japan: Edo Period   111

The Mughal Empire: Sacred Symmetries   119

Persian Gardens of Paradise   124

CONTENTS

Italian Baroque Styles   127

The Flowering of the Dutch Landscape   133

English Gardens: A Restrained Mix of European Styles   134

French Classical Gardens: The Control of Nature   136

18th CENTURY   147

England: The Development of the Landscape Garden   151

The Landscape Garden in France   164

China: Qianlong's Imprint   165

Early American Gardens: Homeland Traditions   171

19th CENTURY   177

England: The Victorians and Their Plants   181

France: Republics and Empires   186

Landscape Architecture in America   189

20th CENTURY   203

The Gilded Age: Extremes of Wealth and Poverty   207

The New Aesthetic of Modernism   211

Environmental Art: Nature as Medium   219

Artistic Trends in Landscape Design   220

Environmental and Ecological Design   222

Postmodern Landscapes   223

21st CENTURY   231

A Sustainable Earth: Ten Ideas   232

Endnotes   245

Bibliography   251

Index   255

Acknowledgments

This work would not be possible without the significant contributions of Tim Mollette–Parks. His input was critical throughout the entire project. Tim provided invaluable assistance in visualizing a poetic format that married word and image, and offered insightful comments on the text. His research on current work formed the basis of the final chapter.

A residency at the MacDowell Colony was absolutely essential to our completion of the manuscript. We very much appreciated the opportunity to work without distraction in a truly creative and inspiring environment.

Heartfelt thanks are due to professors Randy Hester, Joe McBride, and Marc Treib for their belief in our approach. We are indebted to Marc for his comments on the Japanese garden sections. We thank, too, Elizabeth Byrne and her staff at the College of Environmental Design library, who helped direct us to important sources within the extraordinary collection.

Elizabeth's gratitude extends to Professor Heath Schenker, for first giving her the opportunity to teach landscape architecture history at the University of California, Davis; to Gerrie Robinson, whose commitment to teaching is admirable and whose moral support was constant; to her students, who enthusiastically embraced her approach to the subject; and to Pamela Cunningham, for expert wordsmithing. In addition, Elizabeth would like to acknowledge John Furlong, former director of the Radcliffe Seminars Landscape Design program, whose inspired teaching was instrumental in helping her discover her passion for landscape architecture.

Chip would like to thank the Department of Landscape Architecture and Environmental Planning at the University of California, Berkeley, for nurturing a place for creative expression; his students, who encourage and enrich his visual experimentations; and James Natalie, who provided valuable assistance at a crucial juncture. Additionally, the Beatrix Farrand Research Fund provided important research support for this project. Chip is also extremely thankful to Bill Thomson for publishing his comic strips in *Landscape Architecture* magazine, which set the gears in motion for this work. Finally, he would like to thank all the original artists of *Mad* magazine, who opened the door to a drawing life.

Introduction

The constructed landscape embodies a vision of creative power. The gardens and landscapes of the past serve as an endless source of possibility and inspiration. Discovering how the elements of nature have been recombined in different times and places intrigues us. Our purpose in assembling a visual reference of historic landscapes is to provide to the reader a useful guide that captures our exuberance for landscape design.

We examine landscape history as designers, and through the language of design, which is drawing. Plans, sections, elevations, and perspectives are all useful in communicating form and spatial relationships. To this vocabulary we've added sequential drawings, to capture the dynamic experience of space.

As an art form, a designed landscape is a cultural product, representing the ideals and values of its creator, owner, or patron, and situated within a unique social, economic, and political environment. Studying landscape history can inspire contemporary designers, and help them position their work in relationship to present circumstances. Precedents can be rejected or translated into current idioms. Our experience in leading summer study-abroad programs has taught us the value of firsthand experience of historic sites. Observation and analysis (accomplished through drawing) can inform the design process and elevate the quality of one's work.

Our approach to the material outlined in this book is unique in its design focus, chronological organization, and visual orientation. Presenting landscape history chronologically enables the reader to make cross-cultural connections and to understand how common themes may manifest themselves at different times, and to appreciate design trends that are truly unique. The idea for the graphic format originated with Chip's "creative learning" comic series in *Landscape Architecture* magazine. Visual media dominates culture today. Images transmit ideas. We hope the pen-and-ink illustrations in this book provide an overview of landscape history and encourage people to investigate the landscape through the act of drawing.

The content of the book is organized by century. Each section begins with a pictograph—an idea-drawing that illustrates the important concepts of the time period—followed by an illustrative timeline of some significant events in world history. These provide a broad context in which to examine specific works. Representative examples of gardens and designed landscapes are grouped according to geographic region. Spaces are portrayed through the use of storyboards, case studies, and visual narratives. Sections conclude with summaries of design concepts, principles, and vocabularies, as well as lists of "neat stuff"—historic and contemporary works of art that illuminate a specific era. The first and last chapters depart from this format and are designed as visual chronologies—embellished timelines organized thematically.

Built landscapes tell stories; a picture is worth a thousand words. Our goal is to take the reader on a visual romp through the great garden spaces of the past. We hope our work inspires the reader to further explore the landscape and discover his or her own story.

PREHISTORY TO 6th CENTURY

Early cultures attempted to re-create or express in their built landscapes the sacred meanings and spiritual significance of natural sites and phenomena. People altered the landscape to try to understand and/or honor the mysteries of nature. Early "landscape design" elaborated on humankind's intuitive impulse to dig and to mound. Our ancestors constructed earthworks, raised stones, and marked the ground, leaving traces of basic shapes and axial alignments. The purpose or function of many of these spaces is still conjecture.

Cultural values shifted in later antiquity with the advent of philosophical systems based on a human being's capacity for deductive reasoning. People looked for rational explanations for nature's mysteries. The ancient Greeks respected nature as the sanctuary of the Gods, but equally valued the human domain. Their focus on the role of the individual in relationship to the larger community fostered democratic ideals that were revealed in architecture, in urban form, and in the consideration of the landscape as a place of civic responsibility.

The illustrative chronology presented in this chapter is organized thematically, as follows:

* Cosmological Landscapes characterizes prehistoric earthworks and patterns.
* Ancient Gardens describes early parks and villas.
* Landscape and Architecture illustrates temple grounds, buildings, and important site plans.
* Genius Loci depicts sacred landscape spaces.

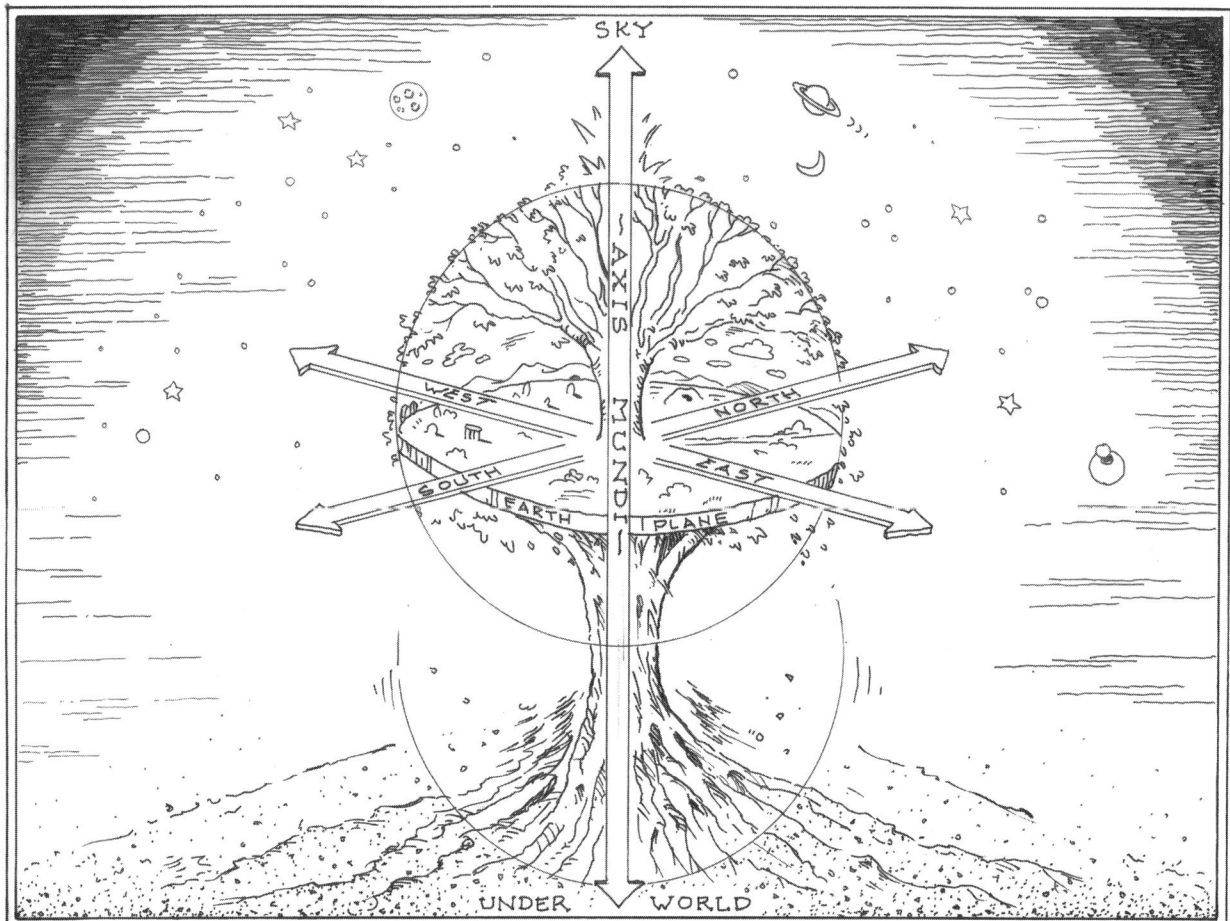

3500 BCE

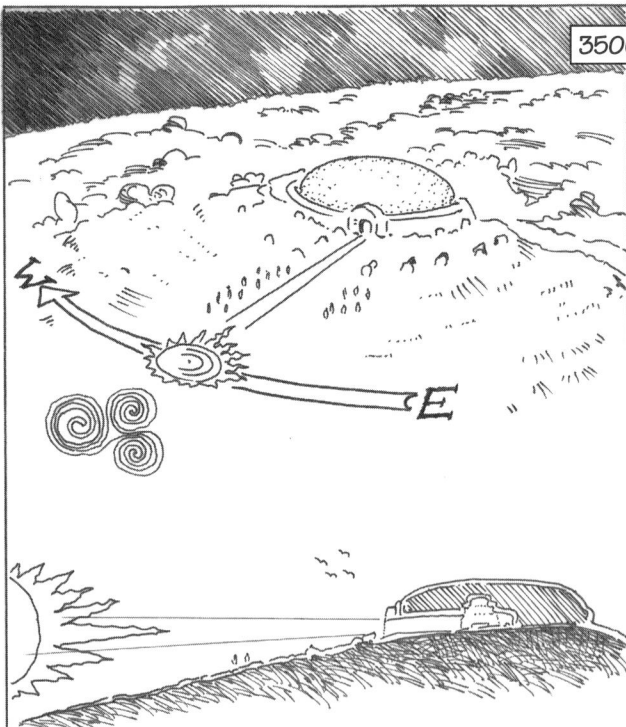

◀ *c. 3200 BCE*
NEW GRANGE, IRELAND
The circular passage tomb at New Grange is over 250 feet wide and contains three recessed chambers. On the winter solstice, the sun rises through a clerestory above the entryway, illuminating the central chamber. A curbstone carved with triple-spiral motifs marks the entryway.

▶ 2950 BCE–1600 BCE
STONEHENGE, ENGLAND
Built by different groups of people at different times, this particular site on the Salisbury plain in southwest England evolved from an earthen embankment, to a wooden structure, to the stone circles we recognize today. A circular ditch and bank (or "henge"), about 330 feet in diameter, marked the first phase of construction. Extant postholes within the circle indicate the position of a wooden structure from about 2600 BCE. The standing stones date from subsequent centuries. All the shapes open to the northeast, framing sunrise on the summer solstice.

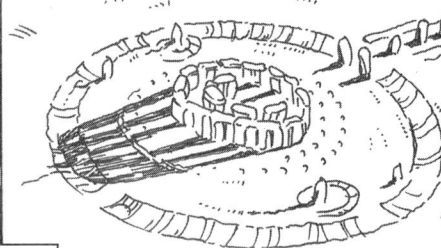

2000 BCE

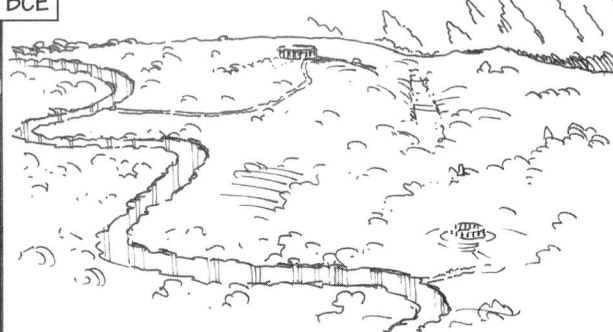

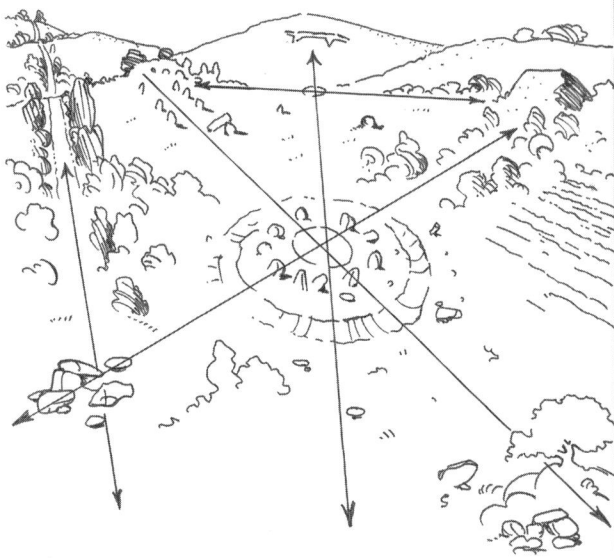

▲ Woodhenge, located about 2 miles from Stonehenge, was a timber circle of roughly the same diameter that marked a burial site dating from the Neolithic era. Sunrise on the summer solstice aligned with its entryway.

◀ LEY LINES, ENGLAND
Some people believe that Great Britain and continental Europe are marked with a network of straight lines that connect geographic features and sacred sites through underlying paths of energy within the earth.

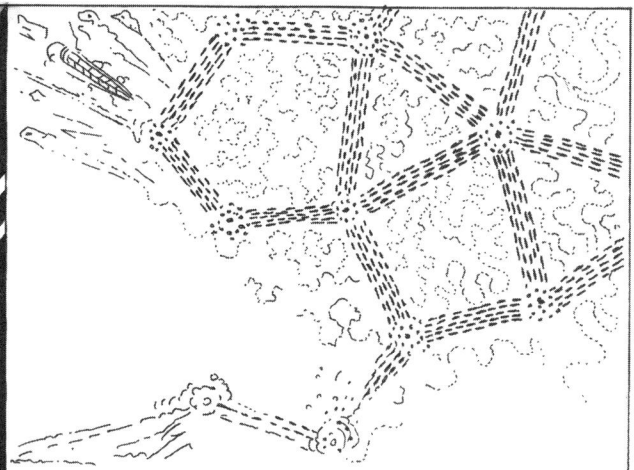

▶ SONGLINES, AUSTRALIA

Indigenous creation myths relate how ancestral beings walked the continent singing the world into existence. Native peoples were believed to have used these songlines as way-finding mechanisms. Traditional paintings illustrate similar spiritual journeys.

200 BCE

◀ 200 BCE–600 CE

NAZCA LINES, PERU

An extensive series of straight lines, geometric shapes, and animal figures were inscribed on the dry lake bed by overturning gravel and exposing the lighter-colored earth below. Archeologists are not certain which culture produced these geoglyphs, nor whether their purpose was related to religion, ritual, water sources, or astronomy.[1]

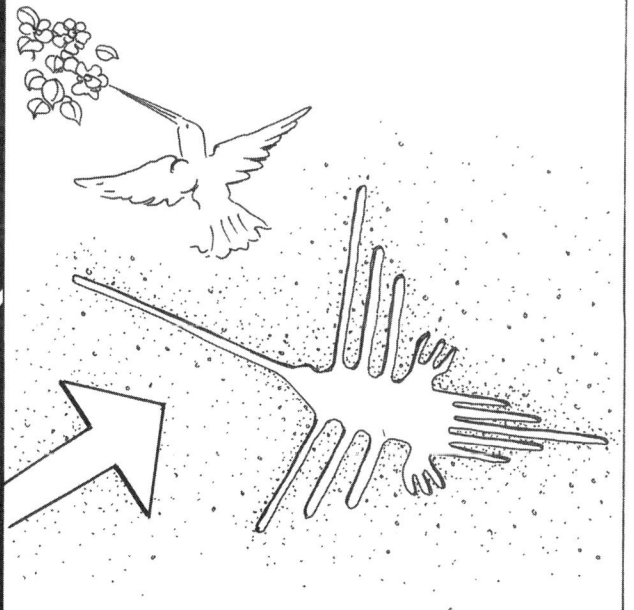

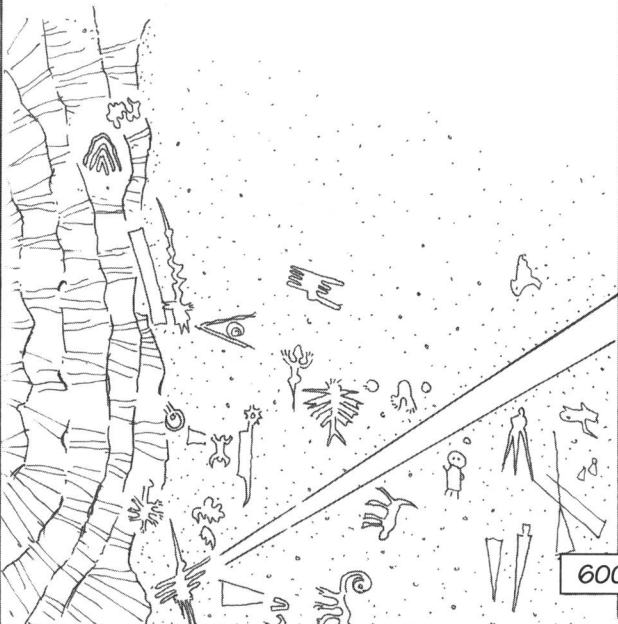

600 BCE

ANCIENT GARDENS

1500 BCE

◀**1380 BCE**
TOMB OF NEBAMUN, THEBES
The gardens depicted on the walls of wealthy Egyptian officials are an important primary source of information about the ancient Egyptian landscape. Shown here is an ordered arrangement of specific plants around a rectangular basin stocked with fish.

▶**2500 BCE–612 BCE**
MESOPOTAMIAN HUNTING PARKS
Written accounts describe the large enclosed parks of the Sumerians, Babylonians, and Assyrians as being stocked with exotic plants and animals—evidence of early management of the landscape. The Epic of Gilgamesh described the ancient Sumerian city of Uruk as being composed of equal parts city, garden, and field.[2]

500 BCE

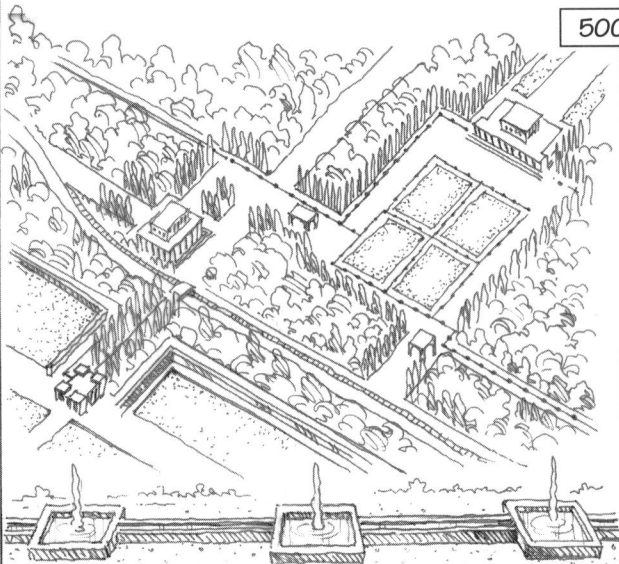

◀**546 BCE**
PASARGADAE, PERSIA
The imperial capital of Cyrus the Great was described by ancient Greeks and Romans as having a geometric division of space defined by water and trees, an early example of the four-square pattern later associated with "paradise" gardens. Existing ruins show the close relationship of buildings and gardens and the decorative use of water. Gardens provided visual and climatic comfort, not spaces for active use.[3]

50 CE

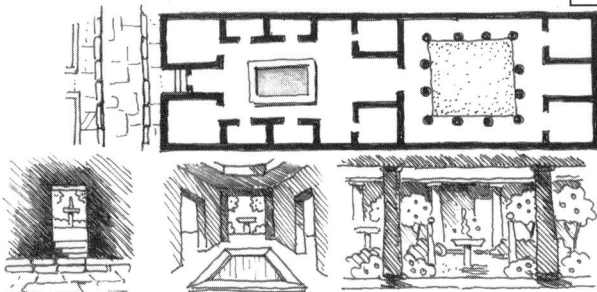

◀▲ *c. 79 CE*
HOUSE OF THE VETTII, POMPEII
The former Greek colony of Pompeii was a popular resort town for wealthy Romans. Forms of 1st-century architecture and landscape were preserved under layers of ash and debris from the eruption of Mt. Vesuvius in 79 CE. A typical Roman town house contained a paved atrium and a garden court surrounded by a roofed colonnade, or peristyle. Garden scenes painted on the walls of the peristyle garden visually extended the space.

100 CE

▲ *c.* 100 CE
PLINY'S SEASIDE VILLA, NEAR ROME
In his numerous letters, Pliny the Younger (61–112 CE) recorded many aspects of his life and times, including detailed descriptions of his country houses and their relationship to the landscape. He planned the rooms of his *villa marittima* according to their functional and climatic requirements, and to take advantage of views. The architectural form of Pliny's villa, as well as its function as a place of escape from urban responsibility, particularly inspired Renaissance designers.

500 CE

▲ 118 CE
HADRIAN'S VILLA, TIVOLI, ITALY
Located 15 miles east of Rome in the foothills of the Sabine mountains, the complex of structures and decorative elements that comprise the imperial villa of Hadrian reflect the emperor's fascination with architecture and his love of Classical culture. Today, ruins cover about 150 acres, or half of what scholars have estimated as the full extent of the villa.[4]

▶ *c.* 540 CE
SPRING OF KHOSROW CARPET (IRAQ)
Woven with gold and precious stones, the carpet made for the audience hall in King Khosrow's imperial palace near Baghdad was over 450 feet long. Depicting a lushly planted garden of rectangular beds divided by paths and watercourses, the carpet, which survives only through written accounts, symbolized an Eden-like paradise in a harsh desert environment.

1400 BCE

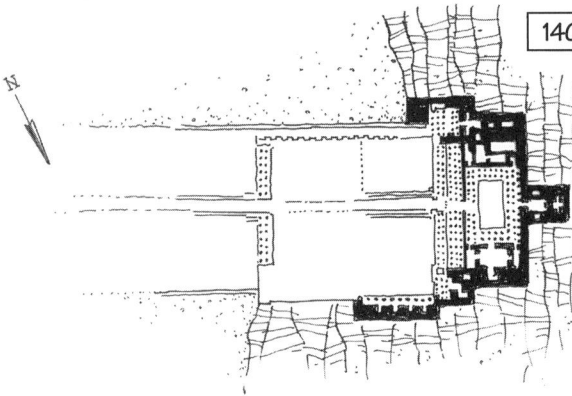

▲ 1400 BCE
MORTUARY TEMPLE OF HATSHEPSUT, DEIR EL-BAHRI, EGYPT

Dramatically sited at the base of a cliff on the west bank of the Nile River, Queen Hatshepsut's tomb comprised a series of monumental terraces and colonnades symmetrically organized around a processional axis. Tomb paintings show frankincense and myrrh trees imported from Somalia; archeological evidence confirms the presence of exotic vegetation on the terraces.[5]

◄ 460 BCE
ACROPOLIS, ATHENS, GREECE

A sacred hilltop site since the early Neolithic period, the acropolis was once the location of a Mycenaean fortress. It remains symbolic of Classical Greek civilization and the architecture of democracy. Following the war with Persia, the Athenian statesman Pericles undertook a major campaign to restore the city and rebuild its temples. The Parthenon dates from this era and represents the Doric order—a proportioning system based on the length and width of the column style.[6] The Panathenaic Way marked the route from the city gates to the acropolis.

400 BCE

▶ 200 BCE
ATHENIAN AGORA

The *agora* was the civic heart of Athens, where people gathered to conduct personal business and participate in municipal affairs. Tracing the use and development of this open space over the centuries frames an informative picture of Greek culture during the Archaic (*c.* 750–*c.* 480 BCE), Classical (*c.* 500–323 BCE), and Hellenistic (323–146 BCE) periods. The shaping of public space became more self-conscious.[7]

200 BCE

◀ **82 BCE**
TEMPLE OF FORTUNA PRIMIGENIA, PALESTRINA, ITALY
This monumental piece of urban design combined Hellenistic principles of movement about an axis with Roman arch technology. The grand staircases, ramps, and arcaded terraces that gracefully negotiated the slope and culminated in an exedra influenced Italian Renaissance designers. The sanctuary was over 1,000 feet above sea level and visible from the Tyrrhenian Sea.

80 BCE

▼▶ **c. 100–225 CE**
TEOTIHUACAN, MEXICO
With a population of more than 100,000 people, Teotihuacan, the cultural center of Aztec civilization, was the largest city in the world during the late 2nd century. The Avenue of the Dead formed the main axis of the orthogonally planned city, which was oriented toward the cardinal directions. The Temple of the Moon was the northern terminus and echoed the shape of Cerro Gordo. The Aztecs sited the Pyramid of the Sun over a cave near the middle of the axis. The large sunken plaza, the *ciudadela*, was located across what is now the San Juan River at the southern terminus of the axis.

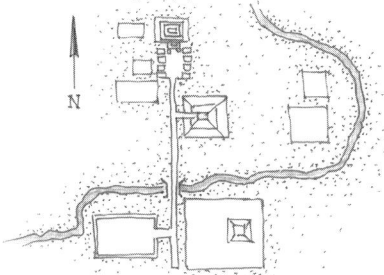

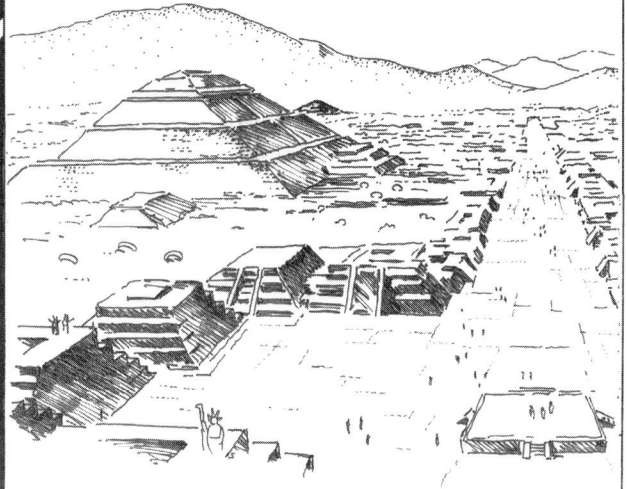

100 BCE

▲▶ **120 CE**
PANTHEON, ROME
Marcus Agrippa constructed a small temple on this site in 27 BCE. The current structure dates from the reign of Hadrian, and until the 15th century was the largest concrete dome ever built. The height of the dome equals its width; its proportions and construction methods were studied by Renaissance architects, particularly Brunelleschi, who designed an even larger dome for the cathedral in Florence. An opening in the center of the dome, the *oculus*, creates dramatic lighting and atmospheric effects.

2000 BCE

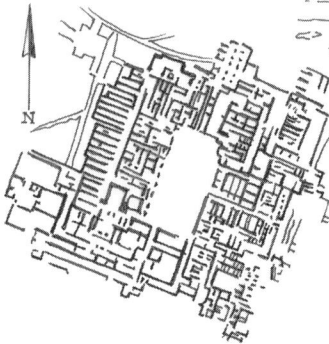

▲ MT. FUJI, JAPAN
Certain natural features, like mountains, were revered in many cultures as sacred spaces. Mt. Fuji was particularly sacred to Shinto followers.

▲ *c. 2000–1470 BCE*
MINOAN CIVILIZATION, CRETE
The unfortified palace at Knossos contained a large open courtyard. "Horns of consecration" placed about the palace represented the bull sacrifice and symbolized the sacredness of the space. A reconstructed pair of horns, interpreted also as the raised arms of the Earth Goddess, frames a view of a distant mountain sanctuary.

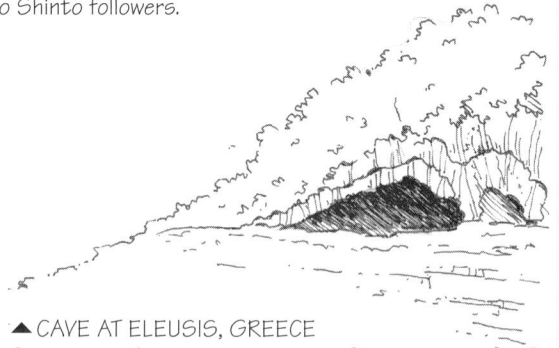

▲ CAVE AT ELEUSIS, GREECE
Caves were also important sites of ancient rites and rituals. The cave of Persephone at Eleusis was the site of the annual celebration of the rebirth of spring, reenacted as the mystery of Persephone's return from the underworld.

600 BCE

◀ *c. 600 BCE*
DELPHI, GREECE
Delphi was the site of a Mycenaean village and an oracular shrine of Gaia, the Earth Goddess. By the 7th century BCE the site had been rededicated to the worship of Apollo by the Greeks.

A

B

C

D

▲ Outside the *temenos*, or sacred precinct of Apollo, was the *tholos*, a circular temple in Athena's sanctuary (A), and the Castalian spring, an important pilgrimage station (B). The temple of Apollo itself (C) enclosed the *omphalos*, or navel of the earth, where vapors emanated from natural fissures. A priestess, perched on a tripod over the *omphalos*, burned laurel leaves in a sacred hearth (D). Attendant priests interpreted her prophecies.

500 BCE

▲ THE GANGES
More than 1,500 miles long, the Ganges River is believed to be the sacred river of salvation by Hindus. The riverside city of Varanasi became the capital of the Kashi kingdom in the 6th century BCE and remains a particularly holy place of worship in northern India. The riverbank is lined with temples, shrines, and steps, called *ghats*.

▲ 563–483 BCE
BODHI TREE, INDIA
According to Buddhist tradition, Gautama Buddha received Enlightenment under a Bodhi tree. The tree was revered by Buddhists as a holy shrine and remains a sacred pilgrimage site.

▲ 331 BCE
SIWA OASIS
Alexander the Great persevered through the Libyan desert by following birds to the western oasis, located in present day Egypt. The Siwa Oasis has been home to Berber tribespeople for hundreds of years, and was established as the site of the sacred oracle of Amun by the ancient Greeks.

300 BCE

▲ 219 BCE
ISLANDS OF THE IMMORTALS (CHINA)
Emperor Qin Shi Huangdi[8] was obsessed with finding an elixir of eternal life. He sent an expedition to the Himalayas to locate the mountaintop dwellings of the mythical Immortals. The Immortals never materialized, but the idea of creating a simulation of their homeland was popularized in the Han dynasty. Within his imperial palace grounds, Emperor Wudi (141–86 BCE) built three artificial mountains in a lake, establishing the influential prototype of the lake-and-island garden.

CASE STUDY: *Hadrian's Villa*

Hadrian (76–138 CE) collected ideas and treasures from places within his vast empire and reassembled them in his imperial estate near Rome. A Roman design vocabulary expressed foreign forms: the *canopus* (named after a branch of the Nile river) is a long rectangular canal, bordered by caryatids on one side and terminated at its southern end by an apsed *nymphaeum* (which possibly served as a dining room) and a semicircular colonnade at its northern end. The long *stoa poekile* (named for the painted stoa at Athens) provided a space to promenade year-round. The Vale of Tempe (a reference to the legendary forest at the foot of Mount Olympus), the Lyceum, and the Academy were other architectural elements of the villa that were inspired by Hadrian's interest in Greek culture.

The charming "maritime theater" is a small, rounded apsidal structure on a round island surrounded by columns and a moat; its function is unknown. Baths, theaters, libraries, guest quarters, and peristyle gardens were interconnected and decorated with artworks.

Set on a prow of land between two rivers, the proximity to water was necessary for the extensive waterworks, fountains, pools, and basins at the villa. Building sites respected the natural contours of the land, while terraces took advantage of views. No organizing geometry unified the site plan, although each self-contained space was organized axially. The site was held together conceptually by its thematic associations.

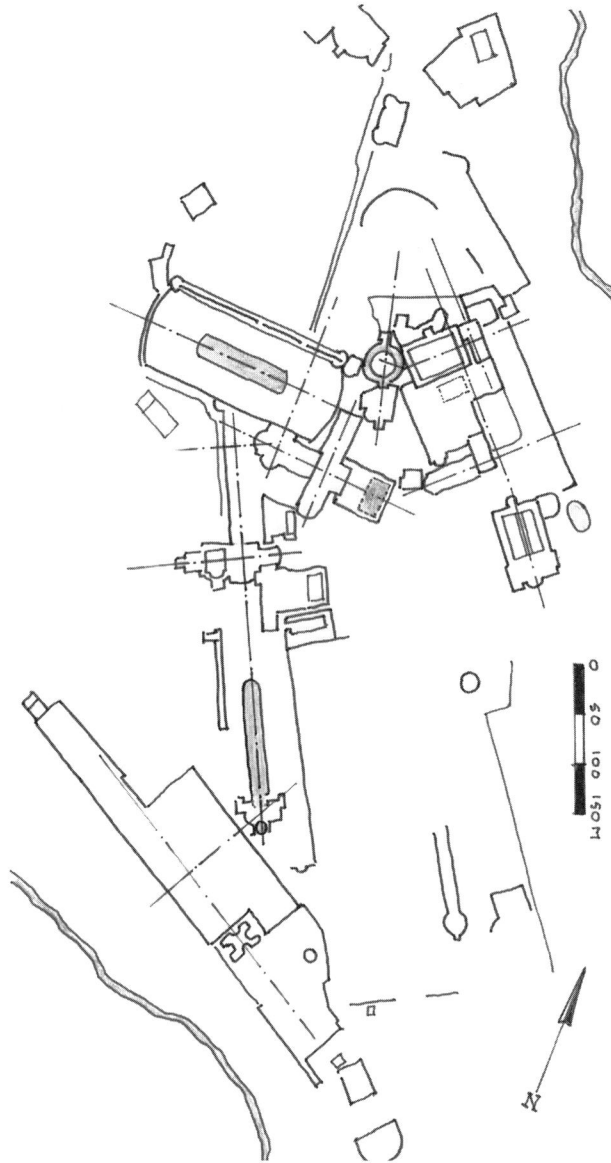

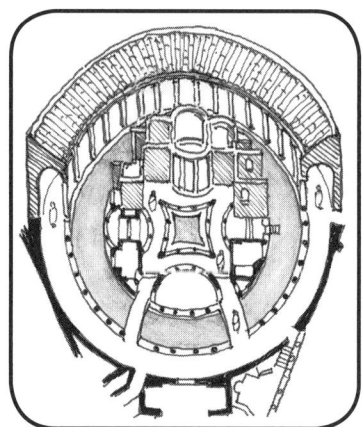

CASE STUDY: *Hadrian's Villa*

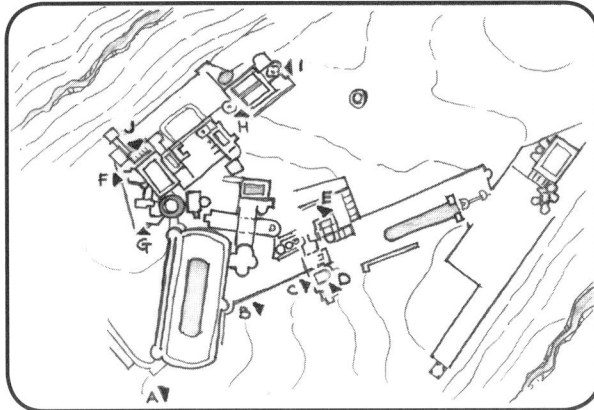

SUMMARY

Around 8,000 years ago, complex social systems began to emerge simultaneously in South and Central America, in Egypt and the Middle East, and in India and Asia.[9] Early civilizations established similar ways of communicating with the sacred spirits inherent in nature. As cultures advanced and humans gained more control over the natural world, we organized the landscape for physical and spiritual comfort. The idea of the garden as a managed pleasure ground evolved from the simple enclosed hunting grounds of Europe and Asia. In ancient Greece and Rome, a new trust in human logic resulted in the substitution of anthropomorphic deities for nature spirits. Sacred structures soon replaced sacred landscapes.

IMPORTANT CONCEPTS

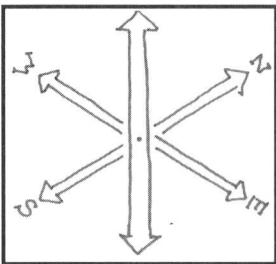

An *AXIS MUNDI* is a symbolic line that extends from the sky to the underworld with the earth at its center. Trees, mountains, pyramids, and earth mounds might all be considered axes mundi.

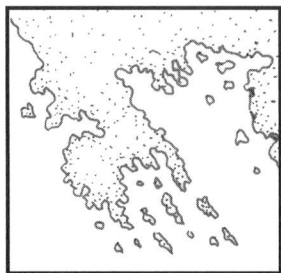

An *EQUINOX* is the day the sun crosses the equator, marking days and nights of equal length. The vernal (spring) equinox is March 20; the autumnal equinox is September 23.

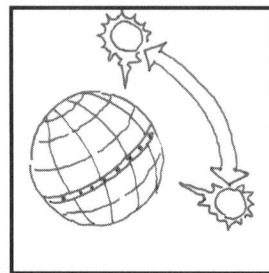

GENIUS LOCI refers to the unique spiritual force inherent in a place.

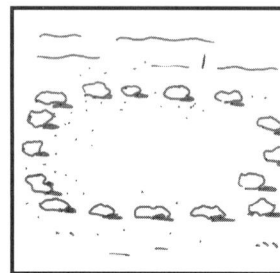

OTIUM is the Roman concept of leisure afforded by a natural setting. It is exemplified by the idea of a country villa.

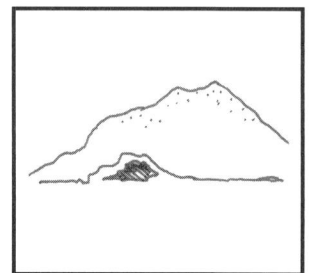

A *POLIS* is an ancient Greek city-state. The mountainous topography and island geography of Greece promoted the formation of independent city-states.

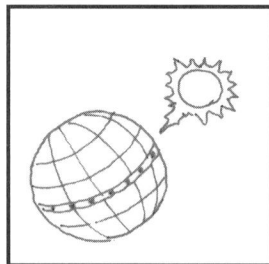

A *SOLSTICE* is the furthest point the sun reaches in the sky. The summer solstice on June 21 is the longest day of the year; the winter solstice on December 21 is the shortest day of the year.

TEMENOS is the Greek word for a delimited sacred precinct.

TOPOS is Aristotle's philosophy of place as defined by specific natural features.

DESIGN VOCABULARY

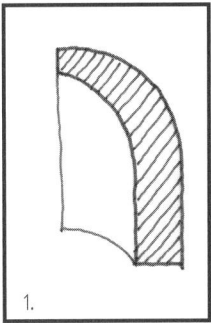

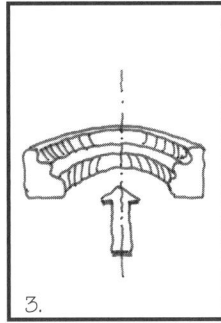

1. An APSE is a vaulted, semicircular recess in a building.

2. A DOLMEN is a stone grouping with a flat, horizontal stone on top. Dolmens were used as primitive graves.

3. An EXEDRA is a semicircular or concave shape terminating a space.

4. GEOGLYPHS are images inscribed on the earth.

5. A KIVA is a sunken or subterranean ceremonial room used in Puebloan cultures.

6. A MENHIR, or megalith, is an individual standing stone.

7. A PERISTYLE garden is a colonnaded courtyard; it was the informal, outdoor living space in a Roman town house.

8. A THOLOS is a circular temple.

9. A ZIGGURAT is a terraced pyramid form.

For further exploration

BOOKS

300, a graphic novel by Frank Miller and Lynn Varley
DE ARCHITECTURA (TEN BOOKS ON ARCHITECTURE), by Vitruvius (27 BC)
EARTH'S CHILDREN, series by Jean Auel
I, CLAUDIUS, by Robert Graves
THE ILIAD AND THE ODYSSEY, by Homer
MEMOIRS OF HADRIAN, by Marguerite Yourcenar
NATURALIS HISTORIA (NATURAL HISTORY), by Pliny the Elder (23–79 CE)
POMPEII, by Robert Harris
SONGLINES, by Bruce Chatwin

FILMS

10,000 BC (2008)
ALEXANDER THE GREAT (1956)
CLAN OF THE CAVE BEAR (1986)
CLEOPATRA (1963)
GLADIATOR (2000)
ROME (HBO TV series, 2005)
SPARTACUS (1960)
TROY (2004)

PAINTINGS AND SCULPTURE

Cave paintings at Lascaux (c. 30,000 BCE)
Venus de Willendorf (sculpture, c. 20,000 BCE)
Ram and Tree from Ur (Sumerian sculpture, c. 2600 BCE)
Minoan Snake Goddess (reliefs and sculptures, c. 1500 BCE)
Charioteer of Delphi (sculpture, c. 470 BCE)
Victory of Samothrace (sculpture, 190 BCE)
House of Livia (interior frescoes, c. 20 BCE)
Marcus Aurelius (equestrian statue, 176 CE)

6th to 15th CENTURIES

The term "Middle Ages" loosely applies to a period from the 6th to the 15th centuries, when cultural advancement in western Europe was disrupted by the decline of Roman imperialism to when the power structures of antiquity were replaced by the humanist ideologies of the Renaissance. But while progress in western Europe paused, other cultures continued to thrive. We use a similar time frame of roughly 900 years to examine not only the landscape traditions of medieval Europe, but also the great gardens of China, Japan, and Islamic Spain. During these nine centuries, enclosed gardens shut out the uncertain dangers of the surrounding landscape. Medieval gardens can be understood as metaphorical constructions, representative of a culture's changing perceptions of nature.

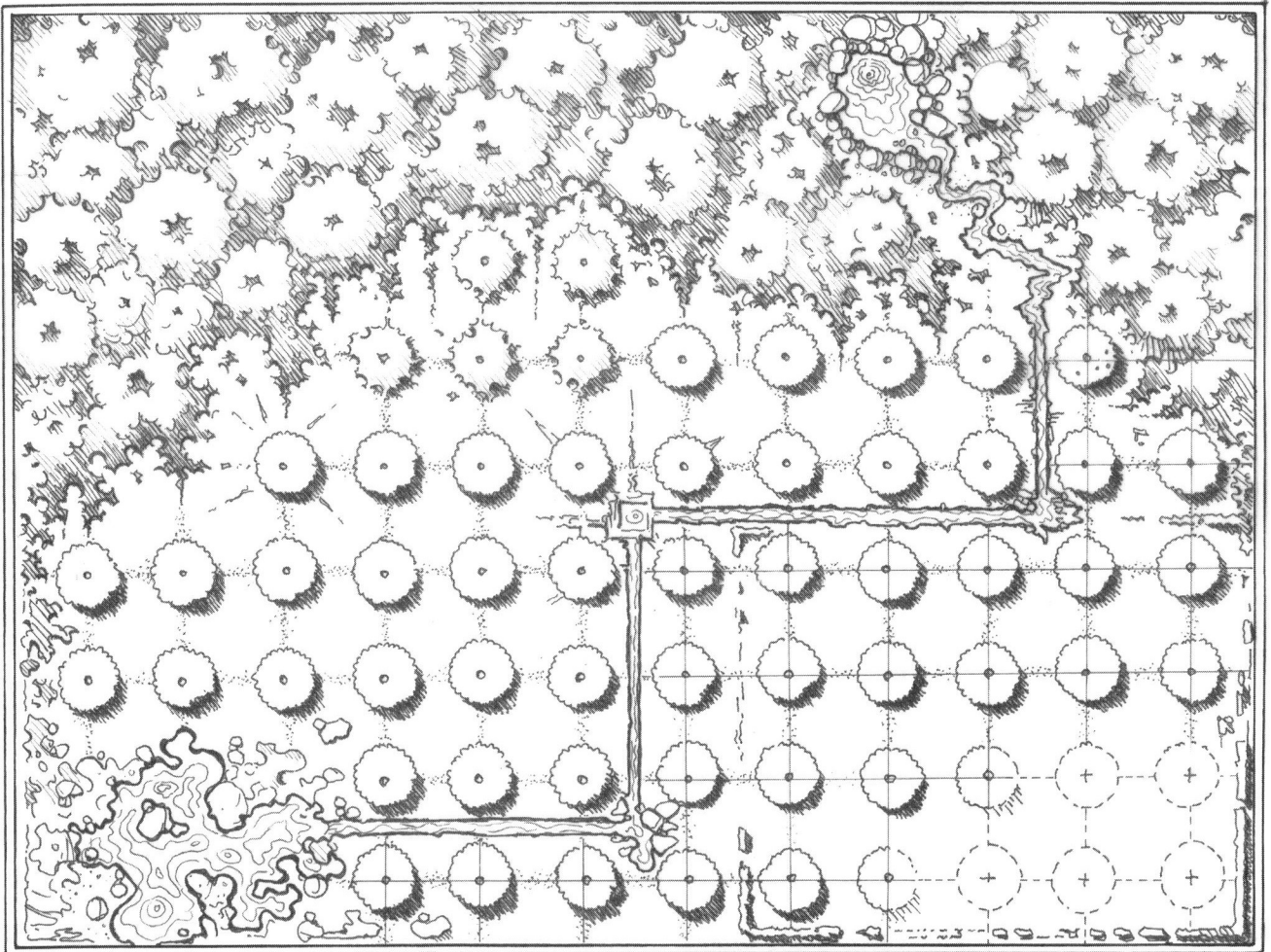

532
CONSTANTINOPLE

752
GREAT BUDDHA

836
SAMARRA

500 600 700 800

c. 750–1035
VIKING AGE

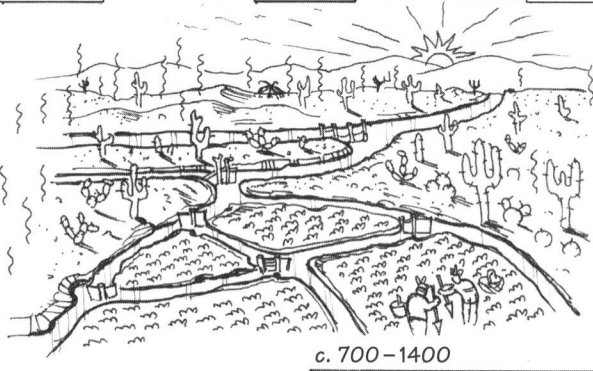

c. 700–1400
HOHOKAM CANALS

c. 1100–1200
CATHEDRALS

c. 1200
ANASAZI

1100 1200

c. 1200–1300
THE "SHAMBLES"

c. 1125
ANGKOR WAT

c.1000
SERPENT MOUND

1074–1291
CRUSADES

| 900 | 1000 |

1070
BAYEUX TAPESTRY

1088
FIRST UNIVERSITIES

1260
FLOWERY MEAD

1346
BLACK DEATH

| 1300 | 1400 |

1305
VILLA MANAGEMENT

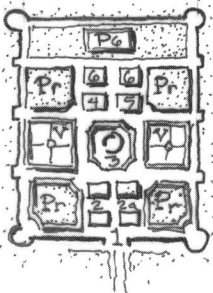

1325
AZTEC CAPITAL

532   CONSTANTINOPLE
Hagia Sophia was rebuilt on the site of a centuries-old basilica in Constantinople (Turkey) by Emperor Justinian I. As the capital of the eastern Roman Empire, Constantinople became the leading European power while Rome declined. About 1 million people lived in Constantinople in the 5th century, second only to Baghdad.

c. 700–1400   HOHOKAM CANALS
The Hohokam peoples of southern Arizona diverted water from the Salt, Gila, and San Pedro rivers in a complex system of irrigation canals that enabled the cultivation of fields more than 16 miles distant from their water source. The more than 250 miles of canals were created with simple tools and human power.

c. 750–1035   VIKING AGE
The constant threat of Viking raids on northern Europe, and the Viking conquests of Britain during the 9th and 10th centuries, made the landscape unsafe and contributed to the medieval European mind-set of seeking protection from nature.

752   GREAT BUDDHA
The Great Buddha, or *Daibutsu*, was constructed by Emperor Shomu at Nara (Japan). Buddhism spread to Japan from India by way of China and Korea, assimilating elements of folk religions along the way.

836   SAMARRA (IRAQ)
The palace city of Samarra, with its iconic spiral minaret at the Grand Mosque, was the administrative headquarters of the Abbasid caliphs for a brief period in the 9th century. Archeologists have found evidence of irrigation channels at Samarra, suggesting the existence of palace gardens.

c. 1000   SERPENT MOUND
Over a quarter mile long, the Serpent Mound, built by the Fort Ancient culture of Ohio, is the largest animal effigy in existence. Snakes were significant in Native American mythology, but the purpose of Serpent Mound confounds archeologists to this day.

1070   BAYEUX TAPESTRY
The Bayeux tapestry was commissioned by Bishop Odo (half-brother of William the Conqueror) to illustrate the events surrounding the Norman invasion of England in 1066. The 230-foot-long embroidered cloth depicts William's victory at the Battle of Hastings, which led to the imposition of the European feudal system on Britain.

1074–1291   CRUSADES
The first crusades were initiated by Pope Urban II to liberate Christian holy sites from Muslim control and to support the Byzantine emperor against threats from the Islamic empire. Although the crusades resulted in an important exchange of information and knowledge between East and West, a wave of violence and persecution ensued, which was particularly devastating to Jewish communities.

1088   FIRST UNIVERSITIES
The University of Bologna, founded around the study of rhetoric, grammar, and logic, later expanded its curriculum to include philosophy and mathematics—subjects first developed by the Arabs and Greeks. In the 12th century, Frederick I (Barbarossa) declared European universities free from the influences of church and state, establishing an enduring model of scholarship that thrived during the Renaissance.

c. 1100–1200   CATHEDRALS
During the surge of large-scale cathedral building projects in Europe, new architectural forms such as the ribbed vault, pointed arch, and flying buttress emphasized verticality and defined the Gothic style. The focus was on the heavenly realm above, rather than the earthly realm below.

c. 1125   ANGKOR WAT
The Khmer empire of Cambodia had its capital at Angkor from the 9th–15th centuries. The temple complex called Angkor Wat was symbolic of Hindu cosmology, with its concentric canals, terraces, galleries, and central temple. The temple's roof structure represented sacred Mount Meru, an *axis mundi* between sacred and profane worlds.

c. 1200   ANASAZI
The cliff dwellings at Mesa Verde, Colorado, are typical of the highly organized Anasazi culture of the American Southwest. Construction peaked at around 1200 CE. The mesas and cliffs were occupied by the Anasazi for over 700 years, but completely abandoned by 1276.

c. 1200–1300   THE "SHAMBLES"
The dense fabric of a medieval city reflected its commercial function. Space was at a premium; workshops and living quarters encroached on public space, creating the intimate streetscape that characterizes medieval European cities today.

1260   FLOWERY MEAD
Albertus Magnus wrote a gardening manual, *De Vegetabilibus et Plantis*, based on ancient Roman and contemporary English treatises. Albertus also described a pleasure garden and included detailed instructions for creating a "flowery mead."

1305   VILLA MANAGEMENT
Piero de' Crescenzi wrote *Liber Ruralium Commodorum*, borrowing extensively from Albertus Magnus. His practical advice on agricultural estate management at various scales was particularly valuable to villa designers of the Italian Renaissance.

1325   AZTEC CAPITAL
The Aztec capital of Tenochtitlan (Mexico City) was founded where, according to legend, an eagle perched on a cactus growing from a rock near a spring.

1346   BLACK DEATH
The plague struck Europe, killing one-third to one-half of the population. The epidemic spread along active trade routes. People abandoned the city and sought refuge in the countryside.

WESTERN EUROPE

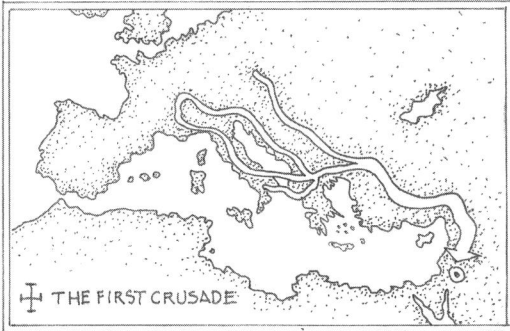

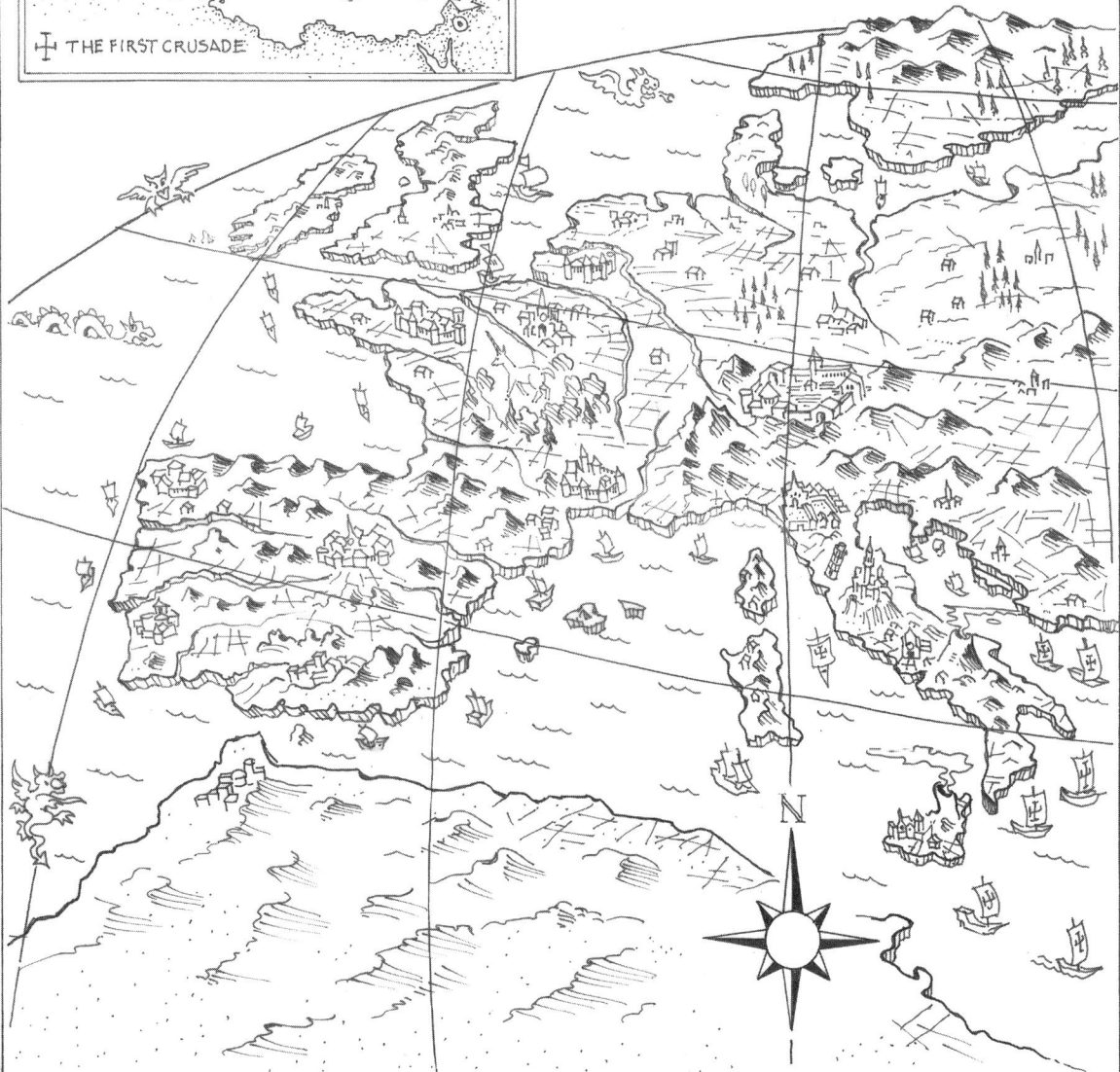

THE FIRST CRUSADE

N

WALLED MINDS, WALLED GARDENS

From the fall of the Roman Empire to the rebirth of humanist ideals in the Renaissance, the focus of western European culture turned inward. Lacking a central authority to maintain the political, social, economic, and physical infrastructure, the landscape fell into ruin. Rival militias battled to establish control over the land. The plague ravaged cities and towns. People sought protection within walled castles, and spiritual fulfillment within walled monasteries. Oppressed by the hardships of a feudal economy, individuals focused on the glorious promises of the next world rather than on the harsh limitations of this one. Society focused inward as the landscape came to represent a realm of insecurity; something to be feared.

The Catholic Church was able to assume a powerful role in the Middle Ages by establishing ecclesiastical seats in formerly imperial towns. The coronation of Charlemagne as Holy Roman Emperor by Pope Leo III in 800 CE brought about a degree of stability to western Europe, and shored up the papacy's hold on its lands. Monasticism flourished as spiritual and mystical communities formed apart from the secular world. In an environment besieged by violence, disease and repression, ancient knowledge was preserved in monasteries, where monks copied both historical manuscripts and the contemporary texts brought by travelers from the east who took shelter within their retreats. Arab scholars also brought new knowledge of plants and horticultural practices to the west.

Some religious mystics sought solitude in the landscape, living as hermits in caves rather than in monastic communities. The landscape, once considered sacred in itself, represented in the Middle Ages a place of penance; a wilderness to be tamed, eventually, within the literal and allegorical confines of the walled garden.

RELIGIOUS FERVOR: Powerful bishops built great cathedrals from the 11th–14th centuries, in the Romanesque and, later, Gothic, style. The cathedral of Notre Dame in Paris was begun in 1163.

Agriculture was the primary activity of life in the early Middle Ages. The many prose poems and treatises on gardening practices written by medieval scholars attest to the importance of a healthy, productive landscape. People were tied to the landscape socially, politically, and economically in a feudal system where entitlement to land equaled power.

The function of the early medieval garden in Europe was primarily utilitarian. People grew vegetables and herbs for food and medicine. In the late Middle Ages, a money economy developed and cities emerged as trading centers. An influential "middle class" began to evolve from the powerful guilds and burgeoning merchant class. As trade resumed and the landscape grew less frightening, people with means built pleasure gardens. The garden became laden with allegorical symbolism both sacred and profane, and was the locus for literary tales of chivalry and courtly love.

Sources of information about early medieval gardens in western Europe are limited. Evidence from the 9th century includes Charlemagne's *Capitulare de villis*, or regulations on the administration of imperial towns; the idealized "Plan of St. Gall"; and poems written by two monks, one containing a detailed list of plants similar to Charlemagne's, and the other a gardening calendar. Later sources include the many paintings, tapestries, illuminated manuscripts, and literary descriptions of gardens that date from the 13th–15th centuries.

KEY SOURCE: The Unicorn Tapestries displayed at the Cloisters in New York date from the 15th century. The story of the hunt of the elusive unicorn can be understood as an allegory of courtly love or interpreted as a metaphor for events in the life of Christ. The garden scenes contain remarkably accurate depictions of plants and flowers.

USES AND SYMBOLISM OF WALLED GARDENS

COMMON ATTRIBUTES:
Medieval gardens typically included a wall or fence, the geometric subdivision of raised planting beds, turf seats, a well or fountain, and grass or "flowery mead."

HORTUS CONCLUSUS: Depictions of medieval walled gardens are laden with religious symbolism. A walled garden is mentioned in the Song of Solomon and is understood as representing the chastity of the Virgin Mary.[1]

The walled garden of the Middle Ages, however simple in concept and form, existed as a place cultivated and tended, a *locus amoenus*, or pleasant place, separated from the dark wild. The *hortus conclusus*, or enclosed garden, the *pleasance*, or pleasure garden, and the monastic cloister garden all are characteristic forms of medieval gardens.

The *hortus conclusus* became symbolic of the Virgin Mary following the religious zeal of the Crusades. Verses taken from the Song of Solomon describe elements typical of a *hortus conclusus*: the "fountain in my gardens"; "a spring of running

PLEASANCE: Pleasance gardens are associated with the cult of chivalry and knighthood that emerged in the late Middle Ages.

CLOISTER: The cloister garden is similar in form to the peristyle garden of the Roman *domus*—a colonnaded ambulatory surrounding a typically square courtyard with a central basin or fountain.

water"; "the closed gate." Symbolic flowers include lilies (purity), roses (martyrdom), and violets (humility).[2]

The *pleasance*, nestled within the castle walls, was a safe place for both reflection and recreation, and served as an escape from the dark confines of the castle. A *herbarium* contained the more utilitarian aspects of the pleasance, like the herb garden and lawn area, while the *viridarium* contained more ornamental plants and trees. Particularly elaborate pleasance gardens contained labyrinths, mounts, topiary, and even menageries.

Monasteries were self-sufficient centers of learning, work, and prayer. Monks had to be knowledgeable about botanical science and medicinal herbs for the sustainability of the community. Kitchen gardens and "physic" gardens yielded food, vegetables, seasonings, and medicines. The monks cultivated flowers, such as the lily and the rose, to decorate altars. They concocted dyes and pesticides from other plant species. The first hospitals and universities in Europe evolved from the monastery paradigm.

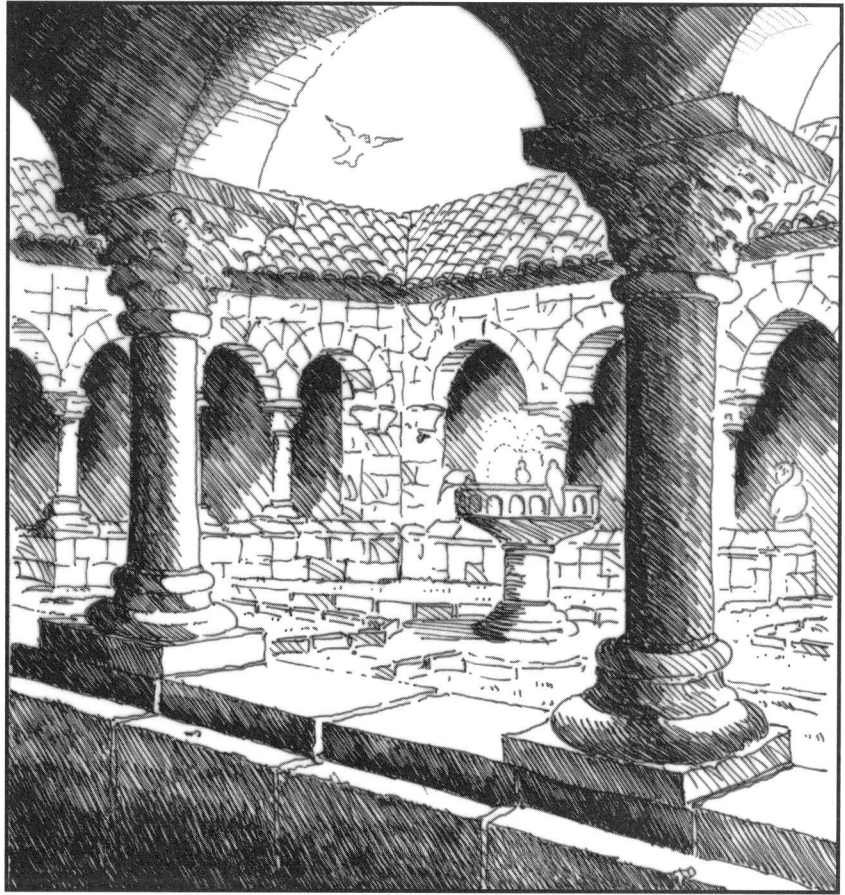

HIERARCHY OF SPACE: The great cloister at the Certosa di Pavia (c. 1396) is surrounded by the individual cells of the monks, each with its own small garden.

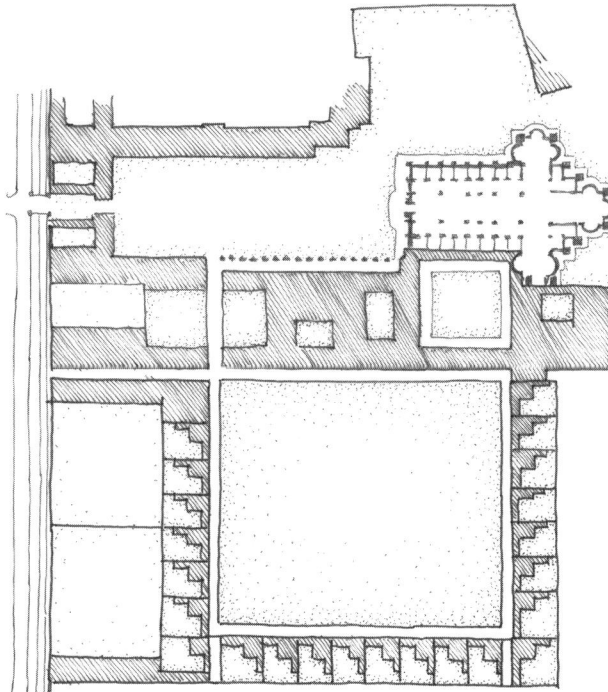

0 20 40 60 80 100M

Roman de la Rose

THE ROMANCE OF THE ROSE is a 13th-century allegory of courtly love begun by the French poet Guillaume de Lorris around 1230 and completed by Jean de Meun 40 years later. The story of love's trials and tribulations was extremely popular—the manuscript was copied for centuries and kept in print until the 16th century. The illustrations and descriptions of the story's setting have continued to be a source of information on all aspects of medieval life, particularly the form and function of medieval gardens.

1 IN MY 20th YEAR I LAY DOWN ONE NIGHT & FELL FAST ASLEEP.

2 DREAMED IT WAS MAY WHEN EVERY THING IS EXCITED BY LOVE.

3 SAW A LARGE GARDEN SURROUNDED BY A WALL.

4 FOUND A SMALL NARROW DOOR. IT WAS OPENED BY A BEAUTIFUL MAIDEN.

5 ENTERED THE GARDEN & BELIEVED MYSELF TO BE IN PARADISE

6 LORD MERRIMENT WAS DISPORTING HIMSELF THERE & HE HAD SUCH HANDSOME PEOPLE WITH HIM THAT I THOUGHT THEY SEEMED TO BE WINGED ANGELS. WITHOUT HESITATION I JOINED IN THEIR DANCE.

7 WANDERED UNTIL I HAD SEEN THE WHOLE GARDEN ALL THIS TIME THE GOD OF LOVE FOLLOWED ME.

VISUAL NARRATIVE

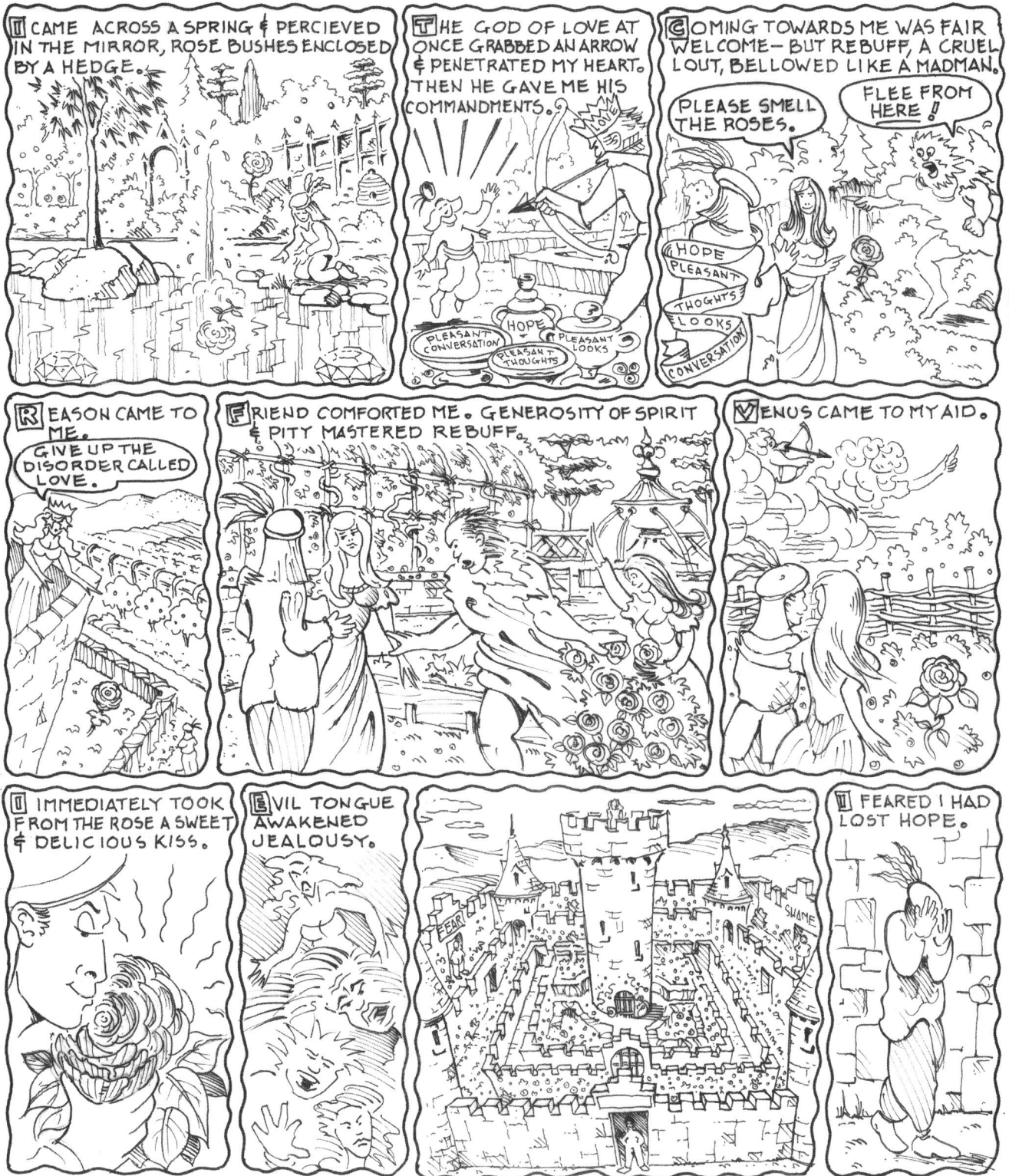

THE SECOND PART of the story contains many long speeches by figures such as Reason, Nature, and Genius, who debate philosophical issues and discuss the events of the times. The Lover remains thwarted in his attempts to reunite with Fair Welcome until the God of Love summons his forces and assaults the fortress. Unsuccessful at first, he calls upon Venus, who attacks the enemies of Love and ultimately enables the Lover to win the rose. "Thus I had the vermillion rose. Then it was day and I awoke."[3]

CASE STUDY: *The Plan of St. Gall*

A VISIONARY MODEL

The Plan of St. Gall, a 9th-century document preserved in the library of the monastery at St Gall, Switzerland, is an important source of information about medieval gardens. The visionary drawing illustrates the layout of a model Benedictine monastery. The site plan was much copied in the following centuries, and is significant for its depiction of functional spatial relationships—its marriage of beauty and practicality. The plan is for a sustainable community; no outside resources are required to support the order. Within the walls of the monastery are its water source, mill, kiln, brewery, gardens, workshops, barns, and animal yards.

Three garden spaces are represented in addition to the cloister. These include the *hortus*, or kitchen garden; the *herbularius*, or physic garden; and the *viridarium*, or orchard, which doubles as a cemetery. All of the individual plants listed on the plan are mentioned in Charlemagne's *capitulare*.

The walled kitchen garden is located in close proximity to the poultry pens and near the dining area. The walled physic garden is sited next to the infirmary. Fruit and nut trees are set between the graves in the cemetery.

A Church
B Cloister
C Kitchen
D Hortus
E Viridarium
F Infirmary
G Physic garden

MOORISH SPAIN

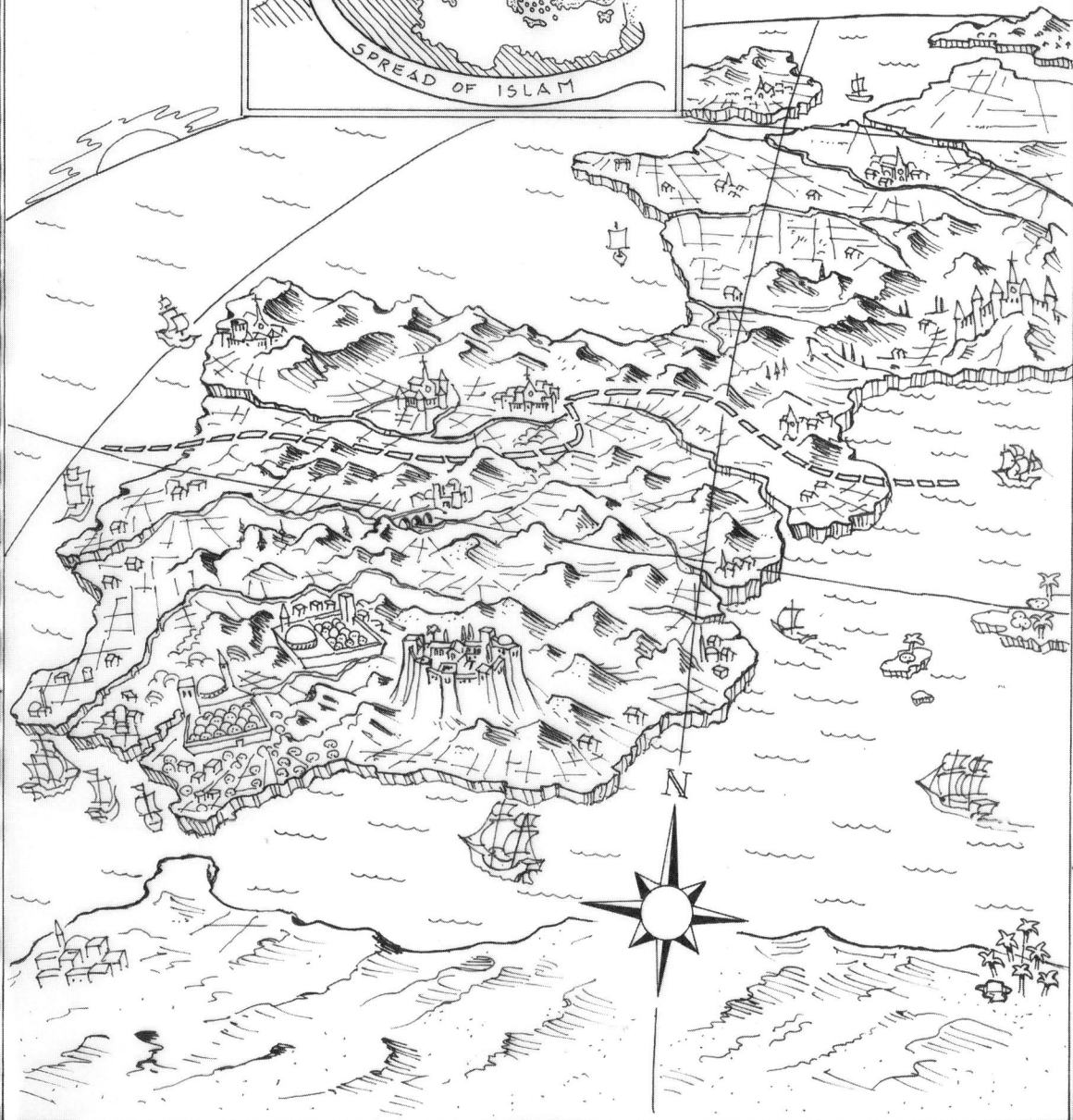

SPREAD OF ISLAM

N

AN INDELIBLE INFLUENCE

The stifled progress of civilization in medieval Europe contrasts sharply with the highly cultured and literate world of the Arabs in the 8th–10th centuries. Islamic culture spread across the Mediterranean, from North Africa to Sicily and Spain. While there are no extant examples of medieval gardens in most of western Europe, gardens from the Islamic era do remain in the Spanish cities of Cordoba, Granada, and Seville.

Much altered over the centuries, the gardens of southern Spain still retain their Moorish (Hispano-Arabic) characteristics. Islamic garden form is well suited to the hot, dry climate of the Mediterranean. The configuration of enclosed patios and courtyards and the presence of water provide cool, shady environments. Attributes of traditional Moorish gardens include the reliance on decorative paving and geometric tile patterns in place of human or animal forms forbidden by the Quran, the predominance of rectangular and axial geometries, and the limited use of plants.

A TYPICAL MOORISH COURTYARD: Water in straight runnels, and simple pools with single jets, structure the geometry. Raised walkways help sunken planting areas retain moisture. Architectural features include a pavilion, arcaded gallery, and mirador, or elevated porch. Often a glorieta or pavilion was placed at the intersection of pathways. We show a glorieta formed of clipped cypress trees.

MOORISH DECORATION: Elaborate floral patterns and intricate geometric arabesques were common decorative motifs executed in carved stone, plaster, and glazed tile mosaics.

WATER MANAGEMENT

The conquest of the Visigoths, who succeeded the Romans in control of the Iberian Peninsula, began in the 8th century when Abd al-Rahman I established an independent emirate at Cordoba, in 756. One of his first tasks was to develop an irrigation system that would allow the building of palaces and gardens similar to those at his ancestral home in Damascus.[4]

Cordoba became an important center of trade and culture. Abd al-Rahman III was a great patron of the arts and sciences, and fostered the study of botany and medicine at Cordoba. The Arabs introduced citrus varieties, date palms, pomegranates, and almond trees to Europe. Sophisticated techniques to

HYDRAULIC ENGINEERING: The excavation of Madinat al-Zahra in a suburb of Cordoba shows evidence of extensive palace gardens built by Abd al-Rahman III in the 10th century. An aqueduct carried water 9 miles from the surrounding foothills to irrigate the garden.[5]

CLEVER IRRIGATION: In the Court of the Oranges at Cordoba, water released from a central source was directed into stone-lined channels for irrigation. Each tree well was flooded in sequence by repositioning wood blocks.

impound and channel water promoted the growth of orchards, vineyards, and gardens across the arid landscape.

The Court of the Oranges at the mosque in Cordoba is one of the oldest examples of a Moorish-style patio. Construction of the mosque was begun in the 8th century, and the patio enlarged to its present form around 976. The correspondence of grid systems—how the orange trees align with the structural columns of the temple—exemplifies principles of unity and order characteristic of all Islamic gardens. The courtyard is subdivided into three rectangles with a basin central to each. Overflow from the fountains irrigated the trees in series, based on an Egyptian design precedent.[6]

VIEW OF THE ALHAMBRA: The palace, as seen from the hills of the Albaicin, against the backdrop of the Sierra Nevada.

DEFINITIVE MOORISH PRECEDENTS

Cordoba declined in the 11th century as the Umayyad caliphate dissolved into autonomous city-states. But Arab influence lingered in Andalusia for another 400 years. Muhammad ibn al-Ahmar established a Nasrid emirate at Granada in 1232, which remained an Arab stronghold until the 15th century. Two beautiful Moorish-style gardens survive from that era, the Alhambra and the Generalife.

ALHAMBRA

The Alhambra is situated on a plateau in the foothills of the Sierra Nevada above the scenic environs of Granada. The palace complex comprises a series of courtyards and patios that connect interior rooms. The scale of the open spaces and their relationship with the architecture create a dynamic experience of movement for the visitor. The Court of the Myrtles and the Court of the Lions are particularly noteworthy expressions of Islamic courtyard form.

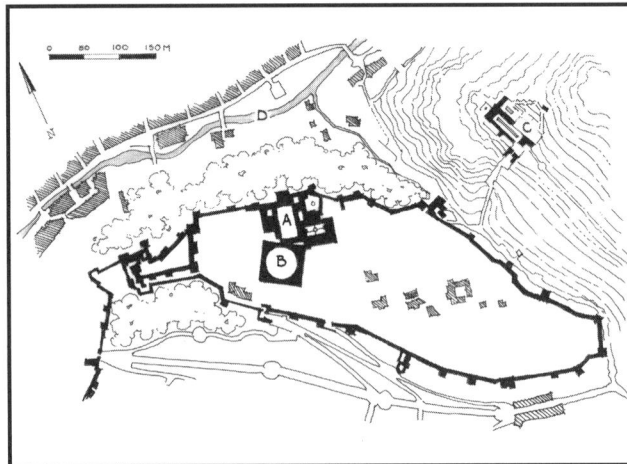

SITE PLAN: The fortified palace of the Alhambra showing the 14th-century courtyards (A), the Pavilion of Charles V (B), the Generalife gardens (C), and the Darro River (D).

The major feature of the Court of the Myrtles, built in the mid-14th century for Yusuf I, is the long rectangular reflecting pool, which visually connects an arcaded wing of the palace with the audience hall below the Tower of Comares. Small, round basins with single water jets terminate each end of the pool. The long sides of the pool are bordered by clipped hedges of myrtle, a modern addition.

The adjacent Court of the Lions, built later in the 14th century for Muhammed V, contains a slender alabaster arcade that frames the space and forms two delicate porticos on the east and west

ends. Two highly decorated pavilions open to the north and south sides. Small circular pools, each with a single bubbler, are located inside the pavilions and beneath the porticos. Four narrow rills of water extend to each pool from a central fountain surrounded by 12 carved lions.

GENERALIFE

Across a ravine and up a steep slope to the east of the Alhambra sits the Generalife, a daytime retreat built in the early 14th century by the founding Nasrid rulers of Granada. The Generalife consists of a series of seven lush garden terraces, each with distinctive water elements. The intimate scale of the courtyards and the privacy afforded by their dense plantings are spatial counterpoints to the experience of openness and views exposed by the many balconies, alcoves, and galleries.

At the lower level, a long narrow canal forms the spine of the picturesque Patio de la Acequia. Low scalloped-edged basins sit at both ends of the axis. The space is contained on the western slope by an arcaded gallery with a belvedere that affords views of the Alhambra palace and the Darro River valley. Arcaded pavilions enclose the courtyard to the north and south. A *mirador*, or viewing porch, extends from the pavilion to the north. Reconstructed after a fire in 1958, the patio retains its historic quadripartite form, although the original level of the planting beds was much lower, creating a floral carpet effect from the walkways.[7]

The Court of the Cypresses lies parallel to the slope above the Patio de la Acequia and is contained by an extension of the two-story arcade to the north. Dark green cypress hedges and unclipped cypress trees shade the U-shaped canal, adding to the cooling effect of the space. A unique water staircase located at the uppermost level of the garden is also an original feature of the Generalife. Water once cascaded down the steps as part of the great waterworks system that irrigated the garden.

Although the remaining garden terraces were later additions, the site plan of the Generalife reflects many of the principles discussed in a 14th-century treatise on agriculture by Ibn Luyun. He wrote that an ideal country villa should be located on high ground, have shady canals, be planted with a mix of evergreen trees and flowers, contain vine-covered trellises and covered walks, and be of a proportion no longer than it is wide "so the eye will not tire in its contemplation."[8]

GENERALIFE SECTION: Rather than occupying the hilltop as a fortress, the gracefully terraced gardens of the Generalife take advantage of views.

THE GENERALIFE, GRANADA: **A**. Patio de la Acequia, **B**. Mirador, **C**. Court of the Cypresses.

CASE STUDY: *The Alhambra*

A   Mexuar Hall
B   View from prayer room in Mexuar Hall
C   Looking from the loggia into Cuarto Dorado
D   Cuarto Dorado
E   Passage to Court of the Myrtles
F   Court of the Myrtles
G   Passage to Court of the Lions
H   Looking from loggia into Court of the Lions
I   Court of the Lions
J   Looking at the Lindaraja *mirador*
K   View of the patio of Lindaraja from the *mirador*
L   Patio of Lindaraja

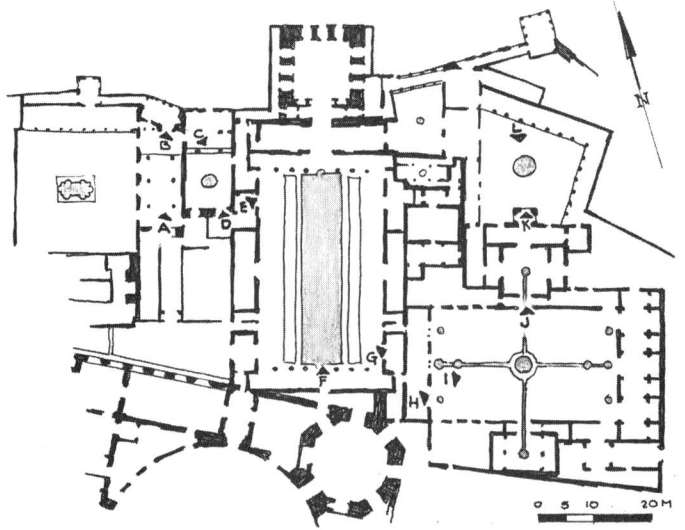

33

OVERLAPPING CULTURES AT SEVILLE

The application of Islamic design elements and principles to structures and gardens by Moorish craftsmen under Christian authority is referred to as being in the *mudejar* style. Seville was conquered by the Arabs in 712, and reconquered by the Christians in 1248. The Alcazar (the royal palace and garden complex) at Seville exemplifies the *mudejar* style.

The original 12th-century palace was rebuilt in the 14th century by Pedro the Cruel, King of Castile. In addition to the traditional Moorish patios adjacent to the palace, 16 acres of gardens remain. The walled gardens are divided into three sections, bordered on the north side by the elevated walkway of Don Pedro. The first terrace consists of small enclosed courtyards, with central fountains

and glazed tile work. The second level is subdivided into eight rectangular planting areas defined by clipped hedges and raised walkways. The third section is designed as a large patio with orange trees and glazed tile benches surrounding the 16th-century pavilion of Charles V. The Alcazar in Seville has been greatly amended since its establishment, but its Moorish spirit remains.

THE ALCAZAR: A diagrammatic reconstruction of the gardens showing the relationship between the interior spaces, early courtyards, and openness of the later parterres. Elevated walkways connect the garden to the architecture.

0 10 20 30 40 80 M

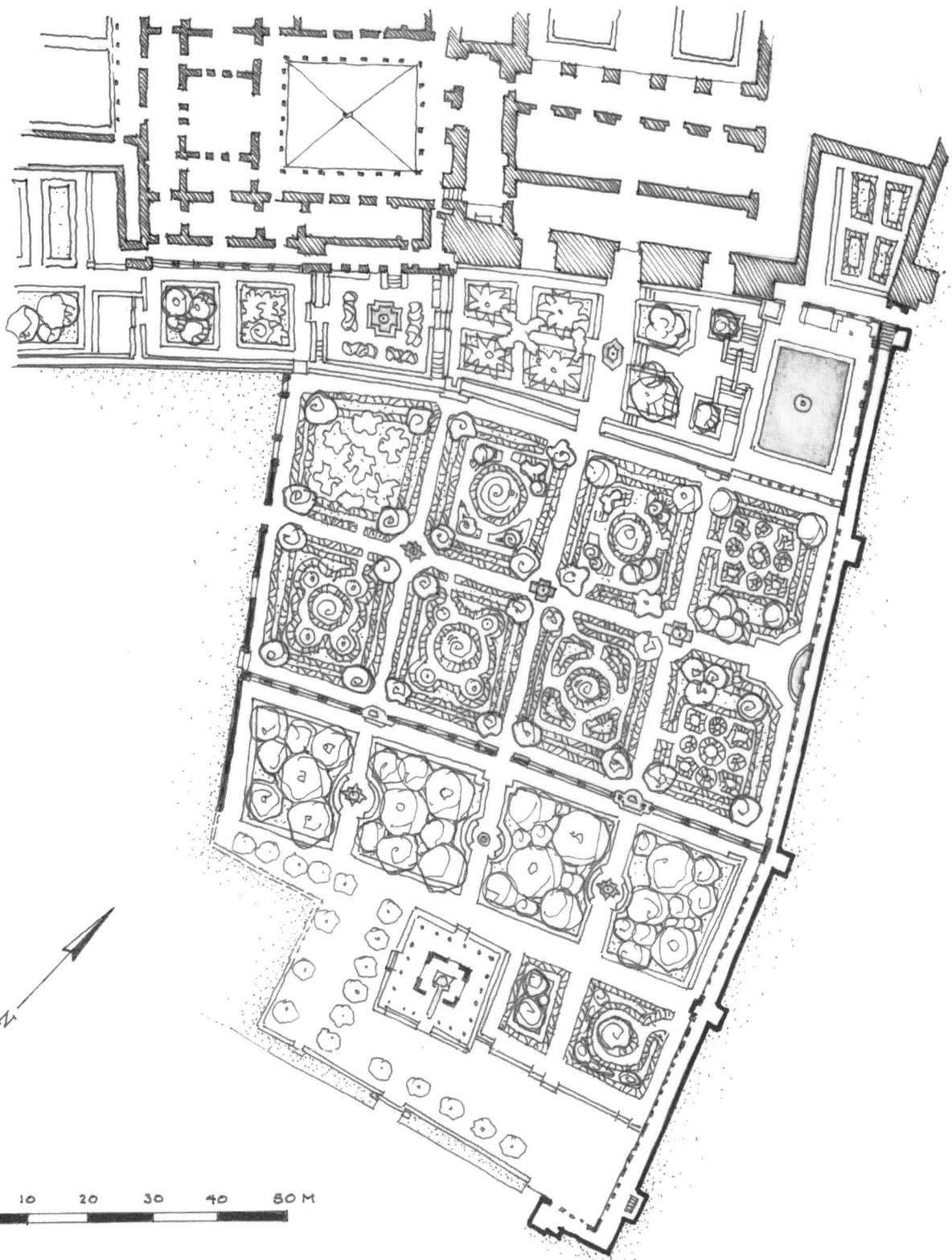

ALCAZAR PLAN: The palace gardens maintain their Moorish character through the geometric division of space into small-scale garden rooms defined by raised walkways.

The Court of Oranges at the mosque in Seville dates from 1171. A large central fountain used for ritual washing was also used for ir-rigating the trees. Runnels in the brick pavement link the grid of orange trees, similar to the system at Cordoba. The drawings below compare the urban contexts and site plans of the two courtyards at the same scale.

SEVILLE: The Great Mosque at Seville was conse-crated as a Christian church in 1248, and remod-eled as a Gothic cathedral in the 15th century.

CORDOBA: Still referred to as La Mezquita, the mosque at Cordoba was converted to a church by the Christians in 1238.

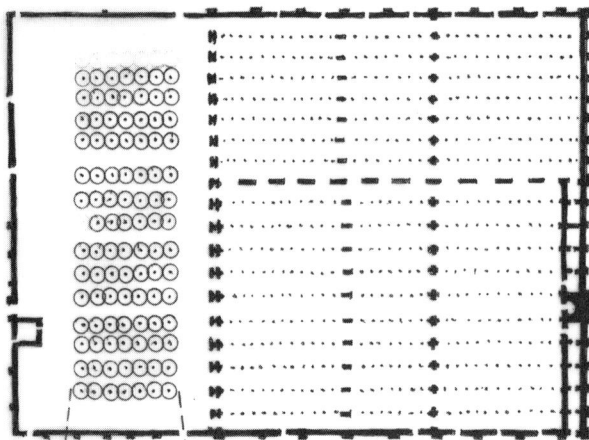

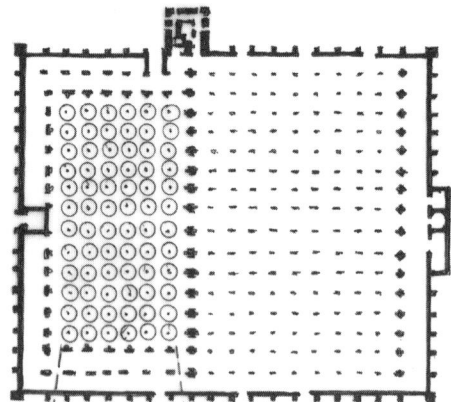

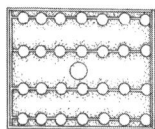

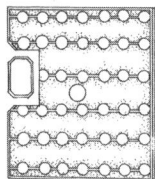

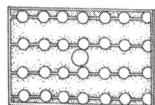

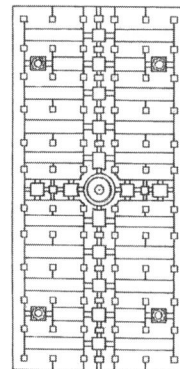

CHINA

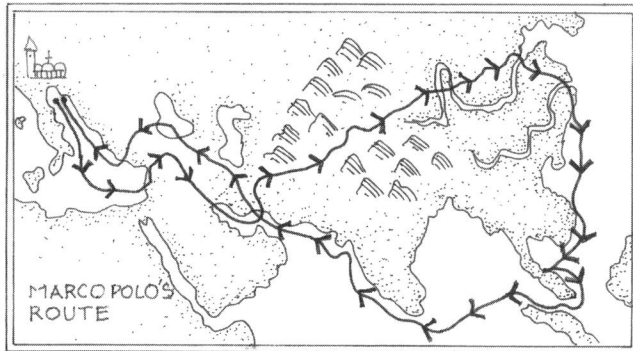

MARCO POLO'S
ROUTE

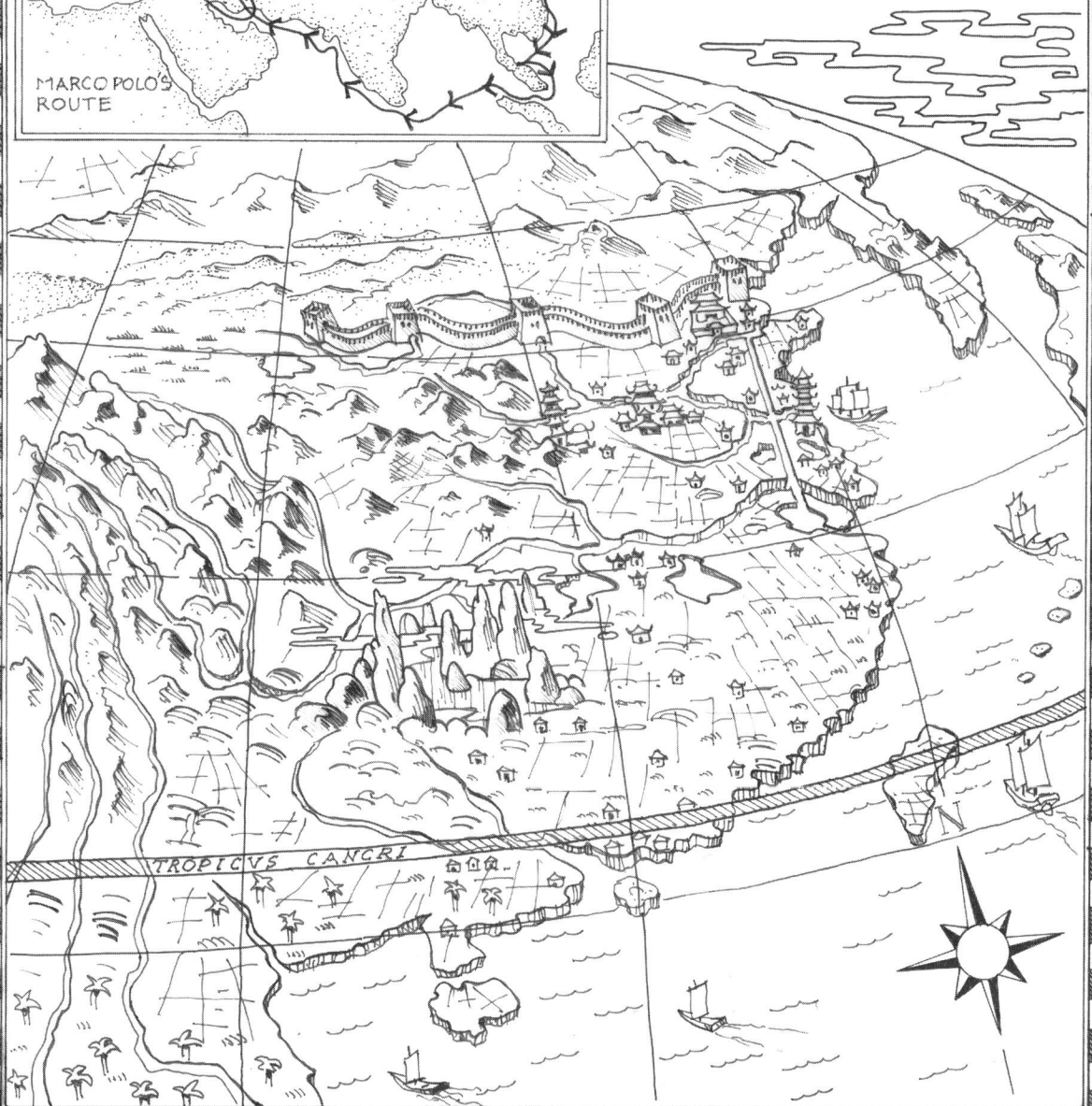

TROPICVS CANCRI

NATURE'S SPLENDOR IN A GARDEN

ROCKS AND WATER: The defining natural features of China—mountains and lakes—are represented in its gardens.

As much as Moorish gardens provided a respite from harsh nature, the gardens of China and Japan provided an affirmation of nature's largesse. The landscape of China is characterized by steep mountains, bountiful plains, peaceful lakes, and dramatic waterfalls. Chinese gardens reference all of the country's natural treasures.

The history of gardening in China extends back to the ancient dynastic emperors who built hunting parks and pleasure gardens as expressions of royal power. Governments were often weakened by excessive spending on lavish imperial gardens. When Yangdi, heir to the Sui dynasty (589–618), ascended the throne in the late 6th century, he undertook several large-scale public works projects, including the construction of an extravagant palace garden at Loyang. A fantasyland over 75 miles in circumference, the garden reportedly contained mechanical figures, mature trees that were artificially enhanced for seasonal effect, and 16 pavilions surrounding a man-made lake 6 miles long.[9]

SHIH TZU LIN: The Lion Grove garden at Suzhou dates from 1342. The "mountain" shaped by the rockery is evocative of the Lion Cliff at Tien Mu mountain.

Chinese gardens expressed a cosmology based on a fusion of Confucian, Daoist, and Buddhist tenets. While each religion advocated different strategies for achieving spiritual freedom, all shared a common respect for nature. Historic Chinese gardens imitated the balance of opposites found in nature, referred to by Daoists as the forces of yin and yang. Rock and water structured the garden: rocks symbolized mountains, a male force (yin), and water symbolized yang, a female force. In fact, the word for "landscape" was composed of words that meant "mountain" and "water"—shan shui. The principle of yin and yang can also be seen in the contrast of the rectilinear geometry of cities, structures, and decorative elements (representing human artifice) with the free-flowing irregular forms of gardens (representing nature).

Daoism advocated the idea of eternal life through contact with mystical Immortals who inhabited mountainous islands in an eastern sea. Thus, gardens contained lakes and rockery that imitated the mountain dwellings of the Immortals. These lake-and-island estates set a precedent for garden form and had particular influence on later Japanese gardens. Rocks themselves had powerful associative meanings in Chinese gardens. Rock formations, flowers, paving patterns, and architectural features all communicated the theme of a garden.

Confucian society was ordered by a moral imperative for civil service and a pursuit of the cultural arts. As a traditional art form, garden making in China was studied along with painting, poetry,

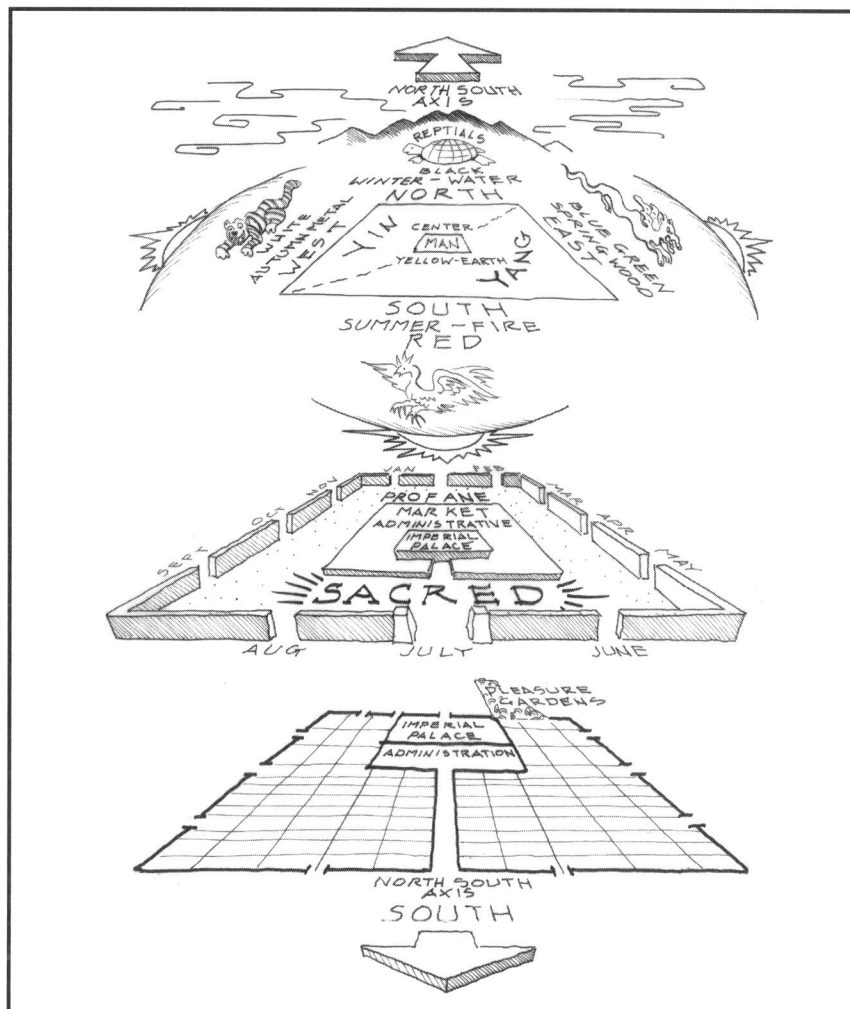

COSMOLOGICAL AND FUNCTIONAL DIAGRAM: The 6th-century grid layout of Chang-an was based on geomantic principles and reflects Chinese political hierarchy.[11]

and calligraphy by scholar-officials seeking status. Confucian order can be read in the urban form of imperial cities, such as Chang-an (Xian, today). During the Tang dynasty, Chang-an was home to more than 1 million people and created a metropolitan aesthetic that was later adopted by the Japanese.[10]

POETIC GARDENS: Like a hand scroll unrolls from right to left, revealing a succession of individual scenes, a Chinese garden is experienced as a series of visual events. These three scenes represent Wang Wei's villa and are combined with lines of his poetry.[12]

Lakeside Pavilion

A light boat greets the honored guests,

far, far, coming in over the lake.

On a balcony we face bowls of wine

and lotus flowers bloom everywhere.

WANG CHUAN: The 8th-century villa designed by Wang Wei was a poetic construction of hills, streams, and forests.

SCHOLAR GARDENS OF SUZHOU

During the Tang dynasty (618–907), China was at its peak of national power. Trade and culture flourished. The thriving city of Suzhou was located on the great canal system that eventually linked the Yangzi River (Chang Jiang) in the south with the Yellow River (Huang He) in the north. Economically prosperous and rich in scenery, Suzhou was known as the "Venice of the East."[13] Here, scholar-officials retired from government service and built rustic country estates, embracing an aesthetic of solitude, learning, and poverty. "Scholar gardens" were private retreats, places for self-development and communion with intimate friends, distinct from elaborate imperial gardens. Suzhou itself remained a haven for artists, particularly during the Ming dynasty.

An example of a typical scholar's garden from the Tang era is the riverside villa of Wang Wei, a painter, poet, musician, and Buddhist scholar. Wang Wei painted 20 views of his estate, showing pavilions set amid the hills of the scenic Wang Chuan valley, 30 miles from the capital at Chang-an. Neither the garden nor the original paintings survive, but extant copies illustrate how he composed the garden as a series of individual views set within the larger context of the landscape.

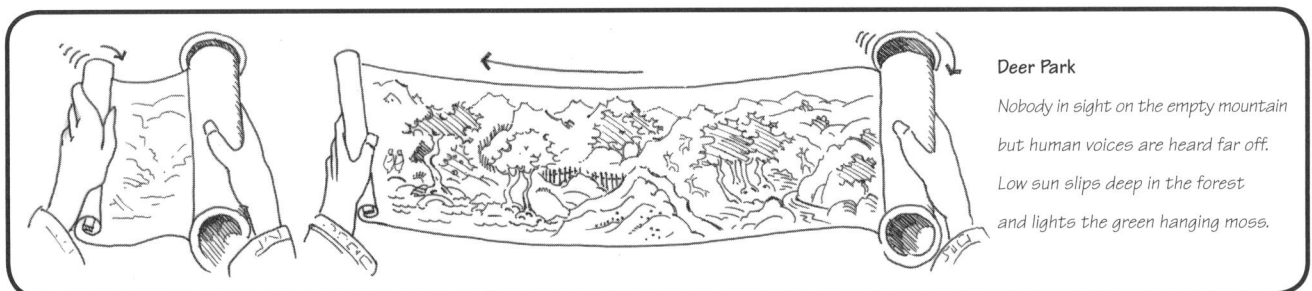

Deer Park

Nobody in sight on the empty mountain

but human voices are heard far off.

Low sun slips deep in the forest

and lights the green hanging moss.

PAINTING AND GARDENING

The height of landscape painting and gardening occurred during the cultural and economic prosperity of the Song dynasty (960–1279). After 50 years of turmoil following the collapse of the Tang dynasty, the first Song emperor reunified the country and established a capital in the northern city of Kaifeng. The centralized power of the Song emperors facilitated urban and economic growth, and made possible extraordinary achievements in technology, such as the invention of movable type.

The Northern Song emperor Zhao Ji (Song Huizong, ruled 1100–1125) was a painter, patron of the arts, and avid collector of rocks and trees. Built in accordance with the geomantic principles of feng shui, his palace garden, Gen Yue, included an artificial mountain over 200 feet high to block the evil forces that he believed kept him from producing a male heir.[14]

When Kaifeng fell to a rival clan in 1126, the Songs were forced south and eventually established a new capital at Hangzhou, on the picturesque shores of the man-made West Lake. Here, rugged peaks gave way to rolling hills; the landscape was more gentle and lyrical, as represented in the poems and paintings of the period. Daoism and Buddhism were stronger

ROCK ROOM: The most valued rocks came from Lake Tai, where unique forces of erosion created the characteristic apertures and shapes prized by Song collectors.

THE PLUM DOOR at Shih Tzu Lin frames a view of the courtyard.

influences in the south. The Daoist belief in a universal flow of energy can be seen in the mania for placing rocks in the garden. Rocks formed the skeleton of the garden like mountains formed the skeleton of the earth. Individual rocks were appreciated and collected during the Tang dynasty, but rock adulation reached its ultimate expression in the Song dynasty. To the Buddhist, rocks represented the creative forces of nature—the more weathered, the more magical.

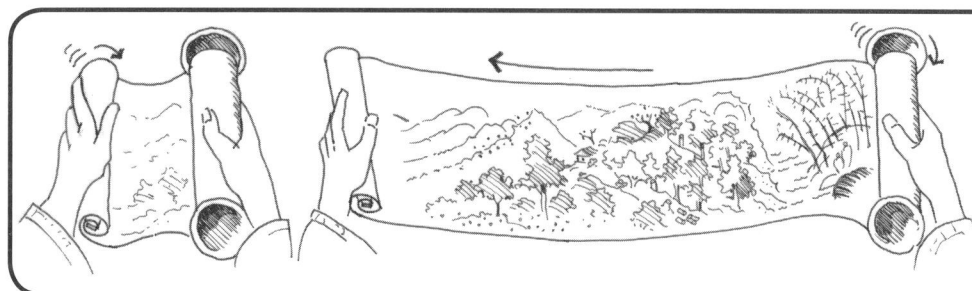

Magnolia Basin

On branch tips the hibiscus bloom.

The mountains show off red calices.

Nobody. A silent cottage in the valley.

One by one flowers open, then fall.

Garden design and landscape painting shared a language of visual conventions that was established during the Song dynasty. Garden layouts were inspired by compositional techniques used by landscape painters. Landscape paintings of the Northern and Southern Song dynasties expressed different attitudes toward nature.[15] Northern Song paintings were intended to be realistic portrayals of nature's awesomeness. Southern Song paintings were more personal expressions of nature, evoking mood. Artists brought the subject matter closer to the viewer. Unessential elements were reduced; space was implied by large voids in the composition. Song paintings are referenced in medieval Japanese literature and had a profound influence on Japanese garden design.

The "Golden Age" of the Song dynasty ended in the early 13th century. Genghis Khan conquered territories in Persia, Russia, and China, and over a period of 75 years the rest of China fell to the Mongol rulers. Kublai Khan captured Hangzhou in 1279 and formed the Yuan dynasty. He moved the capital to Beijing and built extravagant palace gardens and hunting parks to rival those of any former emperor. Literary accounts, including those of Marco Polo, described an artificial mountain covered with rare trees and green stones.

During the successive Ming and Qing dynasties, large-scale imperial parks were again built by the emperors in Beijing. As trade with the West resumed, a new merchant class built impressive gardens of their own; these are discussed in subsequent chapters.

NORTHERN SONG: The "mountain scrolls" of Northern Song paintings often show a diminutive human figure within a vast landscape dominated by natural features. Atmospheric effects created a layering of vertical space—trees were outlined against misty voids. Distance and spatial depth were captured through the manipulation of foreground, midground, and background elements.

SOUTHERN SONG: Detailed portraits of birds and flowers were common themes in Southern Song paintings. The imperial painting academy founded at Hangzhou focused on the intimate observation of nature.

PLUM : ENDURANCE

ORCHIDS : GRACE

CHRYSANTHEMUM : NOBILITY

BAMBOO : RESILIENCE

THE SYMBOLISM OF PLANTS:
To communicate the theme of a Chinese garden, gardeners chose plants more for their physical and symbolic attributes than for their sensual qualities. For example, the lotus, whose roots thrive in the muddy bottoms of ponds and whose blossoms reach up to float on the surface of the water, represented spiritual freedom. The "three friends of winter"—the pine, plum, and bamboo—signified longevity, endurance, and resilience. Plants representative of the four seasons—the orchid, bamboo, chrysanthemum, and flowering plum—also represented the traits of an ideal gentleman: grace, resiliency, nobility, and endurance.[16]

THE SYMBOLISM OF POETRY:
Poets, painters, and philosophers found inspiration in nature and symbolized the emotional relationship between art, nature, and humans in their work. The meaning of a Chinese garden is difficult to comprehend without understanding the literary context in which it was produced.

The courtyard deserted, the moon rises over the steps—shadows of the balustrade all over the ground.[17]

THE TRAVELS of MARCO POLO

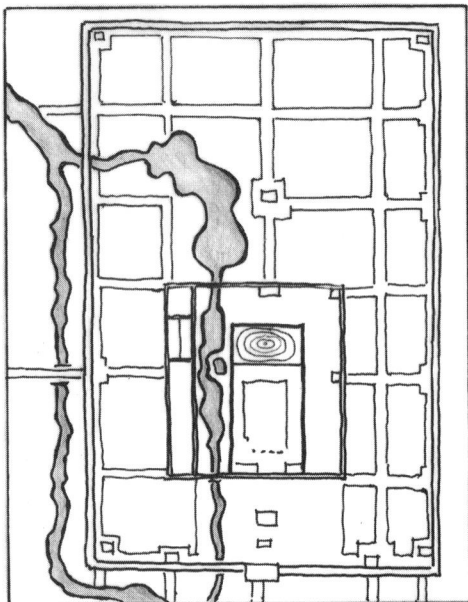

MARCO POLO

KUBLAI KHAN

Concerning the Palace of the Great Khan in the capital city of Cathay, which is called Cambaluc, stands his great palace. It is enclosed all around by a great wall forming a square, each side of which is a mile in length. The great wall has five gates on its southern face. Inside of this wall there is a second, enclosing a space that is somewhat greater in length than in breadth.

Between the two walls of the enclosure which I have described, there are fine parks and beautiful trees bearing a variety of fruits. There are beasts also of sundry kinds, such as white stags, fallow deer, gazelles, roebucks, and fine squirrels of various sorts. Parks are covered with abundant grass; the roads through them being all paved, the rain flows off into the meadows, quickening the soil and producing that abundance of herbage.

From that corner of the enclosure which is towards the northwest there extends a fine lake, containing a foison of fish. A river enters this lake and issues from it, but there is a grating of iron put up so that the fish cannot escape that way.

Moreover on the north side of the palace, about a bow shot off, there is a hill which has been made by art from the earth dug out of the lake; it is a good 100 paces in height and a mile in compass. This hill is entirely covered with trees that never lose their leaves, but remain ever green. Wherever a beautiful tree may exist, it is transported bodily and planted on that hill. In this way the emperor has got together the most beautiful collection of trees in all the world. He has also caused the whole hill to be covered with the ore of azure, which is very green. And thus not only are the trees all green, but the hill itself is all green; and hence it is called the Green Mount.[18]

JAPAN

45

IN THE SPIRIT OF NATURE

A central spine of steep mountains with dense forests rises from the ocean to create the small islands and rocky coastlines of Japan. Warm ocean currents foster a temperate climate with hot summers and mostly mild winters. Streams, waterfalls, and an abundance of moisture in the atmosphere support a wide variety of vegetation. An awareness of natural patterns and seasonal change is integral to Japanese culture.[19]

VIEWS OF NATURE

Nature was perceived in the Japanese imagination not as a harsh or hostile reality, but as an expression of the divine. The Japanese recognized the sanctity of a particular landscape by binding natural features with straw ropes (*shimenawa*) or demarcating space with *torii* gates. The ground plane in front of a temple was often emphasized by an apron of white sand or gravel and was considered purified ground. The form persisted in later Japanese gardens as a ceremonial and decorative forecourt.[20]

The ephemeral qualities of nature appeared as literary themes and sub-

SHINTO SHRINE: The "wedded rocks" (*meteo iwa*) at Ise are joined by a *shimenawa*.

jects of poems. Scenic descriptions of idealized landscape features such as "wild rocky coasts" or "deep mountains" became embedded in the collective imagination.[21] Garden designs were inspired by these poetic concepts, first

as subtle allusions to nature, and later as more overt scenography. As a garden could be a place to write poetry, the influence was circular—iconic imagery took form in the garden, and garden scenery inspired poetry.

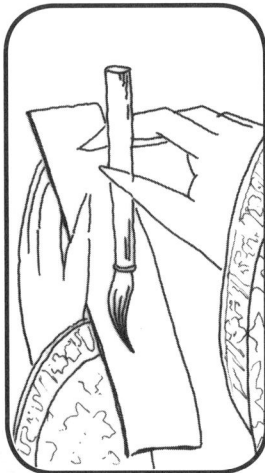

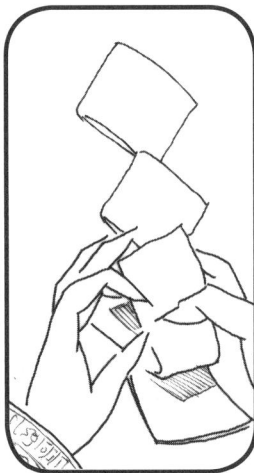

TREE SPIRIT: Shinto religious traditions venerated natural formations such as rocks, trees, and mountains as domains of ancestral spirits, or *kami*. Prayer strips communicated mortal intentions to the divine.

MAINLAND INFLUENCES

Many cultural influences reached Japan via the Korean peninsula, which at its closest point, is only about 300 miles from the island of Honshu. Chinese beliefs and artistic styles had a huge impact on Japanese designers, who adapted mainland ideas to local customs and blended foreign styles with vernacular traditions.

In the mid-6th century, the first Buddhist missionaries arrived in Japan. Buddhist cosmology deemed mountains sacred, a concept sympathetic to Shinto beliefs. Early Buddhist retreats occupied forests and peaks—sites often revered in the Shinto tradition. Empress Suiko and her regent, Prince Shotoku (574–622), promoted Buddhism as the state religion in an effort to unify the population and strengthen government influence.

CHINESE PRECEDENTS

In an attempt to create a strong, centralized government, political reforms of the mid-7th century abolished the private ownership of land and established the primacy of the Fujiwara clan as imperial regents. The capital, which previously had been relocated with each successive emperor, now moved to Nara, and remained there for 75 years. The city's strict geometric layout was modeled on the Chinese capital of Chang-an. The concept of an urban lifestyle and a sophisticated municipal bureaucracy also came from China, and contrasted with the self-sufficient, family-oriented, agrarian settlements in Japan.[22]

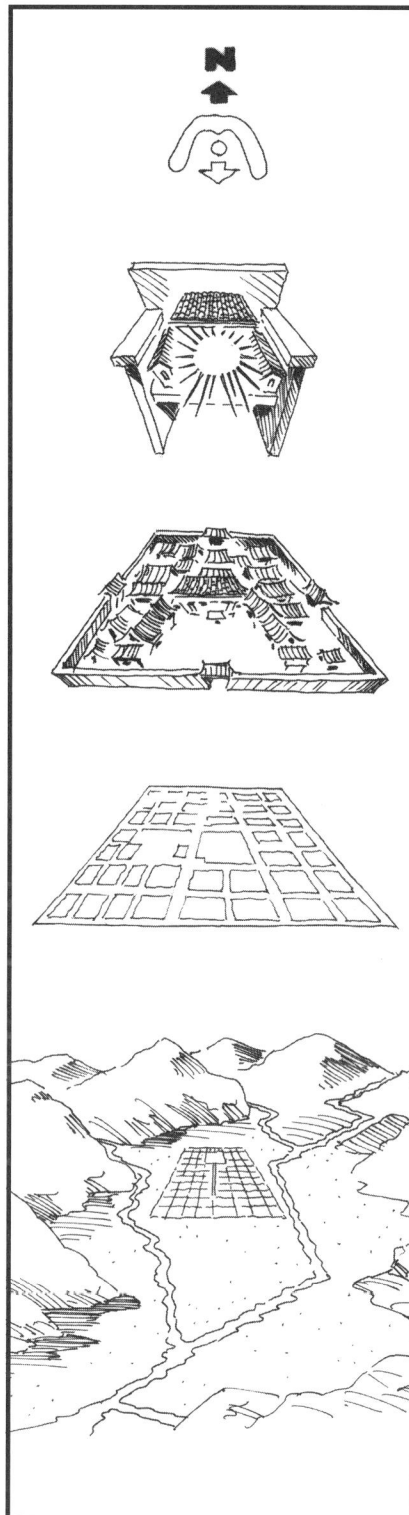

Chinese Tang culture dominated the court at Nara in the 6th and 7th centuries. Early diplomatic missions to the continent were recorded in the Chronicles of Japan (the Nihon Shoki, c. 720), which also described the naturalistic form and immense scale of Chinese imperial palace gardens, including Yangdi's park. The emerging aristocracy in Japan eagerly adopted as a style the large lakes and pleasure pavilions symbolic of the power and authority of the Chinese emperor. Little archeological evidence remains of Nara gardens, but surviving scroll paintings, and poems collected in the 8th-century anthology Manyoshu, document the pond-and-island type gardens of the period and serve as a record of the activities and entertainments that took place there. Chinese influence waned in the early 10th century as the Tang dynasty declined. The last Japanese envoy was sent to China in 894, and Japan entered a period of isolation that lasted until the 12th century.

DESIGN FOR A NEW CAPITAL:
The siting of the palace and city of Kyoto is based on geomantic concepts similar to those at Chang-an. The divine source of power lies to the north. The mountains to the north of Kyoto embrace the city like an armchair, providing a seat for the emperor—the refuge of a "bright courtyard" in Chinese.[23]

THE GOLDEN AGE OF GARDENS

SHINDEN-ZUKURI: Heian gardens were settings for poetry contests, flower-viewing festivals, boating parties, and musical events.

TRAVELING POETRY: The women at Prince Genji's mansion compete for his attention. They exchange poems extolling the virtues of their seasonally themed gardens. Here, autumn versus spring:

AUTUMN: "Your garden quietly awaits the spring. Permit the winds to bring a touch of Autumn."

SPRING: "Fleeting, your leaves that scatter in the wind. The pine at the cliffs is forever green with Spring."[24]

Under threat from the increasingly powerful Buddhist priests at Nara, the imperial court moved once more, in 794, to the politically neutral territory of Kyoto. The new capital, known then as Heian-kyo, or the City of Peace and Tranquility, was planned on a grid like Chang-an and Nara.

The Heian period is marked by a flourishing of aesthetic pursuits and cultural refinement. By the 10th century, the Fujiwara regents assumed complete administrative control of the government. The aristocratic classes, now powerless in affairs of state, turned their attentions to advanced forms of poetry, literature, music, fashion, and landscape design.

The excavation and restoration of actual Heian gardens is ongoing. The *Sakuteiki*, a garden manual written in the early 11th century by Tachibana no Toshitsuna, half-brother of the regent, provides an additional source of information about medieval gardens in Japan. The author describes theories and concepts of rock placement, borrowed scenery, and geomantic principles of estate layout, and even categorizes 10 different types of waterfalls. A spiritual and philosophical approach to garden making, the work blends common-sense advice with knowledge of local environmental conditions.

TALE OF GENJI: The medieval mindset and attitude toward nature is characterized in the *Tale of Genji*, a novel written in the Japanese vernacular by Lady Murasaki Shikibu in the early 11th century. The story unfolds in a princely garden and details the highly structured life at court.

SHINDEN-STYLE COURTYARDS

BYODO-IN exemplifies a shinden-style temple of the period. Originally built in 1052 by Fujiwara no Yorimichi, a devotee of Amida Buddhism, the main structure (called the Phoenix Hall) contains a large statue of Buddha and faces east so the devout would face the western paradise to pray.

Architecture provided the framework for gardens in the Heian period. Large central courtyards, open to the south, were defined by the shinden-zukuri building form. The shinden hall was the main residence and audience chamber. Ancillary pavilions were joined to the shinden by covered walkways. Structures were made of unpainted wood. The main hall opened onto a pond-and-island-type garden—a precedent that alluded to the mythological islands of the Immortals, legendary in Chinese folklore. In Japanese gardens, the ponds often referenced actual coastal scenery, and the islands symbolized the myth of the turtle and the crane. The turtle island represented Mt. Shumisen, the sacred center of the

universe in Buddhist doctrine; the crane island symbolized longevity; together they formed an auspicious balance of nature.

Buddhist temples of the Heian period were also built in the shinden zukuri style. The Amida form of Buddhism reached its peak of popularity during the 11th and 12th centuries. The focus of Amida Buddhism was devotion and the reward of paradise—a "pure land of the west"—for the virtuous. Thus, temple gardens became earthly recreations of paradise. Aristocratic estate gardens were often converted to temple gardens in the 11–12th centuries as the nobility now entered the priesthood and under-

took garden design as a form of artistic expression.

Shinden-style palaces and temples had south-facing pavilions and balustraded verandas that bordered large central ponds. Water flowed through the garden in constructed streams that mimicked natural drainage patterns, moving across a site in an auspicious pattern from east to south to west. Carefully placed rocks along the convoluted shorelines masked the full extent of the ponds, creating an illusion of distance. Other landscape elements in a shinden-style garden included earth mounds, vermillion-colored bridges, and a minimal number of rocks and trees.

SECOND WAVE OF CHINESE INFLUENCE

Agricultural production improved at the end of the Heian age. As trade increased, markets developed and a merchant class was established. Provincial landowners formed hierarchical power structures independent of the capital, further weakening the central government. Civil war ensued. The Fujiwara were ousted by the Taira; the Taira were deposed by the Minamoto. The Minamoto clan moved the seat of the new military government northeast, to Kamakura, near Edo, although the cultural capital remained at Kyoto. Contact with China was renewed, and a second wave of Chinese influence ensued. Japanese priests visited Chinese monasteries, and Chinese artists and intellectuals immigrated to Japan as the Mongolian invasion persisted. In particular, Zen Buddhism and Song period art entered Japan and had profound influences on garden design.

The height of Song painting in China corresponded to the late Heian/early Kamakura period. Painting was as much an intellectual pursuit as it was a technical skill; this aspect of Song culture appealed to the priests and the military class, whose members sought new ways to define their cultural ambitions in opposition to Kyoto society. Creating an illusion of space and conveying the essential spirit of nature were common attributes of Song painting.

ZEN AND THE SAMURAI SPIRIT

The Kamakura period is marked by a spirit of self-discipline and control, evidenced by the growth of religion (Zen Buddhism) and a new military class (the samurai warrior) dedicated to a provincial warlord, or shogun. Amid the political and social instability of the 13th and 14th centuries, a turning inward can be seen not only in the wide acceptance of Zen Buddhism with its emphasis on

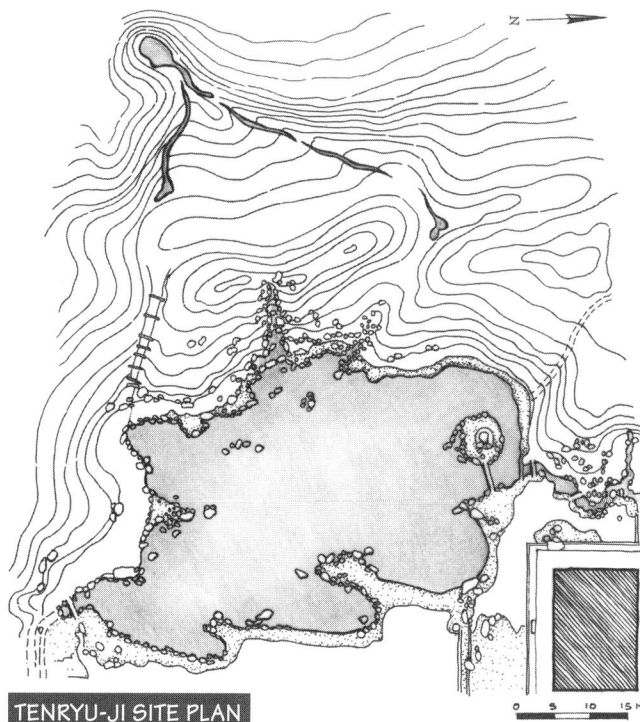

TENRYU-JI SITE PLAN

0   5   10   15 M

FRAMED VIEW: The garden at Tenryu-ji as seen from the abbot's quarters—a single vantage point where the landscape itself becomes the subject matter.

meditation, but also in garden design, where only "essential" characteristics of nature were re-created. Gardens contained "empty" spaces, just as Song landscape paintings contained voids.

During the Kamakura period, the military government sponsored Zen Buddhist temples—austere centers of learning and intellectualism that contrasted with the lavish imperial palaces built during the Heian period. Temple gardens were designed by monks and itinerant "rock-setting priests" who had visited Buddhist monasteries in China.[25] The Zen priest Muso Soseki (1275–1351, given the honorific title Muso Kokushi), promoted gardening as a religious activity. He is credited with the layout of several temple gardens, including the redesign in 1339 of Tenryu-ji and Saiho-ji, former aristocratic estates outside Kyoto.

SEQUENCE OF SPACE: The upper garden at Saiho-ji contains arrangements of flat-topped rocks representing a turtle island, a zazen-seki, or meditation seat, and a dry waterfall.

▲ **DRAGON GATE:** A waterfall with its upright carp stone can be understood as an allegory of achievement and enlightenment—the carp becomes a dragon if it can climb the falls—referencing success in the civil service examinations or the attainment of Buddhahood.

▶ **IMMORTAL ISLAND:** The vertical arrangement of seven stones at Tenryu-ji shows early Chinese influence, possibly representing the islands of the Immortals. Rock arrangements in Japanese gardens would evolve to form more horizontal compositions.

TENRYU-JI

Tenryu-ji represents an important transition between the pond-and-island-style gardens of the Heian court and the contemplative style gardens of the later Kamakura/early Muromachi period. The garden is less than 1 acre in size and contains a pond with a single arrangement of vertical rocks. Just beyond this grouping of upright stones is a "dragon gate" waterfall. A horizontal stone in the foreground of the falls bridges a narrow outlet and serves as a visual counterpoint to the high stack of vertical rocks in the background—creating an illusion of distance and a layering of space similar to that represented in Song paintings.[26]

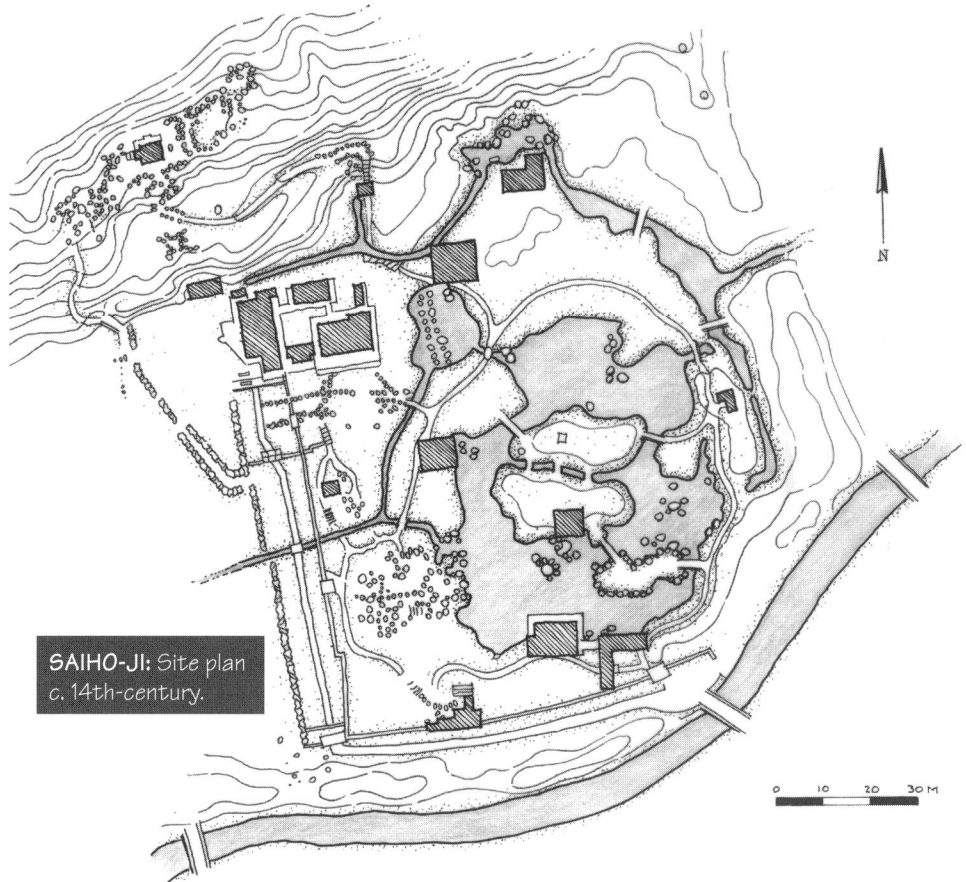

SAIHO-JI: Site plan c. 14th-century.

0   10   20   30 M

SAIHO-JI

Built on the site of an 8th-century temple, and converted to temple grounds by Muso Kokushi, Saiho-ji is another transitional garden of the Kamakura period. The dry cascade of stone illustrates the development of *kare sansui*, a concept originally mentioned in the Sakuteiki, which creates the illusion of streams and waterfalls through the placement of rocks and gravel.

MOSS TEMPLE: Saiho-ji contains an early paradise garden around a lower lake and an upper garden of horizontal, flat-topped rocks, now covered with moss.

NEW WAYS TO CONTEMPLATE THE LANDSCAPE

In the mid-14th century, a less symmetrical, more informal architectural style developed, called the *shoin-zukuri*, or "reading room" style. A *shoin* was an alcove that projected out from the exterior wall and sometimes contained a writing desk and "picture window" that faced the garden. The often diagonal arrangement of interior spaces enabled the garden to be approached from an oblique angle, creating a variety of framing possibilities. The garden now became something to be seen more intimately, from a fixed point of view. The idea of borrowed scenery, or *shakkei*, also mentioned in the *Sakuteiki*, became a guiding principle of landscape design, as did the aesthetic of *kare sansui*. Other features of the *shoin-zukuri* style were *tokonoma* alcoves for the display of art; sliding doors with paper insets, which enhanced the flexibility of interior spaces; and *tatami* flooring mats.

The end of the 14th century saw the rise of the Ashikaga clan and the return of the shoguns to the Muromachi district of Kyoto. The Ashikaga accumulated power and wealth by heavily taxing the peasants. They embraced the subtle aesthetics of the Song dynasty and could afford to be generous patrons of the arts. Many Chinese artists immigrated to Japan during this time and taught calligraphy and poetry to the samurai.

KINKAKU-JI

The third Ashikaga shogun, Yoshimitsu, converted a shinden-style estate to a picturesque retreat in the northwest sector of Kyoto beginning in 1397. Kinkaku-ji, or the Garden of the Golden Pavilion, blends elements of a Heian paradise garden with Song painting conventions. The landscape is carefully composed to manipulate perspectives and vistas, particularly when seen from a boat. An island and small peninsula divide the lake; trees and shrubs on the distant banks are kept small, to visually extend the space. The 4½-acre garden contains many symbolic elements, including turtle and crane islands, ship mooring stones, and a dragon gate waterfall. The three-story pavilion itself functions in accordance with Zen tenets: the lowest floor was for reception, the middle floor for conversation and study, and the top floor for meditation. The shift from outward contemplation to inward contemplation reaches its fullest expression in the garden during the later Muromachi period.

KINKAKU-JI: One important garden that fuses the ethics and aesthetics of the early Muromachi period is Kinkaku-ji, situated in the northwest sector of Kyoto.

SUMMARY

The gardens examined in this chapter responded to a wide range of environmental and cultural conditions, but despite their different contexts, they expressed a similar desire to create areas of significance through the functional and aesthetic modification of nature.

During the Middle Ages, nature was largely uncontrollable, and political order was unstable. Whether for protection or defense, to mitigate forces of nature, or to create a more perfect representation of nature, medieval gardens were enclosed. The act of enclosing space creates a realm distinct from its surroundings; a *locus amoenus* that in the Middle Ages often symbolized an idea of paradise.

DESIGN PRINCIPLES

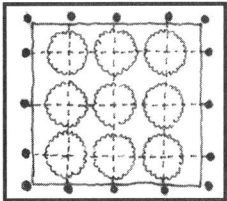

UTILITY

The medieval cloister is an embodiment of utilitarian geometry. A simple square bounded by an arcade becomes an ambulatory to facilitate prayer. A square, subdivided by raised planting beds, becomes a living encyclopedia of herbs and flowers.

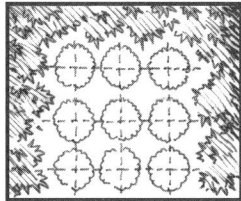

CONTRAST

A small plot of pleasure amid a landscape of labor—the carefully tended pleasance is set in opposition to its untamed surroundings.

SCALE

The Moorish courtyard is an outdoor living room—human-scaled open space defined by architecture. The transition between inside and outside is mediated by architectural elements; porticos and loggias provide secondary thresholds.

BALANCE

The Chinese garden is a microcosm of nature where inherent forces are balanced visually, symbolically, and experientially. An intuitive equilibrium is created between rock and water, solid and void, word and image.

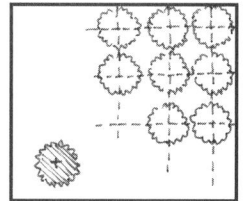

APPROPRIATION

Shakkei is the principle of "borrowed" scenery. The landscape beyond a garden's borders is appropriated to become a visual component of Japanese gardens.

DESIGN VOCABULARY

WESTERN EUROPE
Fences, Walls and Fountains

MOORISH SPAIN
Runnels and Raised Paths

CHINA
Rocks and Water

JAPAN
Courtyards, Lakes, and Islands

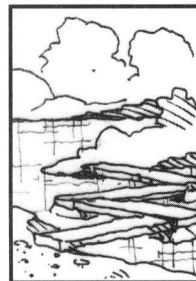

For further exploration

BOOKS
ADVENTURES OF MARCO POLO
CANTERBURY TALES, by Geoffrey Chaucer
THE DECAMERON, by Giovanni Boccaccio
THE DIVINE COMEDY, by Dante Alighieri
INVISIBLE CITIES, by Italo Calvino
THE NAME OF THE ROSE, by Umberto Eco
ONE THOUSAND AND ONE NIGHTS
   (various English translations)
THE ROMANCE OF THE ROSE, by Guillaume de Lorris
TALES OF THE ALHAMBRA, by Washington Irving
THE TALE OF GENJI, by Murasaki Shikibu
THE TALE OF HEIKE,
   translated by Helen Craig McCullough

FILMS
THE ADVENTURES OF ROBIN HOOD (1938)
BRAVEHEART (1995)
EL CID (1961)
GENGHIS KHAN (1954)
KINGDOM OF HEAVEN (2005)
THE LION IN WINTER (1968)
THE SEVENTH SEAL (1957)

PAINTINGS
EMPEROR MING HUANG'S JOURNEY TO SHU,
   artist unknown (8th century)
EARLY SPRING, by Kuo Hsi (1072)
SIX PERSIMMONS, by Mu Chi (13th century)
SCROVEGNI CHAPEL FRESCOES, by Giotto (1305)
THE EFFECTS OF GOOD AND BAD GOVERNMENT
   ON THE CITY AND COUNTRYSIDE,
   by Ambrogio Lorenzetti (1338)

15th CENTURY

The 15th century was an age of exploration—a period of expansion and cultural advancement that proceeded at a different pace, however, across the world. New discoveries and new lands reshaped medieval worldviews. Europe emerged as a world power, with Italy at the center of early Renaissance thought. The new merchant class challenged aristocratic power structures and church authority. But the desire for economic hegemony led to the exploitation of many cultures, particularly those in the Americas and Africa.

As horizons broadened, gardens became places to contemplate nature, not escape from it. Garden prototypes established during the Middle Ages reached maturity in the 15th century. The Zen garden became the ultimate expression of *kare sansui* in Japan; the *chahar bagh* epitomized Islamic garden form; and the Italian villa evolved as the physical representation of a philosophical ideal.

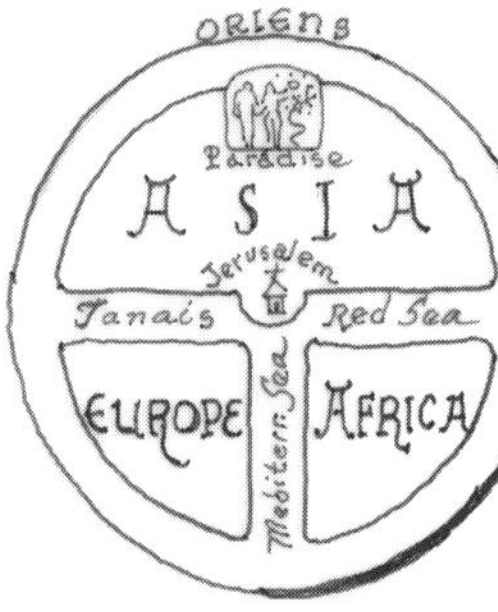

c. 1400
MAPPA MUNDI

1405–1433
CHINESE NAVY

1427
SPATIAL REALISM

1400

1410

1420

1374
PETRARCH

1419
OSPEDALE DEGLI INNOCENTI

1420
OIL PAINT

1426
MING WORKS

1465
THE SONGHAI

1459
HANGING GARDEN

1460

1470

1459
TOWN PLAN

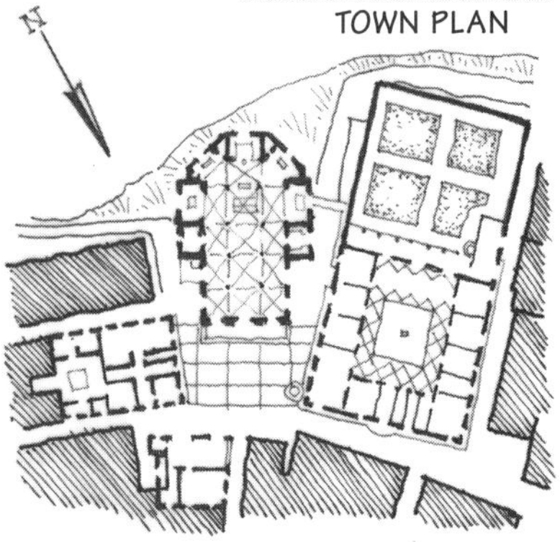

1469
FERDINAND & ISABELLA

1474
THE STRIFE OF LOVE
IN A DREAM

1453
ACQUA VERGINE

1438
TENOCHTITLAN

1436
DUOMO

1430

1440

1450

1435
PERSPECTIVE

1440
PRINTING PRESS

1453
ISTANBUL

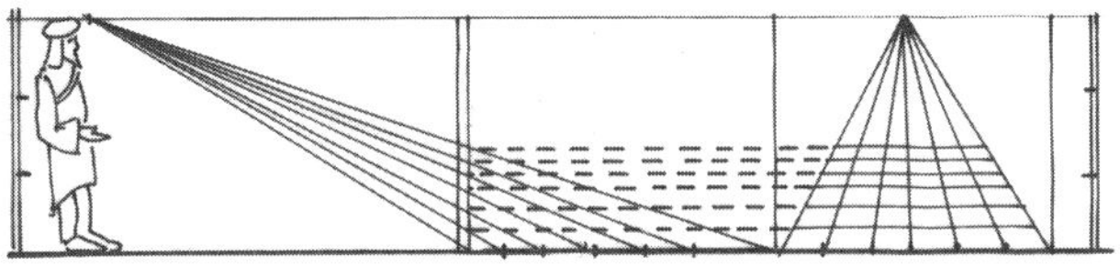

1494
ACCOUNTING METHODS

1480
ALLEGORY OF SPRING

1498
WORLD TRAVELER

1480

1490

1500

1490
VITRUVIAN MAN

1492
DISCOVERY?

1500
THE INCA

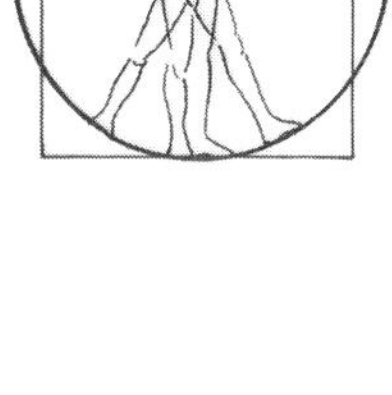

1374 PETRARCH
Petrarch, an Italian poet and early humanist, studied the art and literature of antiquity. He fostered scholarship based on classical ideals.

c. 1400 MAPPA MUNDI
Early medieval maps drawn by Christian cartographers were centered on Jerusalem and illustrated a world of three continents: Asia, Europe, and Africa. East, the direction of paradise, was at the top.

1405–1433 CHINESE NAVY
Ming Emperor Yongle sent naval commander Zheng He on diplomatic and trade expeditions that circled the globe.

1419 OSPEDALE DEGL'INNOCENTI
Filippo Brunelleschi (1377–1446) applied a classical architectural vocabulary to his design for the Foundling Hospital in Florence. The delicate Corinthian colonnade with rounded arches displayed a clear, rational proportioning system.

1420 OIL PAINT
Oil painting was invented by early Netherlandish painters. Artists like Jan Van Eyck captured realistic details, rich colorations, and deep modeling with the new slow-drying medium.

1426 MING WORKS
Ming dynasty rulers restored the Great Wall and the Grand Canal, and developed trade connections with Europe. Ming textiles, lacquer work, and ceramics, particularly blue-and-white porcelains, were highly coveted by Europeans.

1427 SPATIAL REALISM
Masaccio (1401–1428) first depicted one-point perspective in the *Holy Trinity*, a fresco he painted in the church of Santa Maria Novella, Florence. The realistically placed vanishing point created a sense of drama and an illusion of space.

1435 PERSPECTIVE
Leon Battista Alberti described how to construct a perspective grid in his treatise on painting, *Della pittura*.

1436 DUOMO
Brunelleschi completed the design of the dome on the Cathedral of Santa Maria del Fiore, Florence. The double-layered octagonal dome was the largest masonry dome ever built. His firsthand study of ancient Roman ruins may have influenced his success with this engineering marvel.

1438 TENOCHTITLAN
Cultivated islands called *chinampas*, along with an extensive network of canals, dikes, and causeways, helped Mexico's capital city expand.

1440 PRINTING PRESS
Johannes Gutenberg (1398–1468) perfected movable type in the first printing press in Germany. The more efficient way of publishing accelerated the dissemination of knowledge in the Renaissance.

1453 ISTANBUL
The Ottomans conquered Constantinople and renamed it Istanbul, converting the church to a mosque.

1453 ACQUA VERGINE
Pope Nicholas V restored the ancient Roman aqueduct, and established the Vatican Library to house the papacy's growing collection of ancient manuscripts.

1459 TOWN PLAN
Pope Pius II rebuilt his native Tuscan village, Pienza, as one of the earliest models of Renaissance town planning. He organized palace, church, and town hall as a single urban entity embodying the classical concept of *civitas*—the balance of people, nature, and government.

1459 HANGING GARDEN
Palazzo Piccolomini was designed by Bernardo Rossellino, a student of Alberti's, as part of Pius II's urbanization project in Pienza. A terraced garden on the south side of the palace is framed by a loggia affording stunning views.

1465 THE SONGHAI
King Sonni Ali consolidated the Songhai Empire; it became the leading power in western Sudan and upper Africa under later dynastic rulers.

1469 FERDINAND AND ISABELLA
Ferdinand and Isabella symbolically united the kingdoms of Castile and Aragon, and in 1492 completed the reconquest of Spain when Granada fell to the Christians. Ferdinand and Isabella saw non-Catholics as a threat and initiated a long period of intolerance and persecution known as the Inquisition.

1474 THE STRIFE OF LOVE IN A DREAM
The extensive woodcuts in the novel *Hypnerotomachia Poliphili* became a sourcebook of design ideas for future gardeners. Friar Francesco Colonna's detailed descriptions of plant species shed light on the horticultural content of early Renaissance gardens.

1480 PRIMAVERA, BY BOTTICELLI
Mythological subjects were interpreted as humanistic allegories and became part of the secular iconography of the Renaissance.

1490 VITRUVIAN MAN
Leonardo diagrammed the proportional relationships of the human body according to classical ideals, illustrating his point that man is the model of the world.

1492 DISCOVERY?
The Italian navigator Christopher Columbus convinced Ferdinand and Isabella to sponsor an expedition to India by sailing west. He landed in the Bahamas and named the islands the "West Indies."

1494 ACCOUNTING METHODS
Fra Luca Pacioli wrote *Summa de arithmetica, geometria, proportioni et proportionalita*.

1498 WORLD TRAVELER
The Age of Discovery continued with Vasco da Gama's voyage from Portugal, around the Cape of Good Hope, to India.

1500 THE INCA
The Inca empire at its height included 6 million people. Cuzco, the regional capital, was thought to be mapped with sacred lines called *ceques* that radiated from the temple of the sun.

MUROMACHI ERA

Gardens of the Muromachi era (1333–1573) were characterized by a reduced scale, a refined purpose, and a distinct architectural setting that reflected the values of the military regime of the Ashikaga shoguns, who returned the capital to Kyoto. The samurai knights obeyed a code of fearlessness, loyalty, and service. Estate and temple gardens no longer served solely as pleasure palaces or allegories of paradise, as they did for their Heian predecessors. Muromachi gardens now focused on aspects of form and artful composition.

Zen Buddhism, first introduced during the Kamakura era, was widely promoted by the ruling shoguns. Since Zen practice is an individual pursuit concerned with meditation and the development of the interior self, large ceremonial spaces were less critical. Priests established individual subtemples within larger temple compounds. Small temple gardens became sites for seated contemplation, not ritual, and were meant to be seen from fixed points of view. The sliding partitions of the *shoin* provided unique opportunities for framing landscape views.[1] Gardens, engaged only visually, became aids to meditation, not sites of active use.

A MINIMALIST AESTHETIC

Large landscapes were represented in small spaces. Garden elements were abstracted and reduced to their essential characteristics, expressed in the form of *kare sansui*, or dry landscape gardens, and conceptually similar to tray landscapes.

Kyoto was substantially destroyed during the Onin Wars of 1467–1477. Feudal lords called *daimyo* rose to power in the provinces in the 15th century as the power of the Ashikaga declined. A dispute over imperial succession arose

between the *daimyo* and the shogun, leading to the decade of civil war. Despite an entire century of political turmoil, the arts flourished in 15th-century Japan, including Noh drama, gardening, painting, and the early practice of the tea ritual.

A distinct Japanese painting style developed during the Muromachi period, as did a distinct social class of gardening specialists. Both influenced the design of gardens. Sesshu (1420–1506) was a Buddhist monk who elaborated on Chinese ink painting techniques, devising his own vocabulary of short angular strokes and dots. Like Song dynasty artists, he captured the immensity and depth of the landscape within the confines of a hanging scroll.

NATURE ABSTRACTED: Miniature tray landscapes became accepted art forms during the Kamakura period, and may have influenced the development of Zen gardens. *Bonseki* are tray gardens composed solely of stones and sand; *bonsai* are dwarfed plants grown in tray like containers.

LANDSCAPE BY SESSHU: *Sesshu depicted the essence of the Japanese landscape with an economy of line and form.*

LANDSCAPE BY SESSHU: *The flat-topped, straight-sided rocks used in the dry landscape gardens at Daisen-in resemble the painter's rendering of landforms.*

One group of garden designers not connected to the nobility or the priesthood gained the respect of the military-minded Ashikaga shoguns and established themselves as garden building specialists. The kawaramono were poor people, not bounded to landowners, who lived by the untaxed riverside. They did the "unclean" work of tanning and grave-digging. Zen'ami (c. 1386–1483) was one such person who gained respect and status for his ability to arrange rocks as they appeared in ink paintings.[2] He is often credited with the placement of the rocks at Ginkaku-ji.[3]

Examples of Muromachi-period gardens include Ginkaku-ji and the Zen gardens of Ryoan-ji and Daisen-in.

GINKAKU-JI

Ginkaku-ji dates from 1480 and was built by the eighth Ashikaga shogun, Yoshimasa, grandson of Yoshimitsu. The pond-style garden of Ginkaku-ji (called the Garden of the Silver Pavilion) was created on a more modest scale than Kinkaku-ji (the Garden of the Golden Pavilion). Yoshimasa was inspired by the restrained beauty of the garden at Saiho-ji, which he often visited, and he sought to duplicate many of its same features at his villa.[4] The garden contained a tea pavilion, chapel, and bridges leading to an island with flat-topped rocks. The two-storied Silver Pavilion (its name derives from an unrealized project to cover the ceiling with silver leaf) contained a meditation chapel and Buddha hall, and afforded superb views of the garden. The large sand mounds—the Sea of Silver Sand and the truncated cone of the Moon-viewing Platform—were added during later restorations.

ZEN GARDENS

RYOAN-JI

The well-known temple garden at Ryoan-ji was rebuilt in 1488 following its destruction during the Onin War. The enigmatic arrangement of rocks and sand occupies a walled courtyard on the southern side of the abbot's quarters. The 15 rocks, unremarkable in themselves, are arranged in five groups that create a dynamic spatial composition. Visual forces are balanced in asymmetrical relationships that can be perceived within each group and within the total ensemble. The meaning of the abstraction is unclear; perhaps, in keeping with the spirit of Zen inquiry, the interpretation is left to the viewer.

DAISEN-IN

Although Daisen-in was built very early in the 16th century, it is included in this chapter as part of the discussion of Zen gardens. Daisen-in was built in 1509 as a subtemple of the large Zen monastery complex of Daitoku-ji. A kare sansui style garden surrounds the shoin-style temple. The most famous garden, on the northeast side, uses rocks and sand to narrate an allegory of life's challenges and resolutions, beginning with the sacred mountain and concluding in the endless void.[5]

Daitoku-ji held a large collection of Song art. The Japanese artist Soami (1472–1523) created the landscape paintings on the interior walls, and is thought to have influenced the design of the garden, although no documentary evidence supports this claim.

GINKAKU-JI: Unlike its Heian predecessors, this pond-and-island-style garden was experienced by walking, not boating. Particular vistas were meant to be contemplated from fixed points on the path around the lake.

CASE STUDY: *Daisen-In*

Observing the garden from the temple's interior, the visitor's gaze moves from left to right. The dry course of water appears to fall from a high mountain gorge, becoming a river flowing by rocks, under bridges, and finally out to sea.

The large stone parallel to the edge of the veranda serves as an eye-drop, bringing the viewer into the scene. The layering of objects in this small 12 foot by 47 foot space creates a sense of depth similar to that captured by the Song dynasty painters.

The entry garden on the south side of the temple features two simple cones of sand; their form probably derives from earlier utilitarian functions.[6] A wall (not shown) that now bisects the garden was added in the 20th century based on evidence that such a structure existed in the original garden.

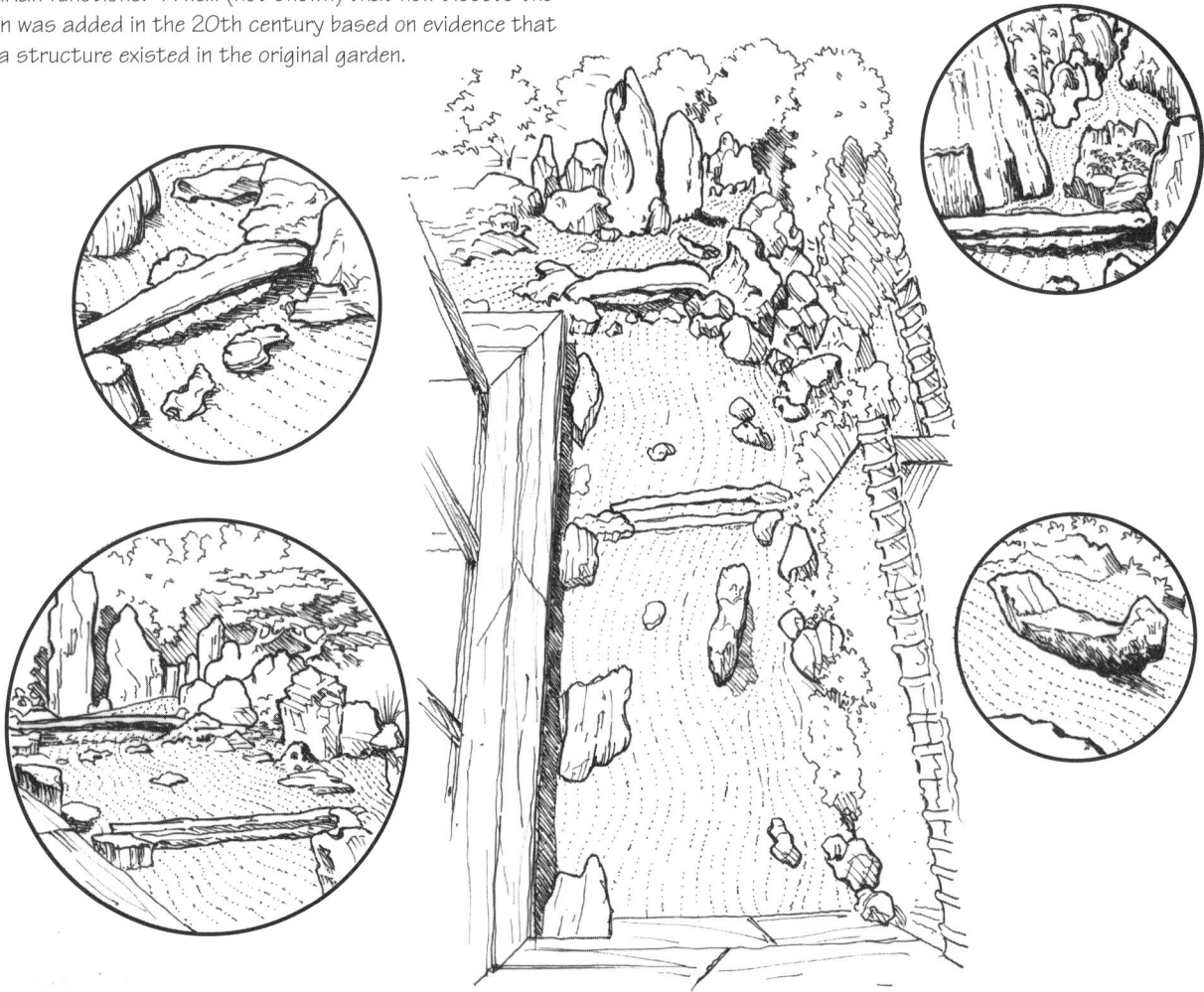

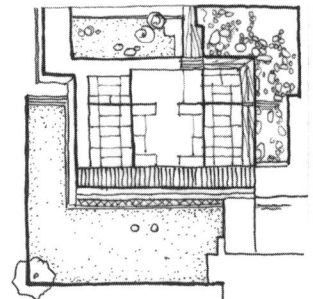

MING DYNASTY

The Yuan dynasty collapsed in 1368 when rebels defeated the Mongol rulers. The Chinese reestablished themselves as indigenous rulers during the Ming dynasty (1368–1644). In 1403, the third Ming emperor, Yongle, moved the capital back to Beijing and began construction of the Forbidden City, on the foundations of what remained of Khublai Khan's destroyed palace complex.[7] It remained the imperial capital until 1912.

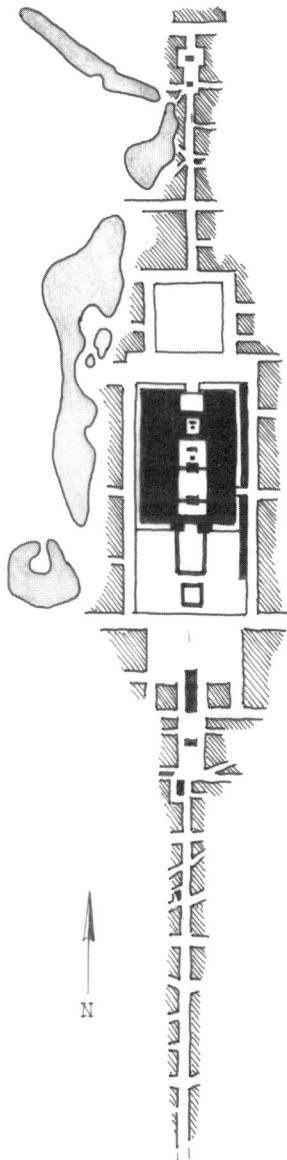

PERFECT HARMONY: Hierarchically ordered spaces emphasized the divine power of the Chinese emperor, who was always positioned at the center.[8]

IMPERIAL CAPITAL: The present form of the Forbidden City was established during the Ming dynasty.

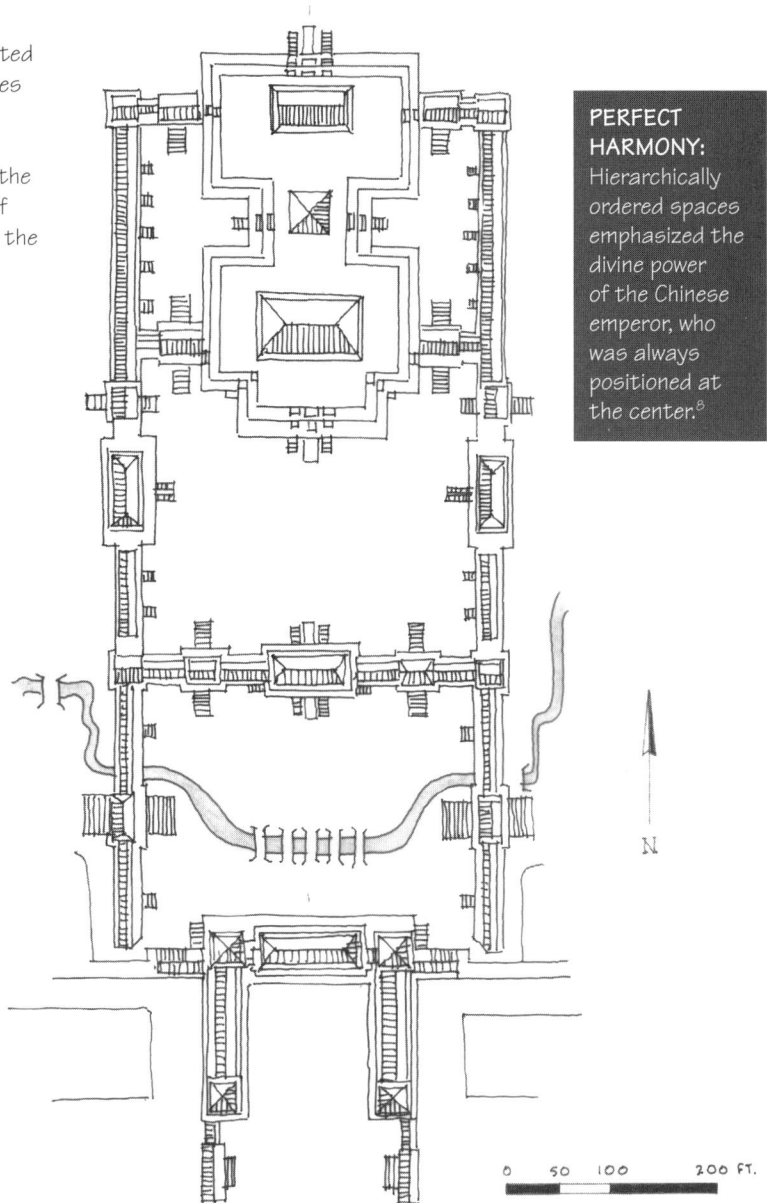

FORBIDDEN CITY

The Forbidden City consisted of hundreds of buildings and courtyards symmetrically arranged around a north-south axis. All buildings faced south. A moat and a wall surrounded the Forbidden City, which was contained within the boundaries of the Imperial City. The emperor and his family occupied the inner court; the outer court was used for ceremonies and by lesser officials. Yongle further excavated the lake originally developed by the Khan in the western section of the city, and as part of an irrigation project created two other lakes that formed the three "sea palaces" of the imperial park (Nanhai, Zhonghai, and Beihai). Earth dredged from the moat formed an auspiciously located hill, called Coal Hill (now Jingshan Park), at the north end of the city.

TIMURID GARDEN CITIES

The close relationship between gardens and urban form in 15th-century Central Asia is exemplified by the planned city of Samarkand, where the managed landscape formed an integral part of the ordered city. Located on the important Silk Route between China and the Mediterranean, Samarkand reveals the influences of many different cultures. Founded by the Persians in the 8th century BCE, the city was conquered by Alexander in the 4th century BCE, overrun by the Turks in the 6th century CE, and dominated by the Arabs in the 8th century, when it became a center of Islamic scholarship. Samarkand was sacked by the Mongols in 1220. Timur (1336–1405, also known as Tamerlane) established Samarkand as the capital of his empire in 1370, and rebuilt the city as a cultural mecca.

A nomadic tribesman from Central Asia, Timur wanted to control lucrative trade routes, and through ruthless warfare subjugated lands from India to Turkey, including parts of Russia. He weakened Mongol power in Central Asia and crippled the Ottoman Turks who were threatening Europe. The King of Castile (northern Spain) sent an envoy, Ruy Gonzalez de Clavijo, to establish diplomatic ties with Timur. Clavijo's descriptions remain an important source of information on the lush gardens and fertile plains of Samarkand.[9]

The court moved to Herat after Timur's death. The Timurid period, from the late 14th to early 15th centuries, was described by Timur's descendent Babur as the Golden Age for art and science.[10] Observatories were built and constellations mapped; Herat and Samarkand blossomed under the leadership of Timur's heirs.

FOUR-FOLD GARDEN GEOMETRY

Once surrounded by forests, orchards, and meadows, the gardens at Samarkand have vanished. But the pleasure gardens and royal encampments described by Clavijo and Babur established a prototype for later gardens: the four-square garden with water axis and central pavilion. Although the rectangular subdivision of space is evidenced in ancient Persian gardens, the first reference to this form as chahar-bagh (literally, "four gardens") was during Timur's reign.[11]

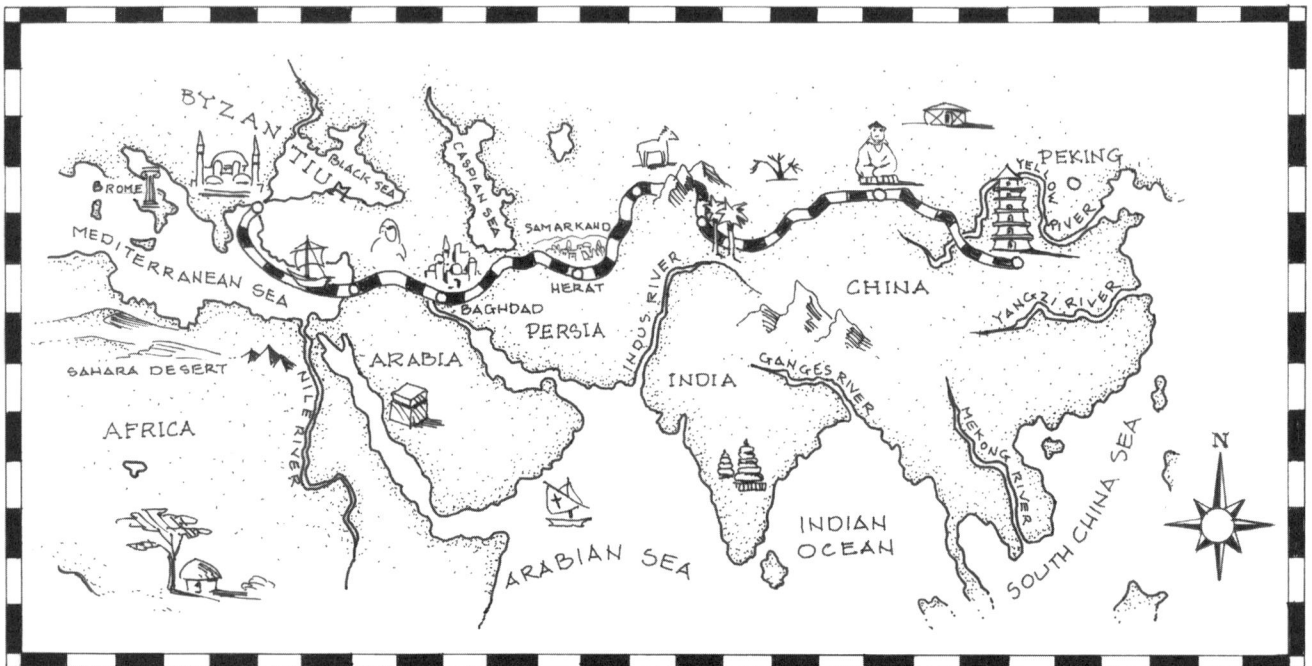

SILK ROUTE: Material goods, scientific concepts, and philosophical ideologies were transferred between continents, enriching cultures worldwide.

In Islam, as in many other religions, paradise is symbolized as a garden. A *chahar-bagh* is often called a paradise garden (its runnels representing the rivers of milk, honey, water, and wine mentioned in the Quran), but the symbolic geometry predates the advent of Islam. In pre-Islamic Persian iconography, crossed axes represented the four corners of the world, marked with a spring at its center. The evolution of the *chahar-bagh* as a model of paradise parallels the etymology of the English word paradise: its Greek root, *parade-isos* (park) derives from the Persian *pairidaeza* (walled enclosure). The elaborate paradise gardens of the Mughal Empire in India and Kashmir, founded by Babur, are described in chapter five.

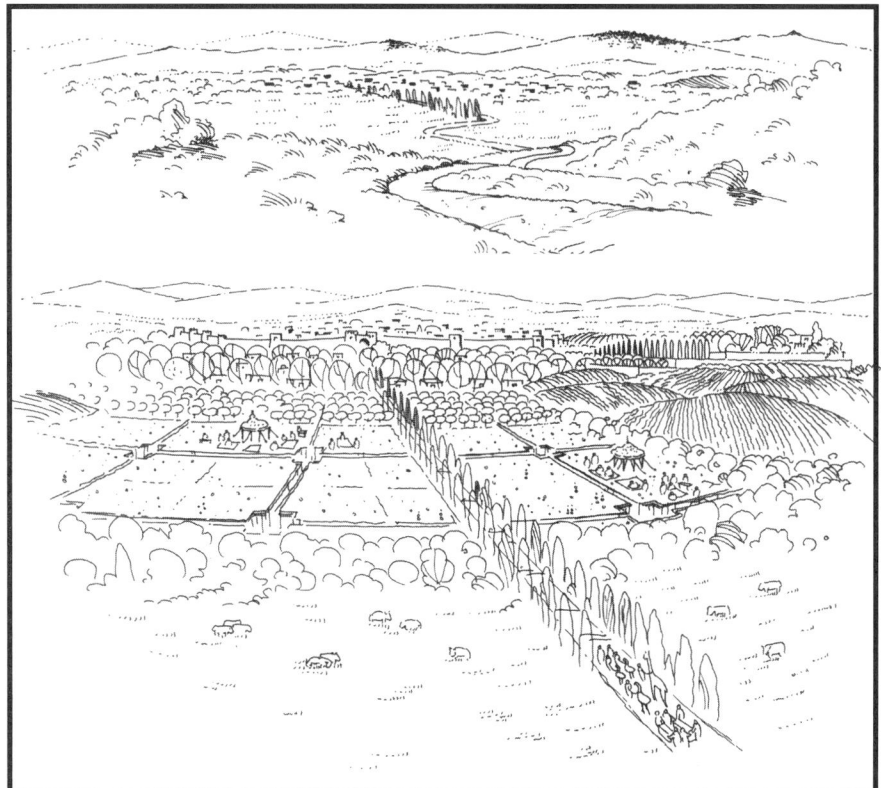

TRANSOXIAN VALLEY: Clavijo described the city of Herat: "It stands in the plain, and on all sides the land is well irrigated by streams and water channels, while round and about the city there are orchards with many homesteads."[12]

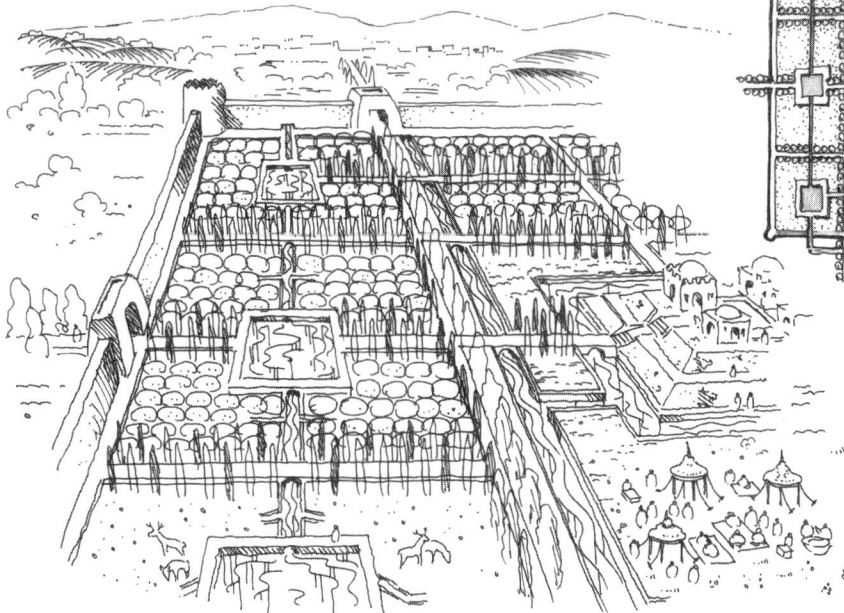

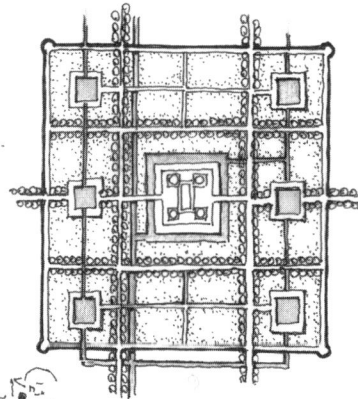

FOUR-SQUARE FORM: Clavijo described the site of one of the many royal fetes held at Samarkand: "The garden is very large…and it is planted with many fruit-bearing trees with others that are to give shade, and throughout are led avenues and raised paths…. In the centre of this garden there was built a very fine palace the ground plan of which was a cross."[13]

CURIOUS MINDS, BROADENED VISTAS

Italy was the locus of transformation from the close-mindedness of medieval thinking to the expansiveness representative of 15th-century thought. Many factors contributed to this cultural shift. Geographically, the Italian peninsula benefited from connections to both the East and the West. New ideas and goods entered Italy as a result of the Crusades. As the economy changed, feudal estates dissolved, enabling land ownership by the rising middle class.

Florence was the center of humanist thought, the cradle of early Renaissance activity. Humanism described a trust in human intellect, a belief in the creative abilities and rational capacities of human beings. The focus of inquiry was not so much on the next world, on the nature of God or of heaven, but on the present context of earthly life and on the social and political relationships of the real world. People's views of nature changed accordingly. Humanists believed that the divine could be perceived in the order of nature. Gardens could be composed to express that order, and landscapes could be appreciated for their scenic value. Gardens focused outward.

The rebirth of classical forms of education and inquiry that characterized the Renaissance was in part a result of the influx of Greek scholars who left Constantinople after the Ottoman conquest in 1453. In addition, Nicholas V, a humanist pope who governed from 1447–1455, sought to restore Rome to its former glory. Ancient Roman ruins, newly excavated, served as valuable sources of inspiration.

Humanist ideals were also expressed by sculptors and painters, who achieved lifelike modeling of form. The development of linear perspective led to an awareness of spatial volume. Order and geometry became the bases of design. Leon Battista Alberti (1404–1474) wrote influential treatises based on the teachings of antiquity, and defined beauty as a harmony of parts. In his ten books on architecture, *De re aedificatoria*, Alberti restated Pliny the Younger's theories on villa design: hillside elevations should be exploited for views, air, and sunlight.[14]

CITY-STATES: In 16th-century Italy, political fragmentation led to the establishment of independent city-states, where identities were defined regionally and power resided with wealthy families.

THE VILLA AS AN EXPRESSION OF HUMANIST IDEALS

The 15th-century garden opened itself to the landscape, relieved of its function as food source, hunting ground, or sanctuary. House and garden formed a single unit, related through geometry, proportion, and use. Loggias and porticos provided architectural transitions between inside and outside spaces. Later Renaissance gardens contained sculpture and more refined architectural settings, as illustrated in the *Hypnerotomachia Poliphili*, a 15th-century novel attributed to Francesco Colonna, a Dominican monk.

The *villa suburbana*, consisting of house, garden, and agricultural component, embodied the ideal of country living as promoted by Alberti. Visual links from the garden to the surrounding landscape, and from the villa to the city, were important contextual references from a humanistic perspective.[15] Nature was understood in terms of varying levels of organization, from uncultivated to controlled, with emphasis on humans at the center. A conceptual framework of the villa acknowledged the close relationship between wild woods ("first nature"), orchards or vineyards ("second nature"), and ornamental flower gardens ("third nature").[16]

FLORENCE: EPICENTER OF CULTURE

Florence, the center of the wool and cloth trade, was the cultural capital of 15th-century Europe. Merchants accumulated great wealth, and banking became a major industry. The Medici family emerged as the controlling force in Florentine

affairs, with power assumed initially by Cosimo the Elder (1389–1464). Cosimo was a great patron of the arts and supporter of humanistic studies. His efforts to gather around him the great minds of the day at his country estates led to the consideration of the *villa suburbana* as a place for productive leisure. The escape from the city to the countryside (the concept of *villeggiatura*) embodied both the classical values of *otium* (withdrawal) and *negotium* (engagement). The Medici villas at Careggi and Fiesole serve as good examples of early Renaissance gardens that functioned as philosophical retreats.

CASE STUDY: *The Villa Medici at Careggi*

The renovation of the Villa Medici at Careggi shows how the typical medieval castle and farmstead evolved into the distinct planning ideal of the *villa suburbana*. Cosimo hired Michelozzo di Bartolommeo (1396–1472) to remodel an existing medieval castle according to new humanist impulses. In about 1457, Michelozzo removed the fortified towers and added a double loggia that defined a small private garden space. House and garden were integrated. The idea of the villa was now fully formed.

The garden at Careggi was the site of Cosimo's original Platonic Academy, where he went to "cultivate not his fields, but his soul."[17] Marsilio Ficino, the mathematician, scholar, and proprietor of Careggi for Cosimo, was instrumental in promoting Florence as a center of classical scholarship.

CASE STUDY: *The Villa Medici at Fiesole*

Michelozzo was again commissioned by Cosimo for the new construction of the Villa Medici at Fiesole, which was completed in 1461 and remains an excellent example of an early Italian Renaissance villa. He engineered the steep site "in rapport" with the landscape so views are possible from many angles, conferring a sense of openness to the gardens.[18]

The architect created two south-facing terraces; a pergola at the base of the 40-foot wall that retains the upper terrace provides an intermediate level. Living spaces opened to each terrace, but access between levels was through an interior stairway. There is no courtyard. An enclosed "secret garden" on the west side of the house affords views to Florence and the surrounding agricultural fields. The *hortus conclusus* of the Middle Ages became the *giardino segreto* of the Renaissance, where Cosimo's grandson, Lorenzo the Magnificent (1449–1492) relocated the Platonic Academy after Cosimo's death.

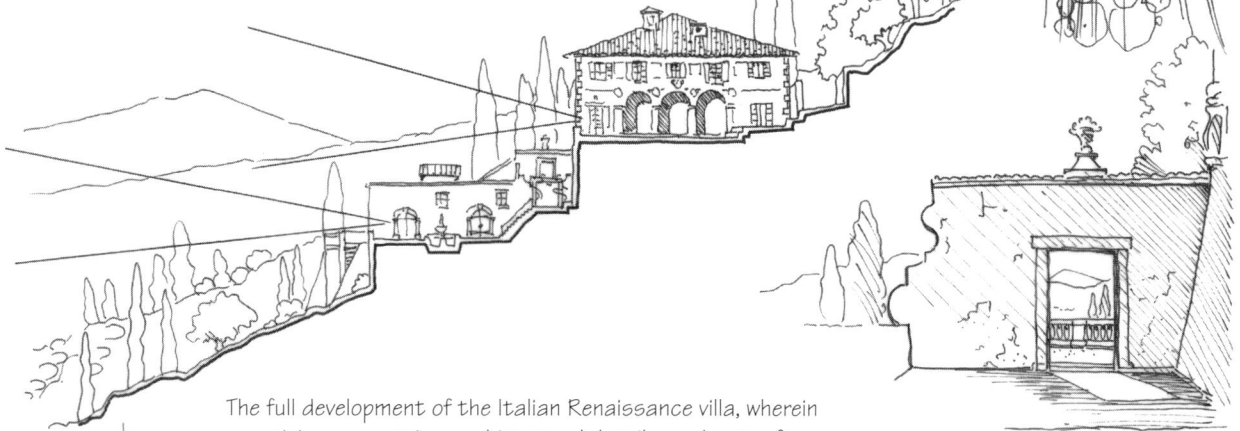

The full development of the Italian Renaissance villa, wherein organizing geometries, architectural details, and water features served to create a unified site plan, occurred in the 16th century and is discussed in the next chapter.

SUMMARY

Intellectual horizons expanded along with political territories in the 15th century. The landscape became manageable as horticultural practices improved and designers better comprehended site planning principles. Landscape spaces were ordered in service to human desires: as aids to meditation, as places of repose, and as signifiers of an idealized agrarian model.

DESIGN PRINCIPLES

REDUCTION
Tray landscapes eliminate the unessential to create a powerful minimalist aesthetic.

ABSTRACTION
Kare sansui gardens express the characteristics of rivers and streams using a selective language of stone and sand.

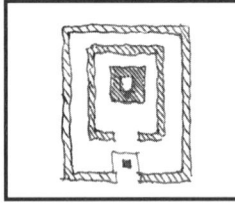

HIERARCHY
Nested geometries concentrate power at the center, as illustrated by the plan of the Forbidden City.

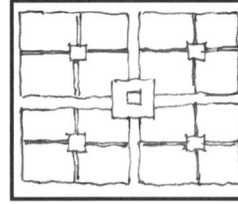

SYMMETRY
Perpendicular axes subdivide space in a chahar-bagh, or four-square garden.

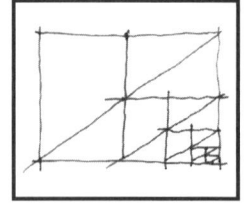

PROPORTION
According to Alberti, the parts must equal the whole—nothing can be added or taken away without destroying the integrity of the design.

DESIGN VOCABULARY

ZEN GARDENS
Raked sand and Rocks

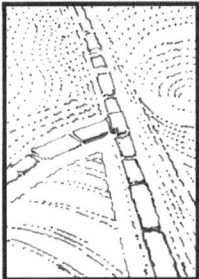

IMPERIAL CITIES
Gates, Courts, and Platforms

ITALIAN VILLAS
Terraces, Loggias, and Porticos

For further exploration

BOOKS
THE BIRTH OF VENUS, by Sarah Dunant
THE LADY AND THE UNICORN, by Tracy Chevalier
THE PRINCE, by Niccolo Machiavelli
TRES RICHES HEURES DU DUC DE BERRY, by the Limbourg Brothers

FILMS
1492: CONQUEST OF PARADISE (1992)
HENRY V (1989)
HUNCHBACK OF NOTRE DAME (1939)
JOAN OF ARC (1948)
TOWER OF LONDON (1939)

PAINTINGS AND SCULPTURES
BRANCACCI CHAPEL, frescoes by Masaccio (1424)
DAVID, by Donatello (1425)
GATES OF PARADISE (DOORS TO THE FLORENCE BAPTISTERY), by Lorenzo Ghiberti (1425–1452)
PORTRAIT OF GIOVANNI ARNOLFINI AND HIS WIFE, by Jan van Eyck (1434)
SAN MARCO CONVENT, frescoes by Fra Angelico (1436)
BATTLE OF SAN ROMANO, by Paolo Uccello (1445)
MAGI CHAPEL (PALAZZO MEDICI-RICCARDI), frescoes by Benozzo Gozzoli (1460)
THE BIRTH OF VENUS, by Sandro Botticelli (1482)
ST. FRANCIS IN ECSTASY, by Giovanni Bellini (1485)
MANTIQ AL-TAIR (THE LANGUAGE OF BIRDS), Timurid miniature (1486)

16th CENTURY

Cumulative changes in the 16th century marked the gradual transition to the modern era. Political power was consolidated across many parts of the globe as individual countries formed distinct national identities. Definitive monarchies emerged in Europe and England; Japan was unified during the reigns of three successive generals; and the Mughal empire spread across parts of Central Asia and India. The Reformation and Counter-Reformation marked a period of commitment to ideals in western Europe. Individual creative pursuits were valued by society; artists gained prestige. All these factors influenced the design of the built landscapes examined in this chapter.

For Europeans, the 15th century was a time to celebrate the rediscovery of nature. In the 16th century, nature became constructed. The idea of the garden as a "third nature" was implicit in more defined styles. Rome was the new authority for Renaissance gardening, art, and architecture. Italian styles spread across the continent and beyond.

1508
DE REVOLUTIONIBUS

1521
OTTOMAN EMPIRE

1500   1510   1520

1521
CORTES CONQUERS MEXICO

1517
PORTUGUESE TRADING NETWORKS

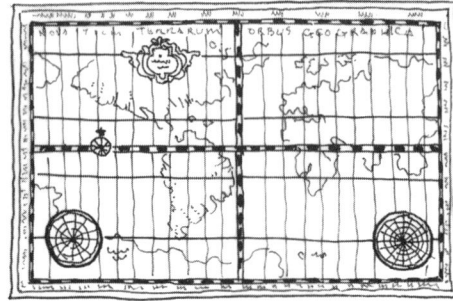

1569
MERCATOR PROJECTION

1550   1560   1570

1554
TULIPS REACH EUROPE

1565
ST. AUGUSTINE, FLORIDA

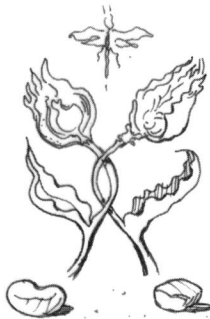

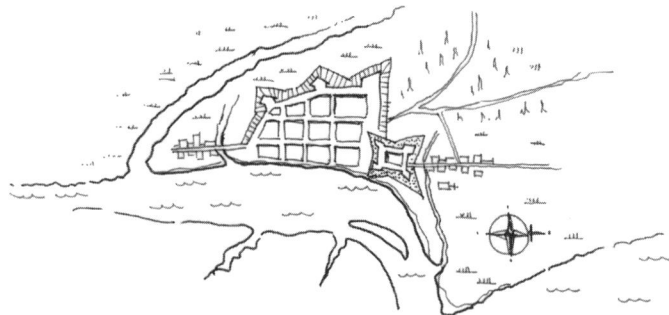

1524
SAFAVID DYNASTY

1530

1536
IL CAMPIDOGLIO

1539
SPANISH CONQUER PERU

1540

1543
PORTUGUESE MERCHANTS
LAND IN JAPAN

1542
LAWS OF THE INDIES

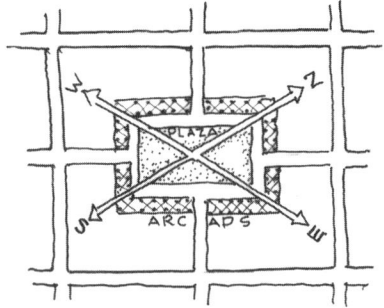

1595
DWARF BOX

1580

1588
SPANISH ARMADA

1590

1599
GLOBE THEATER

1600

1508 DE REVOLUTIONIBUS
Nicolas Copernicus proposed a helio-centric model of the universe.

1517 PORTUGUESE TRADING NETWORKS
Despite initial blunders, the Portuguese established a trading colony in Canton province, China. The meticulous cartography and expert shipbuilding of the Portuguese enabled them to form a vast naval empire.

1521 CORTES CONQUERS MEXICO
Believing that a prophecy had been fulfilled, Moctezuma initially welcomed the Spanish. But Hernan Cortes captured the ruler, seized Aztec lands, and eventually overthrew the entire Aztec empire.

1521 OTTOMAN EMPIRE
Suleiman the Magnificent took Belgrade; the Ottoman Empire reached its greatest extent and its apogee of cultural development under his reign. Imperial production houses imposed particular styles of calligraphy, textile design, and architecture.

1524 SAFAVID DYNASTY
Shah Ismail reestablished native rule in Persia, adopting Shi'ism as the state religion. Magnificent paintings and calligraphy date from this era.

1536 IL CAMPIDOGLIO
Michelangelo's redesign of the medieval civic space in Rome involved the construction of a monumental stepped ramp, the addition of a new building, and the design of new facades for existing buildings. The resultant trapezoidal space was unified by the identical facades, the oval paving pattern, and the placement of an equestrian statue of Marcus Aurelius as a focal point.

1539 SPANISH CONQUER PERU
Francisco Pizzaro was able to exploit internal conflict within the Inca Empire and subjugate the territories around Cuzco. He established a new city at Lima.

1542 LAWS OF THE INDIES
The physical form of the Spanish colonies in America was codified by King Philip II. As one of the first city planning documents, the Laws of the Indies addressed political, social, and economic issues and provided guidelines for developing military fortresses (*presidios*), civilian communities (*pueblos*), and missions.

1543 PORTUGUESE MERCHANTS LAND IN JAPAN
The Portuguese established a very successful trading colony in Kyushu. Jesuit missionaries typically accompanied explorers on their voyages of conquest and conversion. Christianity and weapons were two significant Portuguese exports to Japan.

1554 TULIPS REACH EUROPE
The director of the Leiden Botanic Garden, Carolus Clusius, received a shipment of tulip seeds from Istanbul. He was first to discover how variations in petal color were produced.

1565 ST. AUGUSTINE, FLORIDA
The oldest, continuously occupied European settlement in America was founded by the Spanish 42 years before the English colonized Jamestown and 55 years before the pilgrims landed at Plymouth Rock.

1569 MERCATOR PROJECTION
Gerhardus Mercator developed a formula to portray spherical space on a flat surface. Straight vertical lines of longitude are spaced equidistant; straight horizontal lines of latitude move closer together toward the equator.

1588 SPANISH ARMADA
England defeated Spain in an upset, initiating the ascendancy of English maritime power.

1595 DWARF BOX
The compact form of evergreen boxwood, *Buxus sempervirens* 'Suffruticosa,' allowed gardeners to develop tight, swirling patterns in parterres and knot gardens.

1599 GLOBE THEATER
William Shakespeare's theater-in-the-round illustrated the significant cultural achievements made possible during the reign of Elizabeth I.

THE REBIRTH OF ROME

TEMPIETTO, ROME: Bramante designed the church of San Pietro in Montorio using a classical vocabulary of design and proportion. It is considered the first Renaissance building.

The power center of the Renaissance shifted from Florence to Rome in the 16th century. Dynastic families supplied the Church of Rome with wealthy princes who were able to employ the greatest artistic talents of the era to create works that expressed the status of their patrons. The classical design vocabulary applied by these artists enabled popes to associate their authority with that of the ancient Roman emperors.

Renaissance designers such as Donato Bramante, Jacopo Barozzi da Vignola, and Pirro Ligorio studied Roman architecture and sculpture and were inspired by the logic and rationale behind these forms. Classical principles of order and symmetry organized space. Characteristics of Italian Renaissance gardens include the axial arrangement and architectural framing of landscape space, the abundant presence of water, the use of decorative sculpture, and the development of iconographic programs.

Architects used sophisticated geometries to unify a site plan and relate interior and exterior spaces. They subdivided the ground plane of a garden into compartments (later called parterres) that formed patterns near the house. Sebastiano Serlio's influential books on architecture, *Tutte l'opere d'architettura* (1537, 1540) included drawings and diagrams of intricately symmetrical parterres.

MANNERIST RESPONSES

Rome was sacked in 1527 by mercenaries of Holy Roman Emperor Charles V in retaliation for the pope's alliance with France against the Habsburgs. The city was restored soon after, but these events led to a restlessness and insecurity that was expressed in the arts through the Mannerist style.[1] Nature was ordered though artifice—by the human hand (*mano* in Italian)—representing an individual's imagination and creative power rather than a divine order. Landscape designers' ideas were manifested though the use of freer geometries and allegorical iconographies that flattered the patron and owner of the garden. Spatial relationships were less straightforward; the logic of perspective became less static as experiences varied according to one's position in space.

The Counter-Reformation of the mid-16th century was an attempt by the papacy to inspire faith through artworks. The Reformation initiated by Martin Luther in 1517 was a response to the increasing worldliness of the Catholic Church and its policy of treating salvation as a commodity that could be sold. Protestant communities spread across Europe, forming state churches independent of the Holy Roman Empire. Rome countered with a spiritual and moral renewal of the Church that was popularized through the commissioning of great paintings, sculptures, and building projects, turning the city into a cultural capital once again.

ART-INSPIRED DEVOTION: The Catholic Church commissioned astounding works of art, such as *The Conversion of St. Paul*, by Caravaggio, to attract parishioners.

RENAISSANCE VILLAS AND GARDENS

The list of significant Italian Renaissance gardens is long. We have chosen to concentrate on major works in the environs of Rome that best illustrate the fundamental principles of the time. These projects include: the Cortile del Belvedere, Villa d'Este, Villa Lante, Villa Farnese, Villa Giulia, and the Sacro Bosco at Bomarzo.

CORTILE DEL BELVEDERE, VATICAN CITY (ROME)

The Cortile del Belvedere is often cited as the work that established a new vocabulary of design in the Renaissance.[2] Pope Julius II commissioned Donato Bramante (1444–1514) to link the hillside pavilion, called the Belvedere, with the main papal palace, and provide a venue for festivals and the

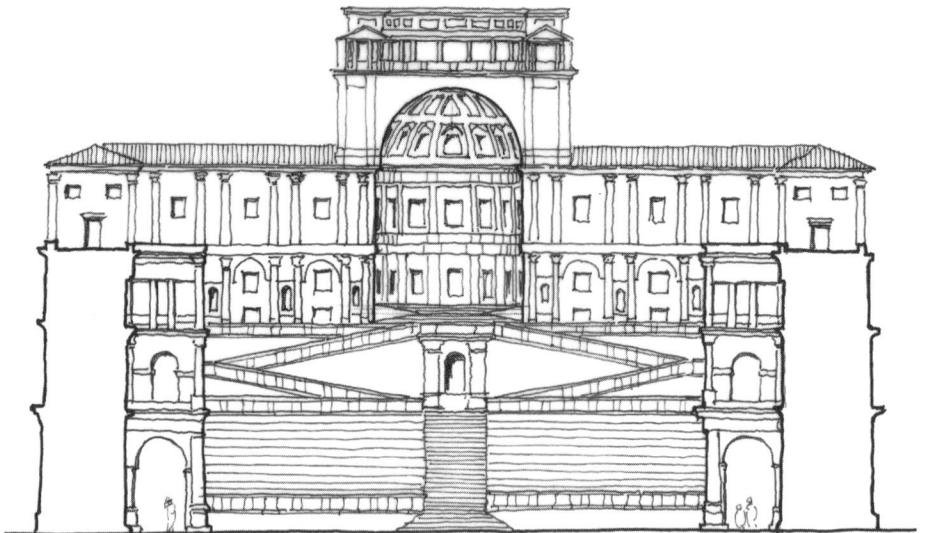

RECONCILING SPACE: The Belvedere courtyard was symmetrical about an implied axis that terminated in an exedra and aligned the irregular geometries of the existing structures.

display of sculpture. The slope was taken up by terraces and negotiated through ramps and stairs that were reminiscent of the Temple of Fortuna

Primigenia (c. 82 BCE). Bramante worked on the Cortile from 1504–1513; modifications were made by others in the following decades.

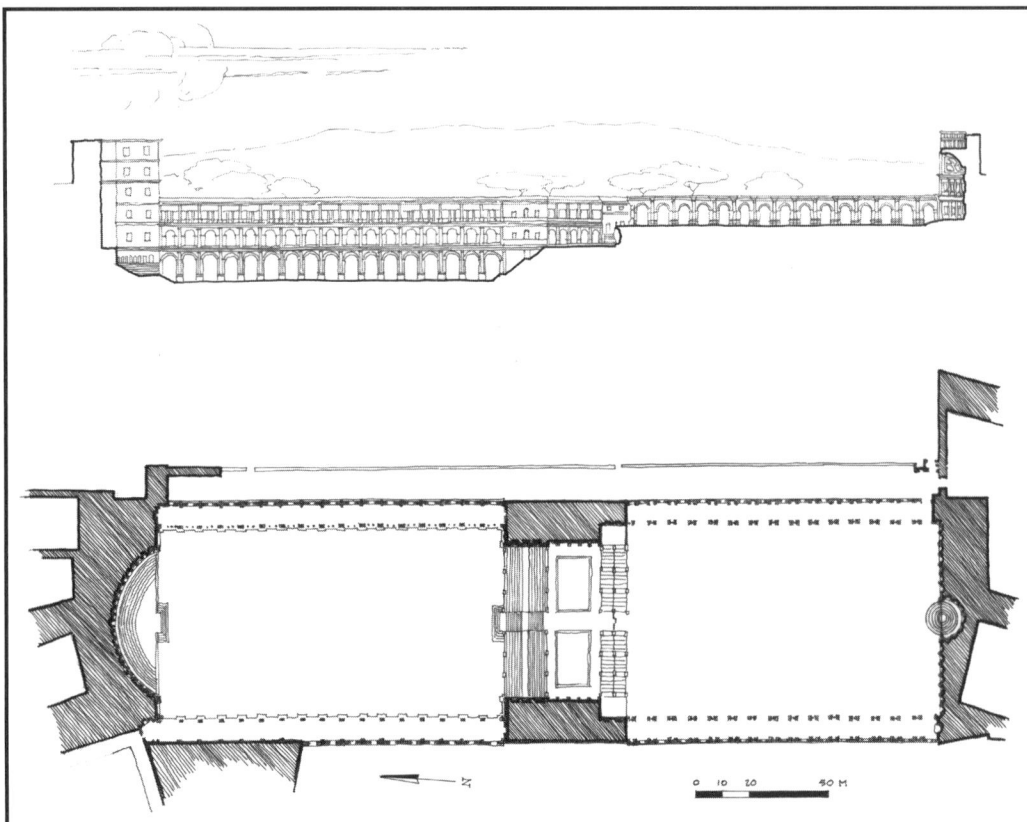

CORTILE DEL BELVEDERE, ROME: Bramante created a large rectangular courtyard framed by a triple loggia, defining a new conception of space through architectural means.

VILLA D'ESTE, TIVOLI

Hercules was the patron saint of Tivoli. The sophisticated iconography of Hercules evident at the Villa d'Este at Tivoli alluded to the guardianship and protection of the people by their governor, Cardinal Ippolito d'Este. The work was undertaken by Pirro Ligorio (1491–1580), who developed the thematic content and engineered the steep slope to create a series of terraces and water features for which the garden is best known today. Ligorio completed the work from 1560–1575; further alterations were made during the 17th century.

The garden's numerous fountains and sculptures narrated the allegory of Hercules. Water diverted from the nearby Aniene River supplied the town and powered the fountains at the Villa. The natural drainage patterns of the Tiber's tributaries were exploited symbolically in the garden—Tivoli (and the Cardinal) supplied Rome with water.

A central axis organizes the space. The first major cross-axis originates in the northeast part of the garden (the town edge) and is formed by water parterres. The cross-axis begins with the Water Organ, where a hydraulically powered wheel struck keys that controlled the flow of air into the organ's pipes, producing the sound of trumpets. Fish ponds continue the cross-axis, which was to terminate in the Sea of Neptune, a feature never built. When the music ended, a deluge of water released from the Water Organ filled the ponds and flowed out to the "sea." Today, the Fountain of the Cascade (created in the 20th century) creates the powerful torrents.

The next major cross-axis encountered in the ascent to the palace is the terrace of 100 fountains, the Cento Fontane, that links the Oval Fountain (also called the Fountain of Tivoli, in honor of the ancient founding of the town) with the Rometta sculptural complex. Above the Oval Fountain is the Pegasus Fountain—where the horse's hoof strikes a rock, bringing

GARDEN COMPARTMENTS: Cross-axes subdivide the garden at Villa d'Este into many *compartimenti*. The upper terraces are linked by ramps and stairs similar in form to those at the Cortile del Belvedere and the ancient Temple of Fortune.

forth the allegorical spring that supplies the Oval Fountain. The three levels of the Cento Fontane represent the three tributaries of the Tiber. The Rometta was a miniature composition of the important temples and structures of ancient Rome; it was seen against a distant view of the ruins of Hadrian's Villa.

Many of the sculptures at the Villa d'Este came from Hadrian's villa, a local source of archeological treasures for Ligorio. No straightforward itinerary

revealed the garden's allegory to the visitor. The grid plan offered a choice of paths and a variety of experiences, but subtle allusions were suggested by the placement of statuary. The easy path led to Venus, profane love; the more arduous route to Diana, chastity. The duality of meaning was implied in other ways, too. Cross-axes afforded views west across the open plain to Rome, contrasting city and country, and the secular and sacred lifestyles of the Cardinal.[3]

VILLA LANTE, BAGNAIA

Begun in 1568 by Cardinal Gian-francesco Gambara, the Villa Lante (named for a later owner) is a superb expression of Renaissance design principles. The garden, an axial composition juxtaposed against an untamed woodland, is schematically similar to the barchetto at Villa Farnese (described next), but differs experientially. Vignola, who was engaged with the Farnese project at Caprarola during this time, is often credited as one of the principal designers of Villa Lante, along with Giacomo del Duca (1520–1601).

Since antiquity, the town of Bagnaia was celebrated for its springs and baths. The cardinal repaired the aqueducts, bringing fresh water to the town in hopes of restoring its ancient status. Tommaso Ghinucci, who is cited as the designer of the waterworks at Villa Lante, revised the urban plan of Bagnaia, creating three new avenues that converged near the lower gates of the villa.[4] He also added a loggia to the bishop's townhouse located near this small junction.

Organized around a central axis of water, the compact garden at Villa Lante presents a unified composition of "part" to "whole." The architectural massing

VILLA D'ESTE, TIVOLI: The original entry to the garden was from the lower end of the central axis, and was visually reinforced by the vertical alignment of loggias on the facade of the palace above.

AUTOMATA: Water pressure forced dozens of mechanical birds to chirp until an owl appeared at the Fountain of the Owl at Villa d'Este. The device has been restored and is operational today.

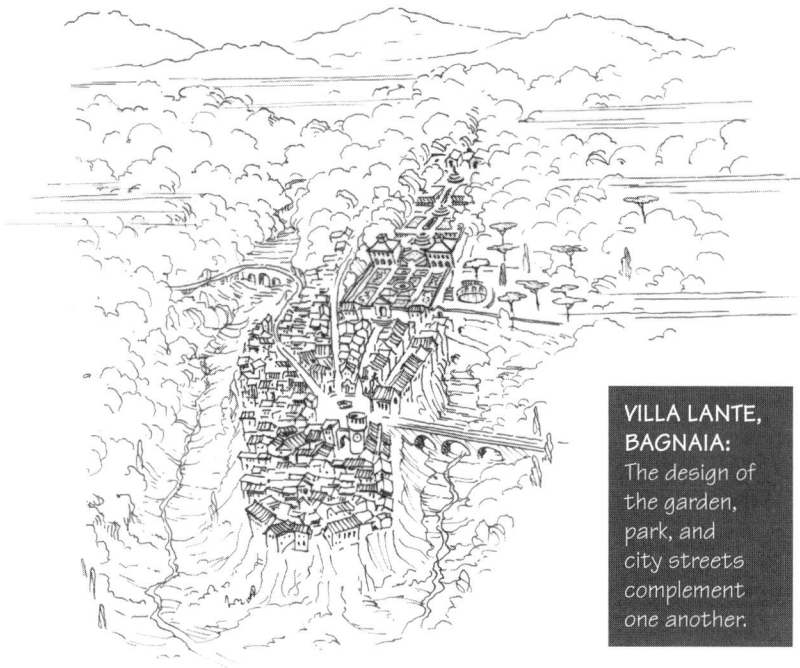

VILLA LANTE, BAGNAIA: The design of the garden, park, and city streets complement one another.

stepped slope, to the Fountain of the River Gods (the Tiber and the Arno). A water table, as referenced in antiquity, occupies the axis on the second level.[5] The concave and convex Fountain of the Lights serves as the transition to the lower terrace. Grottoes of Venus and Neptune are recessed into its retaining wall. Steps and ramps lead to the four-square water parterre on the lowest level. A central sculpture representing the Montalto family emblem terminates the axis. The garden remains a stunning example of Renaissance design to this day.

enforces the perfect symmetry. Two casinos flank the central axis, creating a continuous experience of landscape space. Paths and stairs move the visitor to and from the axis in a subtle choreography of dark to light, open space to enclosed, internal focus to outward view.

An allegory of the control of nature was told through the course of water as it flowed from the upper parts of the garden to the lower parts. Humans mastered nature through art. The narrative began in the *barco* (park), but no predetermined route was prescribed. A fountain of Pegasus marked the entry to the woodland, an allusion to the creation of the home of the Muses on Mount Parnassus. Situated within clearings were mythologically themed sculptures.

A path from the *barco* leads to the upper level of the garden. The water course begins in a grotto, the Fountain of the Deluge, situated between the two Houses of the Muses. The Fountain of the Dolphins marks the uppermost level of the axis. A water chain sculpted with crayfish (a play on the cardinal's name—*gambero* means crayfish in Italian) proceeds down the

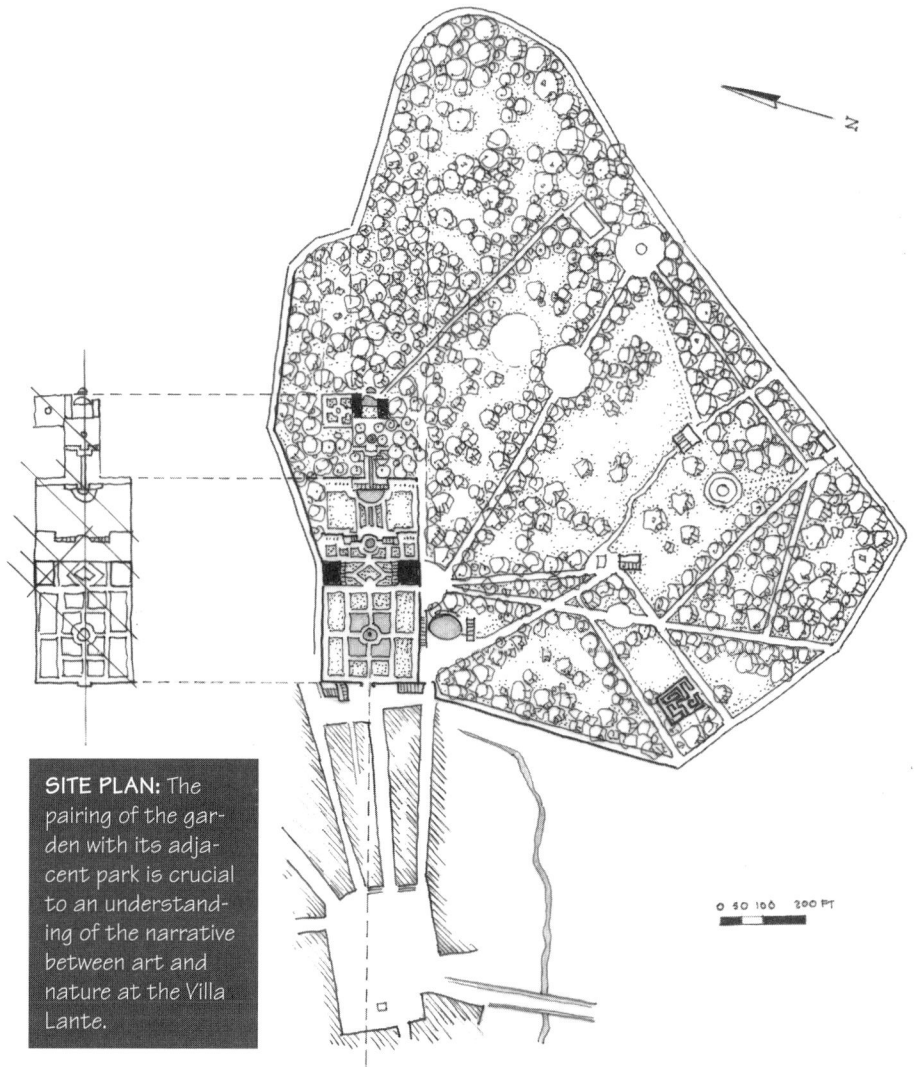

SITE PLAN: The pairing of the garden with its adjacent park is crucial to an understanding of the narrative between art and nature at the Villa Lante.

0 50 100   200 FT

83

VISUAL NARRATIVE: *Villa Lante, Bagnaia*

VILLA FARNESE, CAPRAROLA

Cardinal Alessandro Farnese commissioned Vignola (1507–1573) to complete work on his palazzo at Caprarola in 1556. He redesigned the medieval fortress as a pentagonal palazzo with a central circular courtyard, and added a new entry terrace with curving ramps and stairs. Vignola also planned the seasonal garden terraces below the north and west apartments. These four-square compartments were accessible to residents by a bridge across a moat: the west garden for use in the winter, the north garden in summer.

Around 1584, and at the urging of his colleague Cardinal Gambara, Farnese planned for a separate summerhouse and dining pavilion to be carved out of the wooded slope beyond the palazzo. Called the *barchetto* by the cardinal, this project was probably executed by del Duca.

Located about one-quarter of a mile from the palazzo, the *barchetto* is introduced through an *allée* of trees that opens onto a circular basin within a flat, square clearing. A water staircase bisects a stepped ramp that leads to the Fountain of the Rivers on the upper terrace. (The enclosing walls and twin pavilions at the base of the slope are 17th-century additions by Girolamo Rainaldi.) The two-story casino is flanked by symmetrical *giardini segreti*. (The caryatids that border these parterre gardens also date from the 17th century.) Sculptural staircases lead to a rear court at the upper level. A fountain occupies this quiet terrace, where the second floor of the casino is now at grade. The spacious but gentle slope of the back lawn is retained by low cheek walls decorated with dolphins. An open exedra terminates the axis.

The *barchetto* differs from the garden at Villa Lante in that it is dominated by a main axis with no lateral relief, and experienced as a single event rather than a sequence of individual spaces. The position of the casino directly on the axis creates a distinct division between upper and lower levels.

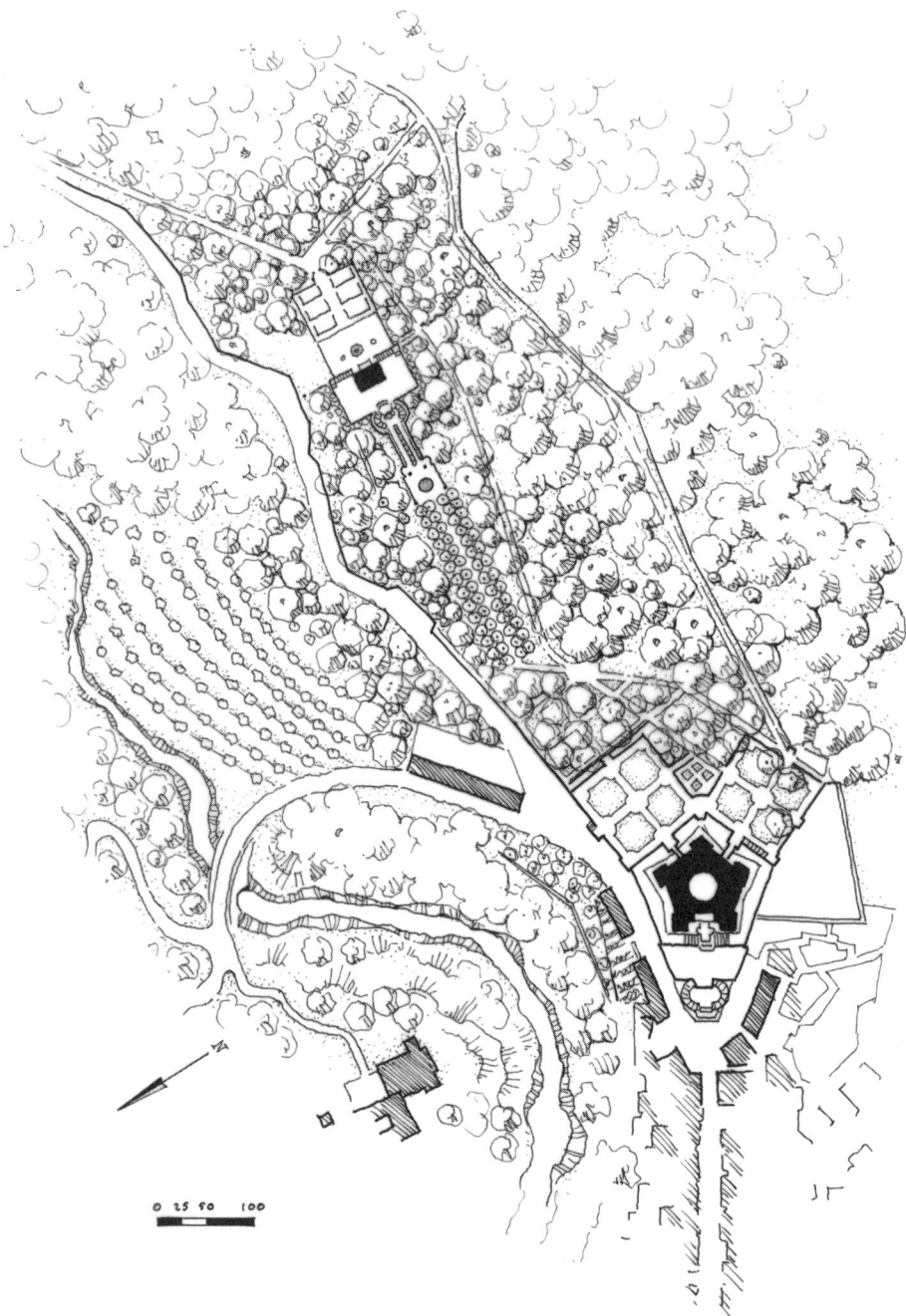

0 25 50 100

BAROQUE DANCE: The architectural emphasis of the 17th-century additions to the *barchetto* at Villa Farnese, Caprarola, introduced a more Baroque design vocabulary based on movement and drama.

WATER AXIS: Similar in plan to the garden at Villa Lante, the barchetto at Villa Farnese is arranged symmetrically about an axis and punctuated by a series of water features.

VILLA GIULIA, ROME

Cardinal Giovanni Maria Ciocchi del Monte enlarged his daytime retreat, a villa suburbana outside the city walls, in 1550 when he was elected Pope Julius III. Many great artists are believed to have had a hand in its design: Giorgio Vasari, Michelangelo, Bartolomeo Ammannati, and Vignola. The linear site plan of Villa Giulia aligns with a shallow valley, a natural low spot amid acres of woods, orchards and vineyards. A long allée connected the villa to a mooring on the Tiber River.

A series of telescoping courtyards frame the garden space. A large semicircular portico defines the first terrace. Views continue through a central loggia to a rear loggia and garden terrace. From the central loggia, one is surprised to discover that the next courtyard is sunken, and a nymphaeum is revealed at an even lower level. The semicircular form of the portico is echoed by the curving stairs that lead to the lower courtyard. Access to the nymphaeum itself is through hidden stairs. The water channel around the perimeter of the nymphaeum was called the acqua vergine after the ancient aqueduct that ran beneath the property. Four graceful caryatids support the upper-level court.

VILLA GIULIA: The garden seen in the context of the barco illustrates the important Renaissance concept of "composed" nature.[6]

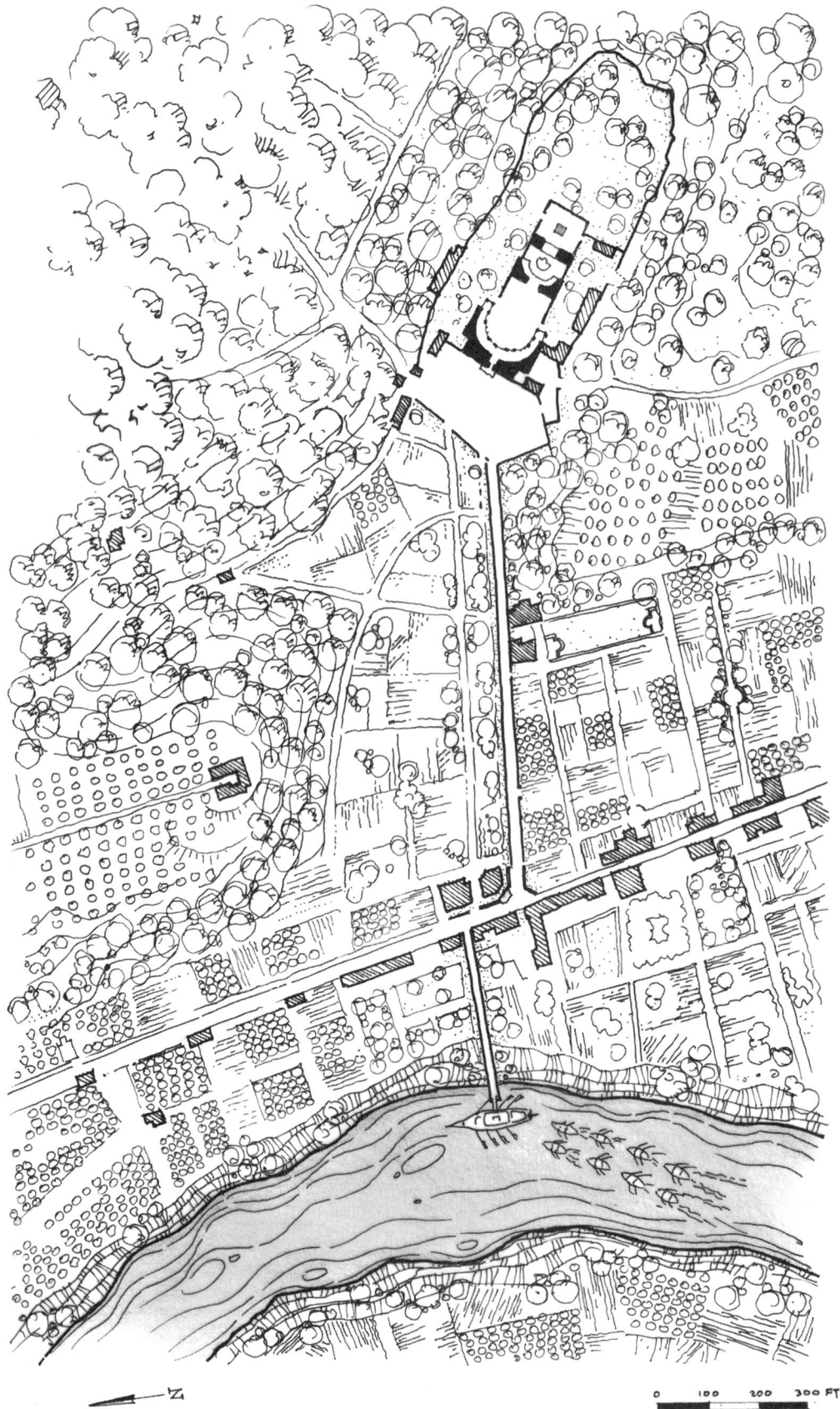

0   100   200   300 FT

CASE STUDY: *Villa Giulia, Rome*

SURPRISE AND DELIGHT: Along the axially arranged space, elements are screened from view, creating a sense of drama.

SECTION ELEVATION: The tension created between the horizontal sight line and the vertical circulation is characteristic of Mannerist design.

FORMS REPEAT:
A dynamic three-part division of space occurs in both plan and section.

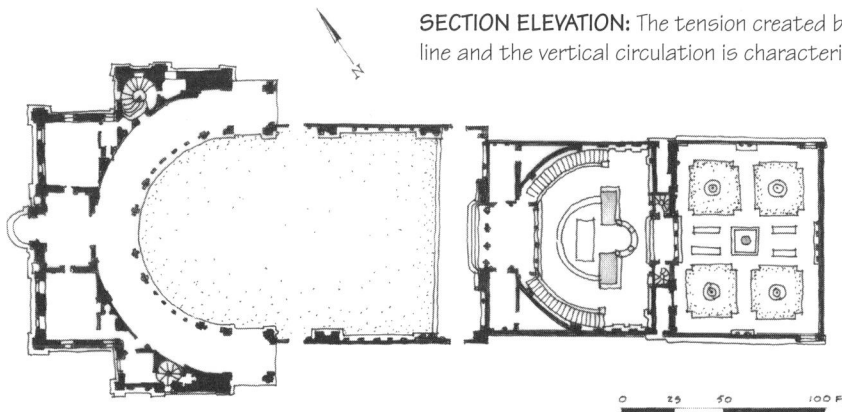

0   25   50   100 FT

SACRO BOSCO, BOMARZO

The most extreme example of Mannerist distortion can be seen in the *Sacro Bosco* (sacred wood) of Count Orsini, constructed at Bomarzo from 1552–1583. Colossal sculptures, some carved out of the stone on the site, dot the valley below the count's hilltop palace. No linear narrative connects these surreal sculptural events. Inscriptions allude to literary themes, but the meaning of this fantasyland is unclear. The park has been variously understood as a critique of Renaissance order and hierarchy, or an interpretation of literary works such as the *Hypnerotomacchia Poliphili*, and *Orlando Furioso*, a story about a man who went mad after the loss of his lover (Orsini's wife died young).[7] The park is known today as the Park of the Monsters.

SACRO BOSCO, BOMARZO: The terrain is largely unaltered in Count Orsini's sacred wood.

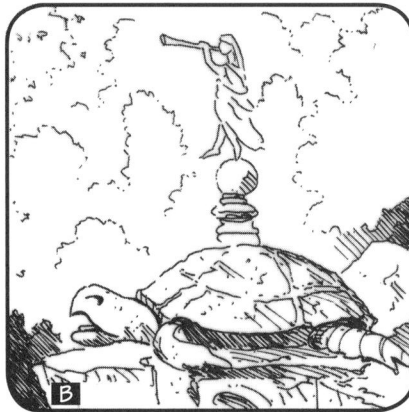

GARDEN OF THE MONSTERS: A) Tilted House—Is the house leaning or the world tilting? B) Fame Rides a Turtle—Fame, like haste, is made slowly; C)Hell's Mouth—*"Ogni pensiero vola"* (Leave every care, you who enter here), a reference to Dante's Gates of Hell, is inscribed on the entry to this grotto with built-in bench and picnic table.

PALLADIAN VILLAS

Different forces affected the development of the Renaissance garden in the Venetian Republic. New trade routes established by the increasingly powerful European monarchies devastated Venice's economy. Attention turned toward the reclamation of agricultural lands in the Veneto region.

Villas of the Veneto are year-round residences and working farms. Andrea Palladio gained a reputation as the preeminent architect of the ideal agrarian villa. He interpreted the classical Roman design vocabulary as a function of space and mass, realized through a rational geometric order. He modeled his four books of architecture, *I Quattro Libri dell'Architettura* (1570), on Serlio's practical treatise, similarly illustrated with plans and elevations.[8]

Palladian architecture is synonymous with a harmony of part to whole. Palladio developed precise ratios for the heights and widths of rooms, and applied the same system to the design of building facades. He arranged functional spaces hierarchically, typically around a central unit, resulting in bilateral symmetry and an A-B-A rhythm.

His villas incorporated elements from traditional farm buildings—dovecotes, long arcaded loggias, stucco finish over brick—and were set amid agricultural fields, staking their claim in the flat Veneto plain. Views of the productive landscape were welcomed. Typical Palladian elements included a square hall, a loggia, a pedimented "temple" front, and steps that led directly to the *piano nobile*. Plinths and platforms elevated buildings above the ground plane. Exterior ornamentation was sober, but interior surfaces were lavishly decorated. Avenues and vistas engaged front and rear courtyards; site planning, rather than garden design, was Palladio's hallmark.

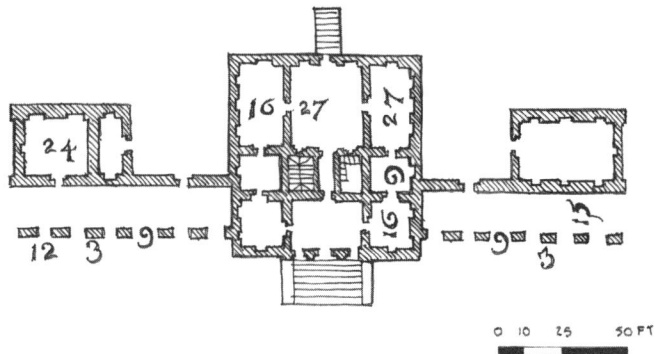

PALLADIAN HARMONY: Plan and elevation were unified by the same proportional relationships.

VILLA EMO, FANZOLO: The villa stretches out as an elongated cross-axis.

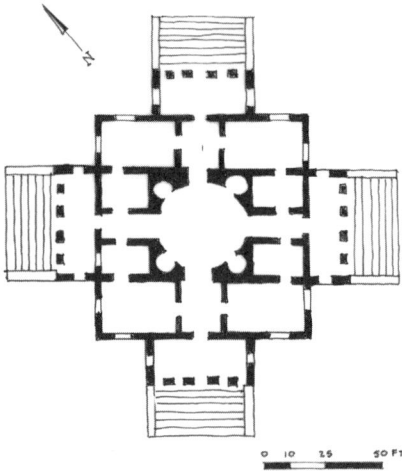

VILLA EMO, FANZOLO

Villa Emo, built in 1564, is a one-story structure with a temple front and a paved entry ramp. Wings extend from both sides of the central block and have an attached colonnade. Long allées define a perpendicular axis and organize the site. The rear courtyard forms a large rectangle.

Of all Palladio's villas, Villa Emo seems to relate most directly to its agricultural context through its low profile and extended arms. Architecture and landscape feel perfectly balanced.

VILLA ROTONDA, VICENZA

Constructed from 1566–1570 on a hill-top very near the town of Vicenza, Villa Rotonda has no agricultural component and most likely functioned as a daytime retreat or entertainment villa. The villa, raised on a platform, occupies the site with authority. The plan is rotated from a true north-south alignment, permitting sunlight to enter each room. Alterations, particularly to the central dome, were made by Vincenzo Scamozzi after Palladio's death.

The square villa displays quadripartite symmetry about a round central hall, with four identical porticos. The repetition of the classical Greek temple front on all four sides is unusual; rather than creating a hierarchical marking of the entrance, it denotes an equality of experience. The dominant axis becomes vertical—the visitor's eye moves up, through the dome. The form of Villa Rotonda was to become an icon in the imagination of future generations of architects and designers.

ARCHITECTURE CONTROLS LANDSCAPE: The Villa Rotonda was carefully sited by Palladio to frame unique views in each direction.

RENAISSANCE GARDENS IN FRANCE AND ENGLAND

As foreign powers made claim to Italian territories, and Italian artists fled Rome after the sack, classical organizing principles spread throughout Europe in the latter part of the 16th century. The new vocabulary of design expressed the regional and cultural characteristics unique to each country.

CHATEAUX OF THE LOIRE VALLEY

France in the 16th century was not as politically fragmented as Italy. After the collapse of the feudal system, power was centralized in an absolute monarchy. Gardens became outsized expressions of royal authority.

The Loire Valley is flatter, more densely wooded, and more spacious than the landscape around Rome and Tuscany. French gardens were sprawling, complex arrangements of ground-plane features. Defensive moats typically surrounded the chateaux of the Loire Valley. When the introduction of gunpowder made fortified medieval castles obsolete and indefensible, the moats, still essential for good drainage, were incorporated into gardens as ornamental canals.

Renaissance gardens in France were mostly additions to existing medieval chateaux, which were year-round dwellings, not summertime retreats. Space was limited, constrained by the moat and the configuration of the fortified castle. The axial arrangements of Italian gardens were ill suited to these irregular spaces. Landowners developed gardens as separate entities, built on adjacent properties not directly related to the house.

The designs of 16th-century French gardens are known today through the engravings of Jacques Androuet du Cerceau. His book, *Les plus excellents bastiments de la France* (1576 and 1579), contained illustrations of important chateaux and their gardens.

LOIRE VALLEY: Royal estates were situated in the Loire valley.

AMBOISE

King Charles VIII of France invaded southern Italy in 1494, asserting his ancestral right to the Kingdom of Naples. His victory was of minor political consequence, but it was enormously influential in bringing Italian Renaissance design ideas to France. He returned to his country with Italian artifacts, artists, and craftsmen. Charles VIII enlarged his garden at Amboise according to the new style, adding 10 compartments and a central water feature along a high terrace within the chateau walls. A gallery along the long side of the rectangular plan defined the edge of the garden and afforded views of the Loire.

FRENCH RENAISSANCE: The chateau at Amboise was redesigned by Italian artists and craftsmen.

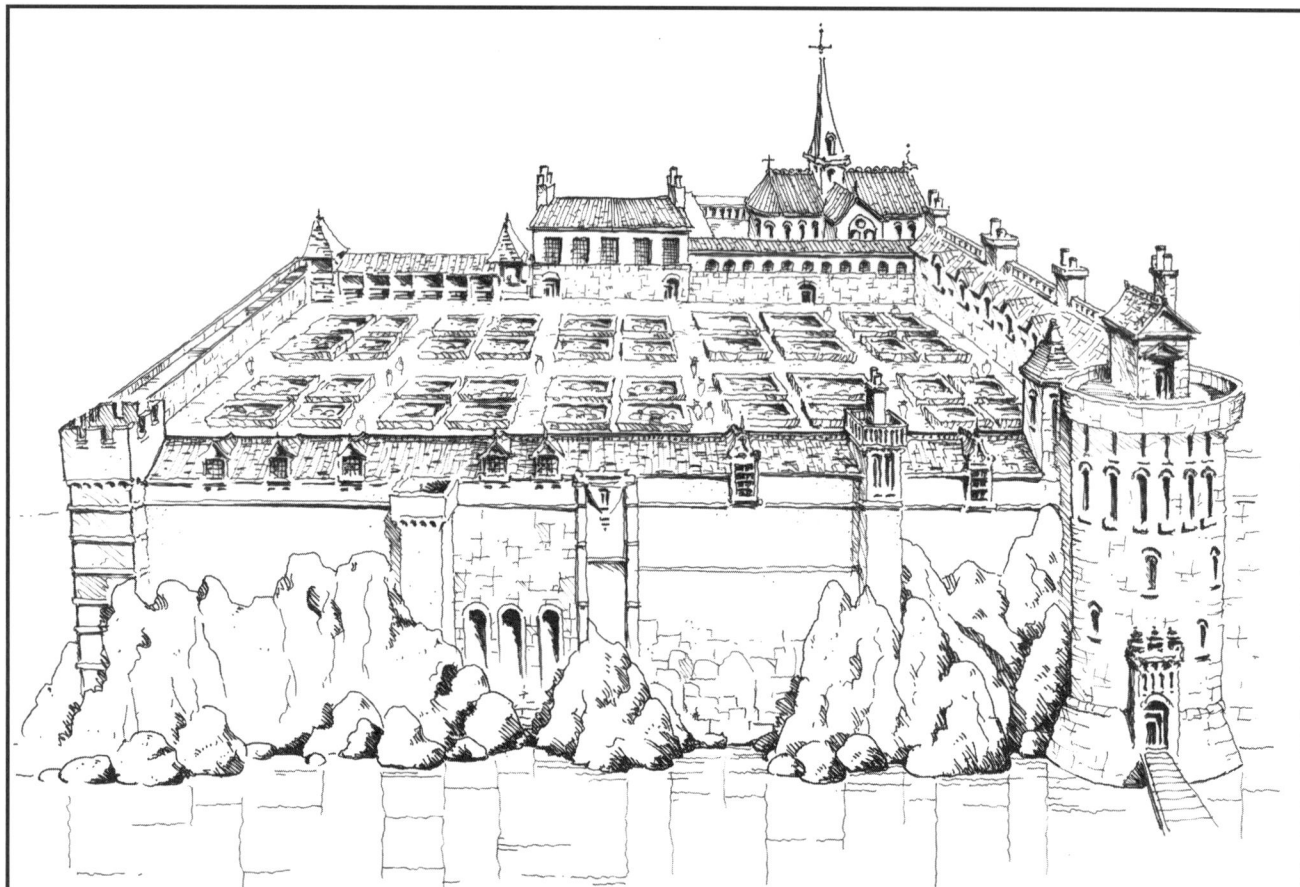

AMBOISE: A garden terrace with 10 symmetrical compartments, called *parterres*, enhanced the medieval castle.

BLOIS

Charles VIII was succeeded by his cousin Louis XII, who not only carried on with Charles's gardening ambitions, but also married his wife. Louis completed work at Amboise, and moved the court to Blois.

The garden consisted of three terraces. The main rectangular terrace comprised 10 garden compartments arranged in two long rows. A central pathway led to a bridge across a moat that connected to the chateau. A fountain within a wooden pavilion marked the intersection of two crossing pathways. The lower terrace is believed to contain one of the first orangeries in France.[9] (The gardens were known for their wide variety of fruits and vegetables.) In 1505, Louis added an upper terrace, probably as an expanded kitchen garden.

FONTAINEBLEAU

When Francis I assumed the throne in 1515 upon the death of his uncle Louis XII, he moved the court to Fontainebleau, near Paris, disdaining the country estates of the Loire Valley. His rebuilding of the chateau has been much altered over time, but the basic structure of the grounds was established in this era. The difference in the scale and variety of landscape spaces, particularly those defined by water, initiated a new phase in French garden design.

The Fountain Court, framed by the old castle, stretched out in front of a new transverse wing. Directly across from the Fountain Court was a large trapezoidal lake. An *allée* of elms on one side of the lake bordered an orchard and recreational fields. On the other side of the lake was a compartment garden of ornamental and utilitarian plants.

The reign of Francis I coincided with the second wave of Italian influence in France. The French court developed into a cultural center, attracting many of the great Italian Renaissance artists, including Serlio, Vignola, Primaticcio, and Leonardo da Vinci, who died in France in 1519. Modifications made to Fontainebleau, most notably during the 17th century, reflected the changing styles and tastes of its royal owners.

FONTAINEBLEAU: Although no comprehensive site plan unifies the various additions to Fontainebleau, sight lines and flat planes of water extended the garden out into the landscape.

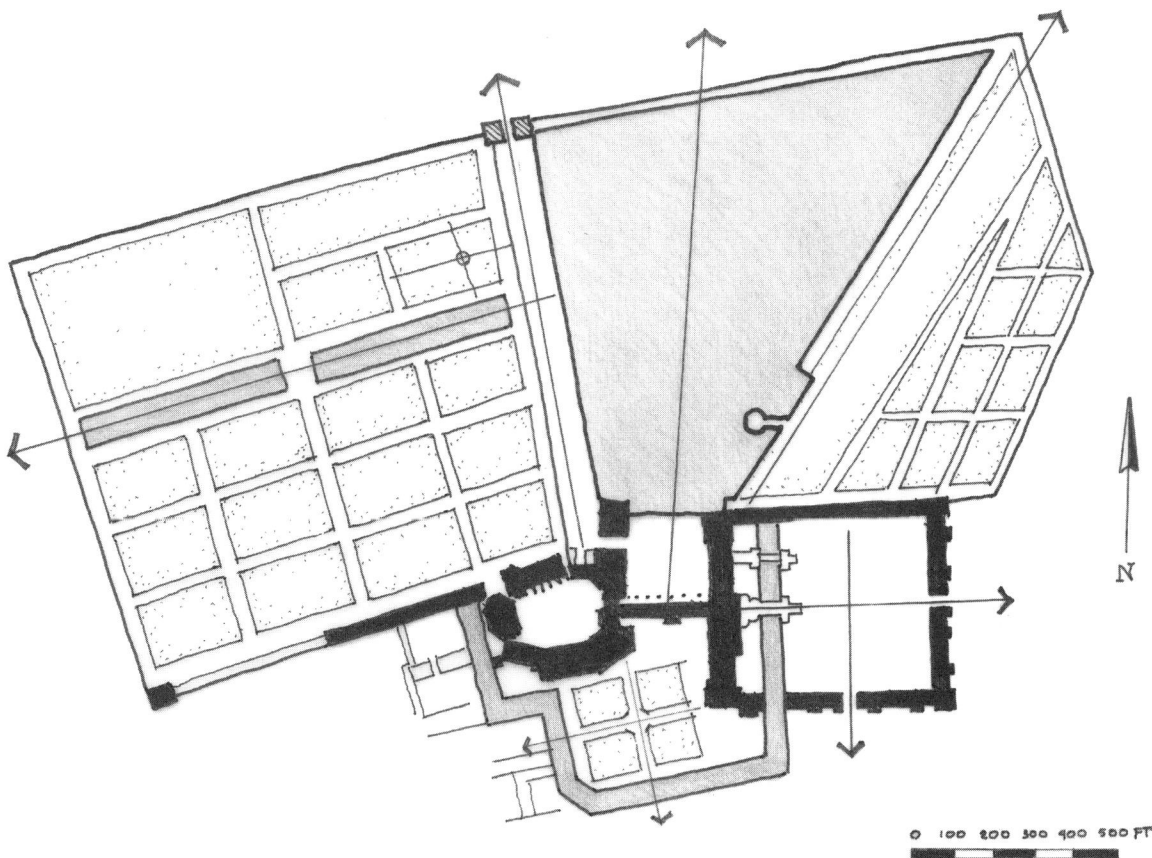

0 100 200 300 400 500 FT

N

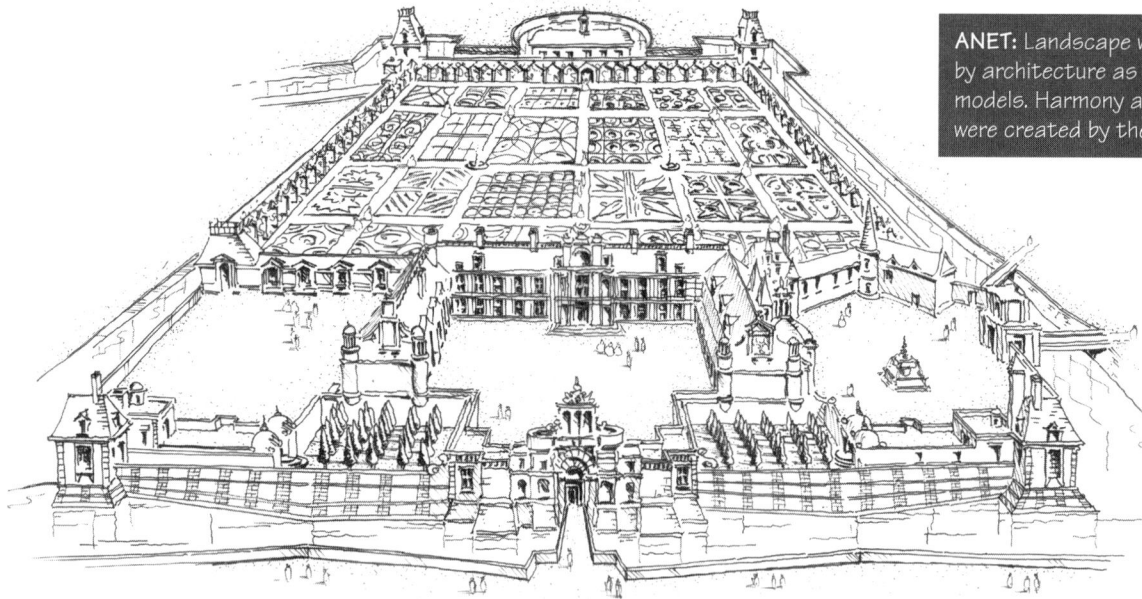

ANET

Francis I was succeeded in 1547 by Henry II. Henry hired Philibert de l'Orme to redesign the chateau at Anet for his mistress Diane de Poitiers. De l'Orme had studied in Rome and developed a symmetrical scheme for the chateau and garden.

A large entry court, called the Court of Honor, was defined by the three wings of the chateau, and bordered on two sides by small plantations, courtyards, and pavilions. Behind the house a semicircular staircase descended to a large garden of compartments, framed on three sides by a gallery and surrounded by a moat. Twin towers marked the far corners of the garden. A pavilion within a semicircular pool terminated the central axis and echoed the form of terrace stairs. De l'Orme developed an iconographic program around the theme of Diana the huntress.

CHENONCEAUX

Diane de Poitiers was also in residence at Chenonceaux. The castle at Chenonceaux is located directly on the river Cher. During the reign of Henry II, Philibert de l'Orme built a bridge to link the chateau to the south bank of the river. A long *allée* of elms leading to the castle was planned at this time, as was a garden on the opposite bank.

Diane had created a large garden terrace on the north bank of the river, to the east of the forecourt, with compartments of flowers, vegetables, and fruit trees. When Henry died in 1559, his wife Catherine de' Medici took over the chateau from Diane de Poitiers. Catherine continued making improvements at Chenonceaux. A second-story gallery was added to the bridge, resulting in the scenic composition recognizable today.

She also planted a garden terrace on the west side of the forecourt.

Catherine's legacy included the reestablishment of the garden as a venue for spectacles and theatrical entertainments. Her lavish parties, which often served political ends, were well recorded.[10] The idea of the garden as theater was expanded upon by the court aristocracy in the 17th century.

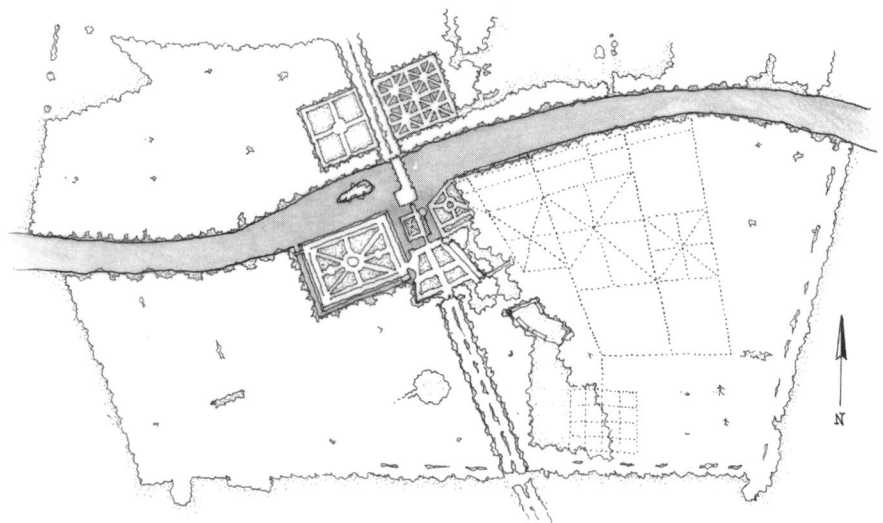

TUDOR AND ELIZABETHAN GARDENS IN ENGLAND

The civil strife between the Houses of York and Lancaster, known as the War of the Roses, ended when Henry Tudor defeated Richard III and assumed the throne as King Henry VII. The most significant garden advancements came during the reign of Henry VIII (ruled 1509–1547), whose rivalry with French King Francis I motivated his interest in the arts and in gardening.[11]

When Henry VIII was unable to obtain a divorce under Catholic church policy, he severed ties with Rome and appropriated the landholdings of Catholic monasteries. His actions had two important effects: a landed gentry class developed, establishing an enduring pattern of land tenure in the English countryside, and northern Europe, rather than Italy, became the source of design influence. Dutch styles had a particular impact on English garden design in the second half of the 16th century. Interest in gardening escalated; ornamental gardens flourished at the country houses of the aristocracy.

The small outdoor rooms of Tudor and Elizabethan gardens (Elizabeth ruled 1558–1603) related to the lines of the house. Sited on a slight rise, to ensure good drainage, they were characterized by intricate ground plane patterns visible from the *piano nobile* or second-floor level of the house. Mazes, mounts, and knot gardens were common elements. Flowers filled the internal shapes created by "closed" knot gardens; colored gravel filled "open" knot gardens.

KNOT GARDENS: *Low, clipped evergreen shrubs and aromatic herbs formed "knots."*

HADDON HALL, DERBYSHIRE: The terraces on the south side of the house date from the Tudor period. The stone balustrade on the second terrace shows Italian influence. The "forthright"—a straight, wide path for walking—became a common garden element.[12]

MONTACUTE, SOMERSET

This Elizabethan garden dates from 1580; its garden compartments cross the straight line of sight created by the entry road and *allée*. Made from local stone, the steps and balustraded walls of the forecourt create a unified architectural ensemble. An 18th-century addition to the northwest facade of the house reversed its orientation. The forecourt is now considered to be at the back of the house.

The sunken garden on the northeast side of the house is an Italian-style compartment garden with an English influence. Paths radiating from a central fountain divide the garden into four squares.

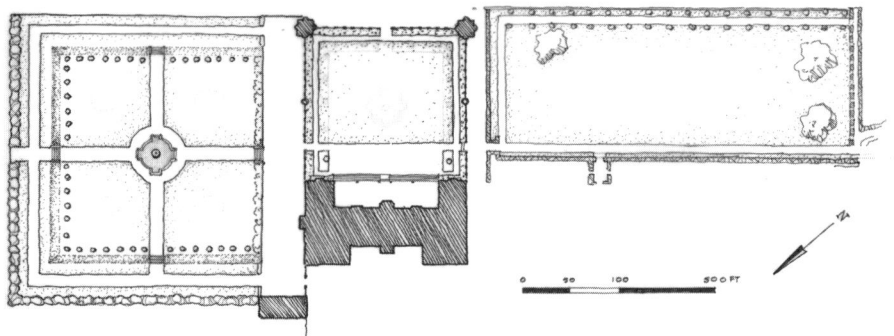

MONTACUTE, SOMERSET: Garden terraces relate to the lines of the house.

HAMPTON COURT, MIDDLESEX

Henry VIII assumed control of Hampton Court in 1531. He immediately enlarged the palace compound to include thousands of acres of parkland and hunting grounds to the north. The Pond Garden and Privy Garden date from his reign. The neat, rectangular Pond Garden included knot gardens, turf banks, arbors, covered walkways, a central fountain, and a banqueting house.

The sunken Privy Garden contained colored gravel parterres, topiary, a maze, and a circular pool with raised turf banks. Most spectacular was the hedged path that spiraled around the mount, crowned by a three-story summerhouse.[13] Painted heraldic beasts, placed throughout the gardens and parks, posed atop poles and held aloft pennants. The design of Hampton Court changed with each successive monarch; the evolution of the garden is illustrated in the following chapter.

ARRIVAL COURT: Stone pavilions decorate the walled terrace, and "banqueting houses" mark the far corners of the forecourt at Montacute.

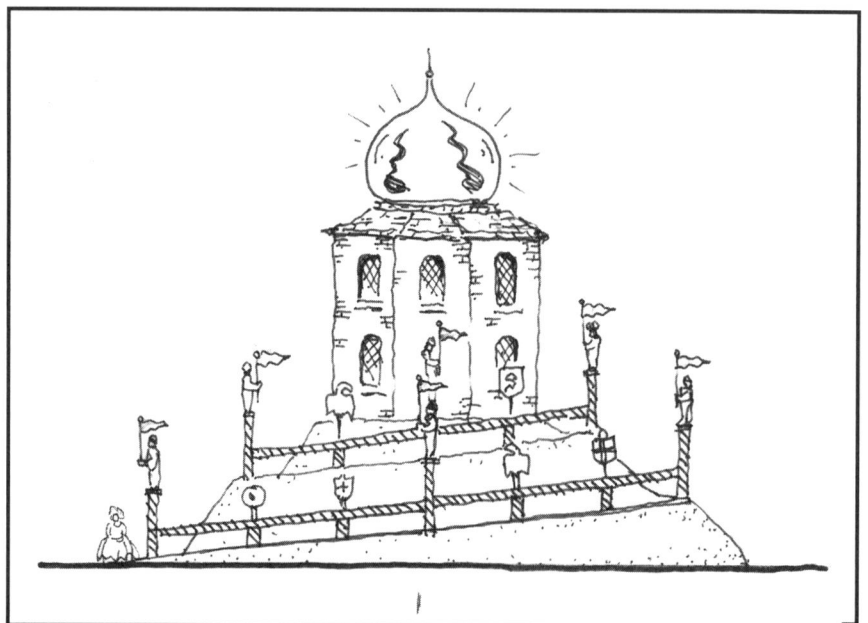

KING'S MOUNT: Henry VIII's summerhouse at Hampton Court.

AN ENCYCLOPEDIA OF PLANTS

In the 16th century, the number of known plants increased twentyfold.[14] Sunflowers, marigolds, sassafras, tobacco, and the potato all entered Europe from the Americas. The first botanic gardens, established in Pisa and Padua around 1543, were still organized as physic gardens, their purpose being to provide useful knowledge about the medicinal, not ornamental, uses of plants. Early botanic gardens also had religious overtones: it was believed that by assembling all the plants of God's creation one could reconstruct the Garden of Eden.[15]

Botanical scholarship was contained in the many herbals published during the period, which were indexed by ailment. Pietro Andrea Mattioli wrote *Commentarii in sex libros pedacii dioscorides* in 1544, summarizing all of Dioscorides's insights from the 1st century and supplementing this knowledge with his own observations. The book, which included woodcut illustrations, was widely influential, as it coincided with the 16th-century boom in printing.

As Enlightenment science evolved in the following centuries, the "garden of the simples" developed into the modern botanic garden devoid of its sacred meanings.

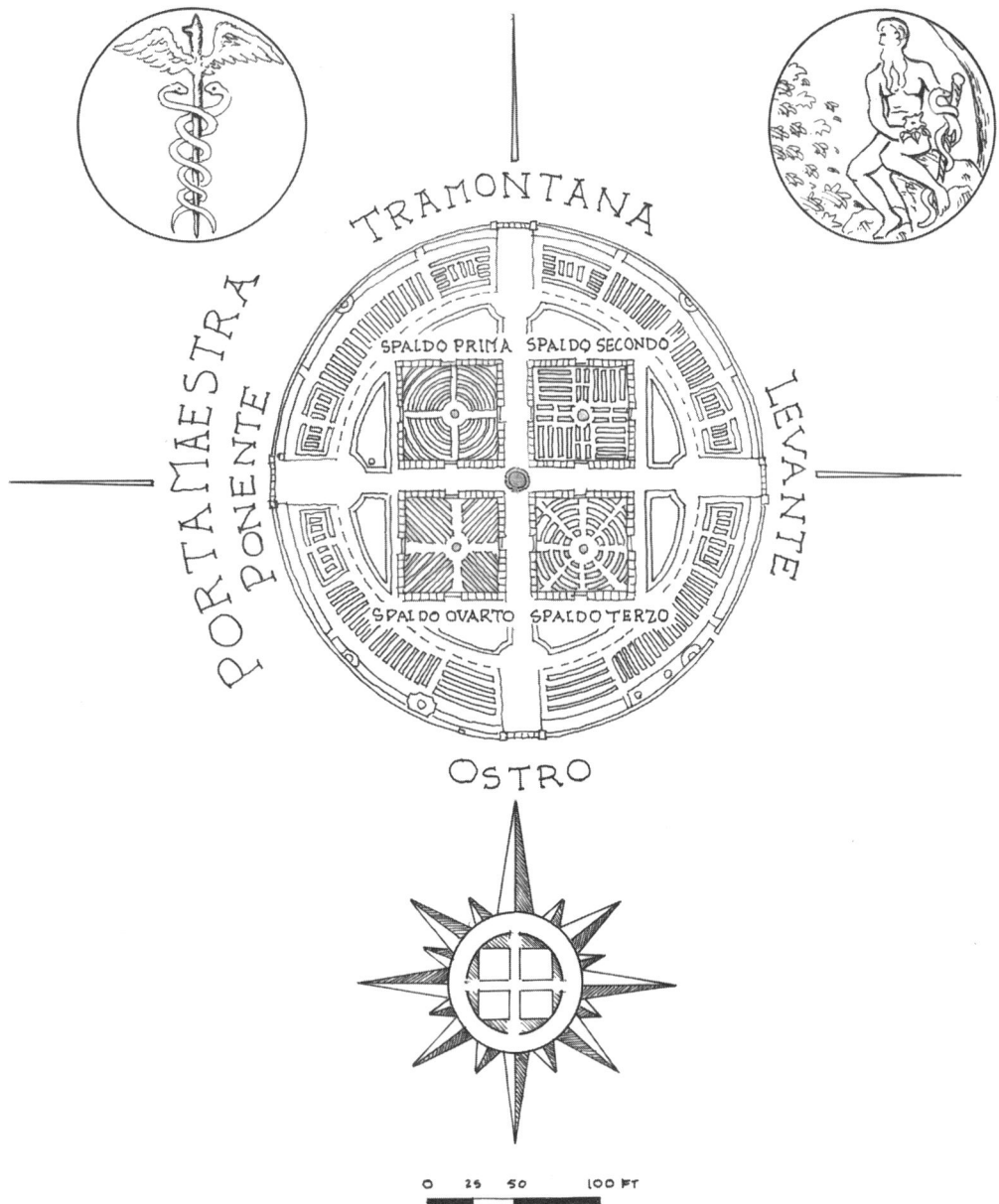

ORTO BOTANICO, PADUA: *"Gardens of the simples" were typically oriented to the cardinal directions, and contained a central well. The organization of the planting beds reflected the order of the universe. At Padua, circular beds are located in square compartments; the four-square compartments are confined within a larger circle.*

PERSIAN ART FORMS TRAVEL EAST

TO THE SOUTH OF KABUL LIES BABUR'S BAGH-E VAFA.

ENTRANCE TO THE GARDEN.

IN THE GARDEN IS AN INCESSANTLY FLOWING STREAM.

BABUR OVERSEES THE LAYOUT OF THE CHAHAR BAGH.

ON THE SOUTHWEST CORNER OF THE GARDEN IS A RESERVOIR OF WATER.

ALL AROUND THE WATER THE GROUND IS COVERED WITH CLOVER. THIS SPOT IS THE VERY EYE OF BEAUTY OF THE GARDEN. AT THE TIME OF ORANGE BLOSSOM THE PROSPECT IS DELIGHTFUL.

BAGH-E VAFA, AFGHANISTAN: The beautiful miniatures contained in Babur's memoirs illustrate his love of gardens and his involvement with their layout.

As a young man, Babur (1483–1530) visited the cities of his Timurid ancestors and was impressed by the artistic ideals expressed there through traditional Persian art forms and gardens. He created gardens in his most beloved city of Kabul and in northern India, based on precedents established at Samarkand and Herat. Babur conquered Delhi in 1526, establishing the Mughal empire. The nomadic ruler traveled throughout his empire, building alliances and consolidating his power. The royal court camped out in orchards, vineyards, and flower plantations, which were watered by springs channeled to the gardens. Babur loved nature and the outdoors. His gardens were conceived of as open-air palaces, with mosques, baths, pavilions, and raised platforms for tents.[16]

Built on a south-facing rise of land, the emperor's Garden of Fidelity, the Bagh-e Vafa, assumed the typical quadripartite form, the chahar bagh. Babur described the numerous varieties of fruit trees planted there and mentioned its water courses. The exact location of this garden is unknown, but the remains of a garden near Jalalabad exhibit many similar features.[17]

The Ram Bagh located along the banks of the river Yamuna at Agra is believed to be Babur's first garden in India. Babur described the ordering of the harsh, dry landscape through the digging of wells, the establishment of water tanks, and the construction of the symmetrical avenues, plantings, and pavilions that constituted the char bagh (chahar ["four"] became char in Hindi).

The forms of Mughal gardens adapted to variations in climate and terrain. Mughal style became characterized by a fusion of Central Asian, Persian, and Indian influences. Babur's grandson Akbar expanded the Mughal empire in the late 16th century. The lush, open-terraced water gardens of Kashmir date from the 1600s and are discussed in the following chapter.

THE MOMOYAMA ERA (1569–1603)

During the Muromachi period, the shoguns moved their political operations back to Kyoto, reestablishing ties with the imperial court that were severed during the Kamakura era. A century of internal conflicts finally ended with the successive reigns of three generals who were able to establish order throughout the country. Oda Nobunaga (1534–1582) seized Kyoto in 1568. To legitimize his power with the cultural elite of Kyoto he had to prove his sophistication. He turned to the preeminent aesthetician and tea master Sen no Rikyu (1521–1591) for advice.[18]

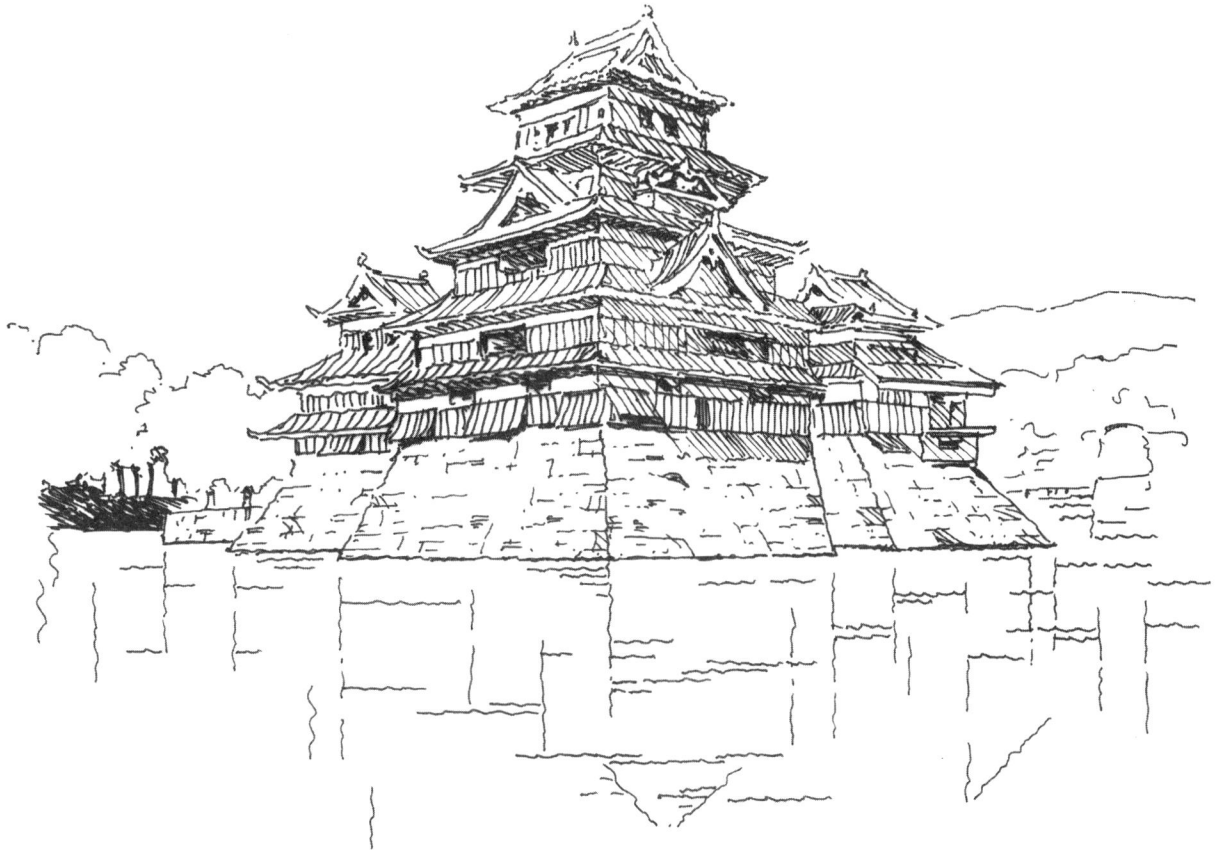

MATSUMOTO CASTLE, KYOTO: Castles were built by wealthy *daimyos* during the Momoyama period.

When Nobunaga was murdered in 1582, Toyotomi Hideyoshi (1536–1598) became shogun. He developed a reputation as an extravagant dictator, perhaps to compensate for his peasant upbringing. Hideyoshi built a castle at Fushimi, south of Kyoto, called Momoyama (Peach Hill). Hence, the latter half of the 16th century became known as the Momoyama period.

During the civil wars, wealthy *daimyos* built fortified castles and used architecture to express their power. Hierarchically arranged castle towns developed as trading centers, and gained a degree of economic independence. A new urban society arose; religion no longer motivated cultural production.

A colorful and flamboyant painting style developed in the early 16th century, distinguished by its use of gold-leaf backgrounds. Works were now executed by professional artists (such as Kano Masanobu, 1434–1530, founder of the Kano school), not by priests or scholars. Also, a new form of poetry emerged, one particularly descriptive of remote landscape imagery.[19]

Opposing expressions of culture characterized the Momoyama period. Against a backdrop of decadence and the ostentatious display of wealth, a ritual of refined etiquette known as the tea ceremony was perfected. The nostalgic appeal of a rustic retreat in the mountains, which in a way the tea hut symbolizes, might have been influenced by the new forms of landscape poetry and the need to provide new venues for social interaction and parameters for social stability.[20]

THE CONCEPT OF THE TEA CEREMONY

Zen Buddhists drank tea to help them stay alert while meditating, a practice also embraced by the samurai elite. One of the first tearooms was built by Yoshimasa at Ginakaku-ji. Later, during the 16th century, Hideyoshi popularized the tea ceremony, promoting its aspects of hospitality and social display rather than its religious functions.

The tea ceremony, or *cha no yu*, involves the performance of specific movements and behaviors in a particular setting, the tea garden, known as *cha niwa* or *roji*. Roji is a reference to the "dewy path" of rebirth in Buddhist doctrine, suggesting that the tea ceremony itself is more about the journey than the destination. The physical form of a tea garden is secondary to its purpose as a place of aesthetic experience. Divided into outer and inner areas, it facilitates the transition from an outer world of distraction to an inner state of composure.

Everything about the tea ceremony is contrived—the proportion of evergreen plants to deciduous plants in the garden, the number of nails in the door, the type of utensils used in the tea hut. Tea gardens became gardens of suggestion, where individual leaves and single flowers were carefully displayed, hinting at the perfection of nature unattainable by humans.

The austere principles of the tea ceremony were codified by Sen no Rikyu, who upheld its virtues of polite restraint and rustic simplicity. The folk aesthetic represented the gracious beauty found within everyday existence. The tea ceremony was practiced by people at all levels of society: Merchants, priests, nobles, and townspeople were all equal within the realm of tea.

FORMS AND ELEMENTS OF THE TYPICAL TEA GARDEN

Tea gardens were small spaces fit into confined property boundaries. Stepping stones, the physical representation of *roji*, regulated speed and direction of movement, while landing stones served to direct attention to a particular feature. The articulation of the path influenced the design of the stroll gardens of the Edo period, discussed in the next chapter.

Wells, basins, gates, and lanterns were prevalent in tea gardens. These elements were points of reference along the path, and had specific functions in the tea ceremony. Guests washed their hands and rinsed their mouths at a basin. Rustic gateways became symbolic thresholds between inner and outer spaces. The types and styles of lanterns, fences, and even stones were carefully chosen to set the tone of the experience.

The floor plan of a typical tea hut accommodated four and a half *tatami* mats, a *tatami* measuring 6 feet by 3 feet. A low door provided entry and forced a humble posture. Decoration was limited to a scroll or subdued floral arrangement within the *tokonoma*. The detached teahouse brought the essence of the countryside into the city, providing sophisticated urban dwellers an escape to an ideal of romanticized nature.[21]

SAMBO-IN, KYOTO

Legend has it that the renovation, in 1598, of the garden at Sambo-in, a former Heian paradise garden within the Daigo-ji temple complex, was motivated by the sudden desire of Hideyoshi to host a cherry blossom festival. The garden is known for its lavish display of more than 700 stones, which are used to define shorelines, form islands, and activate the flat expanses of ground plane. Islands and bridges subdivide the pond into 3 distinct areas. A waterfall is tucked back into a deeply recessed bay, visible from the *shoin*. The garden is meant to be seen from the veranda.

SAMBO-IN, KYOTO: Momoyama gardens are characterized by their exaggerated, highly embellished compositions.

Unique characteristics of Momoyama gardens include earth bridges, lakes with highly convoluted shorelines, and the abundant use of large rocks. One such rock at Sambo-in has a glamorous provenance; its history sums up the values and ideals of the Momoyama era. Called the *Fujito* stone, the large rock was first appreciated by Nobunaga, who had it placed in the shogun's palace with great pomp and circumstance. When Nobunaga died, Hideyoshi had the stone moved to his own palace, and later transported it to Sambo-in.

EARTH BRIDGE DEBUT: Sambo-in contained one of the first earth bridges—wooden posts supported logs covered with soil and grass.

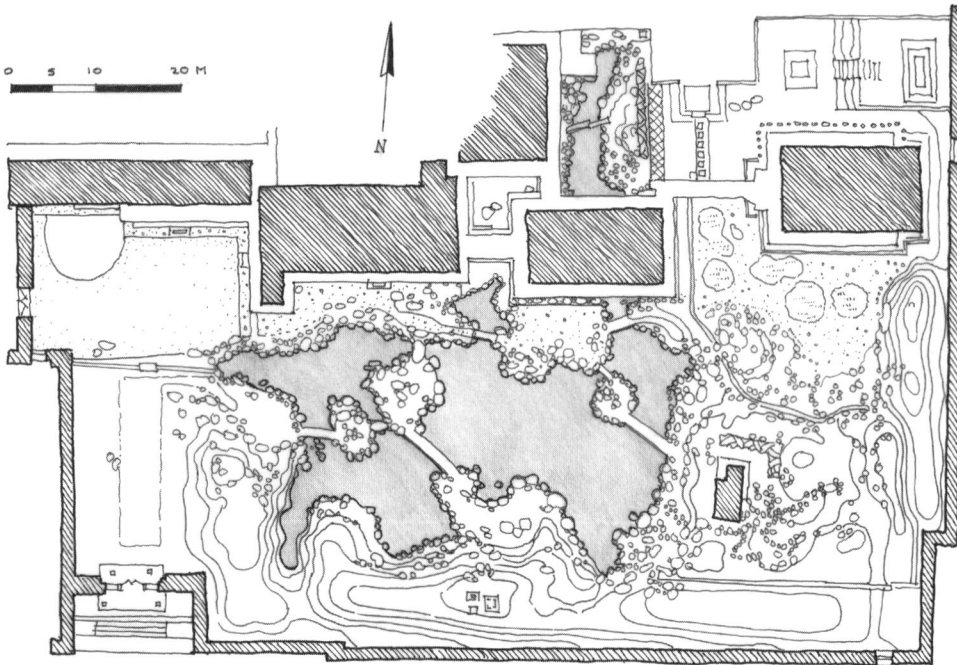

ADDITIVE SCENOGRA-PHY: The sequencing of space around scenic events at Sambo-in marked an important stage in the evolution of the stroll garden.

ATTENTION TO THE GROUND PLANE: Moss in a sea of sand creates gourd patterns at Sambo-in.

SUMMARY

In the 16th century people began to call into question the many assumptions they had made about the way the world worked. Creative forms flourished. Renaissance design principles became manifest in Italian art, architecture, and gardens. Other cultures claimed the landscape in significant ways through similar uses of geometry, water, and the idealization of nature.

DESIGN PRINCIPLES

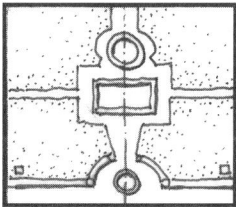

AXIAL SYMMETRY
Italian Renaissance gardens were organized along central lines of sight, creating a geometric ordering of space.

OCCUPYING SPACE
Timurid and Mughal gardens provided spaces for passive enjoyment of the landscape, either on Persian carpets or on flat, elevated platforms called chabutras.

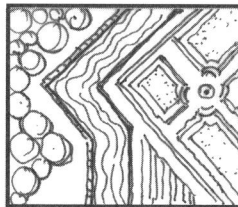

BOUNDARY
French gardens were edged by moats, canals, and galleried walkways, defining ordered ground planes within an untamed landscape.

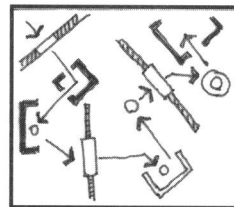

TRANSITION
The sequence and progression of space in a Japanese tea garden represents a psychological as well as physical transition.

HARMONY
Palladio's work demonstrates how all parts correspond to each other through harmonic ratios.

DESIGN VOCABULARY

ITALY
Hydraulics, Compartments, and Sculptures

FRANCE
Parterres, Canals, and Galleries

ENGLAND
Mazes, Mounts, and Topiary

JAPAN
Stepping stones, Basins, and Lanterns

For further exploration

BOOKS
BABURNAMA (THE MEMOIRS OF BABUR)

THE ENCHANTRESS OF FLORENCE, by Salman Rushdie

"THE HISTORIES," by William Shakespeare

THE LIFE OF GARGANTUA AND OF PANTAGRUEL, by Francois Rabelais

THE LIVES OF THE ARTISTS, by Giorgio Vasari

ORLANDO FURIOSO, by Ludovico Ariosto

THE SIXTEEN PLEASURES, by Robert Hellenga

UTOPIA, by Thomas More

FILMS
THE AGONY AND THE ECSTASY (1965)

ANNE OF THE 1000 DAYS (1969)

ELIZABETH (1998)

THE RETURN OF MARTIN GUERRE (1982)

PAINTINGS AND SCULPTURE
DAVID, by Michelangelo (1501)

MONA LISA, by Leonardo da Vinci (1503)

GARDEN OF EARTHLY DELIGHTS, by Hieronymous Bosch (1510)

THE SCHOOL OF ATHENS, by Raphael (1510)

SISTINE CHAPEL, ceiling frescos by Michelangelo (1511)

LAURENTIAN LIBRARY (VESTIBULE AND STEPS), by Michelangelo (1524–58)

BAHRAM GUR IN THE TURQUOISE PAVILION, Safavid manuscript (1524)

PORTRAIT OF HENRY VIII, by Hans Holbein the Younger (1540)

SALT CELLAR, by Benevenuto Cellini (1540)

THE FOUR ACCOMPLISHMENTS, by Kano Motonobu (c. 1550)

RETURN OF THE HUNTERS, by Pieter Brueghel the Elder (1565)

RAPE OF THE SABINE WOMAN, by Giovanni Bologna (1583)

17th CENTURY

From a European perspective, the 17th century is often described as the beginning of the Age of Reason, a period when advances in scientific knowledge challenged beliefs in religious doctrine and Renaissance order. Nature was shaped according to human will, and typically by royal privilege.

Massive colonization of the Americas took place in the 1600s. Jamestown, Virginia, was founded by the English in 1607; Quebec was settled by the French in 1608; Sante Fe was developed by the Spanish in 1609; and New Amsterdam was claimed by the Dutch in 1624. As settlements expanded, native populations suffered and ancient lifeways all but disappeared.

The idea of extension applied not only to geopolitical influence: gardens merged into the landscape with vistas to endless horizons. Large-scale views were part of the drama and idea of mobility that characterized Baroque styles. The earth was no longer the static center of the universe but part of a system in motion around the sun. Politically and culturally, emphasis shifted to France, where the garden became a venue for spectacle, employed as a symbol of the absolutism of the Sun King.

Some of the world's most illustrious gardens, such as the Taj Mahal, Katsura Imperial Villa, and Versailles, were created in the 17th century, and are discussed in this chapter.

1603
VIRGINIA SLIMS

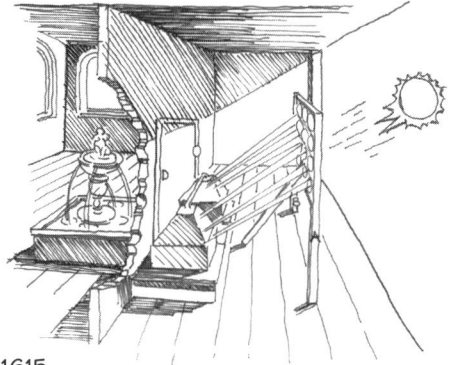

1615
HYDRAULIC WIZARDRY

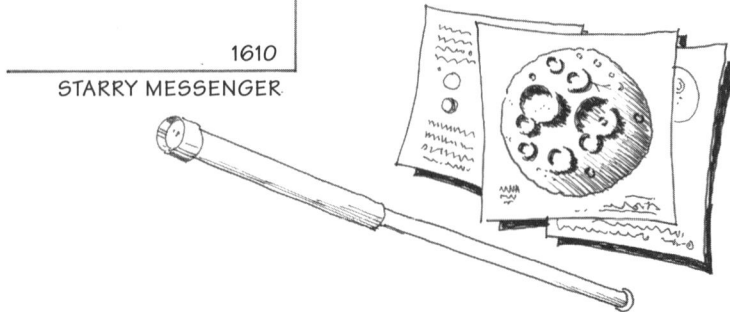

1600 — 1610 — 1620

1610
STARRY MESSENGER

1666
GREAT FIRE OF LONDON

1669
STRADIVARIUS

1650 — 1660 — 1670

1656–1667
BAROQUE EMBRACE

1633
GOING BANANAS

1634
YUAN YEH

1642
THE NIGHT WATCH

1630

1640

1648
LANDSCAPE PAINTING

1677
COGITO ERGO SUM

1682
HALLEY'S COMET

1680

1690

1700

1682
GREEN COUNTY TOWNE

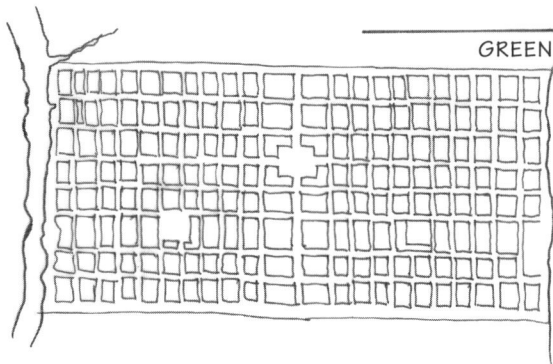

1687
LAW OF UNIVERSAL
GRAVITATION

1603   VIRGINIA SLIMS
Sir Walter Raleigh's initial attempts to colonize Roanoke Island failed several times. He eventually settled the first English colony, Virginia, in 1603. Raleigh returned to England with the Nicotinia plant; by 1617, tobacco smoking was a popular fad at the royal court.

1610   STARRY MESSENGER
Galileo published *Sidereus Nuncius*, the first treatise based on observations made through a telescope. He was tried for heresy because of his theories of a heliocentric universe.

1615   HYDRAULIC WIZARDRY
French engineer and architect Salomon de Caus published a treatise on waterworks, *Les Raisons des Forces Mouvantes*. He and his brother Isaac studied Italian garden design and were influential in introducing Mannerist and Baroque styles to northern Europe and England. Besides his numerous automata, de Caus's greatest built landscape, the Hortus Palatinus in Heidelberg, was called the eighth wonder of the world; it was destroyed in the Thirty Years' War.[1]

1633   GOING BANANAS
The first bunch of bananas imported from Bermuda and ripened in England was displayed in the window of London apothecary and botanist, Thomas Johnson.[2]

1634   *YUAN YEH*
The Ming-period painter and landscape designer Ji Cheng published a gardening manual, the *Yuan Yeh*, in 1634. His main advice for gardeners was that there are "no definite rules for planning the garden."[3] Ji Cheng suggested that gardens should elicit an emotional response and a deep spiritual reverie. His three volumes provided a sort of visual compendium of particular garden elements. But rather than outline specific construction techniques, he gave poetic descriptions of desired effects—for example, rocks should be placed so that they "welcome the clouds and moon."[4]

1642   *THE NIGHT WATCH*
Dutch painter Rembrandt van Rijn was an acute observer of life. His manipulation of light and shadow created dramatic narratives in his paintings.

1648   LANDSCAPE PAINTING
French painter Nicolas Poussin painted idealized views of ancient ruins in the Roman *campagna*. The juxtaposition of classical forms in a landscape setting created a romantic view of nature that became extremely influential in the development of the English landscape garden in the 18th century.

1656–1667   BAROQUE EMBRACE
Gian Lorenzo Bernini was commissioned by Pope Alexander VII to design a new piazza for St. Peter's Cathedral in Rome. The narrowing trapezoidal piazza that leads from the basilica into the large oval piazza is defined by an elegant elliptical colonnade. The work is the consummate expression of Baroque space and urban drama.

1666   GREAT FIRE OF LONDON
Fire destroyed the medieval city within the old Roman walls. Commissioners to King Charles rebuilt London with wider streets and grand squares; property owners reconstructed wood buildings with stone and brick. Christopher Wren's rebuilding of St. Paul's Cathedral exemplified the new style that changed the look of the city.

1669   STRADIVARIUS
Antonio Stradivari refined the shape and proportions of the violin and began crafting string instruments under his own label. The secret to their sweet tones supposedly lies in his (now lost) recipe for varnish.

1677   *COGITO ERGO SUM*
French philosopher, mathematician, and scientist Rene Descartes saw the universe as a mathematical construction. His book *La Geometrie* formed the basis of analytical geometry and outlined how coordinates can define a position in space. His work on optics was equally influential.

1682   HALLEY'S COMET
Edmond Halley used Newton's gravitational theories to correctly predict that the comet then visible in the sky had an elliptical orbit and would reappear in 1758.

1682   GREEN COUNTRY TOWNE
William Penn received a charter from King Charles II to establish a Quaker colony in North America. Penn's grid plan allowed for a central public open space and public greens within each quadrant, and required that houses be placed in the middle of lots as a precaution against fire.

1687   LAW OF UNIVERSAL GRAVITATION
Sir Isaac Newton discovered that the same force governed both the motion of the moon and a falling apple, and proved it mathematically.

EDO PERIOD (1603–1867)

After Hideyoshi died, another of Nobunaga's generals, Tokugawa Ieyasu (1543–1616), established a new warrior dynasty that lasted until the 19th century. He moved the shogunate to Edo (now Tokyo) and issued a series of strict edicts to control all aspects of society. Except for a small Dutch trading colony near Nagasaki, Japan was closed to all foreigners. The Christian missionaries were expelled, and practicing Christians persecuted. Ieyasu endorsed a neo-Confucian philosophy that blended aspects of Buddhism and Daoism; its emphasis on morality and loyalty contributed to his ideal of a strong central government.[5]

model for these new gardens was the tea garden, whose function as a place of passage was realized on a much grander scale. These gardens became known as "stroll gardens."

Stroll gardens were designed to recall the natural scenery of Japan. Since travel within the country was restricted by the shogun, the publication of books illustrating the "famous sights" of Japan became popular.[6] The books contained colorful woodblock prints of scenes such as Mt. Fuji, maple-covered hillsides, and the "eight-bridges" river system. The stroll gardens of the Edo period referenced these famous landscapes.

FOCUS ON THE ARTS

The city of Tokyo expanded dramatically. Trade was now facilitated by a money economy rather than a barter system. Despite their low status, merchants accumulated great wealth and became patrons of new art forms—the Kabuki theater, haiku, and woodblock prints. The merchant class was forbidden to display their wealth. They could not publicly appear in expensive clothing or build large estates. Instead, they built small courtyard gardens, or tsuboniwa, in the open spaces between the rooms of their urban houses.

SOCIAL ORDER AND CULTURAL ISOLATION

The long period of peace and prosperity came at the expense of civil liberties. Society was strictly ordered according to a hierarchical class system where power rested with the shogun, then the daimyos, samurai, farmers, artists, and, lastly, merchants. To limit the potential threat from rival clans in the provinces, Ieyasu required "alternate attendance" of the daimyos—obliging the daimyos to reside in the capital every other year. While they were absent from Tokyo, their families were to remain.

Ieyasu's edicts also prohibited the imperial court's involvement in government and politics, limiting the emperor's activities to aesthetic pursuits only, as was done in the Heian period. The two captive populations, the hostage daimyos in Tokyo and the alienated imperial court at Kyoto, occupied themselves by building large estate gardens. The

TSUBONIWA: Interior courtyard gardens contained evocative elements, as did stroll gardens and tea gardens, but were meant only for viewing, not occupation.

In 17th-century Japan, gardening was a booming business. Nurserymen, rock merchants, and professional garden designers benefited from the thriving economy. Garden design had become a respected, secular profession. Aristocratic gardens no longer alluded to literary or religious themes, but were built on a romantic conception of nature, expressed through individual creativity.[7] The activities of the elite may have been curtailed, but their imaginations were free to soar.

CHARACTERISTICS OF EARLY STROLL GARDENS

The appreciation of the countryside as a place of leisure, rather than toil, and the value of a pastoral vista, were new ways of thinking about the landscape for the elite in 17th-century Japan.[8] Urban dwellers romanticized the distant view: the far landscape represented the appeal of the experience of rustic nature, much like the tea garden did. Stroll gardens surrounded a lake, and often incorporated views of distant landscape features. The route was not hierarchically structured, but designed as a series of independent scenic events that came as a revelation to the viewer. Stroll gardens often contained tea houses, pavilions, sculptural lanterns, and pagodas. Lakes had deeply recessed bays; large rocks emphasized the shorelines. As the visitor moved along the path, views of particular elements both near and far suddenly appeared, set within the garden like scenic tableaux. The principle of hide-and-reveal (mie-gakure) added an element of anticipation and surprise to the experience. In Edo stroll gardens, views were mainly to Mt. Fuji and the harbor; the surrounding landscape was not as picturesque as the environs of Kyoto.

Stroll gardens focused attention both on internal features and outward views. The practice of borrowed scenery, shakkei, involved more than just a visual appreciation of the landscape. Nature was reinterpreted; the picture held a message. Space was composed pictorially according to principles of foreground, midground, and background, extending the limits of the garden visually and conceptually.

IMPERIAL ESTATES IN KYOTO

To placate the imperial family, the shogun gave them land and financed the construction of their villas and retirement estates. These amounted to large landholdings; imperial stroll gardens were on average 10 times larger than the courtyard gardens of their Heian predecessors.[9] Examples of imperial villas include Katsura-Rikyu, Shugaku-in, and Sento Gosho.

KATSURA-RIKYU

Katsura Villa was planned as a countryside retreat in 1620 by Prince Toshihito (1570–1629), the adopted son of Hideyoshi, and finished decades later by his son, Toshitada. The tea master and garden design expert, Kobori Enshu (1579–1649), is often cited as having a hand in its design.[10] Toshihito was inspired by the golden age of Heian culture, and sought to blend in his villa the elegance of that era with the rustic simplicity of tea culture.[11]

Katsura Villa has become the definitive example of the stroll garden as a poetic experience. The path system is carefully contrived around a large lake with an intricate shoreline. Sight lines unfold as the visitor moves clockwise around the lake. Features include a turtle island, a re-creation of the famous land spit Amanohashidate, a monolithic stone bridge, and stone lanterns. A series of tea houses are set within the garden.

The three pavilions of the rustic, shoin-style "palace" are staggered on a diagonal, visually integrated into the landscape. The orthogonal geometry of the architecture plays against the natural forms of the garden.[12] Each room opens onto the garden. The structure is elevated above the ground plane to avoid flooding from the nearby river, and contains a platform for moon viewing.

KATSURA-RIKYU: The densely planted 12-acre garden is adjacent to a river.

CASE STUDY: *Katsura Imperial Villa*

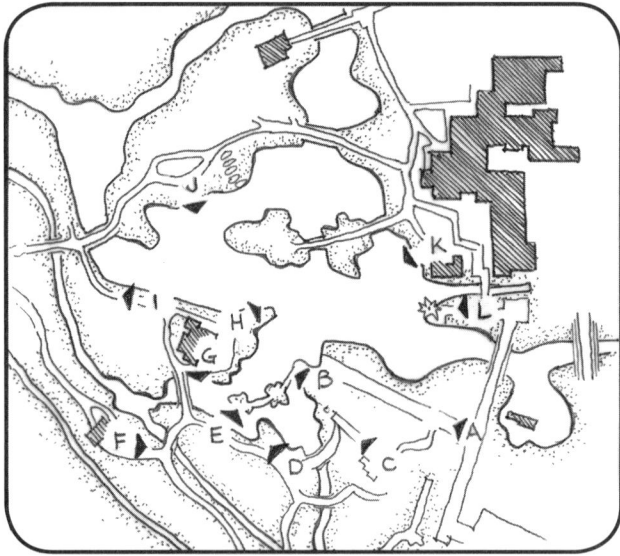

CASE STUDY: *Katsura Imperial Villa*

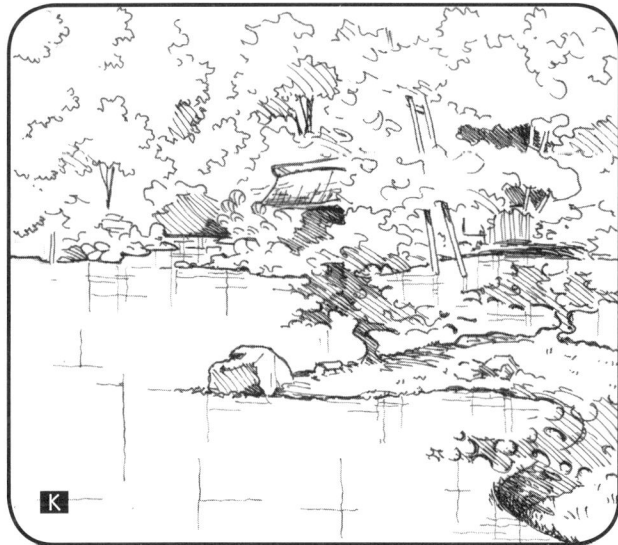

SHUGAKU-IN RIKYU

In 1655, a countryside villa was built by the shoguns for Prince Toshi-tada's uncle, Emperor Gomizuno-o, who was married to Ieyasu's grand-daughter. The estate consists of three villas on different levels set amid woodlands and rice fields.

The lower villas contain small *shin-den*-style gardens and tea houses. Gomizuno-o built an earthen dam to create a sizable lake with a convoluted shoreline. The upper garden is known for its superb application of *shakkei*, where

SHUGAKU-IN: The garden is known for its astonishing incorporation of borrowed views.

an entire sequence of space is manipulated to create a dramatic experience. The visitor enters the upper garden via a stone stair confined by clipped hedges, ascending to the Pavilion in the Clouds (*Rinun-tei*) with his or her back to the view. Turning about, spectacular views of Kyoto emerge over the lake, the contours of which echo the shape of the surrounding mountains.

UPPER GARDEN: Clipped hedges disguise the dam at Shugaku-in, repeating the shape of the rice terraces.

N

0 10 20 30M

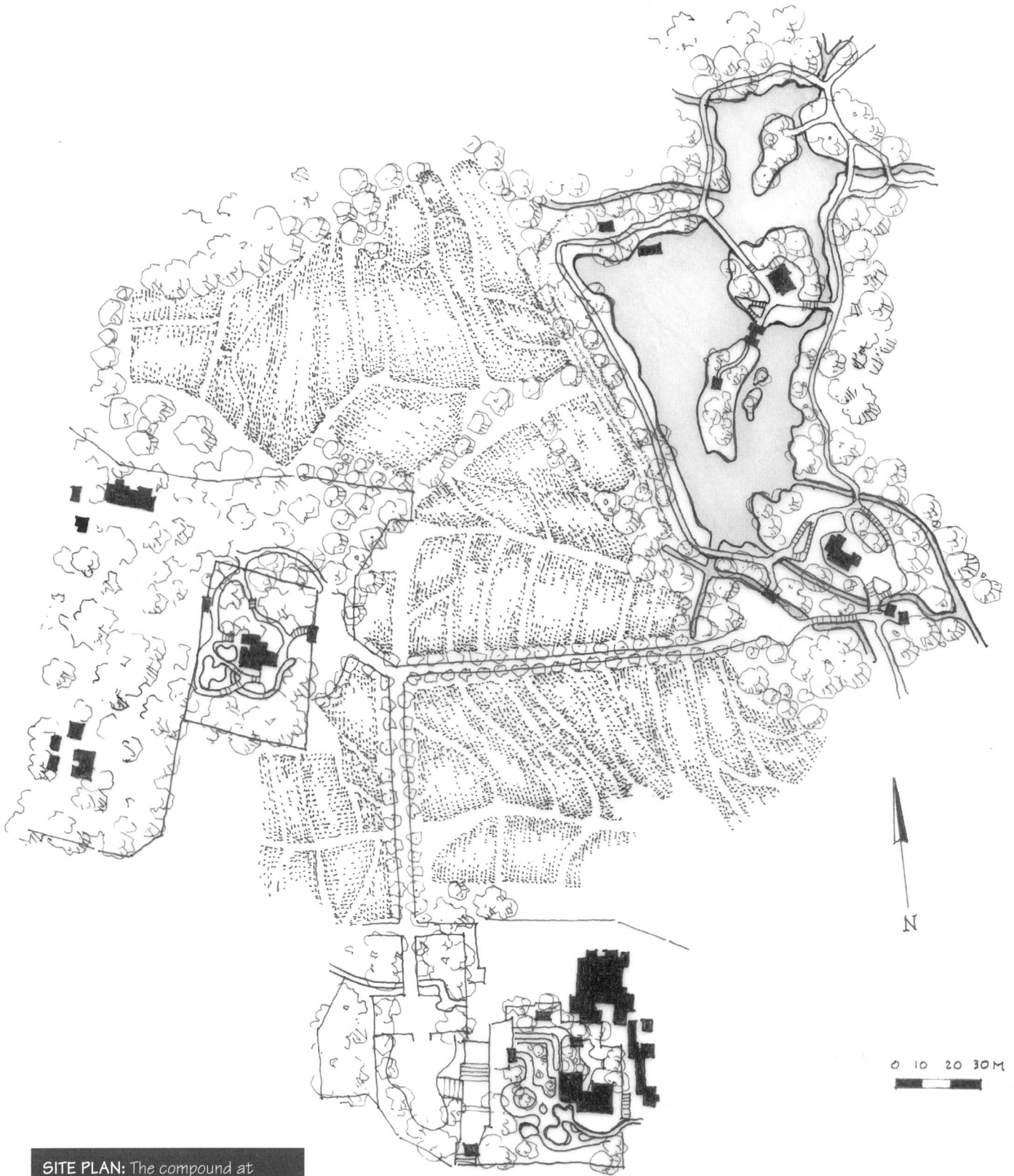

SITE PLAN: The compound at Shugaku-in encompasses three separate villas.

117

SENTO GO-SHO: River-washed rocks form the bank of the lake in the "stone coast" style.

SENTO GOSHO

Gomizuno-o abdicated early; Sento Gosho is the retirement villa he planned with Kobori Enshu in 1634. The garden surrounds a lake and stream and contains a waterfall. Deep bays and peninsulas subdivide the lake, creating a dynamic shifting of space as the visitor moves through the garden. Sento Gosho is distinguished by its pebbled beach, turtle island, and earth bridge.

ESTATES OF THE DAIMYOS

KOISHIKAWA KORAKUEN, TOKYO

Korakuen was a pleasure park built by the Tokugawa daimyo Yorifusa Mito in 1629. The garden was dedicated to Confucius, whose teachings were esteemed by the Tokugawa shoguns. Chinese influences can be seen in several features of the

garden, such as the Full Moon Bridge (*Engetsu-kyo*), and a 30-foot-high artificial mountain, called *Lu Shan*. The garden contains a lake, a large turtle island with a distinctive vertical "head" stone, various bridges, and many imported rocks. Scenes from famous Kyoto temple gardens, as

well as scenes from famous Hangzhou gardens are reproduced here. Korakuen became a model for other daimyo estates which, consistent with the new emphasis on Confucian order, contained more overt interpretations of poetic themes rather than subtle allusions.

KORAKUEN: Shrubs were clipped to look like rocks: low broad lanterns harmonize with the horizontality of the lake.

SACRED SYMMETRIES

The Mughal empire at its height stretched from the base of the Himalayas to the Bay of Bengal, covering territories in present day Afghanistan and northwest India. The landscape differs widely in these regions, from dry desert plains to lush river valleys. Garden forms were adapted to changes in climate and terrain.

Mughal art forms were a blend of Persian, Central Asian, and Indian styles. When Timur conquered Iran in the 14th century, expanding his Central Asian empire, the nomadic Mongols adopted Persian cultural traditions. Persian styles, including the *chahar bagh* form, were carried to India after Timur's descendent Babur captured Delhi in 1526, forming the Mughal dynasty. Babur's grandson Akbar (1542–1605) expanded the Mughal empire when he invaded Kashmir in the late 16th century. Seventeenth-century Mughal art shows the influence of both Hindu and Islamic cultures: aspects of a Buddhist aesthetic based on organic patterns and sculptural ornamentation were combined with the Islamic sense of mathematical order and geometry. These influences can be seen in the architectural features and built forms of Mughal gardens, and in the painted miniatures produced during this period. The tomb garden was a distinctive combination of landscape and architecture that joined aspects of the Islamic paradise garden with the Central Asian tradition of garden burial. Construction of a tomb garden began during an emperor's lifetime; it was used as a park before his death and as a temple ground after.

The greatest Mughal gardens date from the reigns of Akbar's son, Jahangir (1569–1627), and grandson, Shah Jahan (1592–1666).

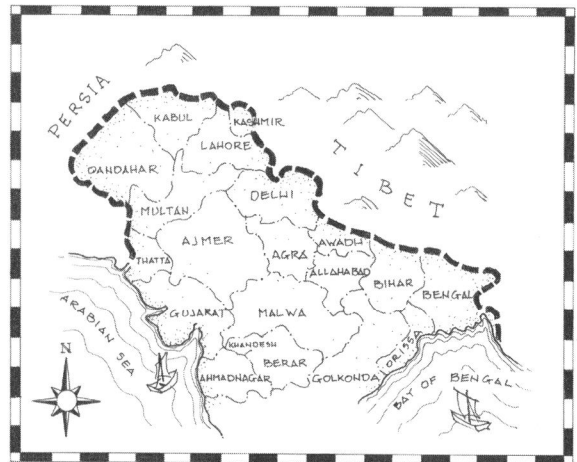

The **Mughal Empire** in the mid-17th century.

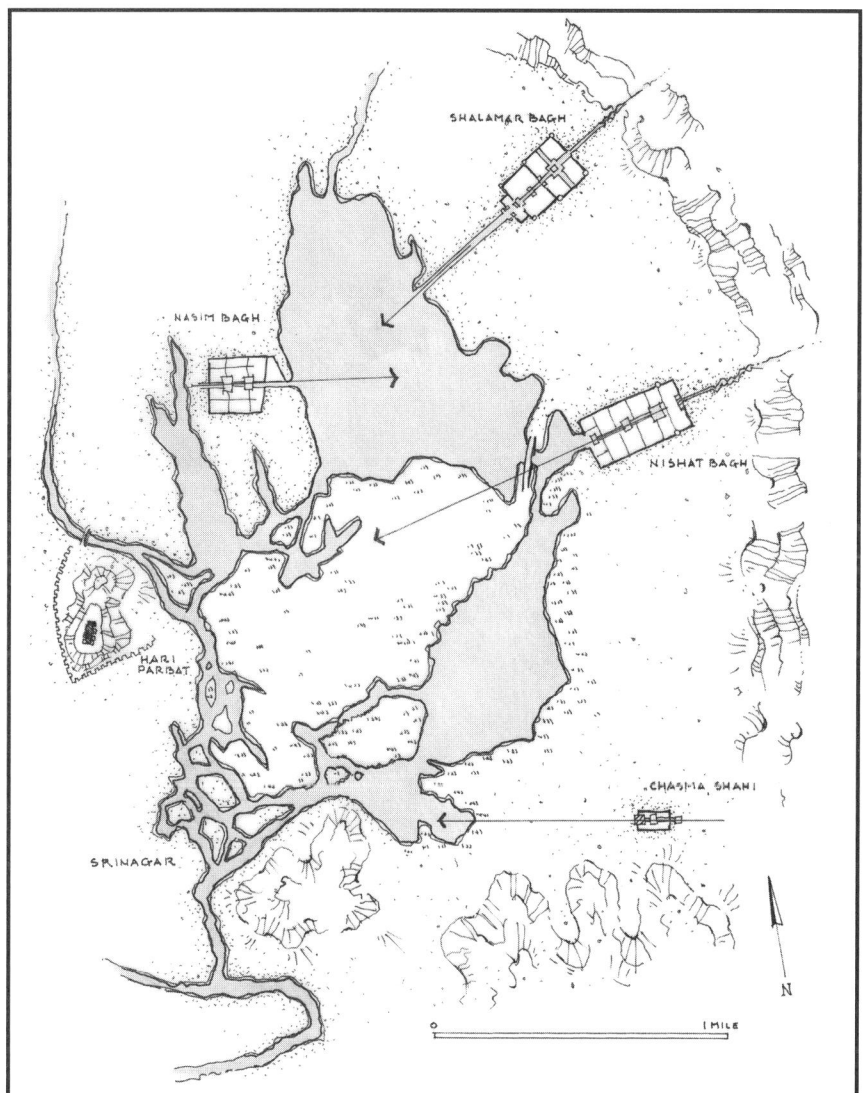

LAKE DAL, KASHMIR: Hundreds of gardens were believed to have been built around Lake Dal and the town of Srinagar during Jahangir's rule.

THE CELEBRATION OF WATER

The lush valley of Kashmir is about 90 miles long. Extant gardens illustrate how the abundance of mountain streams and springs were exploited by the emphatic use of water in Mughal gardens. On these sloping grounds, water flowed with great pomp along a central axis. No longer confined to still pools and narrow rills, water fell in sheets over *chini-kanas* and down *chadars*. A *chini-kana* is a low wall with niches, like a dovecote; a *chadar* is a sloped surface with patterns carved in relief. In addition, raised platforms, called *chabutras*, provided cool resting spots at the intersections of the water channels.

Open pavilions or summerhouses, called *baradari*, built into corners of walled terraces provided comfortable overlooks. Terraces planted with shade-bestowing chenars (plane trees), fruit trees, and fragrant flowers re-created the sights and sounds of an imagined heaven.

Shah Jahan enjoyed the Kashmir valley, but he also appreciated the landscape of the northern plains, perhaps as a reminder of his Rajput heritage.[13] He built gardens in Lahore and Delhi, both named Shalamar Bagh. His great contribution to landscape history was the Taj Mahal, the tomb garden built for his wife in Agra. Shah Jahan also had an impact on the history of city planning, building the city-fort at Agra and the Red Fort in Delhi.

CHADAR: Patterns carved on the surface of the water chute created different effects in the cascade.

CHINI-KANA: Candles or flowers placed in the niches enhanced the effect of the falling water.

TOMB GARDENS AND PLEASURE PALACES

In addition to the Taj Mahal, other representative examples of 17th century Mughal gardens include Akbar's tomb garden at Agra, and the pleasure palaces of Shalamar and Nishat Bagh on Lake Dal.

AKBAR'S TOMB, SIKANDRA (AGRA)

Completed in 1632, this large mausoleum sits atop the center of the two crossing water axes like a monumental *chabutra*. The tomb is built as a series of concentric rectangles: the first three stories are made of red sandstone, the top level is white marble. Four raised causeways subdivide the char bagh. Water flowed across the flat platforms in narrow, shallow runnels from four central basins. Cypress trees (representing death) lined the avenue. Fruit trees (representing life) filled the terraces.

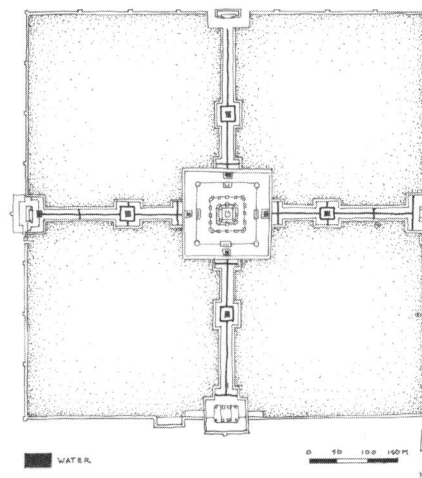

AKBAR'S TOMB: The grounds of the tomb garden typify the char-bagh form.

SHALAMAR, KASHMIR

Shalamar, built as a summer palace along the shores of Lake Dal by Jahangir in 1619, was expanded by Shah Jahan in 1630. Set in a wide ravine and framed by the mountains, Shalamar consists of three terraces connected by a central axis of water punctuated with jets. The main canal is bordered by pathways on both sides, shaded by chenar trees. Turf, flowers, and fruit trees grew on the terraces. At each level change, shallow falls were highlighted by *chini kanas*.

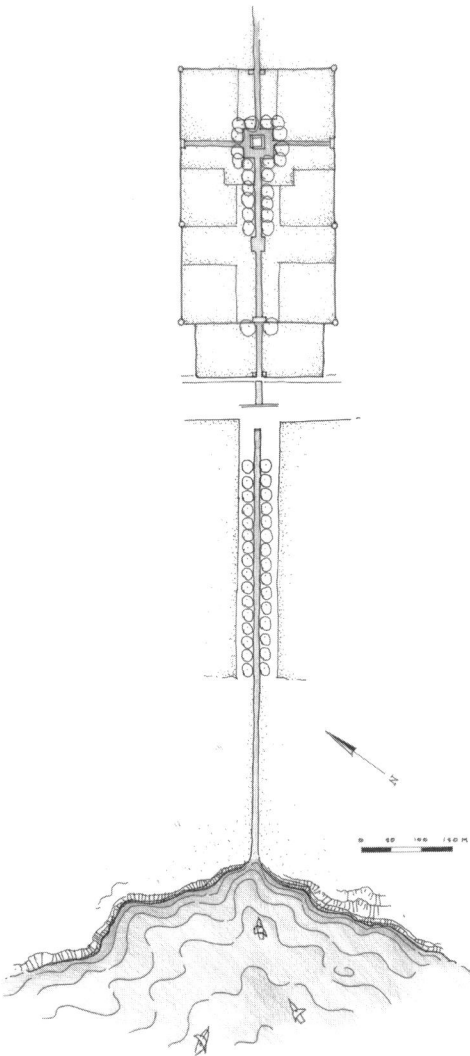

NISHAT BAGH, KASHMIR

Nishat Bagh was built in 1620, most likely by a relative of Jahangir's wife, hence it had no official function. Twelve terraces (representing the astrological signs) climbed up the slope, visually uniting with the distant mountains. Unlike the hierarchical division of space at Shalamar, the terraces at Nishat Bagh formed a large pleasure garden with a separate zenana at the top.

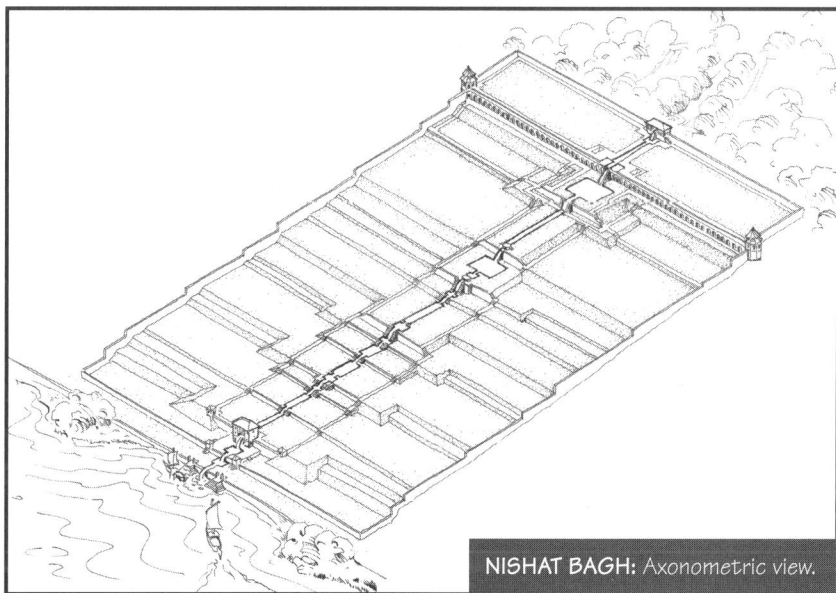

THROUGH FLOATING ISLANDS: Shalamar was approached by boat from a long canal cut through the marshes.

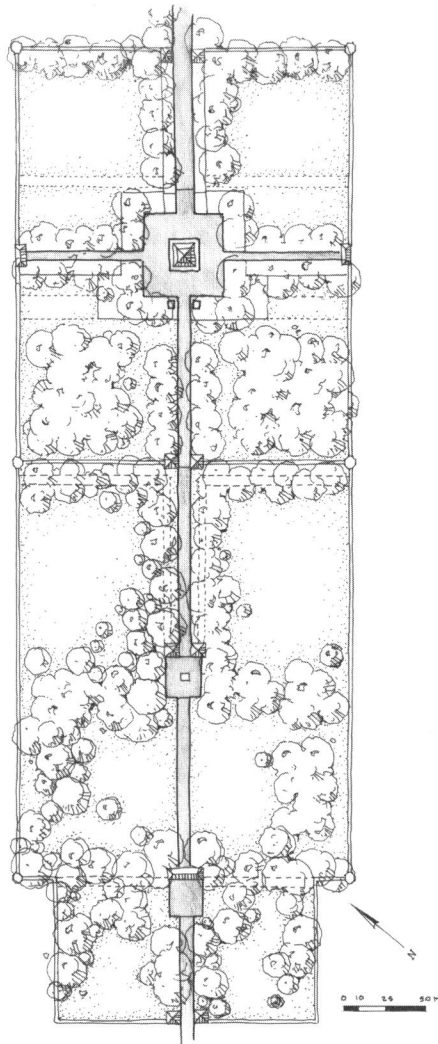

NISHAT BAGH: Axonometric view.

VISUAL NARRATIVE: *Nishat Bagh*

A 13-foot-wide canal, lined with jets, bisects the stepped terraces. Changes in level are marked by narrow *chadars*, steps, pools, and *chabutras*. A tall, arcaded retaining wall forms the base of the zenana terrace. Three-story *baridari* are located at each end of the wall. The watercourse passes right through the pavilion at the top of the zenana.

BUOYANT APPROACH: The garden was entered directly from an inner lagoon separated from Lake Dal by an arched bridge.

TAJ MAHAL, AGRA

The tomb garden for Shah Jahan's wife, Mumtaz Mahal, was begun in 1632 and completed in 1648. It is an enormous *char bagh*, unique in that the tomb is located at the far end of the garden, above the Yamuna river, rather than at the intersection of the water canals. Legend has it that Shah Jahan had one day hoped to build his tomb garden (out of black marble) as a mirror image on the opposite side of the river. Thus the river itself would form the cross-axis, and both tombs would occupy the center.[15]

As it is, a raised tank of water marks the center of the garden at the Taj Mahal, reflecting the white marble dome and its minarets. Tree-lined canals divide the garden into the typical four-square pattern. Trees and flowers once graced each parterre.

The tomb stands isolated on a terrace paved with black-and-white wave patterns. Minarets stand at the corners of the elevated terrace, countering the bulk of the architecture and creating a restful void space. The mosque and assembly hall at either side of the tomb are made from red sandstone, as is the entry gatehouse and the two small pavilions at the end of the cross-axis. The entire 20-acre garden is walled. The round dome over the tomb rests on a squarish octagon; the octagon is symbolic of the union of heaven (the circle) and earth (the square). The number 8 is also significant in Islamic cosmology, representing the levels of paradise and the number of angels supporting the throne of God.

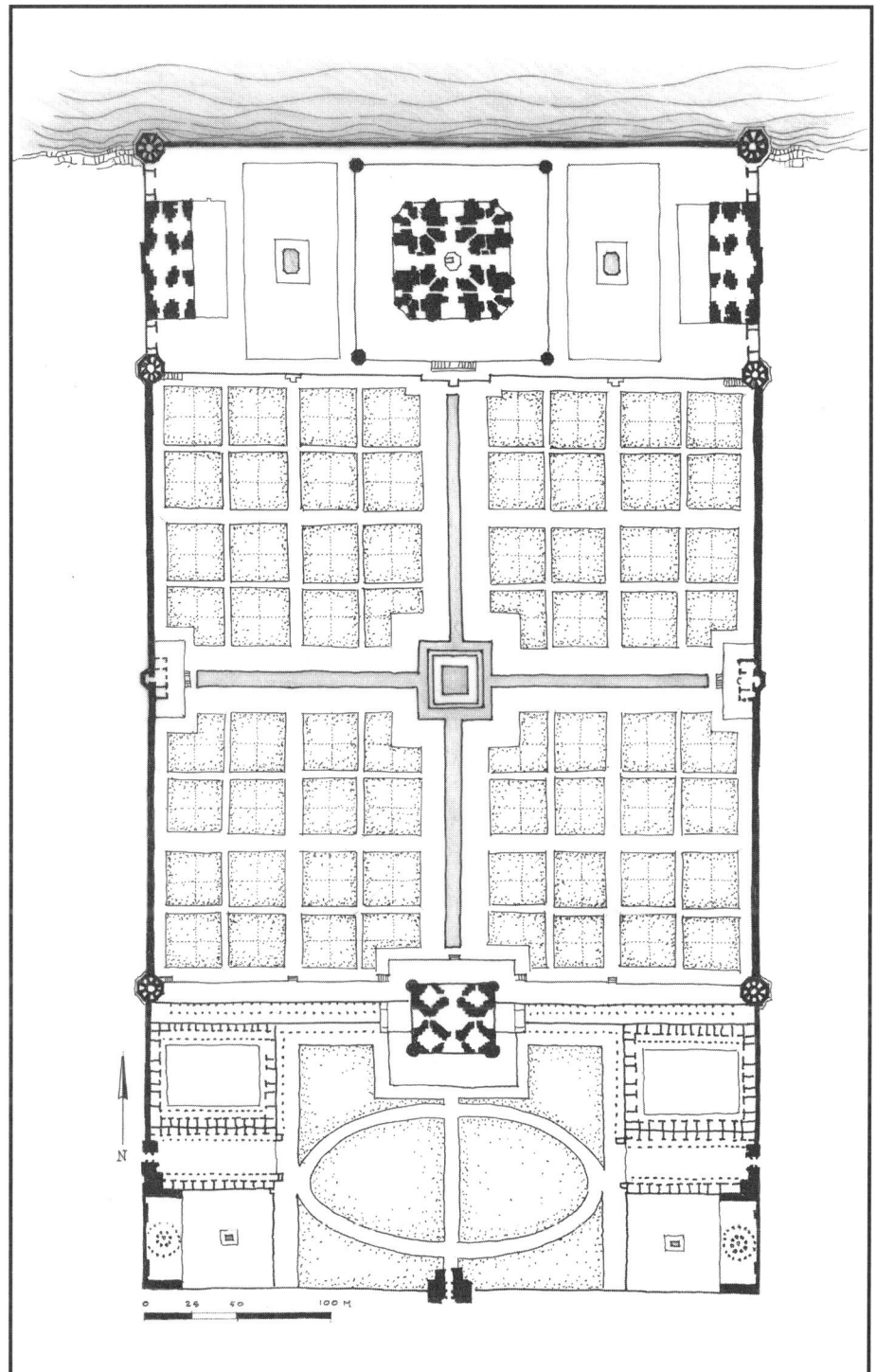

TAJ MAHAL: Historic plans show additional subdivisions of space within each quadrant.[16]

GARDENS OF PARADISE

Shah Abbas I (1571–1629), the great-grandson of Shah Ismail, came to rule in 1587 and led the Safavid dynasty to its height of power. Decisive victories in the first decade of the 17th century gave Iran control over much of the Near East. Wealth accumulated through increased trade fostered by Abbas I's liberal immigration policies and his acceptance of European diplomats. The Safavid empire declined after Abbas I's death, but Safavid rule lasted in some form until Abbas III was defeated in 1736.

Strong geometries, squares, and straight lines signified the order of the Islamic universe. Early Persian hunting parks were divided into quadrants, with a pavilion placed at the intersection. Walled Persian gardens shut out the harsh desert and provided an earthly paradise of shade, water, and colorful flowers. Water was used to irrigate plants and control microclimates, and was always contained in channels and pools. On the dry Iranian plateau,

qanats, or subsurface tunnels, carried water from sources in the surrounding foothills. The form of a garden was determined by its irrigation patterns. Based on traditional garden precedents, the Shah created a splendid imperial city at Esfahan.

THE URBAN GEOMETRY OF ESFAHAN

Shah Abbas I moved the capital to the mile-high city of Esfahan in 1598. By the mid-17th century the city had over half a million inhabitants.[17] Private pleasure gardens continued uninterrupted along both sides of the mile-long promenade between the gate to the royal palace grounds and the Zayandeh river. Called Chahar Bagh Avenue, a central canal lined with onyx formed the axis, which was planted with eight rows of plane trees and poplars. A galleried

bridge built on arched piers continued the main axis over the river, leading to additional royal gardens and parks. One royal park at the far south end of Chahar Bagh Avenue, called Hezar Jarib, was described in the travel journals (1686) of French jeweller Sir John Chardin as consisting of 12 ascending terraces covering 1 square mile.[18]

The shah's construction of Esfahan included the addition of a colossal public square, called the maidan, an imperial mosque, and extensive gardens. The maidan measures about 1500 feet by 500 feet and is defined by a two-story arcade. Shops occupied the ground floor, while the upper arcade served as a gallery for the events and spectacles that took place there. A monumental gateway known as the Ali Qapu overlooks the space on the western edge. Its two-story talar, or covered porch, is raised two stories above the ground and supported by 18 wooden columns. The elevated, shady porch captured breezes, providing a comfortable spot for the shah to preside over activities in the maidan. Directly opposite the Ali Qapu on the eastern edge of the courtyard was the women's mosque. The imperial mosque terminated the southern end of the maidan, although it assumed its own alignment toward Mecca. The Ali Qapu acted as a threshold to the shah's private gardens located behind the structure.

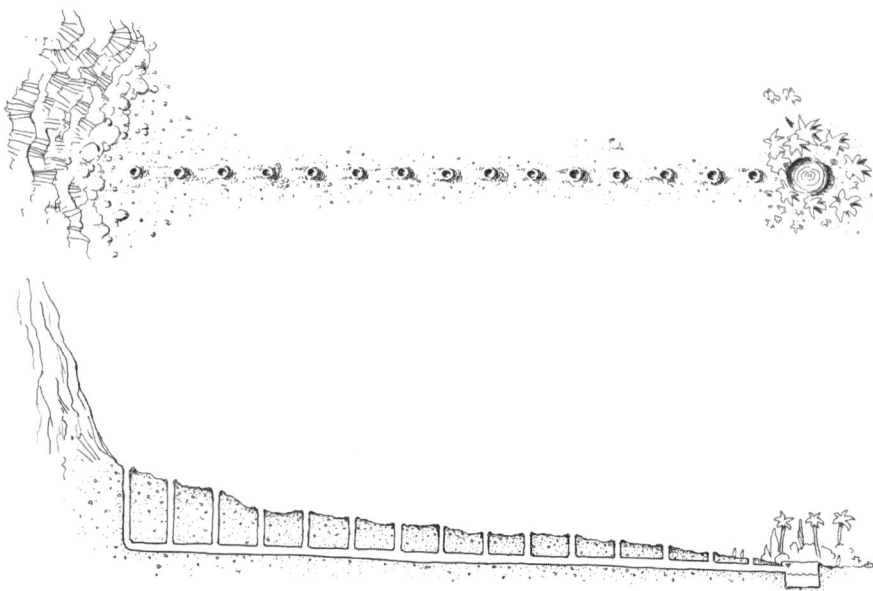

QANAT: Circular air vents formed linear patterns in the landscape and indicated the presence of a qanat.

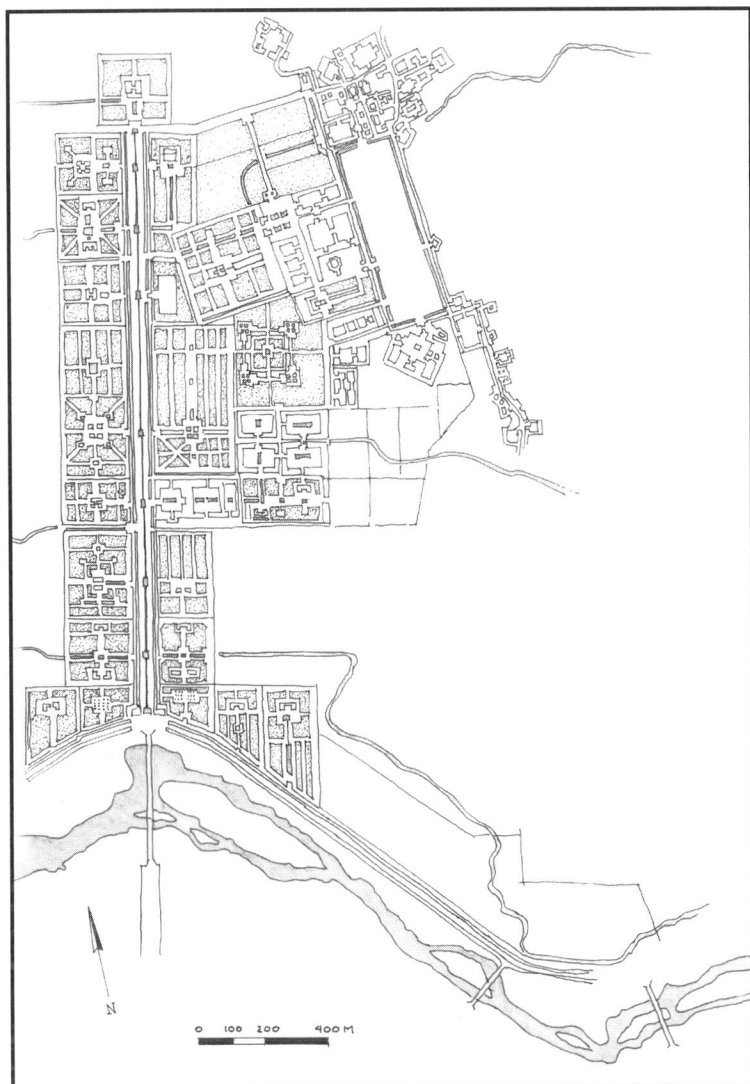

ESFAHAN, IRAN: A grand boulevard of gardens distinguishes the capital city.

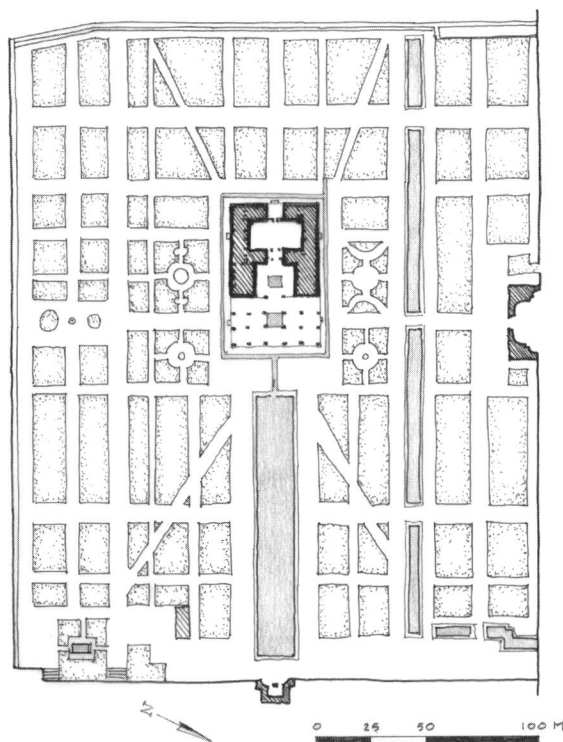

CHEHEL SOTOON: The pavilion occupied the near center of a densely planted 12-acre garden.

ALI QAPU: The six-story pavilion contained a throne room, royal apartments, and reception rooms.

TALAR: Stone lions spouted water into a white marble basin within the porch.

Farther west of the *maidan*, between the Ali Qapu and Chahar Bagh Avenue, a royal pavilion known as Chehel Sotoon was reconstructed by Shah Abbas II in 1647. The 20 tall wooden columns of the *talar* were reflected in a long rectangular pool enfronting the pavilion, hence the name *chehel sotoon* (40 columns).

Overall, the vocabulary used in the royal gardens and pavilions at Esfahan are typical of Persian gardens. Architectural features and garden geometries create an interpenetration of space that is both symbolic and functional. The planting, decoration, and thoughtful use of water combined to create a true paradise on earth.

sented a completely different environment in which to construct gardens. To ease the arduous journey across the desert plains, he had the 300-mile-long route paved, and built resting lodges along the way. The Bagh-e Fin in Kashan (south of Tehran) was the site of a reception for Shah Ismail in the early 16th century. Abbas I improved the gardens in 1587, and Abbas II visited there in 1659.[19]

BAGH-E FIN, KASHAN

A high wall encloses the 6-acre garden. A natural spring and *qanat* supply a

reservoir that feeds the garden by gravity. Other canals irrigate the surrounding fields and farms.[20] From a monumental gateway in the outer wall, a wide avenue containing a runnel leads to a central pool and pavilion, and continues to another pavilion at the far end of the axis. A cross-channel of water emanating from the central pavilion divides the space into four. Pebble-paved paths flank the channels. Interior plots are planted with fruit trees. The sights and sounds of the garden experienced beneath a cover of dense shade create a lush, sensuous oasis. A perimeter canal collects the runoff and delivers it to the village.

SEASIDE PALACES

Shah Abbas I also built palaces and gardens on the southern coast of the Caspian Sea. The well-watered marshy landscape, 100 feet below sea level, pre-

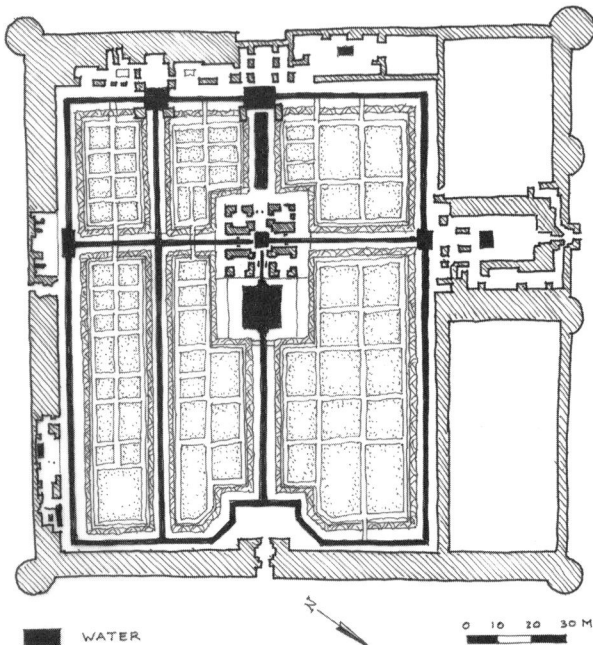

WATER

0 10 20 30 M

BAGH-E FIN: The existing structures date from the 18th century; the garden was restored again in 1935.

SHADY TUNNELS: Four-hundred-year-old cypresses shade runnels lined with turquoise tiles and abundant bubblers at Bagh-e Fin.

ITALIAN BAROQUE STYLES

Toward the end of the 16th century in Italy, the order and clarity of Renaissance styles gave way to a design impulse that expressed the uncertainty and unease felt by society. Space became ambiguous, illusionistic, and distorted. Optical tricks shook one's belief in the order of world. In the 17th century, Mannerist tendencies were taken to an extreme. Baroque styles were characterized by a restlessness and exaggeration of detail. The rational vocabulary of circles and squares was supplemented by the introduction of spiral, oval, and diagonal geometries that kept the eye moving through space.

DETAIL AND DRAMA IN THE GARDEN

Landscape space became more theatrical. Italian gardens of the 17th century were large-scale productions, no longer limited by the conception of villa, garden, and *bosco* as an ensemble complete in itself.[21] Gardens now functioned as places of spectacle and entertainment. Plants and architecture became the set decoration for figurative and literal garden theaters. The use of sculpture and water to animate a space was taken to new levels.

The three gardens described next are characteristic of the Italian Baroque style.

VILLA ALDOBRANDINI, FRASCATI

The town of Frascati, in the Alban hills southeast of Rome, has been a popular location for *villeggiatura*, or summertime escape, since ancient times. Cardinal Pietro Aldobrandini began work on his villa, a gift from his uncle Pope Clement VIII, in 1592. The initial work of Giacomo della

FRASCATI VILLAS: In the 17th century, papal princes tried to outdo one another with the lavish retreats they built in the hills of Frascati. The massive facades of many of the villas were visible from Rome.

Porta was completed by Carlo Maderno in 1603.

The orientation of the hillside villa is to the northwest; views are across the *campagna* toward Rome. The villa is set on a large terrace, creating in the front a platform to launch sight lines and in the back a garden. The rear terrace is carved out of the slope, forming an exedra. The south facade of the villa, the side toward the garden, is more articulated and detailed than the north facade.

The facade of the Villa Aldobrandini has a distinctive "broken" pediment, a Mannerist play on the classical orders. The palazzo looks enormous, but is only two rooms deep (a central foyer affords views to both the garden and the city). A long entrance *allée* helps merge the huge mass of the structure into the landscape. Movement is up along the axis, but deflected to the side as one

enters the villa. Originally, two small *allées* bordered the path, disguising utilitarian gardens and orchards; today, a single massive pleached *allée* leads from the town to the villa. A unique illusion is created at the end of the *allée*—the roof of the villa appears to sit on top of a grotto. Curved double ramps lead up to the forecourt and then to the ground floor. Access to the *piano nobile* can be made directly from the garden level at back.

The highlight of the rear garden terrace is the *nymphaeum*, or water theater. The space is defined by a large semicircular retaining wall, with arched niches containing sculptures of mythological figures. Atlas is at center holding up the world, drenched by a cascade from above. The exedra is terminated by two pavilions, one a chapel to St. Sebastian, the patron saint of the Aldobrandinis, and the other a room of hydraulic wonders.

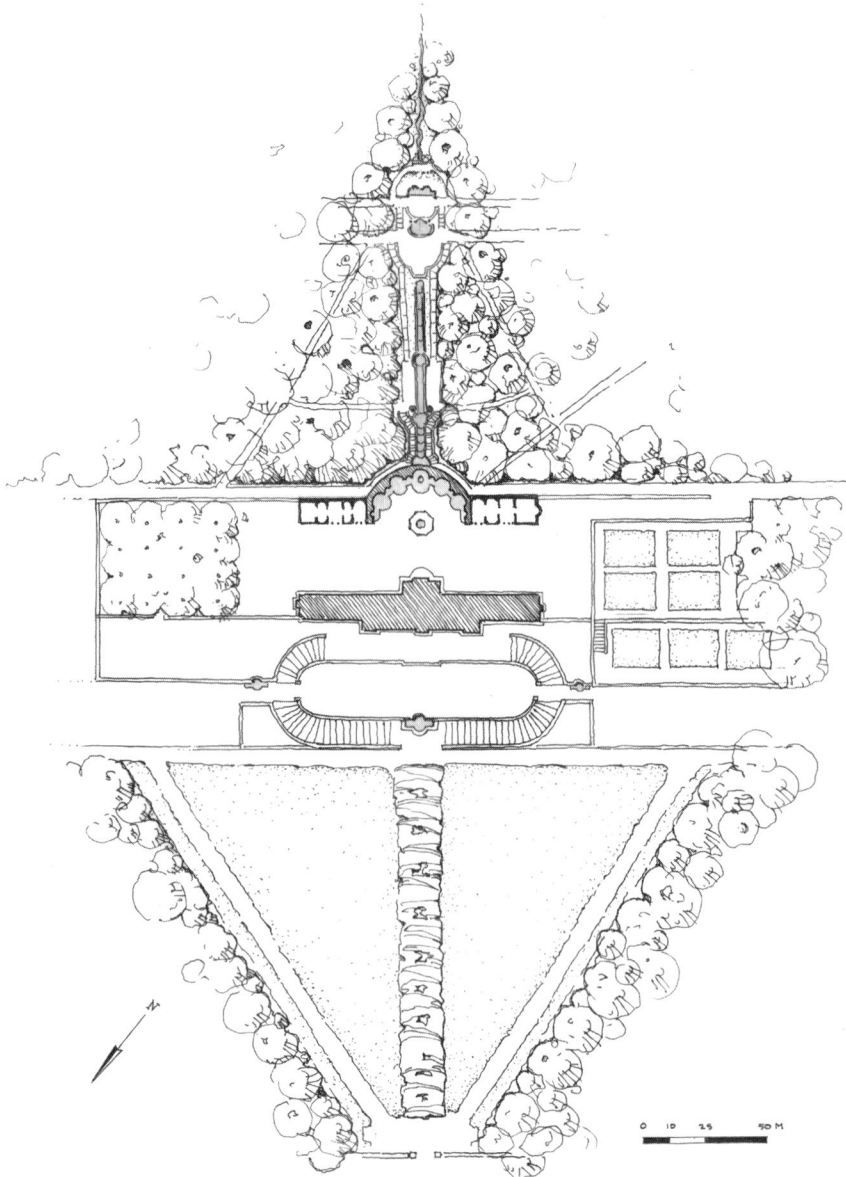

The water features at Villa Aldobrandini were made possible by the construction of several new aqueducts. Water was brought to the villa from Mount Algido, 6 miles away. Giovanni Fontana and Orazio Olivieri engineered the water-works. The cascade begins in the woods behind the villa, in a "natural" grotto at the highest level, and travels down a rough and rocky channel to the second terrace. A "rustic" grotto on the second terrace contains figures of peasants. The water continues along a smooth channel to the cascade, which is framed by the twin Pillars of Hercules. Water spirals down the columns in rills. Optical illusions become evident: The garden terrace disappears and the uppermost loggias of the villa appear to hover over the water staircase, framed by the pillars. Conversely, from the villa, the watercourse, hemmed in by the woods, appears much closer.

The Pillars of Hercules represented the edge of the known world in antiquity. In that context, the design of the Villa Aldobrandini could be understood as an axis mundi, a metaphor for the relationship between heaven and earth.[23] The villa marks the threshold between paradise (the river of life springing from the grotto in the woods) and the world (the city of Rome in the distance).

BAROQUE GEOMETRY: The design of Villa Aldobrandini incorporates site planning principles and architectural features that are typical of Frascati villas.[22]

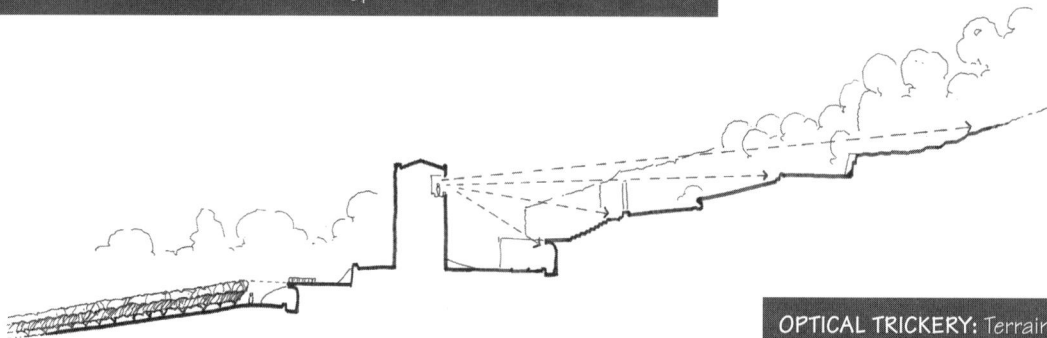

OPTICAL TRICKERY: Terrain was manipulated to create spatial illusions at Villa Aldobrandini.

VISUAL NARRATIVE: *Villa Aldobrandini*

BOBOLI GARDENS, FLORENCE

Niccolo Tribolo began laying out the gardens behind the Pitti Palace in 1549, shortly after the property was acquired by Cosimo I de' Medici (1519-1574). As illustrated in a lunette painted by Giusto Utens at the end of the 16th century, the topography behind the palazzo was manipulated to form a "natural" amphitheater. A large fountain of Oceanus can be seen on the axis. The gardens celebrated the water that Cosimo brought to Florence through his construction of aqueducts.[24] Additions to the gardens continued throughout the 16th century. Ammannati extended the palace in 1558, adding a courtyard and a grotto. To commemorate the wedding of Cosimo's son, Francesco, in 1565,

Giorgio Vasari built a corridor that linked the palace with the Palazzo della Signoria across the Arno.

Beginning in 1618, Giulio Parigi and his son Alfonso extended the garden along a subsidiary axis on the western portion of the site. Called the *Viottolone*, the dramatic, cypress-lined avenue leads down a slope to the *Isolotto*. Here, an oval pond contains an oval-shaped island and the colossal Oceanus sculpture formerly located within the grassy amphitheater. The island, inspired perhaps by Hadrian's Maritime Theater, is surrounded by a stone balustrade and evenly spaced, potted citrus trees. Two bridges connect to the *isolotto* along the path of the axis. The space is surrounded by a dark green clipped ilex hedge.

The Parigis added stone seats to Tribolo's arena, creating a proper amphitheater and a more formal venue for the *fetes*, *masques*, horse ballets, and wedding celebrations staged by the Medicis. They also continued work beyond the amphitheater, adding a horseshoe-shaped terrace with a Fountain of Abundance at the upper limits of the original axis.

From the *piano nobile* of the Pitti Palace, views seem to extend indefinitely along the axis of the amphitheater. The wings of the building appear continuous with the landform. From the reverse view, the distance seems compressed, the sunken courtyard becomes invisible, and the building becomes a ledge for views to the Arno valley. These optical illusions are typical Baroque tricks, reflective of the subversive attitude toward order that characterized the era.

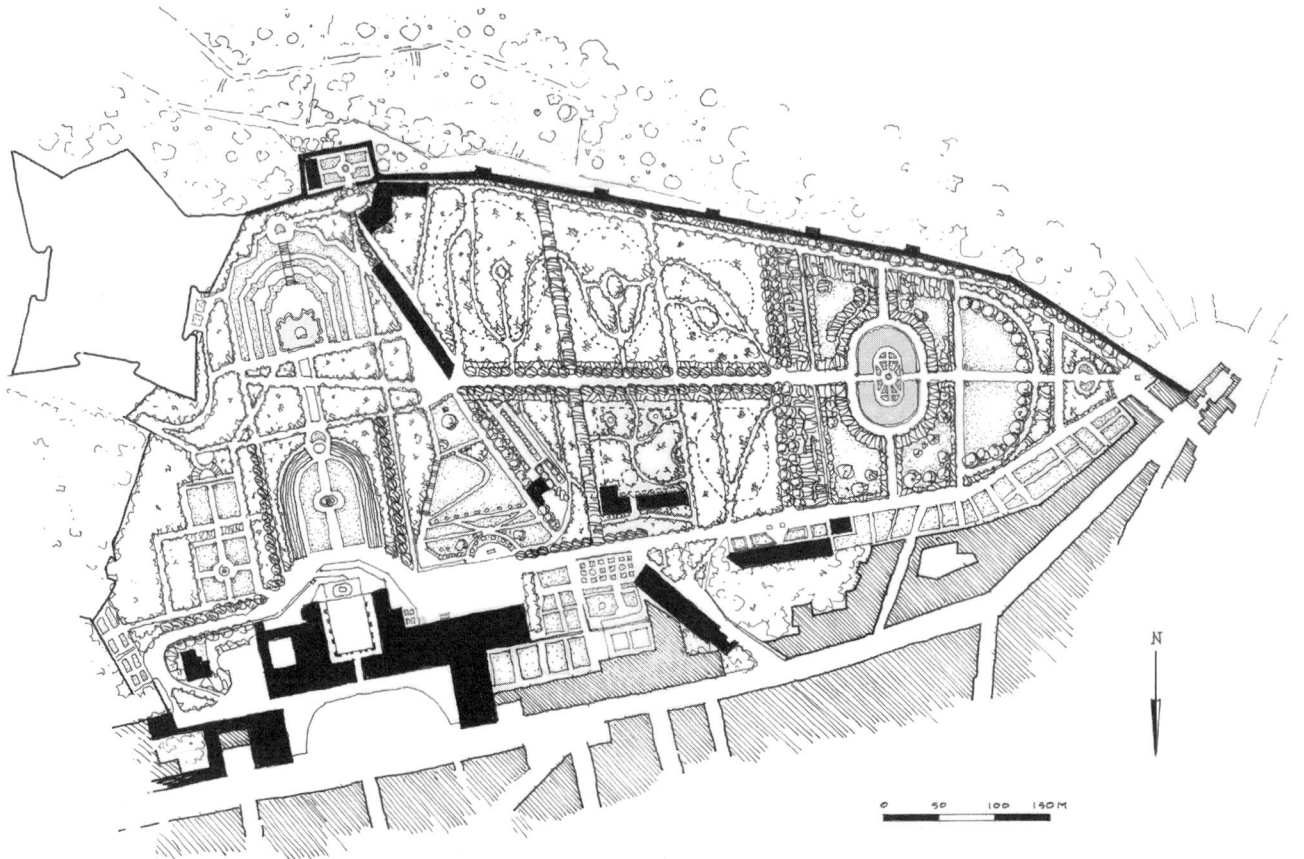

BOBOLI GARDENS, FLORENCE: The garden was enlarged in the 17th century, its redesign expressing a Baroque taste for theatrics and display.

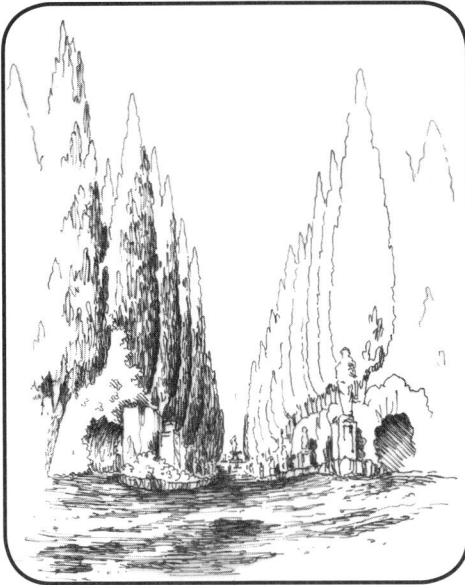

VIOTTOLONE ILLUSIONS: Looking down the *Viottolone* toward the *Isolotto* space seems to expand; yet looking back up the *allée*, the distance appears compressed.

ISOLA BELLA, LAGO MAGGIORE

The palace and terraced gardens that comprise Count Carlo Borromeo's confection on Lago Maggiore were begun in 1630. The architectonic fantasy took over 40 years to complete. Early sketches show Isola Bella as a rigid shiplike form, but some features, such as the "prow" of cypresses, were never constructed.

The palace complex occupies the north end of the island. A fishing village lies to the west. The south end of the island contains 10 rectangular garden terraces. But the axial alignment between the palace and garden could not be made symmetrical. The offset is disguised by curving stairs that accommodate the displacement: The steps on the east side have wider treads and meet the steps on the west side at a point past the centerline.

Entrance to the gardens is through a courtyard at the back of the palace, where a sculpture of Diana catches a glimpse of herself in a basin. The curving steps and staircases lead to the terrace of the camphor tree, on deck six. A large concave/convex staircase is cen-

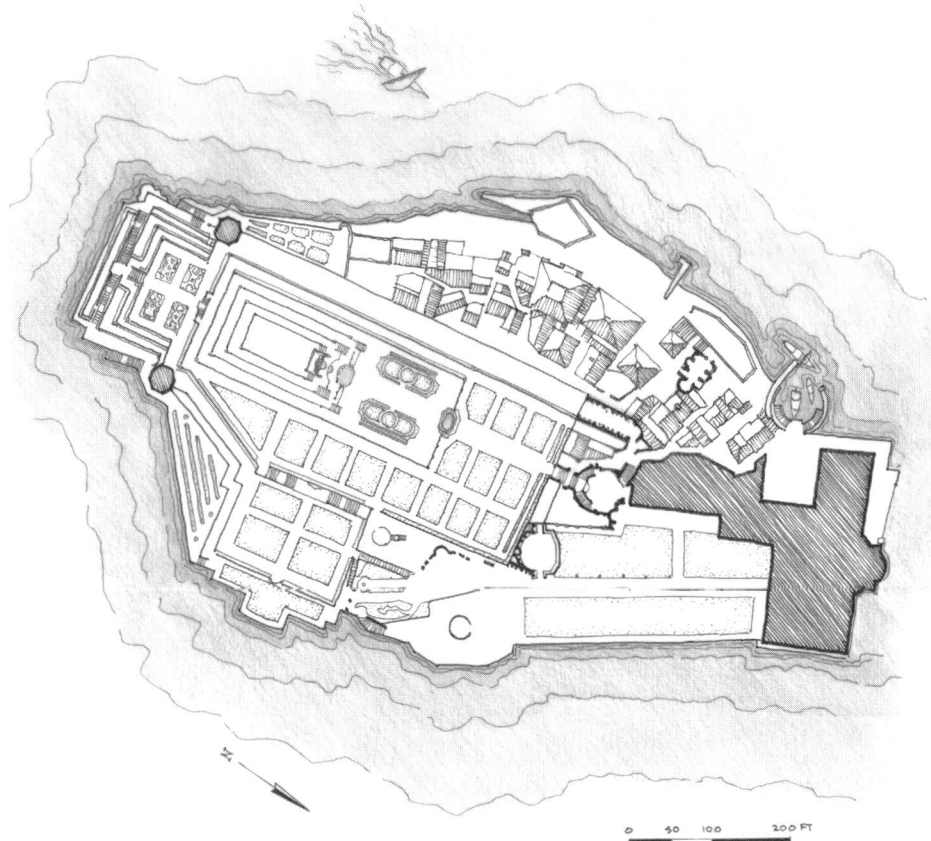

ISOLA BELLA, LAGO MAGGIORE: The main organizing axis is tilted to the west.

FANTASY ISLAND: Isola Bella was always intended to look like a galleon.

tered on the amazing water theater and crowned with a unicorn, the Borromeo herald. The uppermost terrace behind the water theater affords breathtaking views of the lake and the Swiss Alps.

On the south end, octagonal pavilions anchor the widened fifth terrace. The top five levels are oriented with their long sides perpendicular to the lower terraces, elongating the garden toward the palace. The terraces contain parterres of lawn and flowers; peacocks roam free. Every platform is a stage, but the water theater is the star.

In typical Baroque fashion, proportions are distorted. The verticality is overwhelming, creating a sense of tension with the horizontal planes. Typical compositional principles of foreground-midground-background are unsettled by the villa's position on the lake.[25] Water is the intermediary zone. The island confines the visitor, but not the view.

WATER THEATER: A terraced exedra of arched niches is decorated with shells, pinnacles, nymphs, and cherubs at Isola Bella.

THE FLOWERING OF THE DUTCH LANDSCAPE

After the peace of Westphalia liberated Holland from Spanish control, the country emerged as an economic power in the 17th century through the formation of international trading companies and banks. For the most part, Dutch gardens reflected the modest tastes of the middle-class merchants who built them, and not the affectations of an elite aristocracy.[26] By the 17th century, an enthusiasm for horticultural science developed in the Netherlands, building on the research conducted in early botanic gardens. Bulbs, and tulips in particular, were collected with passion. The enduring love of flowers is evident in Dutch garden design.

Dutch garden styles continued the Italian Renaissance tradition of compartments and formal geometries, the orthogonal division of space well suited to the rectangular patterns of land formed from dykes and canals. Vernacular elements included wooden gazebos and berceaux (vault-shaped trellises), parterres de pieces coupées (patterns made primarily with flowers), canals (both functional and ornamental), and large basins of still water (abundant, of course, in the flat Low Countries). Stationary decorations (potted plants, topiary, statuary) magnified the static quality of space. The protracted avenues of the French Baroque were incompatible with the Dutch landscape and mind-set. But French influence can be seen in the intricate ornamentation within the Italian Renaissance framework.

TRIM AND TIDY LANDSCAPES

Het Loo, the royal palace of William and Mary, exemplifies 17th-century Dutch garden style. Prince William was a provincial governor from the House of Orange; his wife, Mary, was the daughter of King James II of England. Garden construction began in 1686 in conjunction with the planning of William's hunting lodge. Dutch architect Jacob Roman and French architect Daniel Marot collaborated on the design. Marot was a Huguenot who fled to the Netherlands after Louis XIV expelled the Protestants from France. His influence can be seen in the parterre design and the expansiveness of the upper garden. Additional work was done on the gardens after the coronation of William and Mary as king and queen of England, in 1689. The garden was completely destroyed during the 18th century when Louis Napoleon covered it over to build a picturesque, English-style garden. Restoration of Het Loo to its original form began in 1979.

The U-shaped lower garden is defined by raised walkways on three sides, opening to an oak-lined cross-avenue. The garden contains intricate parterres de broderie;[27] sculptures mark the intersections of the pathways. The interior decoration of the palace echoes the elaborate arabesque patterns in the King's and Queen's Gardens located on either side of the palace, below the royal apartments. Rectangular planting bands around the parterre displayed new plant species between clipped evergreens.

The large upper garden was built in 1689, reflecting the new trend toward spaciousness. Grass parterres continued the strict geometry and formal symmetry about the central axis. The enormous King's Fountain, fed by a natural spring, marks the center. A semicircular colonnade terminates the axis; a previous configuration of the colonnade created an axial vista to a distant obelisk. The gardens at Het Loo contain numerous fountains, canals, and cascades.

TULIPMANIA: Speculation in tulip markets drove prices to exorbitant levels; fortunes were made and destroyed.

HET LOO: The 15-acre Great Garden, directly behind the palace, is divided into lower and upper sections.

0 50 100   200 FT

N

A RESTRAINED MIX OF EUROPEAN STYLES

Dutch, French, and Italian influences can be seen in 17th-century English gardens. During the reign of William and Mary, garden spaces displayed a compactness characteristic of Dutch gardens. Emphasis was on the planting of flowers, particularly tulips, as well as the creation of topiary forms. At the same time, a classical sensibility informed the architecture of the period, based on the work of Inigo Jones, who had studied in Rome.

England saw an influx of French Huguenot refugees, as did other northern countries. These artists and craftsmen transported continental design ideas, as well as new plants, across the channel. New varieties of fruit trees were of particular interest to the English. They adapted the French idea of the vista, too, but the terrain of England did not permit infinite views. Parterres were also popular, particularly patterns created solely with grass and gravel.

Representative examples include Hatfield House and Hampton Court.

HATFIELD HOUSE, HERTFORDSHIRE

Robert Cecil was given Hatfield House in exchange for a property he owned that was coveted by King James I. In 1611, Cecil began rebuilding Hatfield House. He laid out the gardens around a north-south axis. The house sits between a spacious balustraded forecourt and rear terrace. Garden courts and terraces to the east and west form a cross-axis. A path from a formal parterre on the east side leads to a bowling green and maze. The garden rooms illustrate the continuation of Italian Renaissance styles. Water features were designed by Salomon de Caus. Exotic plants were provided by John Tradescant, the elder.[28]

Pleasure gardens such as Cecil's were popular until Cromwell turned the country's attention to more practical forms of horticulture, enlarging farms

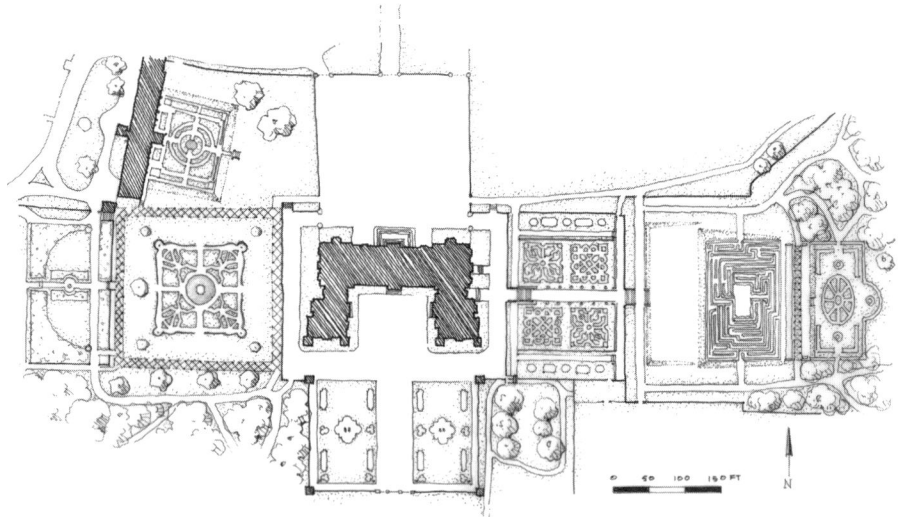

HATFIELD HOUSE, HERTFORDSHIRE: The county manor is typical of early (Pre-Restoration) 17th-century estates.

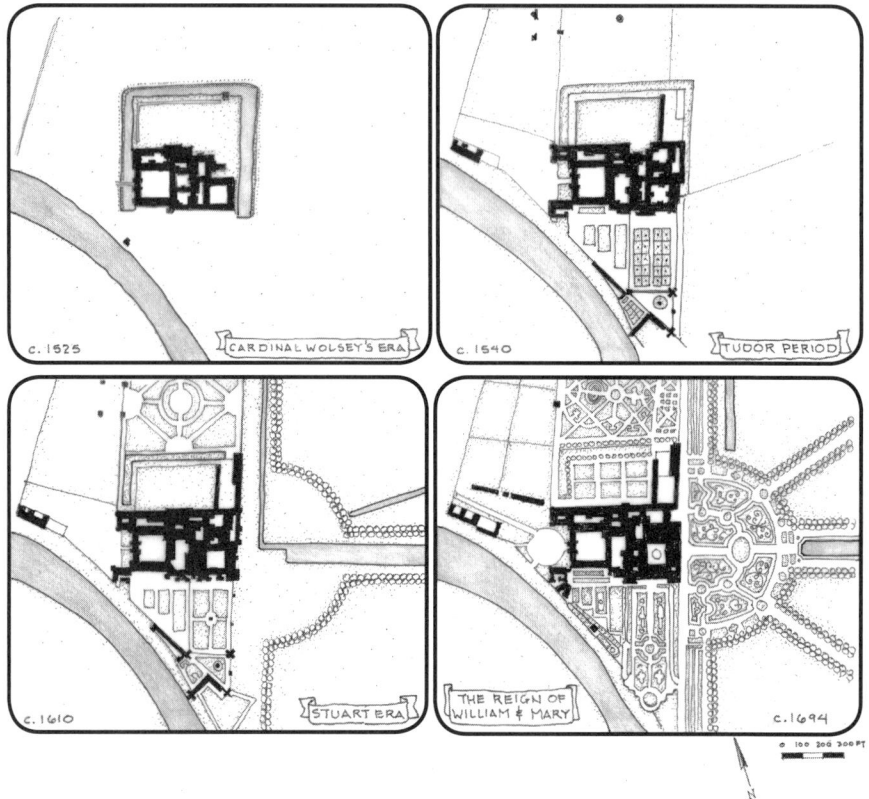

HAMPTON COURT: William and Mary's addition to the palace reflected compact, colorful Dutch styles.

and improving agriculture. Many of the manor houses were destroyed during the Commonwealth of 1649–1660.

HAMPTON COURT, MIDDLESEX (LONDON)

Charles II returned from exile in France and was restored to the throne by a reconvened parliament in 1660. He appointed two French designers, Gabriel and Andre Mollet as royal gardeners, hence French formalism and spatial definition were imported to Britain.[29] William and Mary later enlarged Hampton Court, adding a new block designed by Christopher Wren to the eastern part of the castle. Henry VIII's tudor gardens were altered to reflect Dutch styles.

Modifications made to Hampton Court by Charles II include the Broad Walk, Long Canal, and *patte d'oie*. The tree-lined Broad Walk along the east front of the palace projects out into a semicircular *allée* that intercepts the three arms of the *patte d'oie*—the goosefoot pattern of radial avenues designed by the Mollets. The Long Canal is an extension of the central toe of the *patte d'oie*. The Great Fountain Court, designed by Daniel Marot, dates from the reign of William and Mary. Contained within the semicircular *allée* were parterres de broderie, topiary, fountains, and many sculptures. Late in his life William added the Chestnut Avenue to the north side of the palace, adjacent to the Wilderness. Queen Anne (ruled 1702–1714) obliterated any trace of Dutch garden styles, grassing over the parterres and removing fountains and topiaried trees.

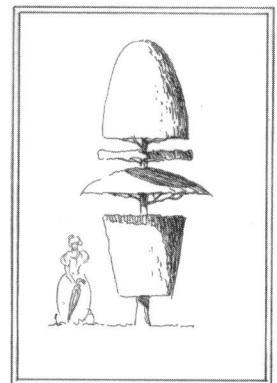

☆ ☆ TOPIARY ALL-STARS ☆ ☆

LEVENS HALL, CUMBRIA: The famous topiary garden was laid out in 1694 by Guillaume Beaumont, gardener to King James II. The plan also included a rose garden, orchard, nuttery, herb and vegetable gardens, bowling green, and a massive beech hedge.

THE CONTROL OF NATURE

In 17th-century France, people's attitudes toward nature changed. Nature was not considered beautiful until human order was imposed upon it: Shrubs were clipped into hedges, trees trimmed to form *palissades*, contours graded with precision, rivers diverted, lands inscribed with straight paths and *allées*, and the ground decorated with *parterres de broderie*. Parterres were best appreciated from a high vantage point, hence the house gained new authority as the symbol of visual control in a garden.

ENDLESS HORIZONS

Axial extensions out into the landscape created a new relationship between building, garden, and landscape. A spatial dynamic developed based on breakthroughs in physics and mathematics. The mathematics of infinity as developed by Rene Descartes implied "limitless" space.[30] A horizon was recognized as being dependent upon one's point of view. Landscape designers applied the science of optics (involving reflection, refraction, and geometry) to the creation of perspectival space, expressing the ultimate control and power that humans had over nature.

The large-scale manipulation of the landscape that characterizes French classical gardens had much in common with the theory and practice of 17th-century military engineering. French military engineers were the first to deal with massive earthworks. A fortress, like a garden, is geometrically controlled space. To ensure security, all parts must harmonize; there can be no weak spot in a defensive fortification.[31] In addition, when distances become so great, measurement becomes crucial. The incredible precision with which landscape designers created flat terraces and canals was made possible by the advanced

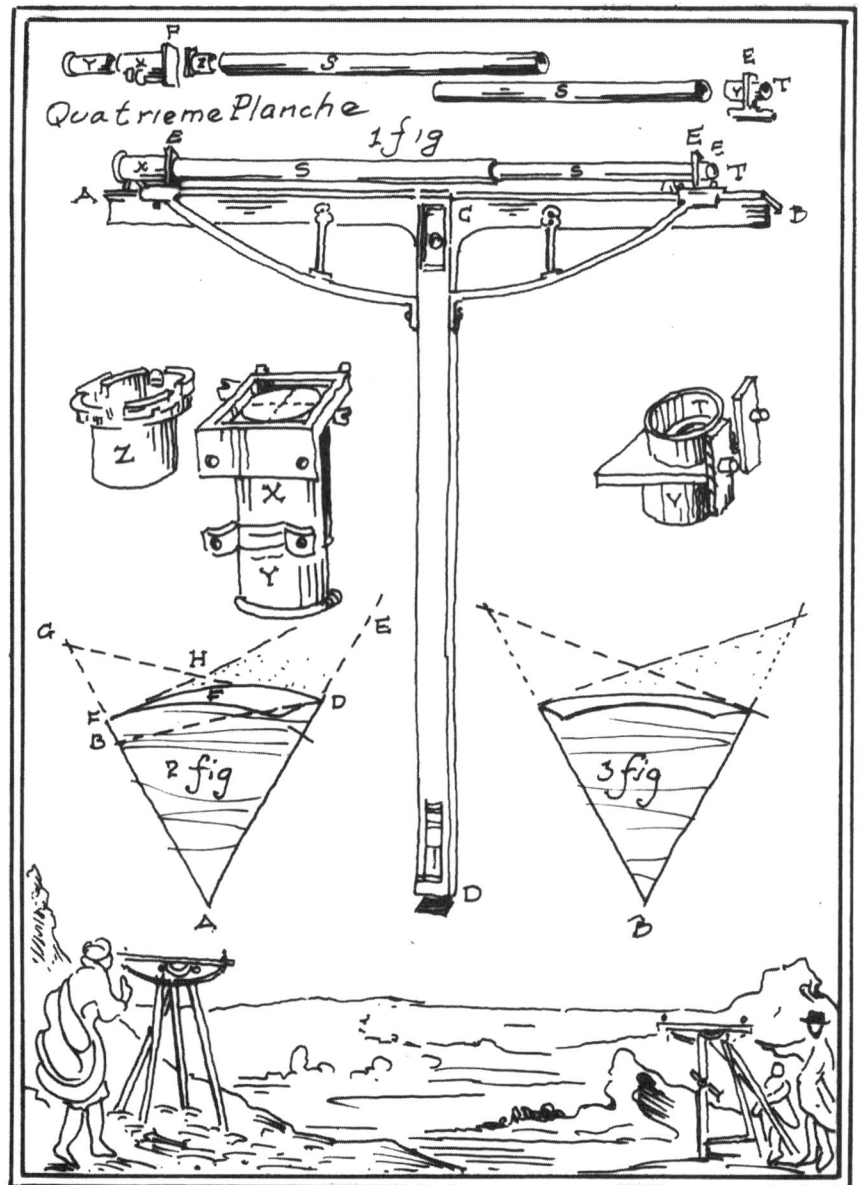

INSTRUMENTS FOR CALCULATING LEVELS, c. 1694: *Large-scale earthworks were made possible by advances in military engineering.*

instrumentation and mathematics of military engineers.

The popularity of the Italian Baroque style remained centered around Rome during the Counter-Reformation. Other European capitals also adopted Baroque design vocabularies to express the dynamism of a world in motion. The 17th-century French garden, on the other hand, was inspired by ideals of grandeur and monumentality represented by classical civilization. Louis XIV compared himself to Augustus; he wanted to create the new Rome.

THE COURT OF LOUIS XIV

France was launched as a leading European power in 1648, when the Peace of Westphalia ended the Thirty Years' War. But a period of social and political unrest followed, called the *Fronde*, in which the French nobility rebelled against the king. Louis XIV (1638–1715) was able to subordinate the dissidents and establish an absolute monarchy; in 1655, he proclaimed "L'Etat, c'est moi" (I am the State). His great garden at Versailles is symbolic of absolute power and control.

To keep an eye on the nobility and quash any potential insurgency, attendance at court was expected of the noble families by Louis XIV. Any kind of advancement or favor required attracting the king's attention. The court was always under scrutiny by the king, and proper etiquette, which dictated everything from dress to facial expressions, had to be observed.[32] The landscape itself conformed to this idea; formal gardens compelled formal behavior. The garden was the stage for the political and social theater of 17th-century France.

To accommodate the entire nobility and the huge retinues that followed the monarch, royal gardens and palaces had to be enormous. Vast volumes of void space were carved out of dense forests. The palace at Versailles stands on a huge terrace, surrounded by parterres; sculptural urns and fountains are the only vertical elements, and they are dwarfed by the expanse of their surroundings. Only crowds in the thousands would make the scale of the place comprehensible. The vista is what made the landscape dynamic.

ANDRE LE NOTRE: The landscape designer's success was due in part to his mastery of court etiquette.

THE WORK OF ANDRE LE NOTRE

Andre Le Notre (1613–1700) grew up in Paris, where his father was superintendent of the royal palace gardens at the Tuileries. (The Louvre was still the seat of government.) Le Notre studied the curriculum for landscape designers suggested by the recognized authority on gardening, Jacques Boyceau: geometry, perspective, drafting, architecture, and horticulture. He studied painting at the studio of Simon Vouet, an early advocate of the French Classical style, where he met fellow student Charles Le Brun.

As a young man Le Notre worked at the Tuileries and Fountainbleau, continuing

the grand traditions first established by Claude Mollet (1563–1650) and Boyceau. He eventually assumed his father's role as superintendent of royal gardens. Le Notre understood space as an abstraction, and was able to impart more clarity and unity on the style of his predecessors. His was an ordered geometry based on Cartesian logic. When designing a landscape, he said "man sets himself up as a little god."[33] He shaped nature with purpose.

Le Notre collected the paintings of Claude Lorrain. Like Lorrain, Le Notre used devices to create spatial illusions. Lorrain's compositions and color palettes created a golden atmosphere that dissolved into infinite perspective. His paintings show mythological figures and classical architecture set in a utopian landscape; an ordered world not unlike the one Louis XIV created at Versailles. (The aesthetics of the pastoral ideal as represented by the 17th-century landscape painters would have particularly powerful implications in the formation of an English garden style in the 18th century.)

At the age of 37, Le Notre teamed up with his artist friend Charles Le Brun and the architect Louis Le Vau to undertake work for Louis XIV's finance minister. Vaux-le-Vicomte was the first in a series of notable collaborations, and epitomizes the spirit of the 17th-century French formal garden. Andre Le Notre died in 1700 at the age of 88. The clarity of the French formal style expressed in his work was imitated across the continent. *La Theorie et le pratique du jardinage* by Antoine-Joseph Dezallier d'Argenville, written in 1709, summarized the elements of the French Classical garden based on Le Notre's work. The book became enormously popular, diffusing the grand style throughout Europe.

VAUX-LE-VICOMTE

Nicolas Fouquet, superintendent of finances for the king, hired the team of Le Notre, Le Brun, and Le Vau to design his new chateau at Maincy (about 34 miles from Paris). Initial site work involved the demolition of three villages. More than 18,000 laborers constructed the project from 1656 to 1661.

Vaux-le-Vicomte is approached through the woods. A semicircular clearing in front of decorative wrought iron gates leads to the moated chateau. The visitor passes into the Court of Honor. Two lower parterres flank the chateau to the east and west. From the terrace behind the chateau, the garden propels itself into the landscape. Space is carved out of the forest, the green backdrop acting like stage wings, or a *coulisse*, that keeps the view focused toward the horizon and provides a dark contrast for sculptural elements. Small clearings and paths hidden within the ornamental groves, called *bosquets*, provide intimate subspaces.

The entire garden appears to be comprehensible from a single perspective point behind the chateau. But as one moves through the garden, its true extents and complexities are revealed. Elements are not what they seemed. The ground is not one flat plane, but a series of subtle level changes and inclines connected by steps. The oval pool is, in fact, circular. A canal cuts across the main axis. The second pool is square, not rectangular. The arcaded grotto, visible from the house, is at a lower level on the far side of another, longer, transverse canal. The grotto forms the base of an upper-level terrace. Opposite the grotto, and hidden from view, one is surprised to find an additional water feature known as the Grandes Cascades. At the terminus of the axis, on the sloping lawn, or *tapis vert* ("green carpet"), the visitor can make an about-face and see the chateau as a central object on the horizon. In this reciprocal view, distances are foreshortened; the gardens appear flat again. Viewpoint becomes focal point; the gardens form a closed system.

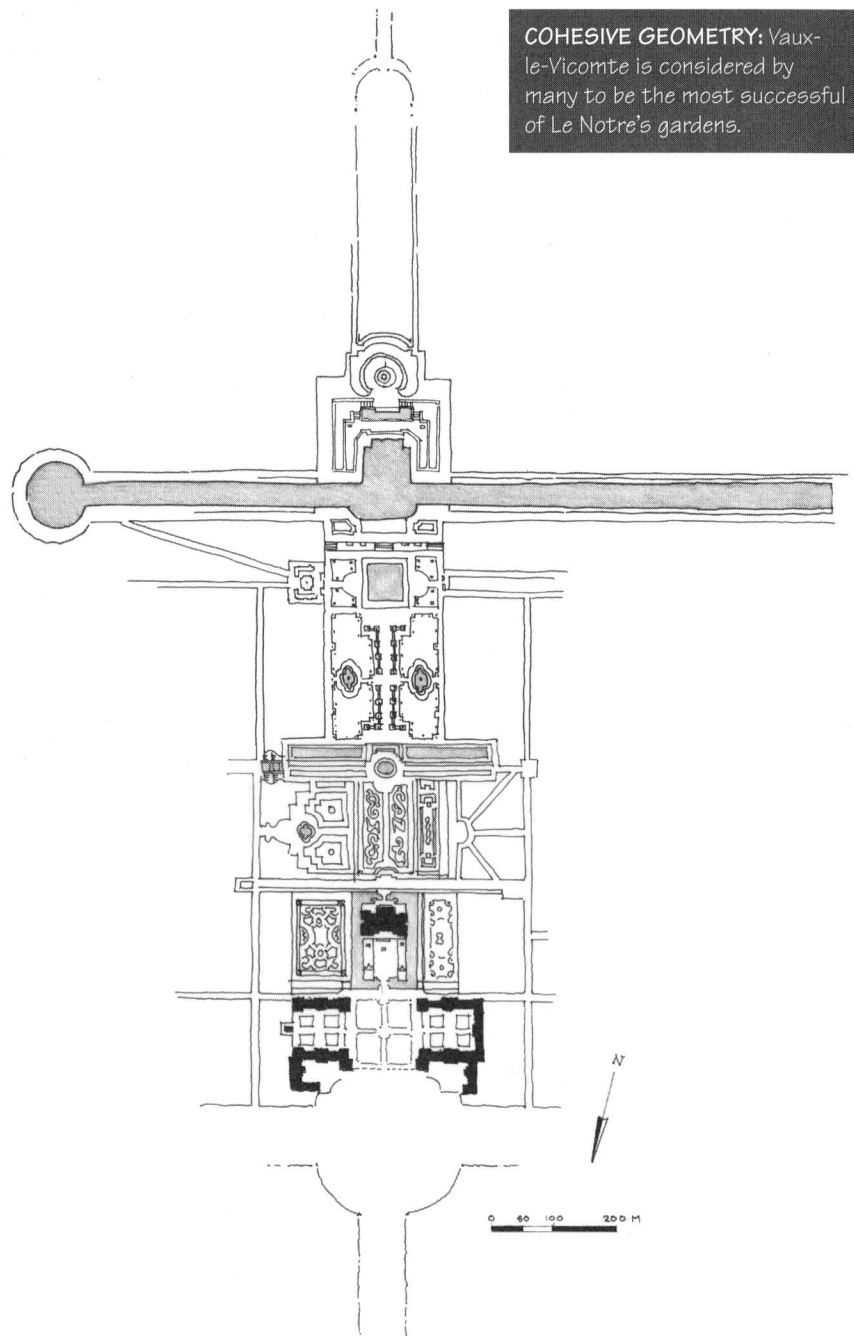

COHESIVE GEOMETRY: Vaux-le-Vicomte is considered by many to be the most successful of Le Notre's gardens.

Vaux-le-Vicomte illustrates Le Notre's understanding of the laws of optics and perspective put forth by Euclid and Descartes. As part of the experience of the garden, Le Notre reveals that reality is an illusion; there are logical explanations for the optical effects.

Fouquet hosted an elaborate fete upon the completion of his gardens, which the king did not attend. Word spread of the garden's magnificence, and Fouquet was obliged to host another party for the king and his court of thousands. Fouquet's lavish display of wealth was his undoing; he was imprisoned for embezzlement soon after the event. The property was looted by Louis XIV, who carted off its sculptural and arboreal treasures to Versailles.

CASE STUDY: *Vaux-le-Vicomte*

0 100 200 300 M

VERSAILLES

Louis XIV hired the same trio of Le Notre, Le Brun, and Le Vau to convert his father's hunting lodge into an entertainment villa and, later, a royal palace. Le Notre reworked Jacques Boyceau's original parterre directly behind the chateau and established the axial structure and geometry of the Petit Parc. Versailles, which is located about 15 miles from Paris, became the seat of government in 1682. Additional work was completed to expand the palace to accommodate the nearly 5,000 people who resided at court. The axis grew to monumental proportions with the later

PETIT PARC: The bosquets between the Fountain of Latona and the Fountain of Apollo form the core of the Petit Parc. Today the Petit Parc at Versailles covers almost 1,900 acres.

THE MATHEMATICS OF INFINITY: *Cartesian space is endless.*

addition of the mile-long grand canal. The vanishing point at Versailles extended to infinity, beyond one's reach.

Louis established his persona as the Sun King at a grand, themed festival held at the Tuileries in 1662, called the Carrousel. Heliocentric iconography, including imagery of Apollo, the god of the Sun, is pervasive at Versailles. The layout of the gardens on an east-west axis records the trajectory of the sun, literally and symbolically. Within the palace, the king's chambers occupy the dominant position on the axis. Fountains and sculptures continue the theme in the garden.[34]

Versailles, located in a lowland marsh, contained thousands of water features and fountains. The magnificent canals were not only an important element of the decorative program, they also

SITE PLAN OF VERSAILLES: The Grand Parc, a woodland crossed with diagonal avenues and rond points, surrounded the Petit Parc. By 1689, the Grand Parc, which included the hunting grounds and the forest at Marly, covered 37,000 acres.

LE ROI DE SOLEIL: Louis performed in ballets dressed as Apollo.

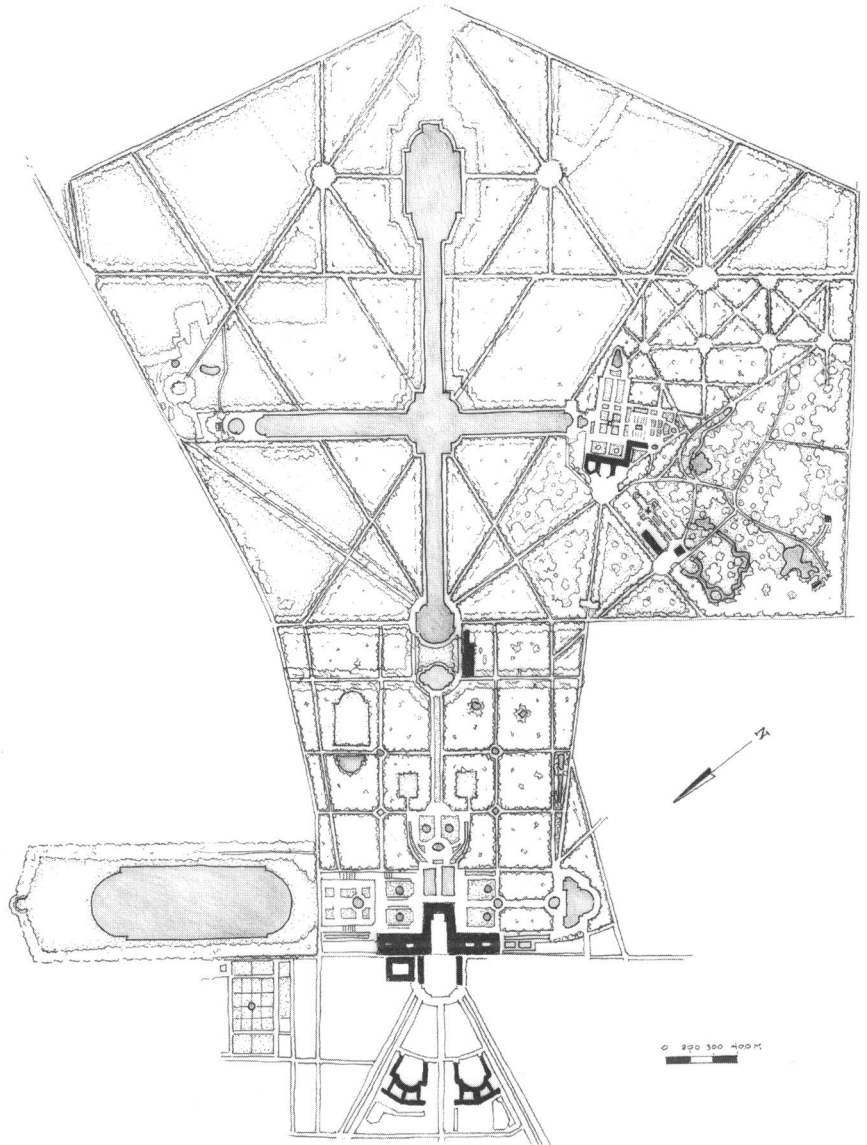

helped drain the swamps. The supply and pressure of water, however, was never sufficient to operate all the water works at once. Gardeners and fontainiers were stationed along the king's route to turn the fountains on and off as he passed. The magnificent Machine de Marly was constructed in 1688 to raise water from the Seine, nearly 4 miles away, and feed the fountains by gravity. Still, the Machine de Marly was not adequate; it mostly supplied Louis XIV's private retreat at Marly.

Parties, banquets, ballets—all kinds of events and spectacles were staged in the bosquets, the garden rooms carved out of the ornamental groves

MACHINE DE MARLY: Fourteen wheels lifted water 528 feet into reservoirs and aqueducts to supply Versailles's waterworks.

in different geometric patterns. In one bosquet, a spectacular water theater, built in 1671 and destroyed in the late 18th century, contained hundreds of single jets capable of creating many different combinations of effects.

The transverse arm of the Grand Canal was terminated by the Trianon at its north end and the menagerie to the south. The Trianon was built to accommodate Louis's need to escape the public atmosphere at the palace. In 1671, the *Trianon de Porcelaine* was built for Louis's consort, Madame de Montespan. The structure was replaced in 1687 with the Grand Trianon, in honor of his new mistress, Madame de Maintenon. The grounds were used for cultivating flowers. Hothouses ensured that Louis would have flowers blooming year-round in the garden.

The retreat at Marly, designed in 1677, was even more secluded than the Trianon. The hillside location enabled the construction of a cascade, *La Riviere*, composed of 53 steps of colored marble. As at the Trianon, the house

FLAGS AND WHISTLES: A crew of behind-the-scenes workers operated the fountains at Versailles.

was at the center of geometrical parterres. *Allées*, hedges, and statues decorated the gardens. At the bottom of the cascade at Marly was the *petit*

parterre. In front of the main structure was the *grand parterre*, where 12 pavilions, 6 for men and 6 for women, lined both sides of a central pool.

BOSQUETS: The bosquets were decked out with proscenium arches, chandeliers, and tapestries as set decorations for performances.

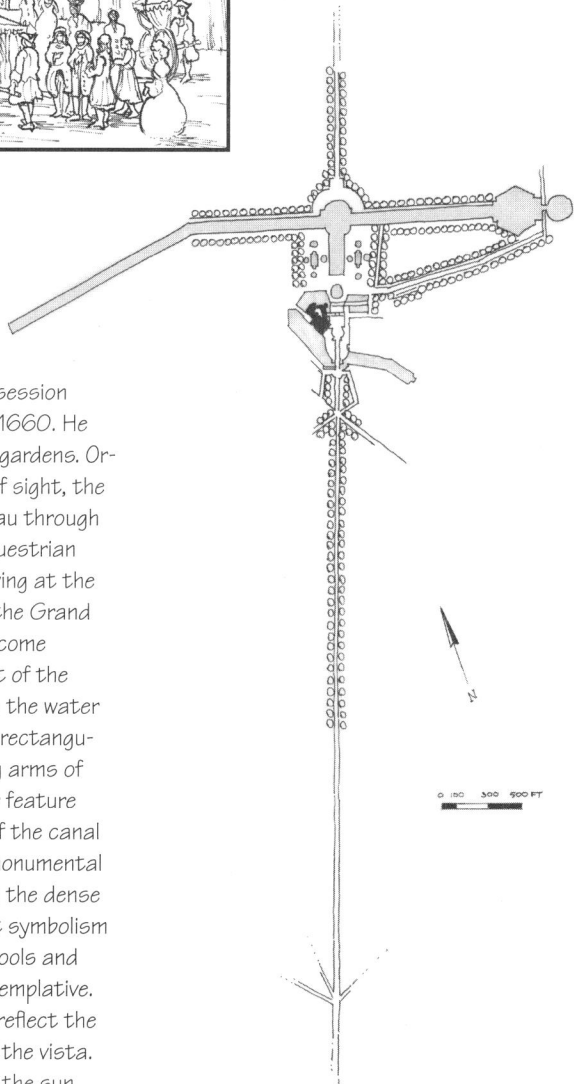

Above the cascade was a primitive roller coaster, large swings, and other play areas. Louis's intimate retreat at Marly eventually contained a 300-acre garden and an 1850-acre hunting park. Le Notre is not believed to have been involved in the planning and design of Marly.[35]

Although organized around a central axis like Vaux-le-Vicomte, the gardens at Versailles were so large and the attractions so numerous that no clear logic existed to visually lead one through the space. When Louis reached middle age, political and familial circumstances discouraged his sponsorship of the huge spectacles of his earlier years. He enjoyed strolling around the gardens and wrote an itinerary for viewing his gardens in a particular order. The king commands: "Enter the labyrinth and after having walked down as far as the ducks and the dog, go up again and leave by the side of Bacchus."[36] The book, rewritten six times, is an excellent record of the alterations made to the gardens throughout his reign.

CHANTILLY

Prince de Conde regained possession of his chateau at Chantilly in 1660. He hired Le Notre to restore the gardens. Organized along a central axis of sight, the visitor approaches the chateau through the woods, focused on the equestrian statue of Montmorency. Arriving at the statue, which is situated on the Grand Terrace, the gardens below become visible. The house is to the left of the axis. Descending the steps to the water parterres, one sees a central rectangular pool connected to the long arms of a transverse canal. The water feature continues on the other side of the canal in a semicircular shape. The monumental axis extends into a clearing in the dense woodland. There is no inherent symbolism in the garden. The reflecting pools and the infinite axial view are contemplative. The pools at Vaux-le-Vicomte reflect the chateau, the station point of the vista. The pools at Versailles reflect the sun, a representation of the former king. The pools at Chantilly reflect nature—the woodlands, the sky, and the limitless imagination of the viewer.

CHANTILLY: The chateau is subordinate to the monumental axis that organizes the landscape.

VISUAL NARRATIVE: *Chantilly*

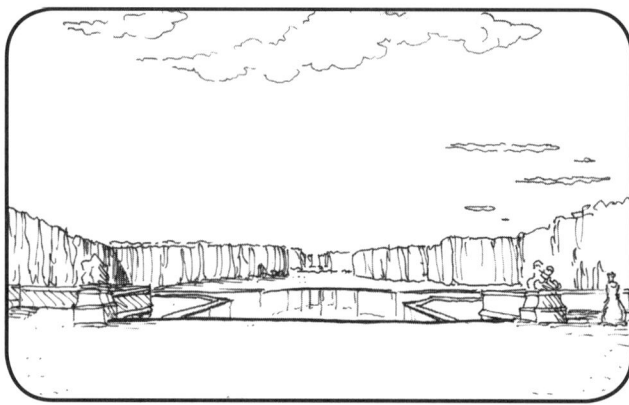 

SUMMARY

Straight lines! In the 17th century, the landscape was ordered by geometries that expressed the power and authority of humans over nature. Whether through monumental axes or lines of sight, as *chahar baghs* or with borrowed scenery, gardens extended into the landscape, literally and figuratively.

GIRL ON A SWING: Nature overtakes the garden in the paintings of Neo-Romantics like Fragonard, Boucher, and Watteau. They captured the decadent gaiety of the fetes galantes that were staged in the decaying French formal gardens at the end of the 17th century.

DESIGN PRINCIPLES

SHAKKEI

Distant landscapes are "borrowed" and incorporated into the pictorial composition of Japanese stroll gardens. Views are framed by vegetation, and garden elements strategically placed in the foreground help place the viewer in the scene.

HIDE AND REVEAL

Space unfolds incrementally as various focal points capture the viewer's attention and imagination in the Japanese stroll garden.

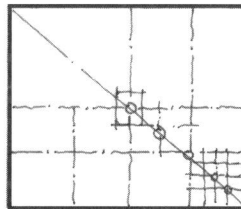

SUBDIVISION

Mughal gardens are characterized by the four-square paradise form. The recursive subdivision of the four-square geometry creates interesting patterns and modulations of space.

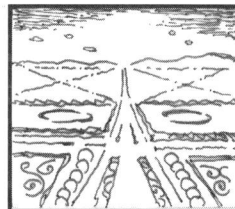

EXTENSION

French gardens of the 17th century were projected into the landscape through monumental axes. Vistas merged with the horizon.

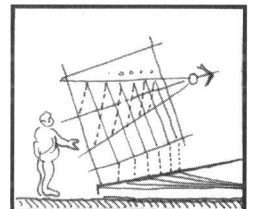

ILLUSION

Perspective was manipulated in Italian Baroque gardens to create theatrical effects and a sense of mystery.

DESIGN VOCABULARY

MUGHAL EMPIRE
Chadars, Chini-kanas, Chabutras

PERSIA
Talars, Chahar baghs, Flowers

ITALY
Water theaters, Stairs, "Stage" management

FRANCE
Reflective pools, Bosquets, Parterres de broderie

For further exploration

BOOKS
THE CRUCIBLE, play by Arthur Miller
DON QUIXOTE, by Cervantes
THE DIARY OF JOHN EVELYN
ESSAY CONCERNING HUMAN UNDERSTANDING, by John Locke
PARADISE LOST, by John Milton
THE SCARLET LETTER, by Nathaniel Hawthorne
TARTUFFE, by Molière
THE THREE MUSKETEERS, by Alexandre Dumas

FILMS
ARTEMISIA (1997)
LAST YEAR AT MARIENBAD (1961)
THE NEW WORLD (2005)
RESTORATION (1995)
RIDICULE (1996)
JAMES CLAVELL'S SHOGUN, TV mini-series (1980)
VATEL (2000)

PAINTINGS AND SCULPTURE
LANDSCAPE WITH THE FLIGHT INTO EGYPT,
   by Annibale Carracci (1603)
PORTRAIT OF CHARLES I HUNTING, by Anthony Van Dyck (1635)
LANDSCAPE WITH THE CHATEAU OF STEEN,
   by Peter Paul Rubens (1636)
PASTORAL LANDSCAPE, by Claude Lorrain (1638)
ET IN ARCADIA EGO (THE ARCADIAN SHEPHERDS),
   by Nicolas Poussin (1640)
THE ECSTASY OF ST. THERESA, by Gianlorenzo Bernini (1645)
THE LETTER, by Jan Vermeer (1666)

18th CENTURY

The great advances in science and technology that defined the Enlightenment changed the way people viewed their place in the world. The spirit of inquiry extended to the contestation of firmly held beliefs in social structures and political systems. Scientific progress shed new light on social relations. The rise of the middle class as an economic and political force brought about the collapse of the *ancien régime*. Philosophers like Rousseau and Voltaire laid the intellectual ground for change. The Scientific Revolution coincided with the American Revolution, the French Revolution, and the so-called revolution of taste in England.

England became the force that shaped garden history in the 18th century. The English "landscape" garden created a new lens through which we see nature. The influence of Chinese garden styles on English trends is examined in this chapter, as is the effect of the landscape garden on early American landscape design.

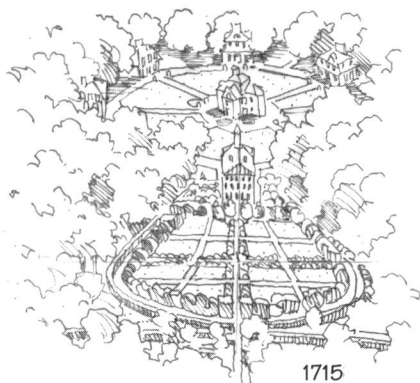

1716
RUSSIAN VERSAILLES

1715
ROCOCO

1700   1710   1720

1717
FREEMASONS

1724
FAHRENHEIT

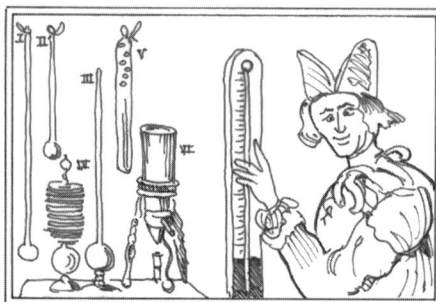

1769
STEAM CART

1773
TEA PARTY

1770   1780

1774
THE SORROWS OF YOUNG WERTHER

1782
FULL OF HOT AIR

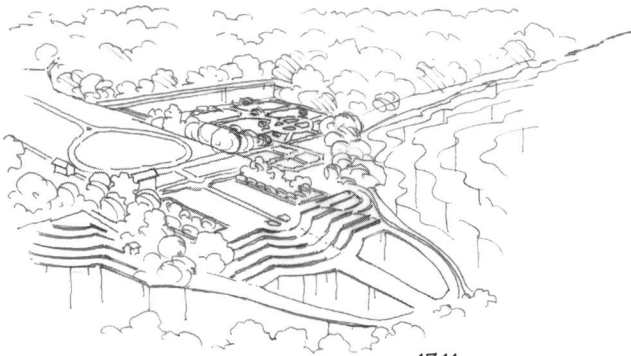

1741
MIDDLETON PLACE

1752
HIGH VOLTAGE!

| 1730 | 1740 | 1750 | 1760 |

1753
SPECIES PLANTARUM

1768
EXPERIMENT WITH AN
AIR PUMP

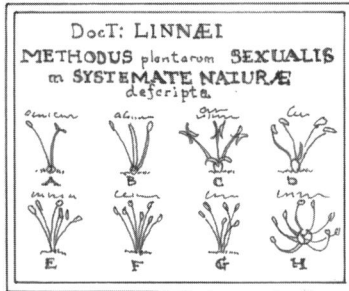

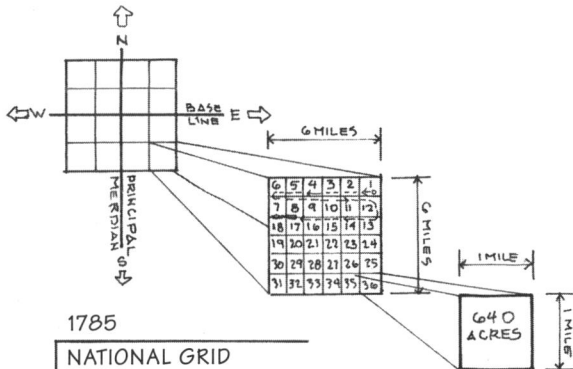

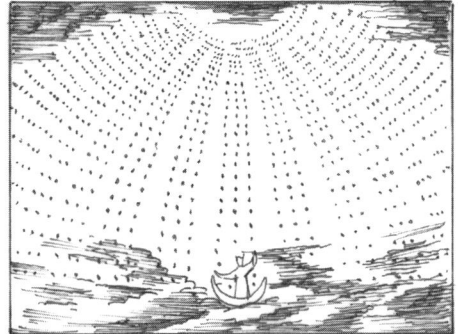

1791
THE MAGIC
FLUTE

1785
NATIONAL GRID

| 1790 | 1800 |

1789
LIBERTÉ, ÉGALITÉ, FRATERNITÉ

1793
COTTON GIN

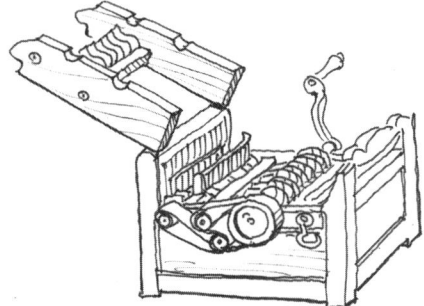

1715 ROCOCO
Following the death of Louis XIV, the grandeur and drama of 17th-century Baroque art forms relaxed into the cheerful exuberance of the Rococo style. Curvy and sinuous Rococo geometries are evident in 18th-century German gardens.

1716 RUSSIAN VERSAILLES
Czar Peter the Great instituted reforms that modernized the Russian empire and made the country a world power. He had his new capital at St. Petersburg designed along European models. Le Notre's pupil Jean-Baptiste Alexandre Le Blond planned the gardens at the czar's summer palace and park, Petrodvorets, to celebrate Russia's victory over the Swedes.

1717 FREEMASONS
Individuals committed to ideals of tolerance and universal understanding inspired by the Scientific Revolution established the first grand lodge of the freemasons in London.

1724 FAHRENHEIT
Gabriel Fahrenheit developed the temperature scale based on a freezing point of 32 degrees and a boiling point of 212 degrees.

1741 MIDDLETON PLACE
Henry Middleton, former president of the First Continental Congress, initiated work on the garden at his plantation near Charleston, South Carolina, in 1741. Slaves labored for 10 years to create the 40-acre formal garden, which is symmetrically arranged along a main axis that begins at the entry drive. Five grass terraces (called the "falls") lead down to the river where "butterfly" lakes help control the water level for the rice paddies. Geometric parterres border the north side of the great lawn.

1752 HIGH VOLTAGE!
Ben Franklin flew his kite in a lightning storm, discovering static electricity.

1753 *SPECIES PLANTARUM*
Swedish botanist Carl Linnaeus (1707–1778) developed a new, binomial system of plant classification based on genus and species names. The simplified system outlined in his book, *Species Plantarum*, was internationally accepted, facilitating the study of botanical research.

1768 *EXPERIMENT WITH AN AIR PUMP*
This painting by Joseph Wright of Derby illustrates how Enlightenment science was simultaneously trusted and viewed with suspicion.

1769 STEAM CART
The first self-propelled road vehicle, invented by Nicholas-Joseph Cugnot, was adapted to many uses in industry and agriculture.

1773 TEA PARTY
American colonists destroyed English tea rather than pay the tax on it. "No taxation without representation" became the clarion call of revolution.

1774 *THE SORROWS OF YOUNG WERTHER*
Johann Wolfgang von Goethe (1749–1832) is known for his poems and plays, including *The Sorrows of Young Werther*, which influenced the development of Romanticism. Equally important was his contribution to natural philosophy. His scientific studies were based on a firsthand encounter with nature, a prelude to the science of phenomenology.

1782 FULL OF HOT AIR
Joseph-Michel Montgolfier's balloon prototype rose 30 meters. He and his brother Jacques-Etienne demonstrated the new technology to the public in the main square of Annouay, France, the following year.

1785 NATIONAL GRID
Thomas Jefferson enacted the Land Ordinance of 1785 to survey the American territories gained in the Louisiana Purchase. The section-township-range system established a grid over 1.2 billion acres of land.

July 14, 1789 *LIBERTÉ, ÉGALITÉ, FRATERNITÉ*
The storming of the Bastille by citizens of Paris was the first move toward the overthrow of the *ancien régime*. The French Revolution brought radical change to the country.

1791 *THE MAGIC FLUTE*
Wolfgang Amadeus Mozart (1756–1791) premiered his last opera, *Die Zauberflote*, in Vienna.

1793 COTTON GIN
American Eli Whitney revolutionized agriculture with his engine that separated cotton fibers from seeds.

THE DEVELOPMENT OF THE LANDSCAPE GARDEN

In the 17th century, English gardens were a mix of French and Dutch styles adapted to different environmental circumstances. In the 18th century, these foreign, formal styles were overthrown in favor of a more English, "natural" style.[1] Landscape gardens, as they came to be called, were equally as contrived as formal gardens, but somehow people interpreted irregular geometries as being more representative of nature than straight lines, a prejudice that exists in the Western tradition to this day.

The development of the English landscape garden occurred in phases that coincided with changing tastes and aesthetic theories. Early 18th-century gardens, while developing their naturalistic form, included numerous architectural features (temples, Gothic ruins, obelisks, etc.) that were the focal points of vistas connected by walks. Later 18th-century English gardens focused on views and prospects to natural features. The final phase was characterized by an increase in tension and variation characteristic of the Picturesque movement.

THE INFLUENCE OF POLITICS, POETRY, AND PAINTING

The 18th-century English garden was influenced by a desire to rid the landscape of the rigid order indicative of French absolutism. These forms were no longer appropriate in England after a constitutional monarchy and a formalized parliamentary system were established following the Glorious Revolution of 1688. Although opposing political parties were united in their efforts to ensure a Protestant succession, the Whigs, who supported constitutional government and civil liberties, often differed with the Tories, who remained loyal to the crown. Thus the lifestyles of the aristocratic Whig landowners became centered on their country estates rather than the royal court. They incorporated classical imagery in their gardens, to represent their elevated status and cultured taste.

To improve the agricultural economy of England, the Enclosure Acts of Parliament put vast tracts of once commonly held land into private hands, increasing the economic and political power of the landed gentry. Property owners enclosed fields and pastures within the boundaries of their private estates, called parks. Timber and grazing land (which was now leased out) were two main sources of income.

Subsequent to their calls for political freedom, 18th-century English poets and philosophers also articulated a case for a freer style of landscape design. Essayists such as Joseph Addison, Alexander Pope, and Anthony Ashley Cooper (first Earl of Shaftesbury) denounced the tyranny of foreign garden styles and practices in England; they especially ridiculed topiary, and advocated nature itself as the ideal. Pope's *Epistle to Lord Burlington* of 1731 states that "good sense" is essential to garden making and that Le Notre "had it not to give." He reminds designers to consider nature as the "genius of the place," the force that "paints as you plant." Finally, he cites the design of Lord Cobham's park at Stowe as an example of good sense.[2] In 1771, Horace Walpole, the son of the first prime minister of England, wrote *Essay on Modern Gardening*, referencing the work of writer John Milton and landscape painter Claude Lorrain as influences on the development of the English landscape garden.

Alexander Pope said "all gardening is landscape painting."[3] The 17th-century landscapes of French painters Claude Lorrain and Nicholas Poussin were revered by the English for their mix of heroic and pastoral imagery. These paintings were collected by the landed gentry who went abroad on "grand tours" to continue their classical education.[4] Wealthy landowners were eager to re-create in their parks the idyllic Arcadia represented in the paintings. Educated aristocrats would have understood the allusions to Ovid, Virgil, and Pliny contained in the Italian Renaissance gardens they visited. Early 18th-century English gardens had similar encoded meanings. Lord Burlington toured Italy and was particularly taken by the scenographic effects and classical vocabulary of the Palladian villa. In 1715, Palladio's books were translated into English, further inspiring ideals of agrarian classicism.

GREEN AND PLEASANT LAND: Common pastures were "enclosed" by acts of Parliament to increase agricultural productivity.

COAST VIEW OF DELOS WITH AENEAS: The composition of a scene at Stourhead is remarkably similar to one portrayed in Lorrain's painting.

VIEW OF PONTE MOLLE: The position of the temple and bridge in Lorrain's landscape was re-created at Castle Howard.

In the second half of the 18th century, English gardens became poetic constructions devoid of earlier moral overtones. Allusions to classical themes were not as readily understood by the new class of landowners, who were not as educated as the landed aristocracy and whose estates were much more modest.

FASCINATION WITH CHINESE STYLES

Other influences on the development of the English landscape garden include the images and descriptions of Chinese gardens brought back to Europe by the Jesuits. The French Jesuit missionary

and painter Jean-Denis Attiret (1702–1768) moved to China in 1737 and sent home illustrated accounts of the imperial gardens. His reports were translated into English in 1752. English designers were receptive to the irregular forms of Chinese gardens that "shunned" the straight line. In 1757, the Scottish architect Sir William Chambers published *Designs of Chinese Buildings, Furniture, Dresses, Machines,* and Utensils. Chinese decorative elements were included in the garden, as well as in the home. Chinoiserie refers to the Chinese-themed textiles, ceramics, wallpaper, and furniture that were now in demand. The fascination with Chinese styles figured in the serious debates over style that engaged English designers later in the century. (The controversy is examined further in this chapter.)

DESIGN ELEMENTS

In addition to their productive agricultural function, the newly enclosed parks were developed by their owners as pleasure grounds to conform to the new ideal of pastoral life. English garden designers shaped lakes and hills and used trees as visual frames. To create the anti-Versailles, they deconstructed the stiff boundaries that separated garden from park. The ha-ha (a sunken fence or ditch) and the tree cluster (variations of belting, clumping, and dotting) were important elements in the transition to the naturalistic style. An organic design vocabulary—gently rolling hills, free-form lakes, and groves of trees—unified site plans. "Professional" landscape designers spread this style across England.

The idea of the ferme ornée—a working farm "decorated" like a garden—accorded with English cultural identity, and was an early attempt to impart a classical theme on a rural aesthetic.[5] William Shenstone developed a ferme ornée at the Leasowes, his estate in Warwickshire. Perimeter walks connected separate scenes of the garden. Latin inscriptions on sculptural elements provided an overlay of classical ideology. Trees, clustered around the boundaries of the site, kept views focused inward. Shenstone was also first to use the terms "landscape gardening" and "landscape gardener" in his essay of 1764 entitled "Unconnected Thoughts on Gardens."

INFLUENTIAL GARDEN DESIGNERS

While key writers and philosophers promoted the revolution of taste, professional landscape designers like William Kent, Lancelot "Capability" Brown, and Humphry Repton remade the country as an English landscape garden. Their work followed that of architect Sir John Vanbrugh and landscape designers Henry Wise and George London, who worked with formal design vocabularies in the early 18th century, and established an English Baroque style. Charles Bridgeman set the stage for the transition to the natural style. He mixed the regular geometry of the parterre with free-form wildernesses. Bridgeman was a masterly site planner; his avenues conformed to the topography and terrain of the site. He pioneered the use of the ha-ha at Stowe, although Walpole's praise of Kent,

AH HA!: The ha-ha is a sunken fence or ditch that permits distant views of fields while keeping grazing animals away from living areas.

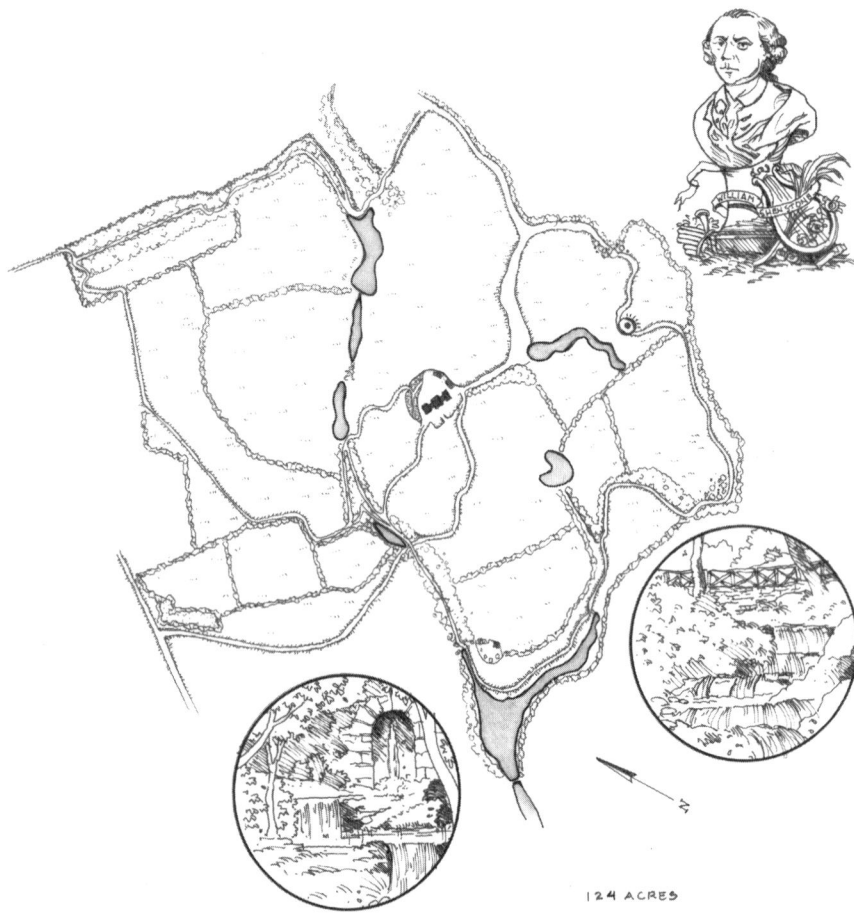

124 ACRES

THE LEASOWES: The ornamented farm of William Shenstone partnered horticulture with agriculture.

who "leaped the fence," has somewhat obscured Bridgeman's contribution.[6]

WILLIAM KENT (1685–1748)

William Kent was a landscape painter and set designer who understood the scenic capacity of the landscape and composed gardens pictorially. Kent is credited with creating the new move toward informality, working "without level or line."[7] He was the ultimate set dresser, incorporating literary allusions and mythological content through naming and inscription—for example, the "Elysian Fields" and "Praeneste Terrace" at Stowe. His gardens unfold in time and space like a performance develops in sequential scenes and acts.

Kent spent almost 10 years studying in Italy. Italian Renaissance gardens made an impression on him, but it was their overgrown, neglected state that he observed—an overlay of disorder on their perfect geometric harmonies. Kent's

vocabulary included the use of serpentine bodies of water and the massing of trees in individual groups. His landscapes contained architectural features such as sham ruins or fabriques that were similar to elements seen in the paintings of Lorrain and Poussin; he even planted dead trees to give "truth" to a scene.[8]

Kent's Italian diaries indicate his understanding of sophisticated perspective construction techniques; he used oblique perspective points that converged outside the "scene" to unify the design and encourage the viewer to move through the space. Scenes were not framed from any single point.[9] The visitor approached architectural features, such as the Praeneste Terrace, from an angle, adding to the element of surprise.

Kent's early work at Rousham illustrates Addison's ideas that an entire estate should be considered a garden. Kent produced a great variety of experiences in a small, awkwardly shaped space by clearing and grouping trees. Delightful surprises awaited the visitor within the confines of the garden.

Rousham, sited along a river bank in Oxfordshire, is a narrative circuit garden Kent composed as a series of landscape pictures. He began work in the 1730s, a decade after Bridgeman had established the framework of the garden. Kent reworked some of Bridgeman's straight paths, and developed a series of sequential visual events. Directly behind the house, a reproduction of a famous antique statue of a lion attacking a horse sits at the edge of a rectangular grassy

STAGE DIRECTION: William Kent employed trees as visual screens. Capability Brown planted trees in belts, clumps, and dots to direct views of the landscape.

SKETCHBOOK: William Kent considered the garden a stage for human activity.

terrace. Views continue down the open slope toward the river and across to a far hilltop crowned with an "eyecatcher"—a fake Gothic ruin placed there by Kent. As the visitor moves through the garden, views of sculptures and architectural features are suddenly revealed, evoking historical and literary themes.

LANCELOT "CAPABILITY" BROWN (1715–1783)

The naturalistic style reached its height of expression through the work of Lancelot Brown, whose reputation (and name) was built on his skill in visualizing the capability of a site to be transformed into a garden and thus "improved." Brown changed the character of the built landscape in England by redesigning existing gardens and parks of country seats in the new naturalistic fashion. He obtained nearly 200 commissions during his career. His early apprenticeship at Stowe gave him a background in practical horticulture that Kent lacked.

Brown was concerned foremost with the harmony of line. Smooth transitions in topographic elevation complemented the flowing curves of lakes and paths. Brown eliminated all traces of the formal parterre and terrace and brought the lawn right up to the house. He disguised any visible aspects of the working farm. The landscape was no longer a vehicle for narrative expression; it became the narrative itself. Brown took the idea of the landscape garden to an extreme. His landscapes were devoid of literary associations. His work was criticized by

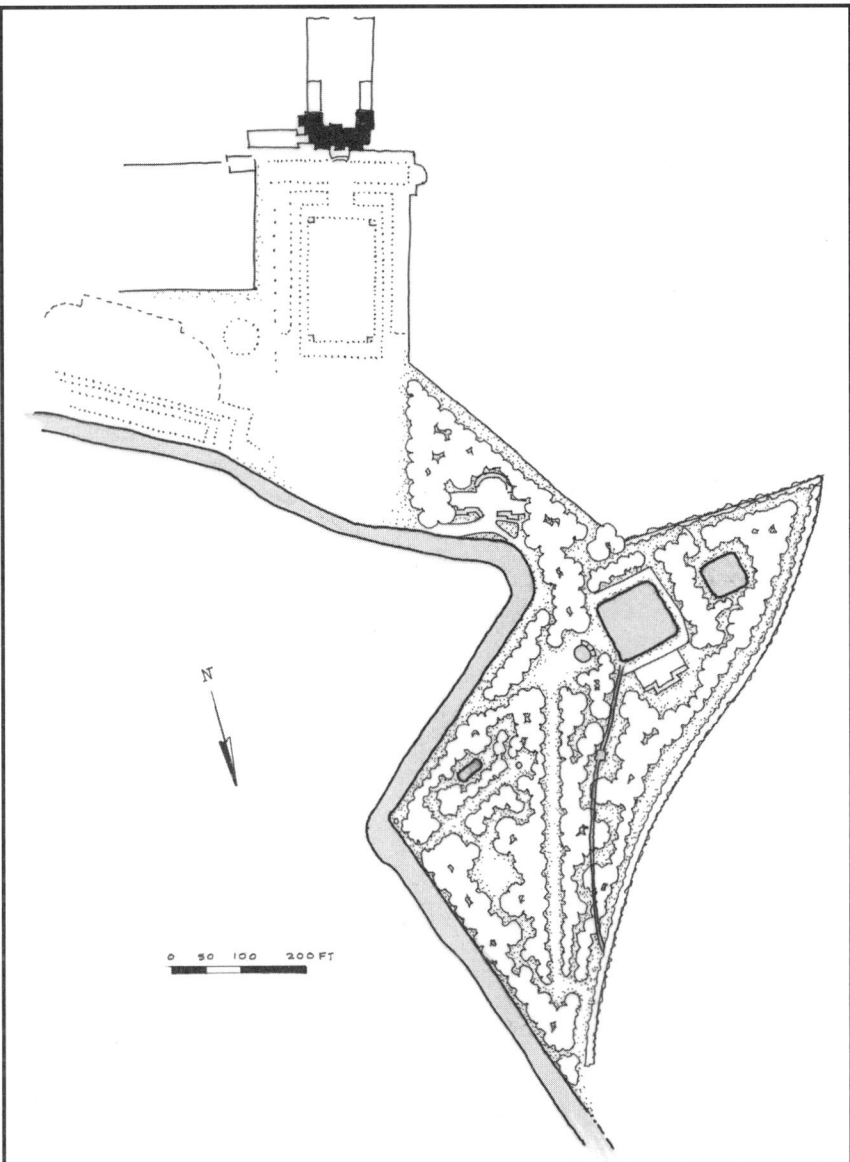

ROUSHAM: Kent added a theatrical overlay onto the framework established by Bridgeman.

S-CURVE: The "serpentine line of beauty" defines Brown's landscape gardens.

advocates of the picturesque as being too "empty"; there was no "nature" to be seen except for the gentle landforms, and the groups of trees creating light and dark spaces.

HUMPHRY REPTON (1752–1818)

Repton changed careers midlife; he was an educated writer and skilled painter who turned his hand to landscape design at the age of 36. He was first to advertise himself as a landscape gardener. He visually merged gardens into the landscape, "correcting" nature's imperfections.

Repton developed a style that combined aspects of formalism and naturalism. As his career matured, he reintroduced geometrically planned garden details around the house to establish a foreground, close-up view, which contrasted with the sculpted landscape park beyond. Repton reintroduced balustraded terraces into his work and planted understories with mixed shrubs and flowers.

Unlike Brown, Repton recorded and published his theories. He joined the stylistic controversy by supporting Brown's style and defending his own work against criticism from the proponents of the picturesque movement, who advocated a more dramatic realization of nature.

Repton was known for the before-and-after scenes he painted for his clients, viewable by raising a hinged flap on the drawing. The works, bound in red leather, were called his "red books." Repton's work was a major influence on the development of Victorian garden styles in the 19th century.

REPRESENTATIVE PROJECTS

STOWE, BUCKINGHAMSHIRE

Bridgeman's work at Stowe began in 1714, when the Enclosure Acts increased Richard Temple's (Viscount Cobham's) property from 28 acres to almost 900

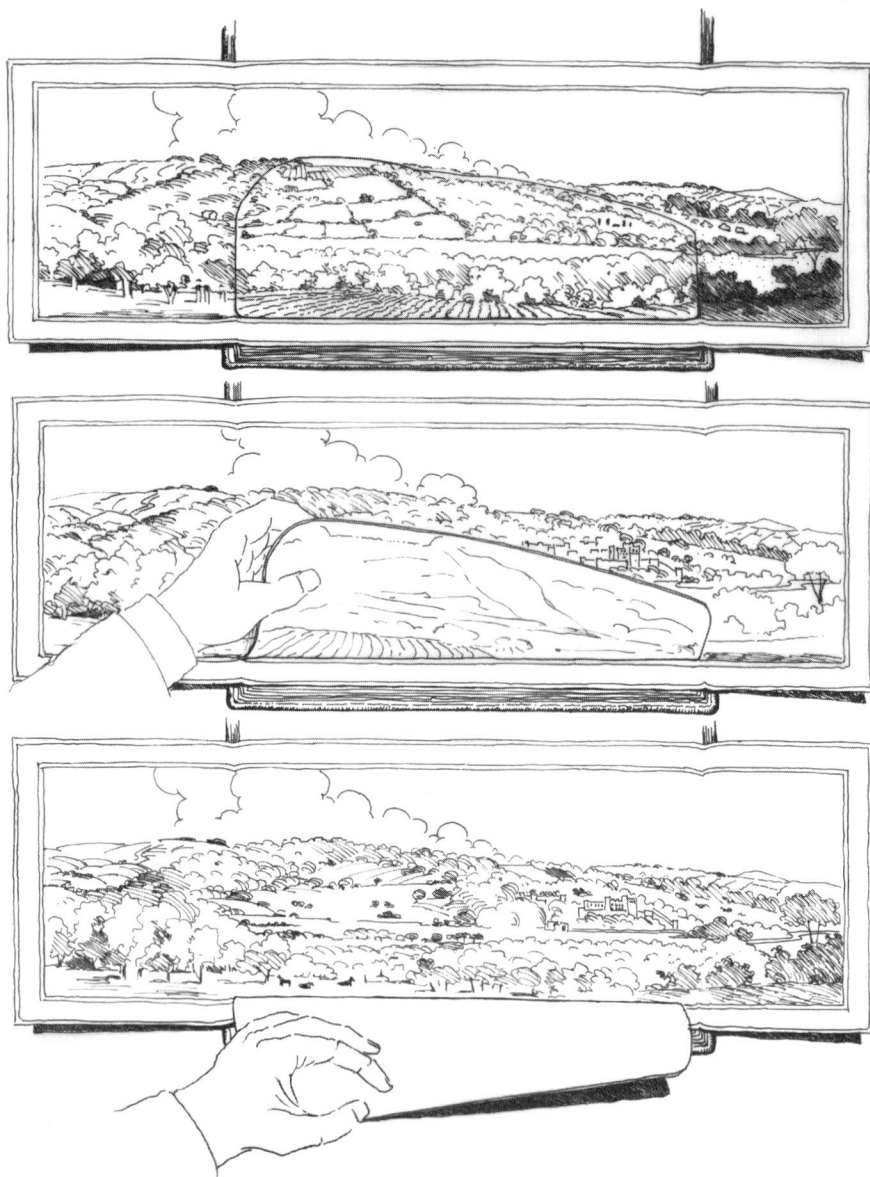

RED BOOK: Repton helped his clients visualize his proposals by preparing books with before-and-after views.

acres. Bridgeman removed the terraces, planted trees along the perimeter, and created axial views terminated by architectural features.

Kent's work began in 1734. He relaxed the geometric boundaries that subdivided the space and used vegetation as visual frames. He divided the large body of water into two irregularly shaped lakes, sculpted the Elysian Fields, and planned the curving pathways and tree clusters. The Elysian Fields were staged by Kent around a triad of temples to Ancient Virtue, Modern Virtue, and the British Worthies. The round Temple of Ancient Virtue is a copy of the Temple of the Sibyl at Tivoli; the Temple of Modern Virtue (no longer extant) was built as a ruin and contained a headless bust— Cobham's political commentary aimed at Robert Walpole, the prime minister. The Temple of British Worthies contained busts of celebrated "heroes, patriots, and wits" and included a commemoration of the family dog.

TEMPLE OF ANCIENT VIRTUE

TEMPLE OF MODERN VIRTUE

TEMPLE OF BRITISH WORTHIES

· ELYSIAN FIELDS ·
BRIDGE OVER THE
RIVER STYX

ROTUNDA

GOTHIC TEMPLE

CORINTHIAN ARCH

LAKE PAVILIONS

TEMPLE OF
CONCORD & VICTORY

· PALLADIAN BRIDGE ·

GRECIAN VALE

ELYSIAN FIELDS: Like the garden at Versailles was used as political theater by Louis XIV, the design of Stowe was politically motivated.

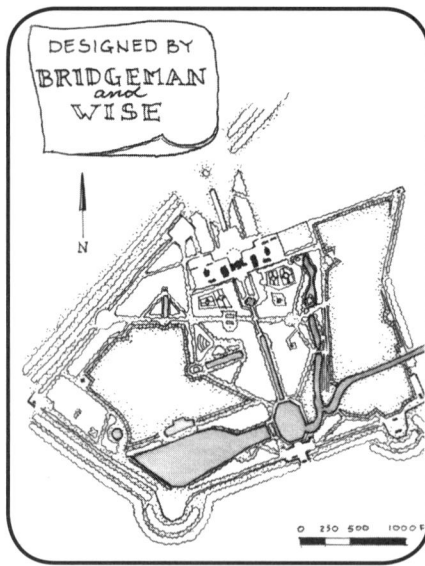

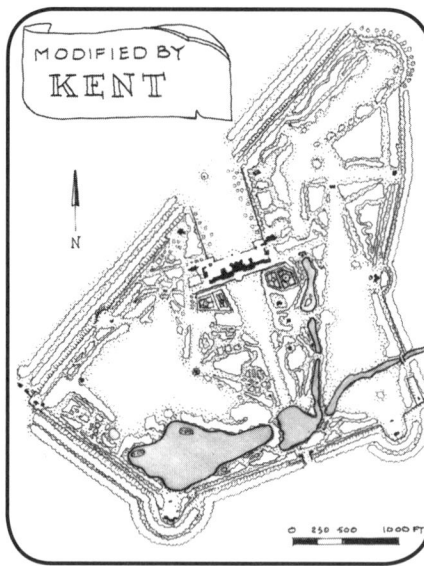

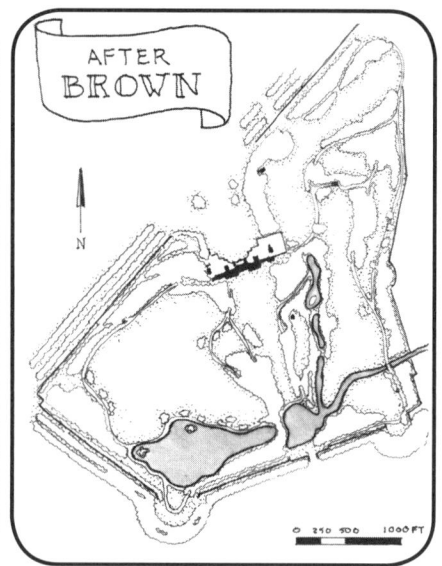

STOWE: The successive site plans are a record of changing garden design styles in the 18th century.

Brown began his work at Stowe in 1741. He extended the Grecian valley and created the south lawn.

BLENHEIM, OXFORDSHIRE

The original plan of Blenheim was completed in 1722 by Henry Wise, who designed a monumental parterre in keeping with the grandeur of the building. An axial alignment of trees along the approach avenue represented the placement of soldiers in the Battle of Blenheim.

Brown's work at Blenheim began in 1764. He dammed the river and excavated the two existing lakes, raising the water level to make the single volume of water more in balance with the heavy architectural mass of the stone house and bridge. He obliterated the parterres and brought the lawn to the base of the huge palace.

BLENHEIM: Brown's changes to the Blenheim plan exemplified the new naturalistic style.

STOURHEAD: Site plan.

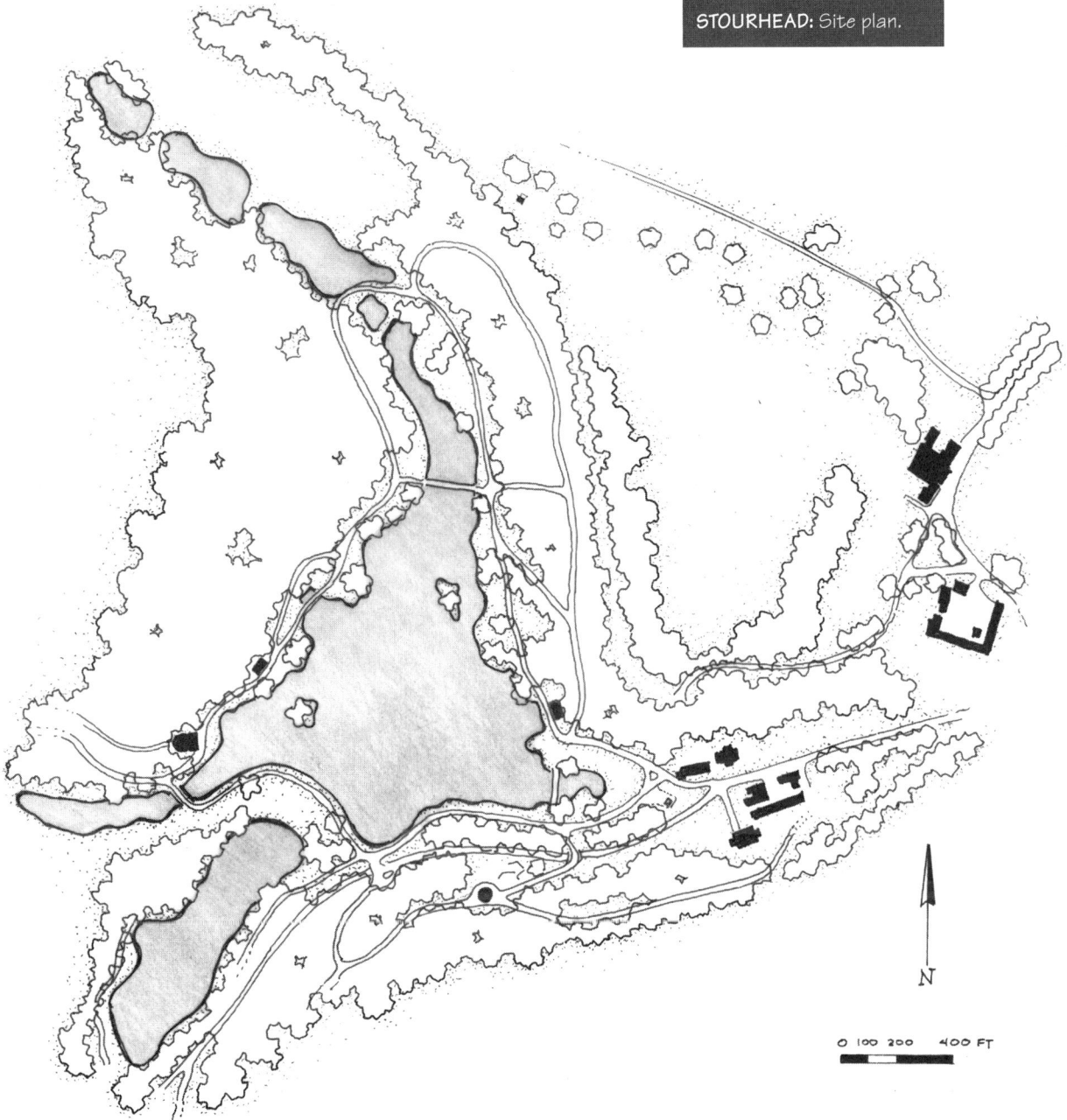

N

0 100 200 400 FT

STOURHEAD, WILTSHIRE

The design of Stourhead was begun by its owner, Henry Hoare II, in 1735. He set the garden in a deep valley around a 20-acre lake, which he constructed by damming a stream.

While the narrative circuit at Rousham incorporated outward views to distant scenes, the garden at Stourhead focused inward, on intimate views across the central lake. The path leads the visitor in a counterclockwise direction, relating a sequence of events from Virgil's *The Aeneid*—the story of the voyage to Rome by Aeneas and the Trojan survivors. From the Temple of Apollo, the ultimate stop on the itinerary, the whole garden becomes visible.

VISUAL NARRATIVE: *Stourhead*

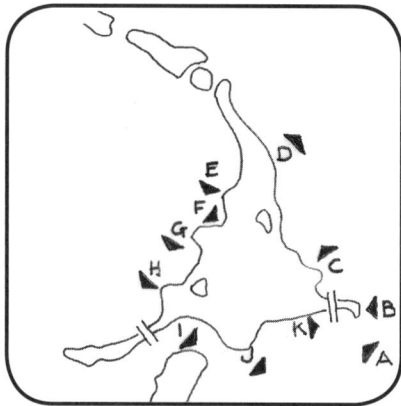

A

B

C

D

E

F

G

H

I

J

K

STYLISTIC CONTROVERSY

What exactly a naturalistic garden should look like became a matter of contention early in its history. The aesthetic rebellion against formalism was interpreted in different ways—as beautiful and as picturesque. The debate about the superior style was taken seriously because taste was critical to position in English society. Added to the mix was the new fad for Chinese decorative styles, and the idea of the sublime.

In addition to the idealized view of antiquity that the landed gentry brought back from their grand tours of Italy, Chinese imagery began to exert an influence on the English imagination. In William Chambers's book *Dissertation on Oriental Gardening*, published in 1772, he suggested a sort of Chinese fantasyland as a counter to the naturalistic movement. He interpreted the emotional effects of Chinese gardens as being "pleasing, horrid, and enchanted," and suggested that a sublime garden should contain some element of terror—like the clamor of a thunderstorm or the threat of a fire. He used the publication to critique Capability Brown's style, complaining that Brown's work was indistinguishable from nature's own. Chambers's book was influential in the development of highly wrought rococo styles in continental Europe and led to the popularity of the *jardin anglo-chinois* in Germany and France.

Artists and critics put forth aesthetic theories to explain the qualities of the landscape most desirable in a garden. The painter William Hogarth published his book *The Analysis of Beauty* in 1753, suggesting that all beautiful forms follow an S-curve. Beauty was expressed in the landscape by the flowing forms and unrestricted spaces defined by a serpentine line. The philosopher Edmund Burke wrote an essay in 1756 entitled *A Philosophical Enquiry into the Origin of Our Ideas of the Sublime and Beauti-*

THE LANDSCAPE—A DIDACTIC POEM: Richard Payne Knight compared a picturesque scene (bottom) to the landscape gardens of Brown (top), "dressed in the modern style."

RUSTIC IDYLL: Estate owners added grottoes and hermitages to their gardens for their poetic associations.

ful, in which he proposed that beauty is characterized by smoothness and gentle transition. The sublime, on the other hand, was characterized by rugged, masculine forms.

Intellectuals such as Uvedale Price and Richard Payne Knight grew discontent with the sameness and lack of distinction within the Brownian landscape garden. Anti-Brownian sentiment reached its apex as Repton entered the profession. Critics called for more rugged scenery—the inclusion of con-

trasting elements that would appeal to a painter. William Gilpin proposed that the landscape should be viewed the same way a painting is viewed, that views of nature should be picturesque.[10] The formal, compositional aspect of pictures, not their thematic content, is what came to define the viewer's experience of nature in the second half of the 18th century. Scenery without statuary was valued; the experience shifted from looking at objects in the landscape to looking at the landscape as an object.

Gilpin traveled the British Isles and published his observations on various scenic spots. In his book, *Observations on the River Wye, and Several Parts of South Wales, &c. Relative Chiefly to Picturesque Beauty; Made in the Summer of the Year 1770*, he expanded the definition of the picturesque to include the requirements of ruggedness, variety, and architectural elements. Gilpin also published touring guides and gave instructions for framing particular views according to compositional techniques used by painters. People sought a more dramatic depiction

CHINOISERIE: In his work at the Royal Gardens at Kew in 1761, Chambers added a 163-foot-high pagoda decorated with gold dragons.

BEFORE TOURISTS EMBARKED ON THEIR SEARCH FOR THE PICTURESQUE THEY SHOPPED AT *SPECIALTY STORES* FEATURING ART PRINTS, TRAVEL GUIDES, ARTISTS SUPPLIES, DRAWING AIDS & ART BOOKS.

GILPIN
◆
GUIDE TO THE LAKE DISTRICT
◆

PLACE	OMISSIONS	DATE	OBSERVATIONS

CUSTOM DESIGNED *DIARIES* WERE FORMATED FOR THE ADVENTURERS TO RECORD THEIR VISUAL IMPRESSIONS.

THE LAKE DISTRICT IN ENGLAND WAS A FAVORITE LOCATION FOR TRAVELERS SEEKING *PICTURESQUE VIEWS.*

A *STIMULUS* TO THE *IMAGINATION*, BUT NATURE HAD TO BE MARKED SO THAT THE *TOURISTS* COULD IDENTIFY AN *EXACT PICTURESQUE SCENE.*

FREE-STANDING WALLS WERE BUILT TO *FRAME* THE VIEWS THAT PEOPLE WOULD *ANALYZE & SKETCH.*

GILPIN'S PICTURESQUE TOURS.

of nature and toured the countryside sketching and analyzing scenery.

A scathing war of words was waged in the press between the two schools. Thrown into the mix was Chambers, with his new requirement of terror to define the sublime. There were now three conceptions of space: the beautiful, the

picturesque, and the sublime. Repton countered that the use and experience of the landscape should be the foremost criteria for evaluation, not its two-dimensional characteristics. Walpole defended Brown against Chambers. Knight and Price later disagreed with each other over matters of taste and what form variety should take.

The abstraction of the landscape yearned for by Price and Knight would develop in the 19th century as Impressionism. The debate had been centered on aspects of the tame and the wild. The argument continued into the next century, when John Claudius Loudon developed another style—the gardenesque.

THE LANDSCAPE GARDEN IN FRANCE

The revolution of taste spread across Europe at the end of the 18th century, about the same time that Attiret's letters from China reached France. The French saw a connection between the Chinese garden and the English garden through their similar vocabularies of winding paths and irregularly shaped lakes. A hybrid style known as *anglo-chinois* became popular in France and Germany.

The appeal of uncorrupted nature was also felt throughout French society in the late 18th century. French writer Jean-Jacques Rousseau wrote a novel, *La Nouvelle Heloise*, in which he described a garden where no trace of human intervention can be found. He evoked poetic images of a glorified wilderness that was later reproduced in actual gardens. The book had a big impact on Marquis Rene-Louis de Girardin, who created one of the best examples of an English landscape garden in France at Ermenonville.

Girardin himself was intimately engaged in the project. The full title of the treatise he published in 1777 summarized his design intentions: *De la composition des paysages, ou Des moyens d'embellir la nature autour des habitations, en joignant l'agreable a l'utile* (*Of the composition of landscapes, or ways of embellishing the land surrounding dwellings by bringing together what is pleasurable and what is useful*). Girardin toured England in 1763 and visited the Leasowes. Ermenonville contained similar kinds of rustic retreats and artificial pastoral elements—*fabriques*—like mills, cascades, tombs, and temples. The grounds comprised four distinct areas: the grand parc, petit parc, farmland, and wilderness, called the *Desert*. Girardin's model farm was both functional and ornamental. Its utilitarian purpose helped create renewed interest in "real" agriculture in France.[11]

ILE DES PEUPLIERS: Jean-Jacques Rousseau's tomb at Ermenonville.

Rousseau left Paris for Ermenonville and died there months later. In an ironic twist, the "man of nature and of truth" was buried in Girardin's garden on an artificial island in an artificial lake. (His body was eventually moved to the Pantheon in Paris.) The romantic image of the Isle of Poplars—the circle of poplar trees and the isolated tomb—was much imitated in later gardens and cemeteries, prompting the 19th-century cult of the melancholy.

The landscape garden remains enormously influential today. The style, as artificial and contrived as French formalism, is for many people synonymous with nature.

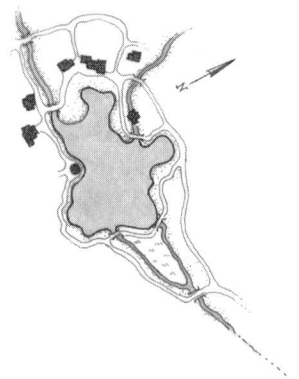

HAMEAU: In 1782, Marie Antoinette commissioned *Le Hameau de la Reine* (the Queen's Hamlet), a model farm, for the Petit Trianon at Versailles.

QIANLONG'S IMPRINT

In the late 17th century, Manchu warriors from the north deposed the last Ming emperor, establishing the Qing Dynasty (1644–1911). The foreign rulers strengthened the country by reconciling various tribes and ridding the court of corruption. Chinese territory extended into Central Asia. In 1710, approximately 110 million people inhabited China; by 1814, the population had reached 375 million.[12] The height of prosperity and expansion was reached during the reign of Qianlong (1736–1795), who also nurtured the development of the arts and sciences. The imperial palace became a repository for the emperor's collection of rocks and paintings from Suzhou.

Qianlong welcomed the Jesuit missionaries and invited them to live at court as his advisors on Western culture. French, Italian, and German priests had lived in the Forbidden City since the 17th century. In fact, German missionary Johann Adam Schall von Bell reformed the Chinese calendar and was appointed director of the royal observatory at Beijing, in 1651.

Parallels exist between Chinese gardens and English landscape gardens. The flow of nature inspired their forms, and both shared similar motives to prompt emotional reactions in the viewer through poetic allusion. The poetic naming of views and their conceptual association with natural scenery was as critical to Chinese gardens as political references were to English gardens.

IRREGULAR BEAUTY

English explorers and merchants related their impressions of the "spontaneous beauty" they saw in Chinese gardens.[13] Chambers, whose tour of China was limited to Canton province, wrote of the asymmetry of Chinese forms. He and the other advocates of the sublime yearned for gardens with gripping visual content. They saw in the Chinese garden a fundamental interdependence of architecture and garden that was lacking in the English landscape gardens of Capability Brown.

More than just the Chinese aesthetic of natural order appealed to the English. Advancement in the Qing court was based on one's knowledge of Neo-Confucian philosophies. Confucian teachings, particularly the idea that status could be acquired through cultural education rather than birthright, were inspiring to the Europeans, who were rebelling against absolutist forms of government and royal privilege.

The wealth and power of Beijing culture during the Qing dynasty is captured in *The Dream of the Red Chamber* (also called *The Story of the Stone*) written by Cao Xueqin in the 1750s. The novel is a good primary source of information on 18th-century Chinese gardens, since a main part of the story takes place in a garden. The daughter of a wealthy aristocratic family has been appointed royal concubine. Her family prepares for her visit by enlarging their garden and adding apartments. The author leads the reader on a tour of the garden, describing its elements and materials—pavilions, rocks, stone bridges, orchards, artificial mountains, and so on. The family is trying to come up with poetic inscriptions for the spaces, because a garden is not complete without them. Their suggestions (such as "pathway to mysteries") were written on paper lanterns and left for the daughter to select.

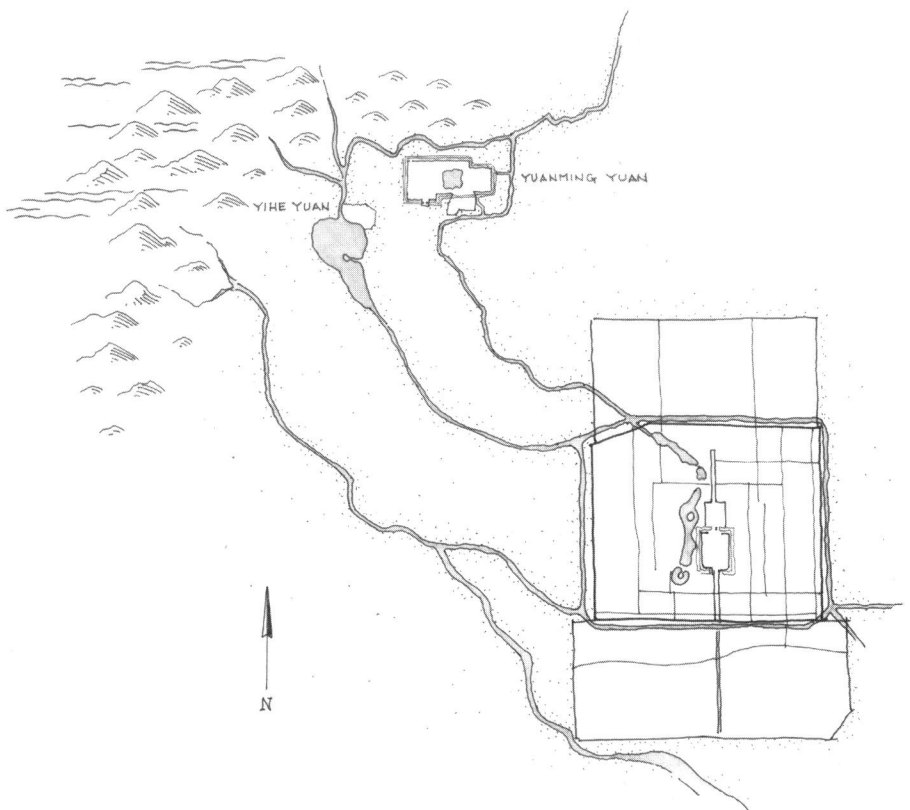

YUANMING YUAN

YIHE YUAN

N

FRAGRANT HILLS: Emperors built imperial villas in the hills northwest of Beijing.

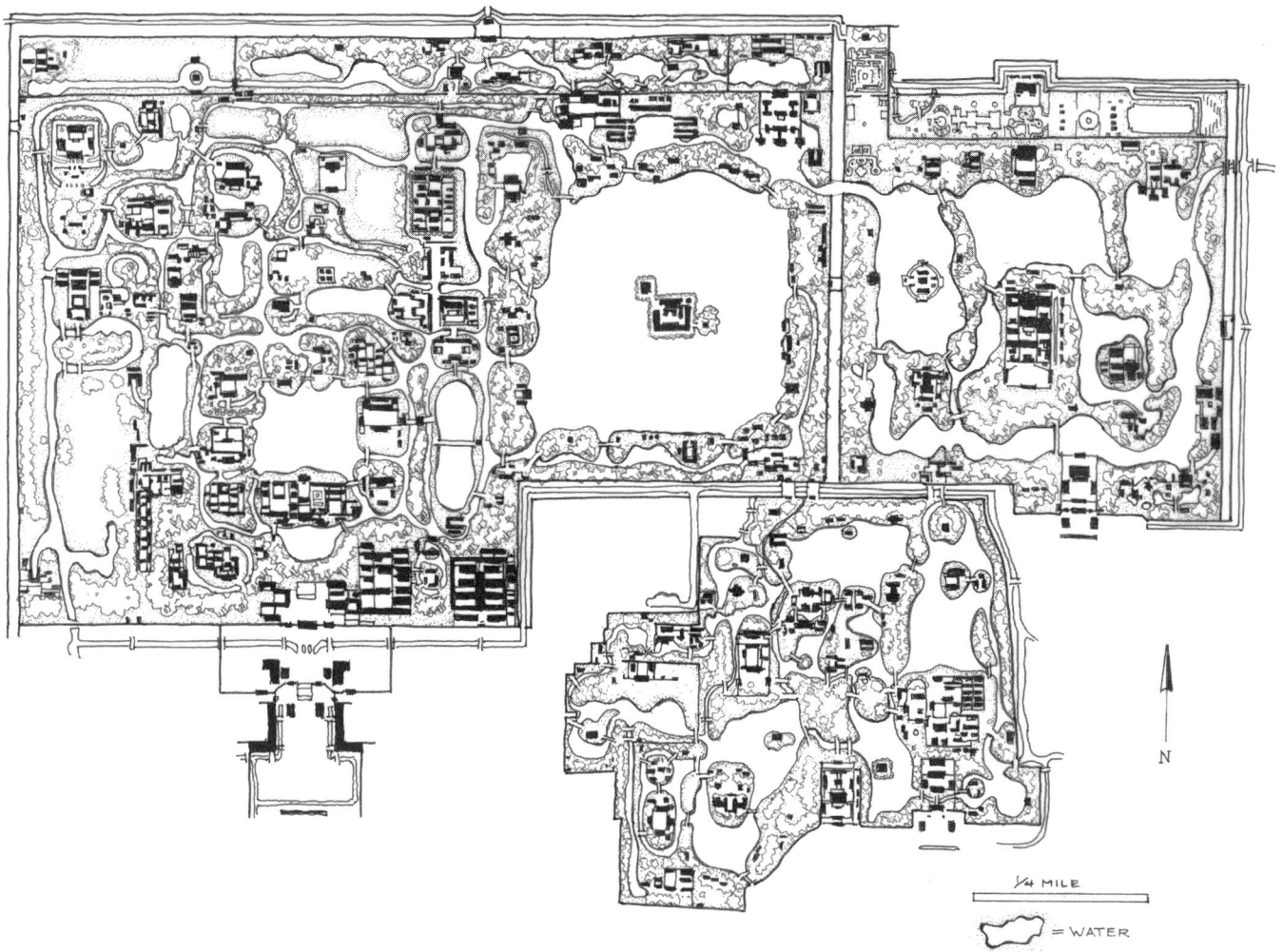

GARDEN OF PERFECT BRIGHTNESS: The garden encompassed more than 700 acres, with water covering about one-third of the site.

During the early Qing period, the emperor built pleasure gardens in the hills northwest of the capital. The gardens of Suzhou, in southern China, served as inspiration. Representative examples of both are described here.

YUANMING YUAN (GARDEN OF PERFECT BRIGHTNESS), BEIJING

The imperial gardens, located in the Western Hills outside the Forbidden City, were first planned by Emperor Kangxi, and further developed by his grandson Qianlong. The Yuanming Yuan has much in common with Versailles. The huge, elaborate garden was established as the seat of government by Qianlong, much like Versailles became the official court under Louis XIV. Both gardens reflect the grand ambitions of their royal patron. The Yuanming Yuan was destroyed during the war with France and Britain in the 19th century.

The Yuanming Yuan comprised three linked gardens, which, through dredging and artificially filling the flat site, recreated the topography and water-scape of the three geographic areas of China—the northwest plateau, the great plains, and the southeast coastal area.[14] Qianlong designated the "40 best views" of the garden. He wrote poems about them and commissioned court artists Tang Dai and Shen Yuan to paint the 40 scenes. The album of silk paintings was completed in 1747 and now resides in the Bibliotheque Nationale, in Paris.

Images of the garden reached Europe in the mid-18th century. French and Swedish publishers reproduced the paintings of the famous scenes as woodcuts in European editions. The scale of the Yuanming Yuan was also described by Father Attiret in his letters of 1743.

Qianlong was interested in foreign garden styles and asked the Jesuits to design a garden in the European style. The work was undertaken by Giuseppe Castiglione, Michel Benoit, and Attiret. They created a baroque garden complete with sculpture, fountains, parterres, a brick maze, and the famous water clock that told time by spouting water from the mouths of 12 different animals.

Qianlong loved gardens and kept building them. The huge complex contained study pavilions, entertainment rooms, audience halls, artificial hills, canals, rockeries, a library, farm fields, and drill fields. Each space had a unique identity, defined by both architecture and landscape.

FORTY FAMOUS VIEWS: The 40 dominant scenes of the Yuanming Yuan were internationally known.

CHINESE VERSAILLES: Emperor Qianlong asked the Jesuit residents of the palace to build a European-style garden within the Yuanming Yuan.

SUMMER PALACE: Over a period of 14 years, Qianlong enlarged Kunming Lake and sculpted hills and causeways at his favorite retreat.

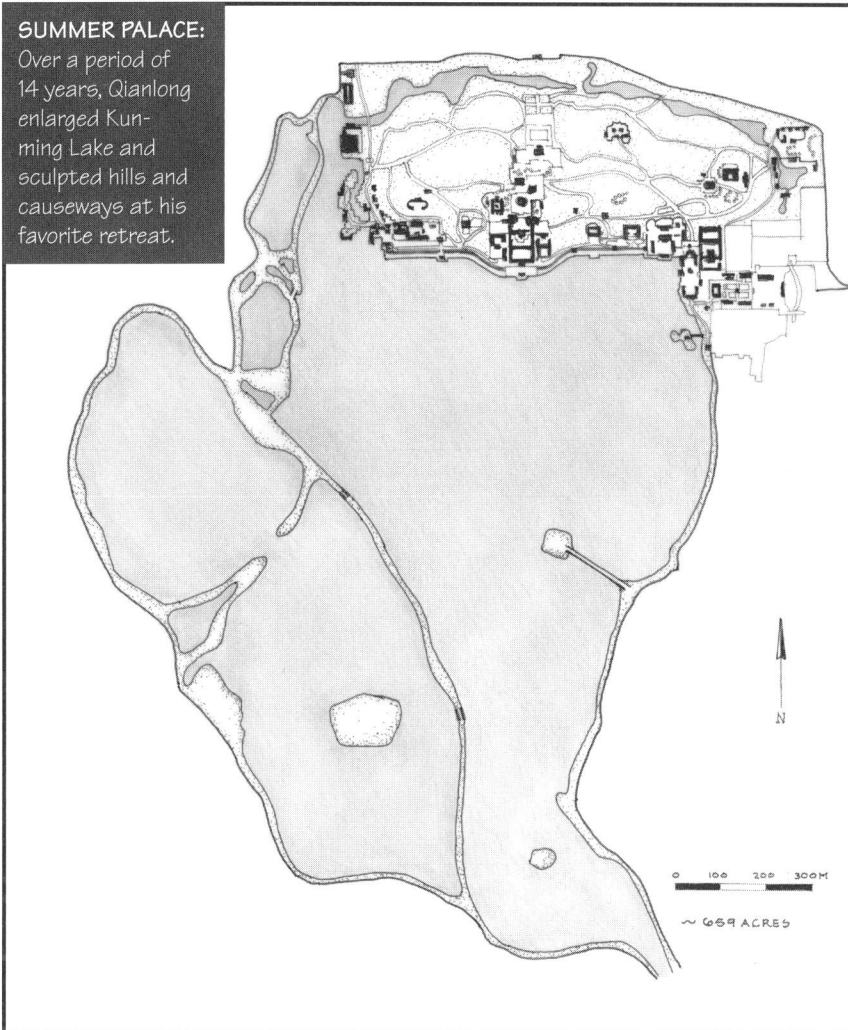

0   100   200   300M

~ 659 ACRES

N

YIHE YUAN (SUMMER PALACE), BEIJING

In 1680, Kangxi began restoring the gardens on what is now called Longevity Hill. Qianlong continued the work, excavating Kunming Lake in honor of his mother's sixtieth birthday, in 1754. The large lake recalled the beauty of West Lake in Hangzhou. The garden was named Yihe Yuan, the Garden of Harmony and Ease, in the 19th century.

A covered gallery, over a half mile long, borders the north side of Kunming Lake. Landscape scenes and floral motifs decorate the crossbeams of the gallery's 273 bays. Picturesque bridges, such as the Marble (Jade Belt) Bridge and the Seventeen-Arch Bridge connect various causeways. Behind Longevity Hill to the north, the emperor had an urban street scene re-created along a canal, in imitation of an actual retail district in Suzhou. Behind the royal palace to the east, a garden-within-a-garden (called The Garden of Harmonious Interest) replicated a famous Suzhou garden.

The original garden was destroyed during the Opium Wars in the 19th century, and has since been rebuilt.

SEVENTEEN-ARCH BRIDGE: The stone bridge leads to the picturesque Island of the Dragon Temple at Yihe Yuan.

169

WANGSHI YUAN (GARDEN OF THE MASTER OF THE FISHING NETS), SUZHOU

Suzhou was the center of learning and creativity during the Ming dynasty. It was said, "Everyone's a scholar and calligrapher in Suzhou."[15] Suzhou reached its current size in the 12th century, when the Song court fled south. Picturesque canals and bridges traversed the walled city. Suzhou remained a cultural capital throughout the Qing dynasty. Wangshi Yuan is an excellent example of the many scholar gardens that were built and renovated during the 18th century.

Wangshi Yuan was built in 1140 and rebuilt in 1770. The 18th-century owner, a retired government official, placed new structures on old foundations around the central pond. The small, 1-acre garden consists of a series of interlocking courtyards and pavilions, each with a different character and configuration. The illusion of space is created by concealing and framing views along a circuitous route around the pond. Views to scenic spots and planting areas are disclosed in sequence. The full extent of the pond is not visible from any one point.

To create a poetic atmosphere, garden owners named spaces in their gardens. At Wangshi Yuan, the "Pavilion of the Accumulated Void" is hidden behind a lakefront gallery; the "Pavilion of the Arriving Moon and Wind" juts out onto the western edge of the pond. This picturesque structure with its stone foundation and flaring eaves is the focal point of the garden. Mirrors inside the pavilion reflect the water.

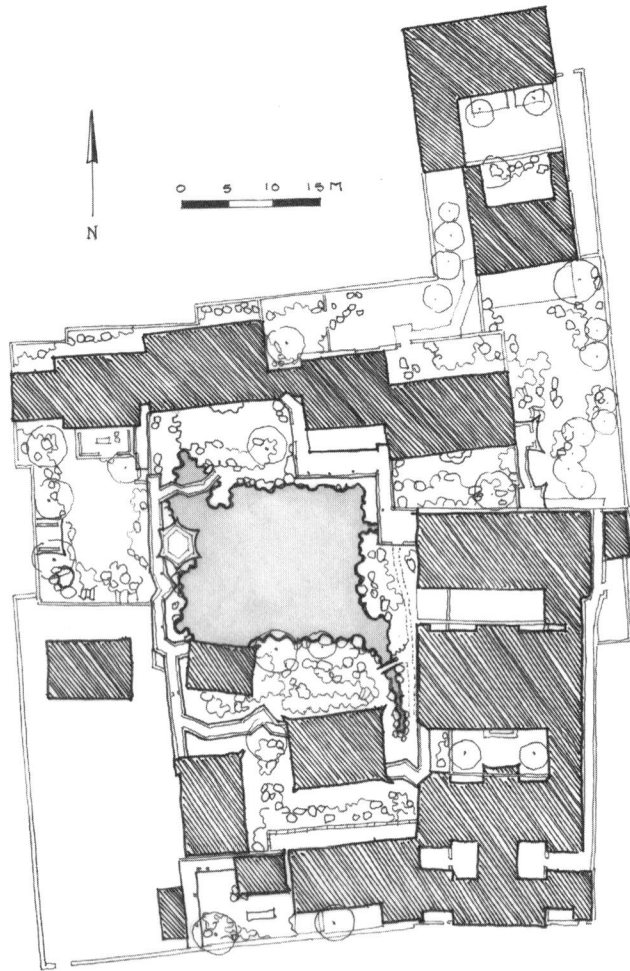

GARDEN OF THE MASTER OF THE FISHING NETS: The visitor is afforded a variety of experiences through the artful manipulation of level changes and controlled views in this small Suzhou garden.

PAVILION OF THE ARRIVING MOON AND WIND: From this central location, all of the garden is visible.

HOMELAND TRADITIONS

Although their war for independence would eventually be won, many settlers were still fighting a war with nature in the 18th century. They struggled to clear the dense forests and put land under cultivation to secure stable sources of food and income—meanwhile destroying Native grounds and food supplies. In established settlements, such as Williamsburg and Boston, the Europeans continued the garden traditions of their homeland. Dooryard and cottage gardens were planted in the northern townships, while the landed aristocracy who settled in the south planted more extensive estate gardens.

Beginning in 1716, Alexander Spotswood, the second governor of Virginia, extended the gardens at the governor's mansion in a style reminiscent of 17th-century English gardens. The formal parterres arranged along a central axis recalled the gardens of William and Mary, and contained garden terraces and canals. Affluent residents copied the formal styles, and included topiary in their gardens. The mild climate encouraged horticultural research. Local plantsmen studied native plants and sent seeds back to botanical gardens in England. The gardens were restored in the 1930s by Arthur Shurcliff in association with the Colonial Williamsburg Foundation.

GOVERNOR'S MANSION: The gardens of Williamsburg, Virginia, exhibit English, Dutch, and French influences.

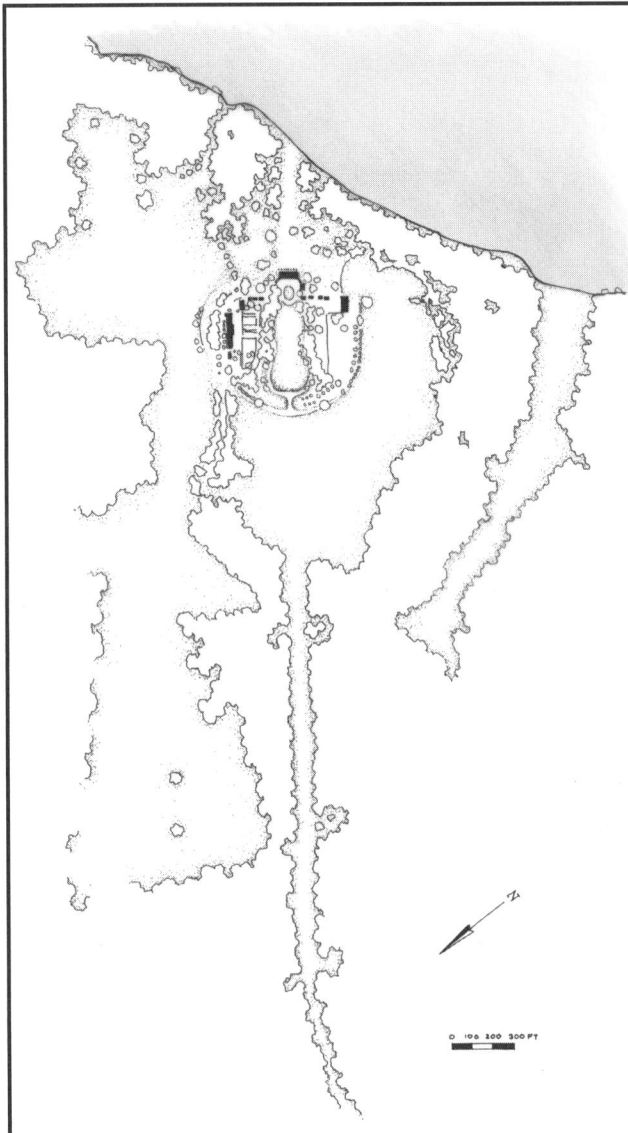

FERME ORNÉE: *George Washington's design for his estate at Mount Vernon was based on both artistic and rational planning principles.*

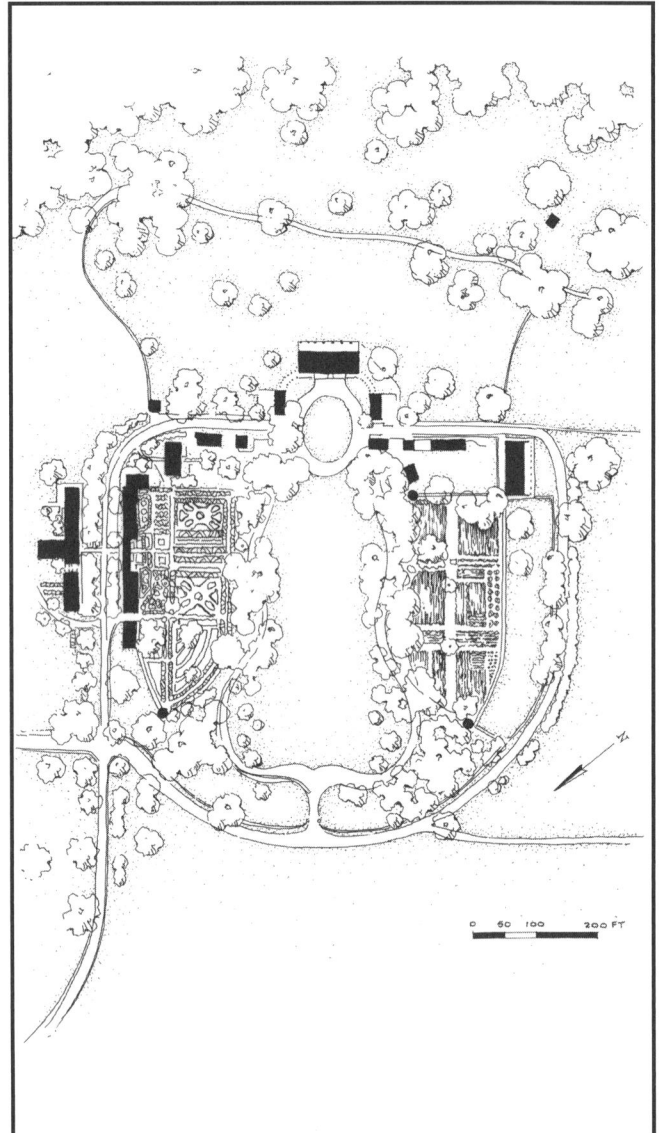

MOUNT VERNON, VIRGINIA: *The modest, coherent plan of Mount Vernon reflects the values of a gentleman farmer.*

A FARMER-PRESIDENT

The Arcadian ideals expressed in the 18th-century English landscape garden appealed to the sons of liberty in the newly formed United States of America. George Washington was a keen plantsman and practical farmer. Although he read the English garden treatises that were illustrated with irregular geometries, his foremost priority in laying out the grounds of his estate at Mount Vernon, Virginia, was the improvement of his farm lands. Still, Washington sited his house to take advantage of picturesque views. A sloping lawn extended from the two-storied portico at the front of the house to the river. The entry drive was at the back of the whitewashed wood house. He unified the symmetrical plan with a curvilinear path, incorporating utilitarian areas and ornamental gardens around a bowling green and orchards. Washington mixed exotic plants with native species.

JEFFERSONIAN VILLAS

From 1784 to 1789, Thomas Jefferson was the American ambassador to France. He visited Marly and Versailles. He went to England in 1786 and toured the landscape gardens. While he was critical of the formality and ostentation at some gardens, he was impressed with the manipulation of sight lines and the prospects of pastoral scenery.[16] He hoped to adapt the naturalistic English garden style to the terrain and climate of Virginia. Beginning around 1771, Jefferson built Monticello as his private retreat, where he could pursue his studies of natural history and architecture. He developed a vernacular style by using local materials within a classical idiom. Jefferson laid out the grounds around a central lawn. Partially sunken corridors connected service buildings to the main house and kept slave activities out of sight.

MONTICELLO, VIRGINIA: Thomas Jefferson's long terraces and promenades introduced a degree of the picturesque to 18th-century American gardens.

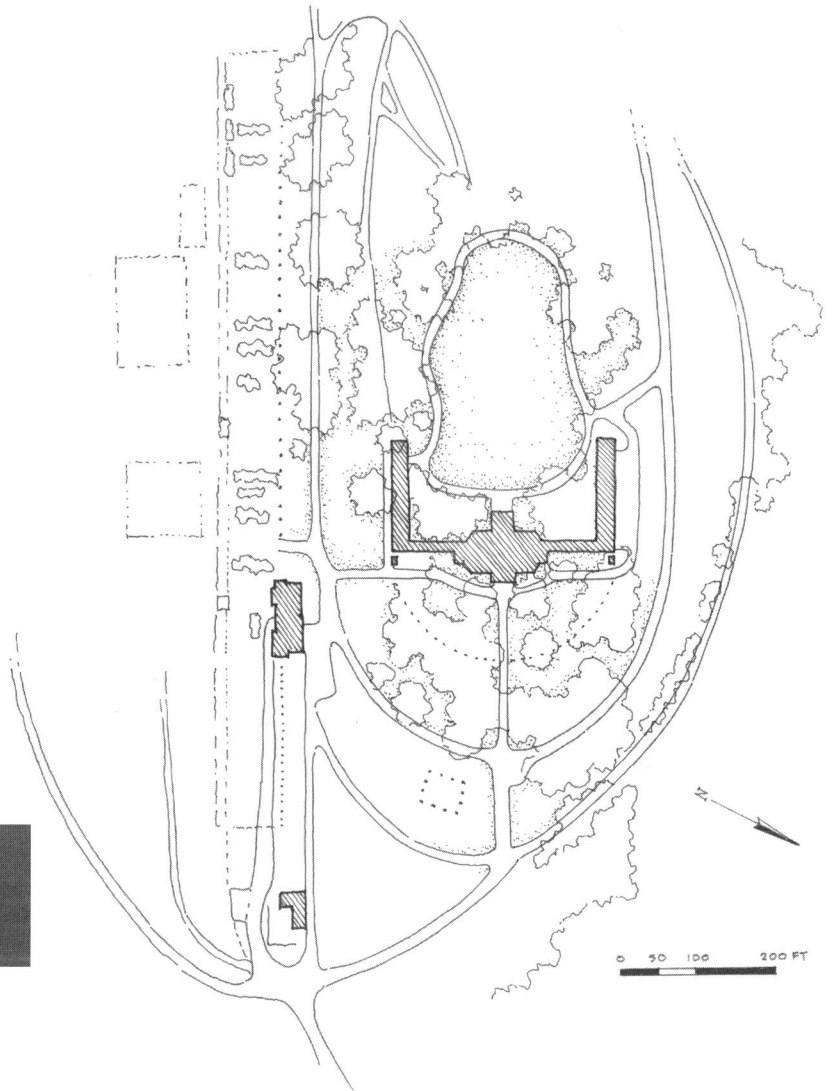

PALLADIAN CLASSICISM: Jefferson's house, with its Greek temple front and octagonal dome, recalled Palladio's Villa Rotonda and its precedent, the Pantheon in Rome.

Jefferson's design of his farm-estate at Poplar Forest truly represented the artful science of the Enlightenment. He referred to the 61-acre property as his "curtilage" or private sanctuary. The 10-acre homestead was a study in sophisticated proportional relationships. The house was sited by Jefferson to take advantage of specific views of distant ridgelines, and was the center point of a 540-foot-diameter circular drive. An axis formed by the entry drive and rear terrace was crossed by an *allée* of trees. The dimensions of the central room of the house were echoed on both sides by willow trees planted in a 20-foot square. The trees stand on 100-foot-diameter circular mounds; the mounds are connected to the house by 100-foot-long tree-lined *allées*. The bowling green behind the house is 100 feet wide.

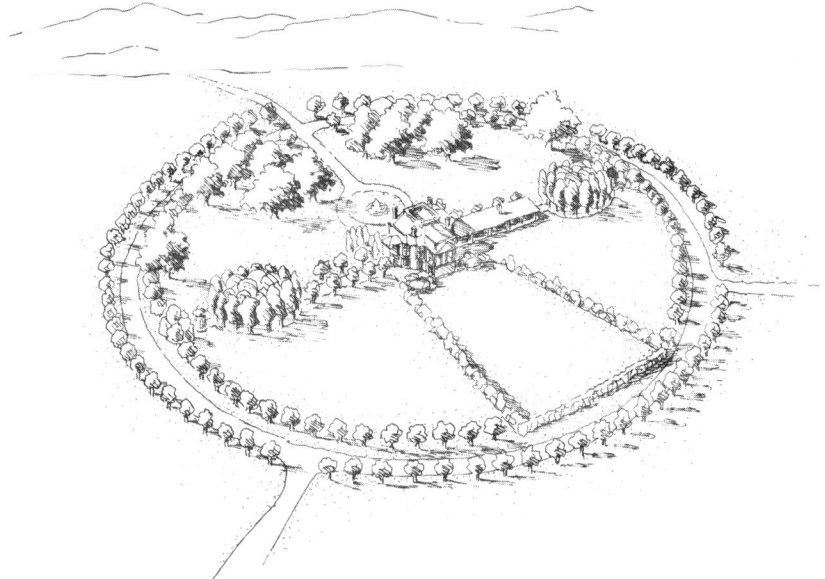

POPLAR FOREST, VIRGINIA: Jefferson's second farmstead was a perfect marriage of architecture and landscape. Archeological investigations at the site are ongoing.

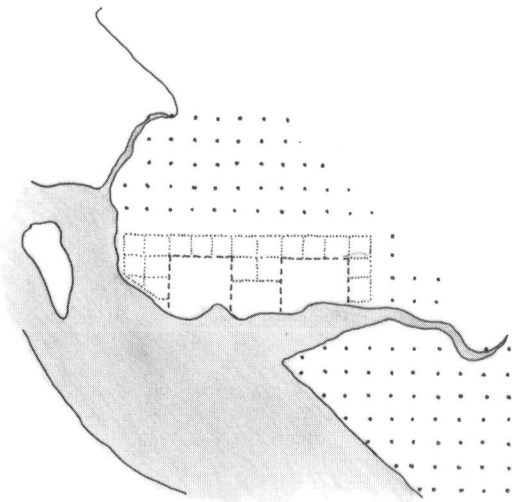

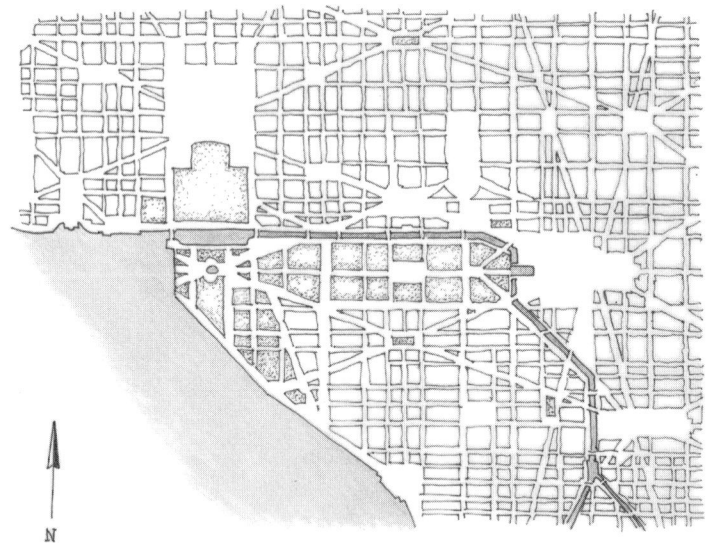

DISTRICT OF COLUMBIA: Jefferson's plan (left) for the proposed capital district shows the president's house and Capitol separated by public walks, and a grid infrastructure for future development. French-born citizen Pierre Charles L'Enfant, a veteran of the American Revolutionary War, developed a plan (right) expressive of French classical design ideas—a monumental grid intersected with diagonal avenues. He sited the president's house and the Capitol at right angles to each other and connected them through sight lines. He named the major thoroughfares after existing states and referenced their actual geographic location by their position within the new federal district.

SUMMARY

Curves, realized as sweeping lawns, serpentine lakes, and billowing trees, defined the "line of beauty" in the 18th-century English garden. Here, "landscape" became an adjective descriptive of an enlightened vision of uncorrupted nature—the garden. The tradition of the pastoral aesthetic as embodied in the English landscape garden influenced early American gardens and continues today in parks, campuses, and residential developments. The relationship between art and nature in 18th century Chinese gardens and its impact on English styles was also examined in this chapter.

DESIGN PRINCIPLES

FRAMING	ALLUSION	NARRATIVE	VARIETY	OBSERVATION
Garden scenes were viewed through intricate latticework windows and screens in Chinese gardens. Trees framed views of fields and hills in English gardens.	Both English and Chinese gardens contained visual references to literary passages. Naming and inscribing scenes assured common interpretations.	The heroic or patriotic theme of an English garden was made explicit through statuary and built form.	Picturesque gardens contained contrasting forms, textures, and lines.	Plants, landscapes, scenery—all of nature was scrutinized and classified during the Enlightenment.

DESIGN VOCABULARY

ENGLAND
Ha-has, Hills, and Lakes

CHINA
Pavilions, Walls, and Windows

AMERICA
Orchards, Lawns, and Prospects

For further exploration

BOOKS
CANDIDE, by Voltaire

DISCOURSE ON THE MORAL EFFECTS OF THE ARTS AND SCIENCES, by Jean-Jacques Rousseau

GULLIVER'S TRAVELS, by Jonathan Swift

MANSFIELD PARK, by Jane Austen

PRIDE AND PREJUDICE, by Jane Austen

ROBINSON CRUSOE, by Daniel Defoe

THE SOCIAL CONTRACT, by Jean-Jacques Rousseau

SYSTEMA NATURAE, by Linnaeus

FILMS
BARRY LYNDON (1975)

BRIDESHEAD REVISITED, television miniseries (1981)

DANGEROUS LIAISONS (1988)

THE DRAUGHTSMAN'S CONTRACT (1982)

MARIE ANTOINETTE (2006)

TOM JONES (1963)

PAINTINGS AND SCULPTURE
EIGHT-PLANKED BRIDGE (FOLDING SCREEN), by Ogata Korin (c. 1701)

PILGRIMAGE TO CYTHERA, by Jean Antoine Watteau (1717)

ROBERT ANDREW AND HIS WIFE, by Thomas Gainsborough (1748)

LANDSCAPE, by Alexander Cozens (1784)

PROJECT FOR A MEMORIAL TO ISAAC NEWTON, by Étienne-Louis Boullée (1784)

GEORGE WASHINGTON, by Jean-Antoine Houdon (1788)

THE DEATH OF MARAT, by Jacques-Louis David (1793)

19th CENTURY

The Enlightenment left in its wake a new concept of time and space. The Industrial Revolution eroded agrarian society. People moved into cities to supply the labor force required by factories. Urban populations swelled, causing concern for public welfare.

Industrial production defined the social, economic, and political order of the western world in the 19th century. The unquestioned belief in technology prompted a backlash: Romanticism became the antidote to the ills of mechanized society. For the middle class, emotion triumphed over reason, imagination was prized more than cultivated scholarship, and nature was elevated as the source of inspiration. Society believed sensitivity to natural phenomena and appreciation of natural beauty to be morally and spiritually uplifting.

The 19th-century landscape was urban, public, and Romantic.

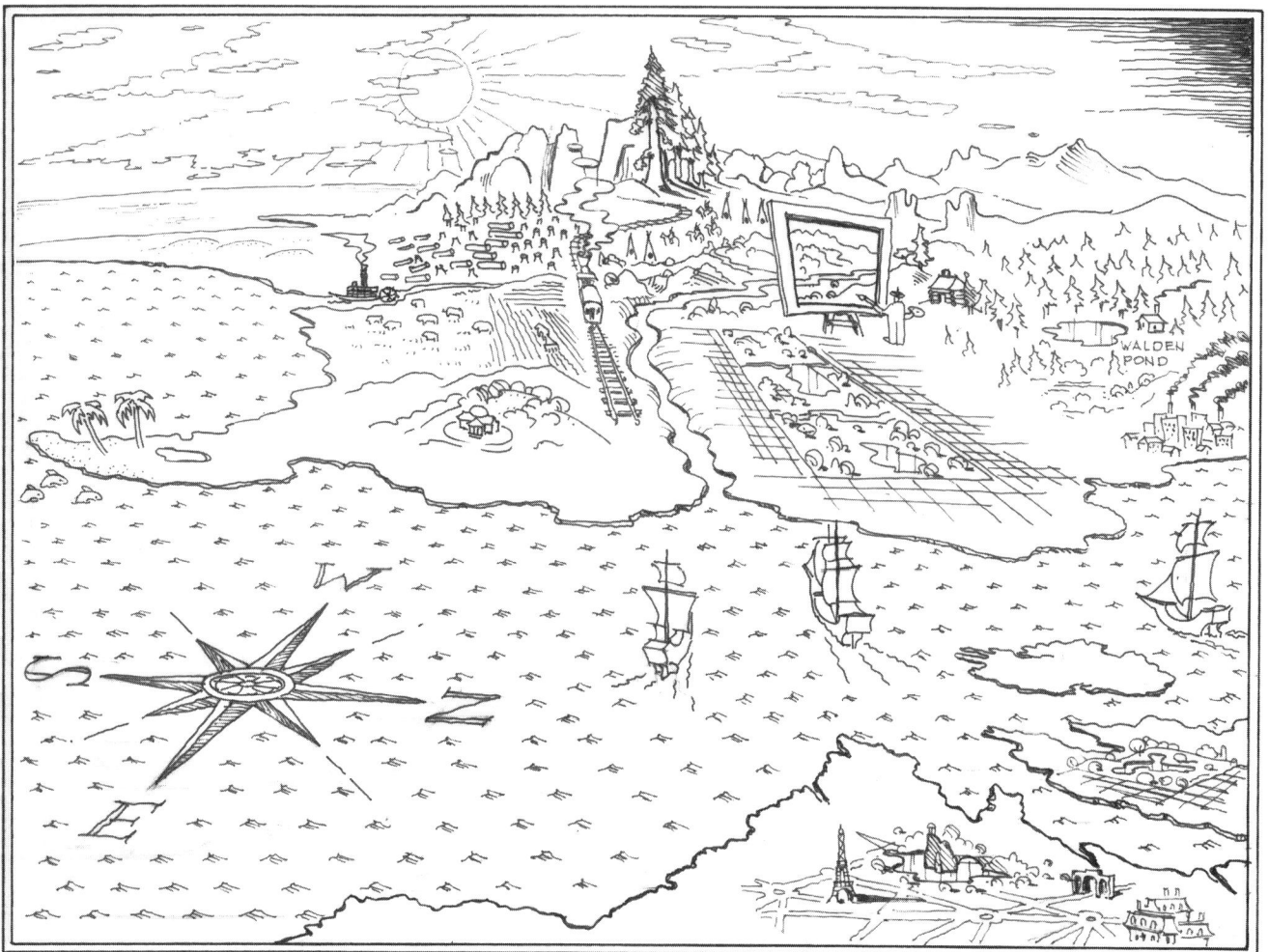

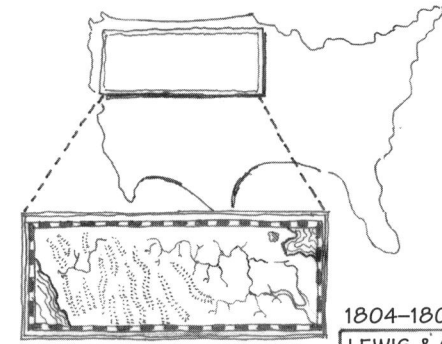

1804–1806
LEWIS & CLARK

1817
FLORILEGIUM

1800

1810

1820

1819
ÉCOLE DES BEAUX-ARTS

1822
JŌHHNY APPLESEED

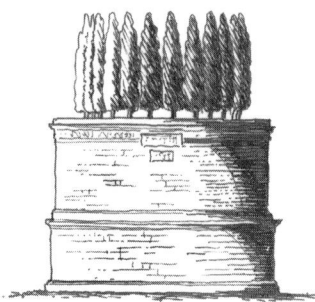

1861–1865
AMERICAN CIVIL WAR

1866
WHIRLED PEAS

1860

1860
OPIUM WAR

1868
MEIJI RESTORATION

1841
KEW GARDENS

1830
UKIYO-E

| 1830 | 1840 | 1850 |

1830
INDIAN REMOVAL
ACT

1859
ON THE ORIGIN OF SPECIES

1869
GOLDEN SPIKE

| 1860 | 1880 | 1890 | 1900 |

1869
SUEZ CANAL

1886
STATUE OF LIBERTY

1893
WATER LILIES

1899
ASLA

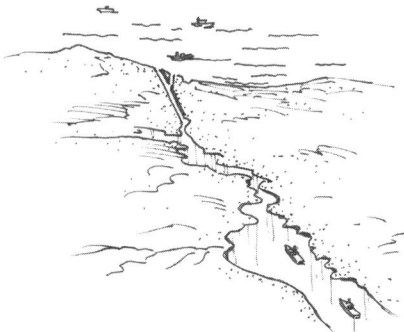

1804–1806 LEWIS AND CLARK
American president Thomas Jefferson sent two explorers out to the newly acquired western territories to inventory the terrain and plant life.

1817 FLORILEGIUM
Pierre-Joseph Redoute painted the 250 species of roses at Empress Josephine's garden at Malmaison, near Paris. *Les Roses* was one of his most famous albums of botanical illustrations.

1819 *ÉCOLE DES BEAUX-ARTS*
Napoleon I established a school of fine arts, training architects and artists in the neoclassical tradition.

1822 JOHNNY APPLESEED
John Chapman (1774–1845), missionary and nurseryman, distributed apple seeds across the Midwestern frontier.

1830 *UKIYO-E*
Hokusai and Hiroshige captured the bohemian life of Japanese actors and courtesans in colored woodblock prints. Later subjects included urban landscapes and nature scenes such as Hokusai's *Thirty-six Views of Mount Fuji.*

1830 INDIAN REMOVAL ACT
The railroad opened the American West to settlers and gold miners at the expense of Native Americans, who were forcibly removed to reservations and unclaimed western territories. In 1876, the Sioux defeated the U.S. Army at Little Bighorn—Custer's last stand. But the Indian victory was short-lived. In 1890, the Sioux were massacred at the battle of Wounded Knee Creek, in South Dakota.

1841 KEW GARDENS
Kew Botanic Gardens, a former royal property, opened to the public. Within five years it grew from 15 to 250 acres, attesting not only to the exponential growth in new plant introductions but also to the popularity of public gardens.

1859 *ON THE ORIGIN OF SPECIES*
Charles Darwin wrote a groundbreaking treatise on evolutionary biology, based on his voyages to the Galapagos Islands on the HMS Beagle in 1831.

1860 OPIUM WAR
The British burned the Yuanming Yuan in retaliation for the abuse of hostage British soldiers.

1861–1865 AMERICAN CIVIL WAR
Eleven southern states seceded from the Union over the issue of slavery, forming the Confederate States of America. Confederate General Robert E. Lee surrendered to Union commander Ulysses S. Grant at Appomattox after five years of bloody warfare.

1866 WHIRLED PEAS
Gregor Mendel discovered the laws of heredity, making possible plant hybridization.

1868 MEIJI RESTORATION
The Emperor of Japan was restored to power after 250 years of shogun rule, ending a long period of isolation and initiating economic and political reforms.

1869 GOLDEN SPIKE
The transcontinental railroad was completed in Promontory Point, Utah.

1869 SUEZ CANAL
An important trade route opened between the Mediterranean and the Red Sea, connecting Europe and Asia.

1886 STATUE OF LIBERTY
Lady Liberty was given to the people of the United States by the people of France in celebration of the 1876 centennial of the signing of the Declaration of Independence.

1893 WATER LILIES
Artist Claude Monet acquired a neighboring property in Giverny, France, to construct a water garden. His garden served as the inspiration for many of his impressionist landscape paintings.

1899 ASLA
The American Society of Landscape Architects was founded by Beatrix Jones Farrand, Warren H. Manning, John Charles Olmsted, Frederick Law Olmsted Jr., Downing Vaux, Nathan Barrett, Daniel Langton, Charles N. Lowrie, Samuel Parsons Jr., George F. Pentecost Jr., and Ossian Cole Simonds.

THE VICTORIANS AND THEIR PLANTS

The landscape garden style, so popular in the 18th century, became less feasible in the changed economic circumstances of the 19th century. Large estates were expensive to maintain, and many property owners had to sell or split their estates into smaller units for development. Panoramic views were curtailed. Whereas Georgian society was dominated by the upper class and their landscape gardens, Victorian society was dominated by the middle class, who built smaller "suburban villas" around industrial centers. People's tastes were changing. Attention shifted from the scale of the wider landscape to the scale of the individual plant.

The Victorians were enthralled by the plethora of new plant species being introduced to England. They collected and displayed exotic plants with fervor. The invention of the Wardian case, the

BUDDING'S LAWN MOWER: Budding patented his lawn mower design in 1832. Its small size made easy work of cutting around intricate planting beds, and made lawns feasible for even the smallest gardens.

development of the glasshouse, and the proliferation of gardening literature all made gardening accessible and fashionable with the middle class.

The naturalist, fern enthusiast, and medical doctor Nathaniel Bagshaw Ward developed his glass case by accident. While studying butterflies, he buried a chrysalis in soil and sealed it in a glass jar. A fern, instead of a butterfly, emerged from this

perfect environment. Wardian cases, essentially miniature greenhouses, enabled live specimens rather than seeds to be transported from China, India, and North America, dramatically increasing the number of plants available to the trade. Ward also thought his case could be used to help the poor, who "might grow flowers, ferns and ivies for pleasure…and raise small salads, radishes, etc."[1]

The repeal of the glass tax in England in 1845 made the manufacture of sheet glass more economical. Small glasshouses were marketed to homeowners who were eager to include tender plants in their gardens. J. C. Loudon first developed the ridge-and-furrow system that Joseph Paxton later adapted to curved glass. The many contributions of these two men are discussed next.

Horticultural industries prospered from the middle-class zeal for flower and vegetable gardens. In addition to new technologies geared to the management of more modest-sized properties, numerous periodicals and magazines were devoted to small-scale gardening. Garden writers focused on botany rather than aesthetic theory. The inexpensive publications were eagerly read by the new class of homeowners. This emphasis on practicality was even recognized by Repton in the last decades of his career. The terraces, cutting gardens, and fountains that Repton added to his later landscape plans reflected his preoccupation with the more intimate functions of a garden.[2]

WARDIAN CASE: Glass cases protected plants displayed in the home from the poisonous fumes of gaslight.

J. C. LOUDON AND THE AMATEUR LANDSCAPIST

John Claudius Loudon (1783–1843) is known for his prolific contributions to the literature of landscape design and his progressive views on public space. He published *Gardener's Magazine* from 1826 to 1843, a popular source of garden information for the middle-class homeowner, who sought advice from periodicals rather than landscape designers. His *Encyclopedia of Gardening* (1822) was a compendium of historical styles and practices, collected from his travels abroad.

↓summary

Dedicated to the causes of the middle class, Loudon developed the gardenesque style as a way for small property owners to enjoy the landscape. He formulated different prototypical garden plans for a variety of lot sizes, which he categorized as first rate (10 acres), second rate (2–10 acres), third rate (1–2 acres), and fourth rate (1 acre and less). Loudon also supported the development of public parks. He designed the Derby Arboretum, which opened to the public in 1840, as an educational and recreational garden. He applied his gardenesque principles to the 11-acre site, which contained a central gravel promenade, a perimeter walk screened by trees, constructed mounds, and amenities such as restrooms,

↓area used for walking

↳free standing structure

pavilions, and benches. Plants and trees were labeled with botanical and common names, country of origin, and height at maturity.

Loudon suffered from rheumatic fever in his early life and eventually had to have his arm amputated. Despite this and other adversities, his career continued, due in part to the contributions of his wife, Jane. After John's death, Jane Loudon went on to publish dozens of articles and books on her own, including the popular *Gardening for Ladies* (1840) which profoundly influenced women's involvement with gardening.

SUBURBAN GARDENER (1838): Loudon believed that sketching the landscape was good practice for women gardeners.

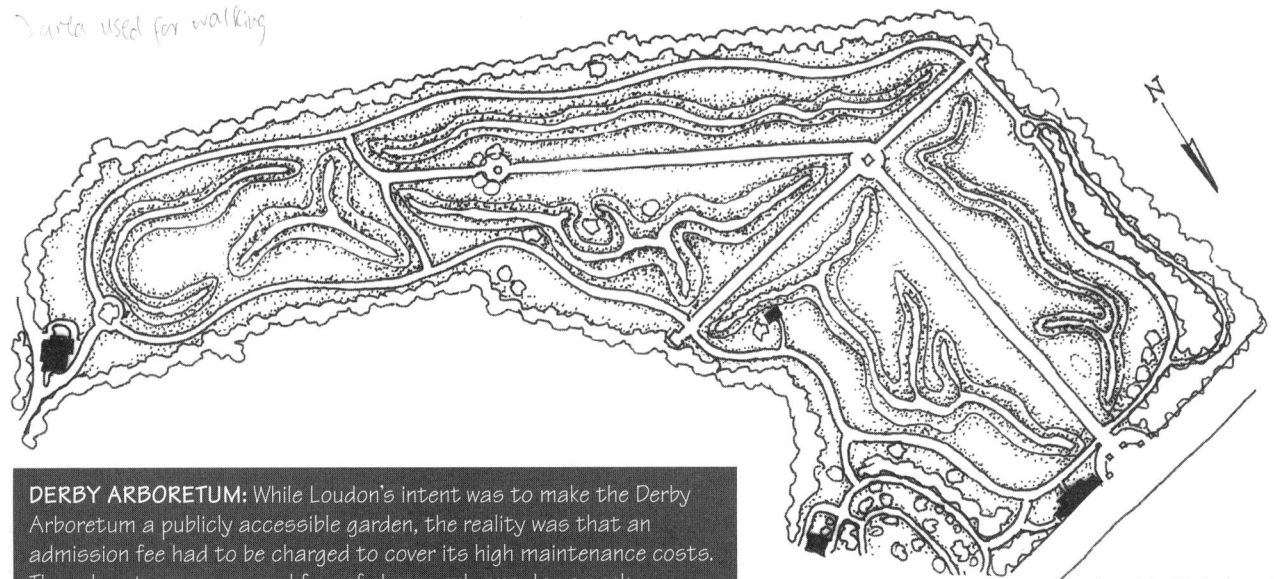

DERBY ARBORETUM: While Loudon's intent was to make the Derby Arboretum a publicly accessible garden, the reality was that an admission fee had to be charged to cover its high maintenance costs. The arboretum was opened free of charge only one day a week.

0 50 100   200 FT

THE PUBLIC AND PRIVATE SECTOR WORK OF JOSEPH PAXTON

Joseph Paxton (1803–1865) wore many hats in his career: He was head gardener and close friend to the sixth Duke of Devonshire; he authored and published several gardening journals; he designed buildings and engineered sites; he was a Fellow of the Horticultural Society, and an elected Member of Parliament. His innovations in glasshouse technology and his advocacy of public parks are two particular contributions we examine here.

Paxton built the conservatory (the "Great Stove") at Chatsworth in 1836, the largest glasshouse ever constructed at the time. He improved upon Loudon's system by replacing wrought iron elements with cast iron and wood. In 1850, he designed the Crystal Palace for the Great Exhibition in Hyde Park. Conservatories and winter gardens displayed rare plants, and were popular public attractions; smaller glasshouses, affordable by middle-class homeowners, were used for entertaining.[3]

The first park publicly funded and maintained, and opened to everyone, was Birkenhead Park in Liverpool, designed by Paxton in 1843. He excavated two lakes in the swampy site, and screened from view the extent of the water to create the illusion of distance. Constructed islands, as well as small hills and mounds, created layers of visual interest. The park opened in 1847. Frederick Law Olmsted visited the park in 1850 and was particularly impressed by its unique circulation system, which separated carriage traffic from pedestrian traffic.

The concern for social welfare in the 19th century was prompted in part by a general awareness of the detrimental effects of industrial development and the paternalistic concept of *noblesse oblige.* Public parks were a response to unchecked urban growth and the unsani-

CRYSTAL PALACE: Built around an existing tree, Paxton's glasshouse was nearly 1,900 feet long.

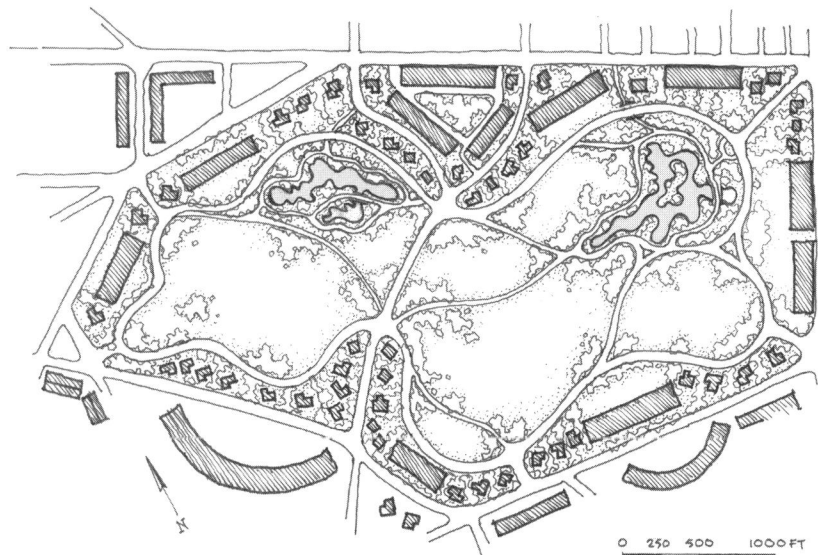

BIRKENHEAD PARK, LIVERPOOL: Paxton's unique circulation system influenced Olmsted's scheme for Central Park.

tary conditions of cities. But in addition to being morally uplifting, parks were also regarded by developers as potentially profitable—housing lots were sold along the parks' boundaries. Paxton was first to develop the idea of "subscription plots" to help make public parks economically feasible.[4]

THE CONTINUING SAGA OF STYLES

The stylistic controversies that raged at the end of the 18th century were stirred up again by garden theorists at the end of the 19th century. The debate this time was centered on aspects of "formal" and "informal" styles.

Formal styles were characterized by the revival of "architectural" gardens—planting areas defined by built elements and strong geometries. Often these parterres contained colorful flowers arranged in mosaic-like patterns and changed seasonally, a practice known as carpet bedding. Hundreds of gardeners were required for "bedding out"—putting tender plants in the open ground during the summer months. Plants numbered in the tens of thousands, a symbol of the status of the owner.[5]

Bedding out was a result of Loudon's idea of the gardenesque taken to an extreme. Loudon, a prolific and influential writer, was at first critical of Brown's and Repton's landscape gardens, siding with Price and the advocates of the picturesque. After traveling to the continent and visiting the great European gardens, Loudon came to appreciate the formal geometries that were so clearly of "art" rather than "nature." He proposed a

THE GARDENESQUE: Plants did not touch each other in gardenesque planting schemes.

CARPET BEDDING: Gardeners clipped dwarf foliage plants and perennials like lobelia, salvia, and verbena into knots, monograms, and clocks.

new style, termed the gardenesque, that reflected popular interest in the aesthetic qualities of plants and the practice of horticulture.

The gardenesque was a particular style of planting wherein each plant was displayed individually, expressing the artistic talents of the gardener, not the ideals of the owner or designer. Lawn was kept away from planting areas, and ample room was provided for cultivation and maintenance. The viewer's focus was on the individual character of a tree or shrub, not on the mass of vegetation or the wider landscape scene. Loudon's theory was that a garden is a work of creative artistry, not an imitation of nature. He believed gardens should be composed with specimen plants of unusual form, particularly exotic species, unified in some ordered scheme. Unfortunately, the result was often an unrelated collection of plants, not the structured composition Loudon envisioned.

Critics reacted against the stiffness of bedding out and the eclecticism of the gardenesque. William Robinson (1838–1935) referred to the geometrical presentation of plants as "degrading the true garden art to the level of the pastrycook's notions of design."[6] He suggested that people inclined to these practices limit themselves to wallpaper and rug design. In his book The Wild Garden, published in 1870, he proposed a natural approach to planting based on the horticultural needs and artistic qualities of the plants. He advocated the use of herbaceous borders mixed with wildflowers as a way to merge the gardenesque with the picturesque. Masses of shrubs could be broken up by outlying plants, softening the perimeter. In his book of 1883, The English Flower Garden, Robinson cataloged all the new plant species introduced in the 19th century and focused on creating low-maintenance habitats. The book ran for many editions.

In opposition to the informal style pro-posed by Robinson, Reginald T. Blomfield (1856–1942) called for a return to formality. In 1892, he wrote *The Formal Garden in England*, citing the Italianate terrace garden as the perfect example of garden art. The controversy raged until art and nature met in the partnership of architect Edwin Lutyens (1869–1944) and landscape designer Gertrude Jekyll (1843–1932). Jekyll was a disciple of Robinson's. She trained as a painter and developed planting design theories based on principles of form, texture, and color. Jekyll was advised to give up painting be-cause of her bad eyesight, so she turned her attention full-time to gardening. She was a steady contributor to *Country Life* magazine in the 1890s, and wrote her first book, *Wood and Garden,* in 1899. Lutyens created the structural geometry for Jekyll's softscape. His highly detailed forms, built with local materials, were the perfect complement to her sweeping strokes of flora.

HERBACEOUS BORDERS: Gertrude Jekyll developed William Robinson's ideas about naturalistic planting. She created distinctive perennial borders with large swaths of single colors.

THE ARTS AND CRAFTS MOVEMENT

The Industrial Revolution brought unprecedented change to the land-scape. Factories replaced home workshops. Trade boomed and popula-tion increased. Ten million people lived in England in 1800; the population had doubled by 1850, and doubled again by 1900. People increasingly moved to cities; London in 1830 was home to 1.5 million people.[7]

Author and critic John Ruskin (1819–1900) was one of the first people to question society's blind faith in tech-nology. He saw traditional landscapes and lifestyles deteriorate and called for the preservation of both. In 1848 a group of artists known as the pre-Raphaelites tried to revive traditional aesthetic values. They were particularly inspired by medieval craftsmanship and regarded the guild system as an answer to industrial order. The Arts and Crafts movement of the 1880s and 1890s was a response to the poor quality of machine-made goods and the process of mass production. Writer, designer, and socialist William Morris founded a decorative arts company whose work was based in the Arts and Crafts style. Morris used organic patterns and floral motifs, finding inspiration in nature. These Romantic impulses can be seen in the cult of the English cottage garden, with its straight paths and profusion of flowers, and in the development of the rural cemetery and garden suburb.

WILLIAM MORRIS & CO.: The floral mo-tifs in Morris's wallpaper designs were inspired by the plants in his garden.

REPUBLICS AND EMPIRES

In 1802, Napoleon Bonaparte (1769-1821) was elected consul for life by representatives of the people of France under the provisions of their new constitution (France's "first republic"). Two years later he appointed himself emperor and sought to dominate all of Europe (the "first empire"). After Napoleon's defeat at Waterloo in 1815, a constitutional monarchy was established by King Louis XVIII. Upon the king's death, his brother, ultra-royalist Charles X, assumed the throne. In 1830, Charles X acted to suppress the constitutional charter; political turbulence and social unrest followed. Liberal opponents of the king forced his abdication in favor of "citizen-king" Louis-Philippe. Rapid industrialization was taking its toll on the country. People wanted reform, and an overthrow of the old order. A Second Republic was formed by the assembly in 1848, and Louis-Napoleon (nephew of Napoleon Bonaparte) was elected president. In 1851 he dissolved the parliament and established the Second Empire, crowning himself as emperor Napoleon III. He ruled until 1871, when liberal opposition prevailed and a Third Republic was formed.

HAUSSMANNIZATION

Baron Georges-Eugene Haussmann (1809–1891) was appointed Prefect of the Seine (city manager) by Napoleon III in 1853. He implemented the emperor's plan for modernizing the city of Paris, which involved upgrading the existing infrastructure and adding new tree-lined boulevards, road junctions, green squares, and parks. The urban renewal campaign came at the expense of the working-class neighborhoods, which were destroyed during the "improvements." Ironically, the ideal of social reform had the effect of displacing the poor, forcing them out of the city limits.

Much like Pope Sixtus V created a system to link important sites in Rome during the Renaissance, the emperor and Haussmann overlaid a formal geometry on the medieval fabric of the city. The new street plan

HAUSSMANN'S PARIS: A geometry of order and control was imposed on the medieval fabric of Paris.

facilitated modern transportation and commerce, but was also a form of social control. Wide boulevards divided the city into manageable districts, and open spaces—places—were traffic nodes. Building codes established uniform heights for new structures. A grand opera house and other cultural institutions were built as part of Haussmann's plan.

An earlier renovation of the Champs-Elysées served as a precedent for Haussmann's urban vision. By 1836, the avenue extended from the Tuileries to the new Arc de Triomphe and was embellished with fountains, streetlights, and benches; theaters and restaurants were planned.[8] In 1858, Haussmann lengthened the avenue toward the Bois de Boulogne.

Haussmann appointed engineer-designer Jean-Charles-Adolphe Alphand (1817–1891) as head of the division of Promenades et Plantations, the agency responsible for carrying out the redevelopment plan. Alphand established a coherent design language for all

public spaces in the city. Between 1867 and 1873 he published two influential volumes on the architecture and urban design of Paris, which contained illustrations of his elegant curvilinear landforms and precisely detailed structures.[9]

PARIS PARKS

Haussmann's plan keyed public parks to the city's geography: Bois de Boulogne to the west, Bois de Vincennes to the east, Parc des Buttes-Chaumont to the north, and Parc Montsouris to the south.

The Bois de Boulogne, a former royal hunting park, was opened to the public by Louis XIV and given to the city in 1851. Radial allées and rond-points typical of French formalism inscribed the dense woodlands. Prior to the French Revolution, it was a fashionable location for the social promenade. Napoleon III was impressed by London's public parks and had Haussmann redesign the Bois de

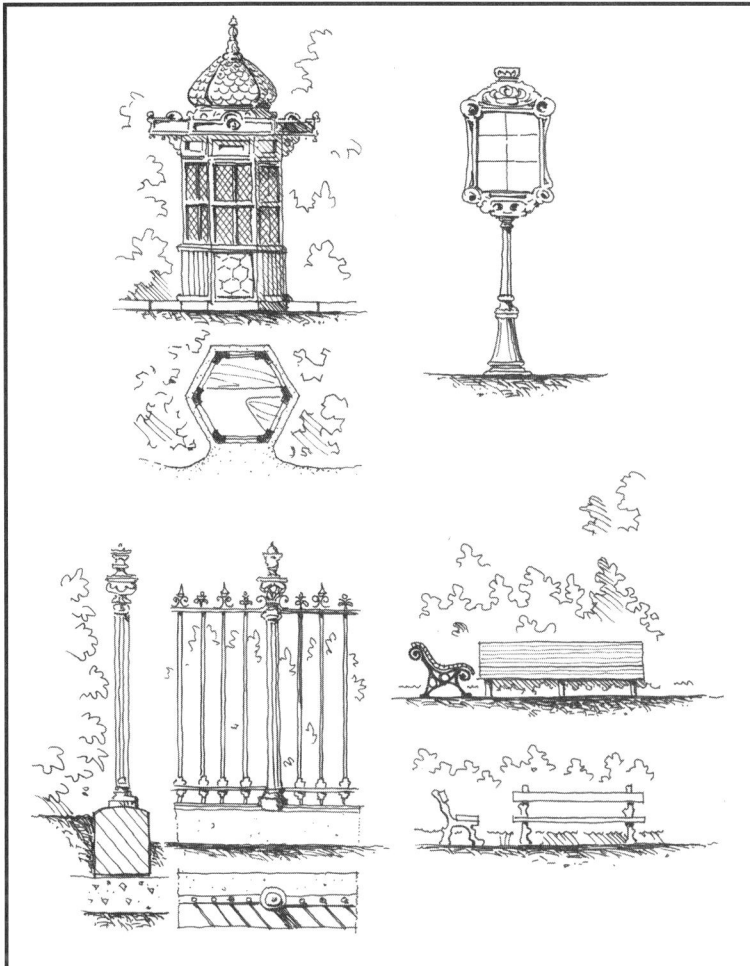

ALPHAND'S VOCABULARY: The highly detailed architectural elements created a unified design language across the city.

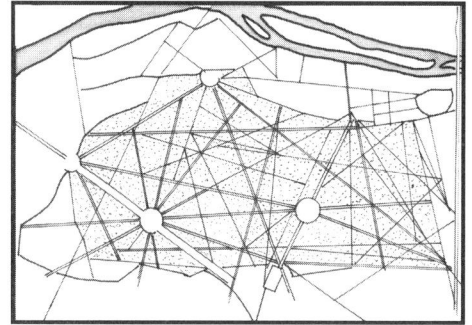

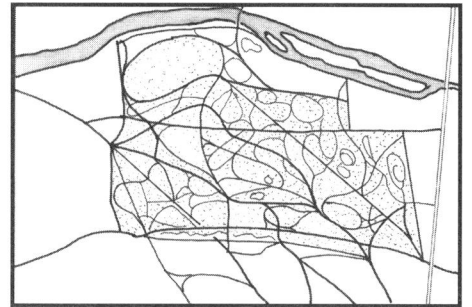

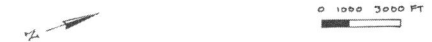

BOIS DE BOULOGNE: A naturalistic, English-style landscape replaced the formality of the 18th-century Baroque design.

PARC DES BUTTES-CHAUMONT: A former quarry was reborn as a public park. Picturesque prospects resulted from the sensuously curving path system and the tree planting scheme, both of which conformed to Alphand's dramatic re-grading of the terrain.

Boulogne in the English landscape style.[10] The refurbished park was a popular attraction; Olmsted met with Alphand in 1859 and toured the Bois de Boulogne.

Haussmann converted the Bois de Vincennes, a former military parade ground, to a public park in 1860. Located in the working-class section east of the city center, the park contained promenades like the Bois de Boulogne, so the "common people" would have equal opportunity to educate and improve themselves by imitating their more privileged neighbors.[11]

A former quarry in the northern section of the city created a naturally picturesque site for Parc des Buttes-Chaumont. Built from 1864–1867, the park contains a steep promontory that rises

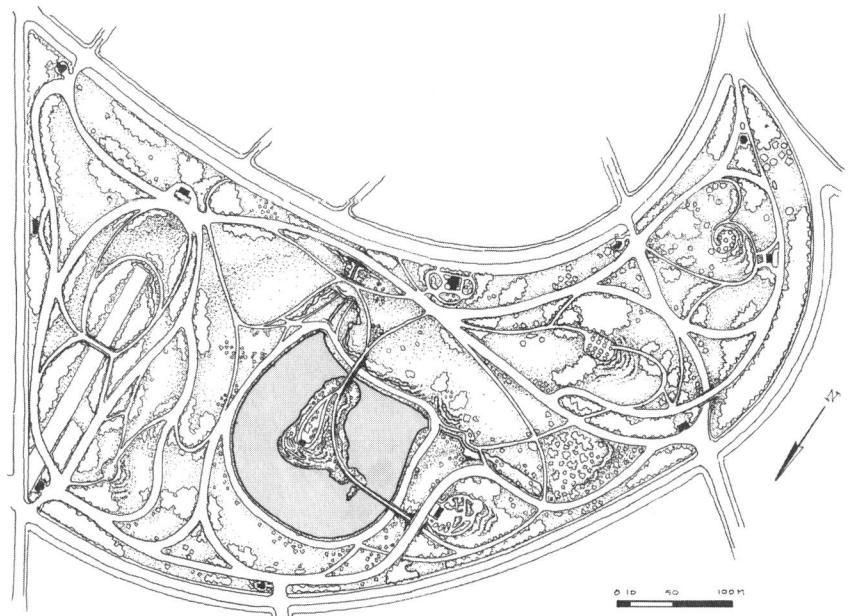

from a central lake. A suspension bridge connects the island with the banks. The cliff is topped with a circular temple. Classically themed follies coexist with grottoes and waterfalls.

Haussmann's plan also included the design of 24 neighborhood parks, decorated with Alphand's gates, streetlights, and furniture.

INTERNATIONAL EXPOSITIONS

During the 19th century, countries held world's fairs and exhibitions to show off their cultural advancements and technological achievements. The Great Exhibition of London in 1851 was followed by international exhibitions in Paris in 1855, 1867, 1878, and 1889. For the exhibition in 1889, celebrating the centennial of the revolution, Gustave Eiffel designed the iron tracery of the Eiffel Tower—at 984 feet high, it remains one of the tallest structures in the world.

"BRIDGE OF SUICIDES": A suspension bridge leads directly to a temple atop a steep cliff creating a thrilling experience for the 19th-century visitor.

TECHNOLOGICAL FEAT: Built for a world expo in 1889, the Eiffel Tower remains an icon of structural engineering.

LANDSCAPE ARCHITECTURE IN AMERICA

America in the 19th century was subject to the same impulses toward industrialization as Europe. People embraced technology as a means to achieve a comfortable lifestyle. In 1803, the size of the United States doubled with the acquisition of former French territories in the Louisiana Purchase.

Large-scale consequences to the environment were hard to imagine in a country of such immense proportions and seemingly infinite resources. But the impact of industrialization was more immediate for the urban dweller. As the century wore on and the frontier drew nearer, people reexamined their relationship to the landscape. The important contributions to the history of landscape architecture in 19th-century America were the public park and the idea of a wilderness aesthetic. What is particularly American about these land uses is the fact that citizen initiative was integral to their creation.

ACROSS THE CONTINENT, WESTWARD THE COURSE OF EMPIRE TAKES ITS WAY (1868): This popular Currier and Ives lithograph of a Frances Palmer painting expressed the nation's belief in manifest destiny.

ENGLISH PRECEDENTS FOR PUBLIC PARKS

England's Reform Bill of 1832 was symbolic of the increased social consciousness that followed on the heels of rapid industrialization. The government acknowledged the need for public green spaces as one aspect of social reform. The crown had opened royal properties to the public in the wealthier West End of London, but no comparable spaces existed in poorer neighborhoods. Parks were part of the housing developments that industrialists built in the 1830s, but these green spaces were surrounded by gates and accessible only to residents. Birkenhead Park in Liverpool, the first nonroyal property opened to the public, was one manifestation of

the progressive trend. However, its motivation was not only philanthropic; profits were to be made from developing adjacent lands.

Similar trends influenced the development of the urban landscape in America. The works of both Andrew Jackson Downing and Frederick Law Olmsted were shaped by the aesthetics of the English landscape garden and the ideals of social reform.

ANDREW JACKSON DOWNING (1815–1852)

Downing grew up in a town along the Hudson River, north of New York City. His early training was in horticulture. His book, *A Treatise on the Theory and Practice of Landscape Gardening, Adapted to North America*, written in

1841, expressed his affection for the "rural" landscape and his dedication to the artful design of middle-class residences (typically single-family country homes). His belief that environment influenced behavior formed the focus of his professional career. Downing's early support of the public's right to open space was crucial to the eventual realization of Central Park in Manhattan.

Downing considered the stylistic improvement of suburban properties a moral imperative and a patriotic duty. He believed that an inventory of finely designed houses and gardens—a mark of civilization and republican virtue—would give America the cultural caché it lacked in the eyes of the Europeans. Downing was an advocate of "taste," which he defined as "good proportions, pleasing form, and fitness for the use intended"—qualities he believed to be embodied by naturalistic-style gardens.[12] Downing reinforced the harmonious relationship between house and

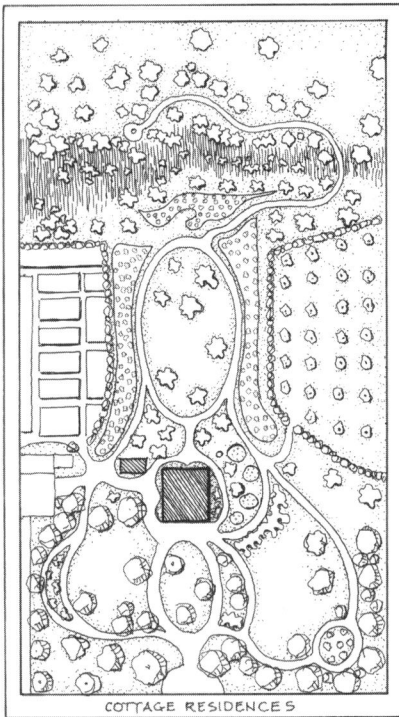

COTTAGE RESIDENCES

COTTAGE RESIDENCES: Downing offered prototypical plans for the design of small-scale gardens in his book, *Cottage Residences* (1842).

THE NEED FOR URBAN OPEN SPACE

With limited opportunity to enjoy outdoor space, people used cemeteries as pleasure grounds. Rural parklike cemeteries addressed the needs of growing urban populations in two ways. They provided access to landscaped space for recreational purposes and they insured public health by keeping burial sites away from populated areas. Church graveyards in cities were filled to capacity. The new, secularized cemetery was seen not just as a graveyard, but as a sentimental and inspirational landscape, much like Rousseau's tomb at Ermenonville. Nondenominational cemeteries became fashionable cities of the dead, ornamented with monu-

ments and sculptures. In 1804, Pere Lachaise Cemetery was planned by the city of Paris as one of the first cemeteries in which plots could be purchased in perpetuity. It was a blend of both formal and informal geometries. Curvy paths surrounded a central grid of straight avenues.

Mount Auburn Cemetery in Cambridge, Massachusetts, was developed in 1831 by the Massachusetts Horticultural Society as an experimental garden, arboretum, and cemetery. Its sweeping lawns, lakes, native trees, and exotic flowers were reminiscent of English landscape gardens, and became the vocabulary of park design. Cemetery administrators prohibited slab tombs; instead, urns, obelisks, and figurative sculpture helped create a picturesque scene. The popular appeal of cemeteries strengthened the lobby for public parks.

garden by suggesting improvements that were based on "beautiful" and "picturesque" principles. Typical elements included lawns, porches, vegetable gardens, and ornamental planting. His forms were based on curvy geometries.

Downing met the architect Calvert Vaux (1824–1895) in England and persuaded him to join his practice in New York. Vaux later formed an equally influential partnership with Olmsted.

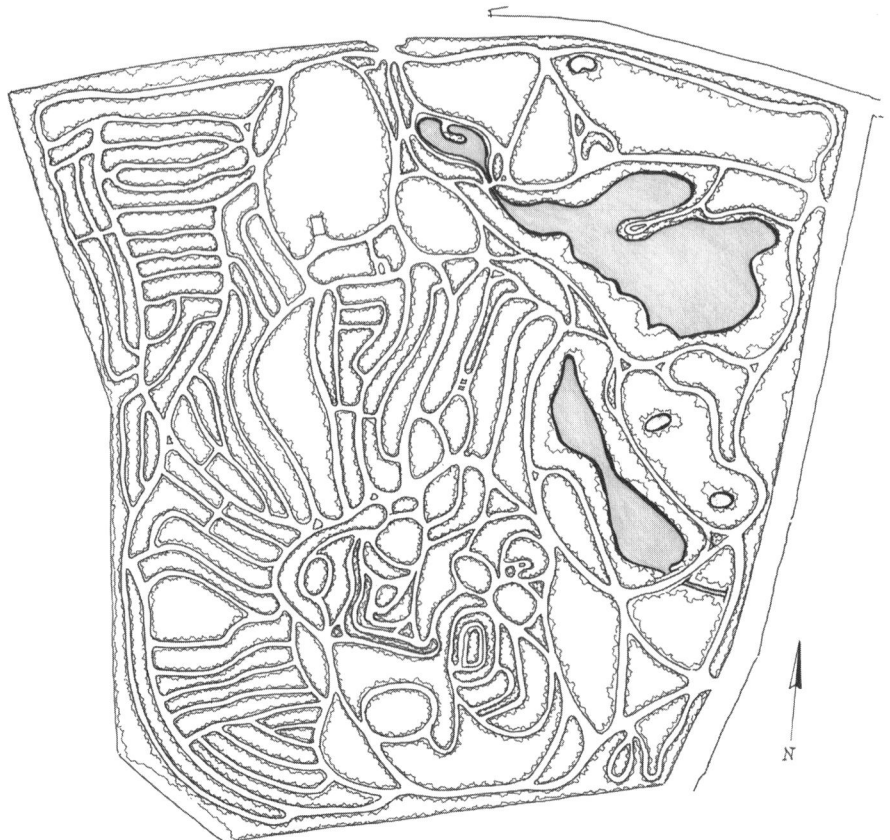

MOUNT AUBURN CEMETERY: Pathways followed the natural contours of the land.

RURAL ROMANTICISM: People used cemeteries as pleasure grounds before public parks were built. Monuments and sculptures created architectonic focal points against a picturesque background. The idea of commemorating a person's earthly life and achievements represented the individualism characteristic of the 19th century.

FREDERICK LAW OLMSTED (1822–1903)

Olmsted was a gentleman farmer who had a keen interest in the cultural landscape. He traveled widely and published his accounts of vernacular landscapes, agricultural practices, and social issues.[14] He toured the English landscape in 1850 and commented on the success of Birkenhead Park.

CENTRAL PARK

Olmsted teamed up with Calvert Vaux to enter the competition for the design of Central Park in New York City. Their winning entry, the Greensward Plan, preserved the wooded area and exposed bedrock in the middle part of the site, south of the reservoir, which they called "The Ramble." Extensive site engineering was necessary to create the many lakes and sloping lawns within the park. They included a formal pedestrian mall and terrace to accommodate society's need to see and be seen. The perimeter they screened with trees. The total area of parkland eventually covered 843 acres—an area about 2–1/2 miles long, and 1/2 mile wide. The project brief necessitated

Waves of European immigration in the mid-19th century added urgency to the campaign for public open space in New York City. The cause was taken up in the press with support from Downing and William Cullen Bryant, poet, and editor of the *Evening Post*. After much deliberation and partisan politics, the city secured state funding and purchased a site. A board of commissioners was set up by the state, and in 1857 they appointed Frederick Law Olmsted to oversee the project. Land values around the proposed park skyrocketed once the existing tenant farmers, squatter villages, and noxious industries were cleared. Seneca Village, an African-American settlement, was destroyed. Many immigrant populations were displaced to make way for the new "people's" park.[13]

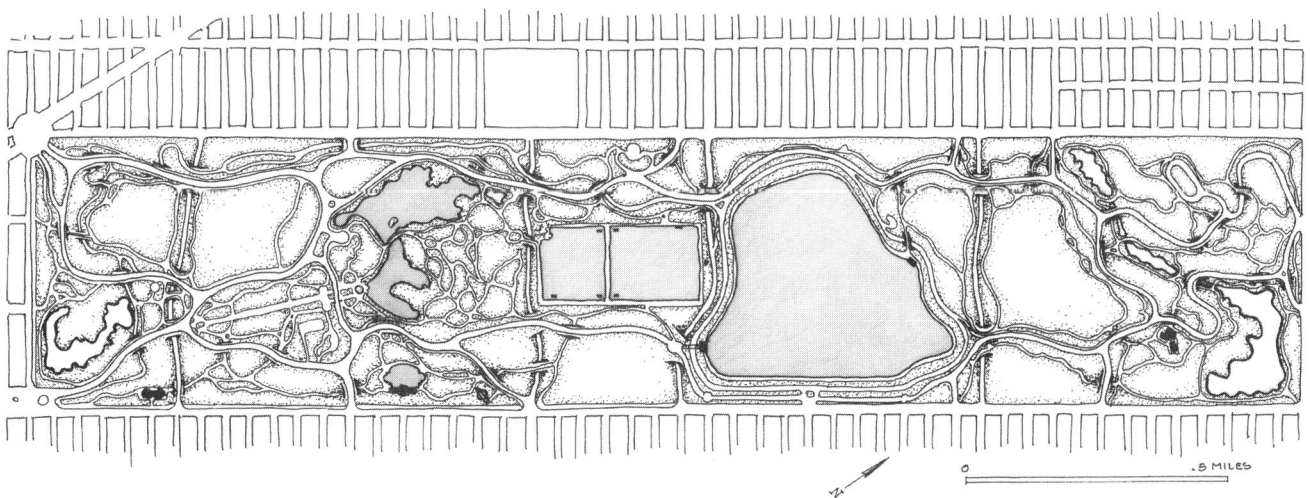

CENTRAL PARK: Olmsted and Vaux overcame the challenges of the orthogonal site and planted an English landscape garden within the grid of Manhattan.

LITTLE NEMO'S AIRSHIP FLIES OVER CENTRAL PARK IN 1910

THIS IS CENTRAL PARK! IT IS A HALF A MILE WIDE, ALMOST 3 MILES LONG & THE MOST BEAUTIFUL PARK IN THE WORLD

AND RIGHT IN THE HEART OF THE CITY TOO

MIDTOWN MANHATTAN, c. 1910.

that four cross streets be included in the plan. Olmsted and Vaux's innovation was to depress these arteries beneath the paths that ran lengthwise through the park, thereby separating all the different modes of circulation—pedestrian, equestrian, and carriage.

Humanitarian ideals motivated Olmsted. He saw public parks as a means of escape from the oppressive conditions of cities. He believed that access to nature was physically therapeutic and psychologically uplifting for the working class.[15] His plan included a dairy, where refreshment was available for women and children. But boating and skating, not the field sports of the working class, were the only organized sports originally accommodated in Central Park. He also disdained the incorporation of monuments and cultural institutions in the park, although the Metropolitan Museum was first included in 1880, and other architectural features, such as the Bethesda Terrace, help structure the landscape space.

Periods of administrative conflict and political turmoil marked the progress of the park's construction. At one point, the designers resigned their posts,

signing their letters with the title "landscape architects." This momentous designation helped define the scope of the future profession.

PROSPECT PARK

In 1866, Olmsted and Vaux collaborated on the design of Prospect Park in Brooklyn. The 526-acre park was constructed over an 8-year period, under much more congenial political circumstances and on a site with much fewer programmatic and topographic constraints. Prospect Park presented opportunities for the scenic choreography of space. The main entrance to the park is through an underpass in the northern boundary. The visitor is drawn into the sweeping space of the Long Meadow; sight lines continue to pull one through the space as new vistas open up around trees and curving lakes.

PARK SYSTEMS

Olmsted's vision was to go beyond the creation of an isolated urban park and develop a continuous network of open spaces within a city. Olmsted and Vaux developed a park system for Buffalo, New York, in 1868. Landscaped boule-

PROSPECT PARK: Picturesque prospects are afforded by the irregular geometries of the site.

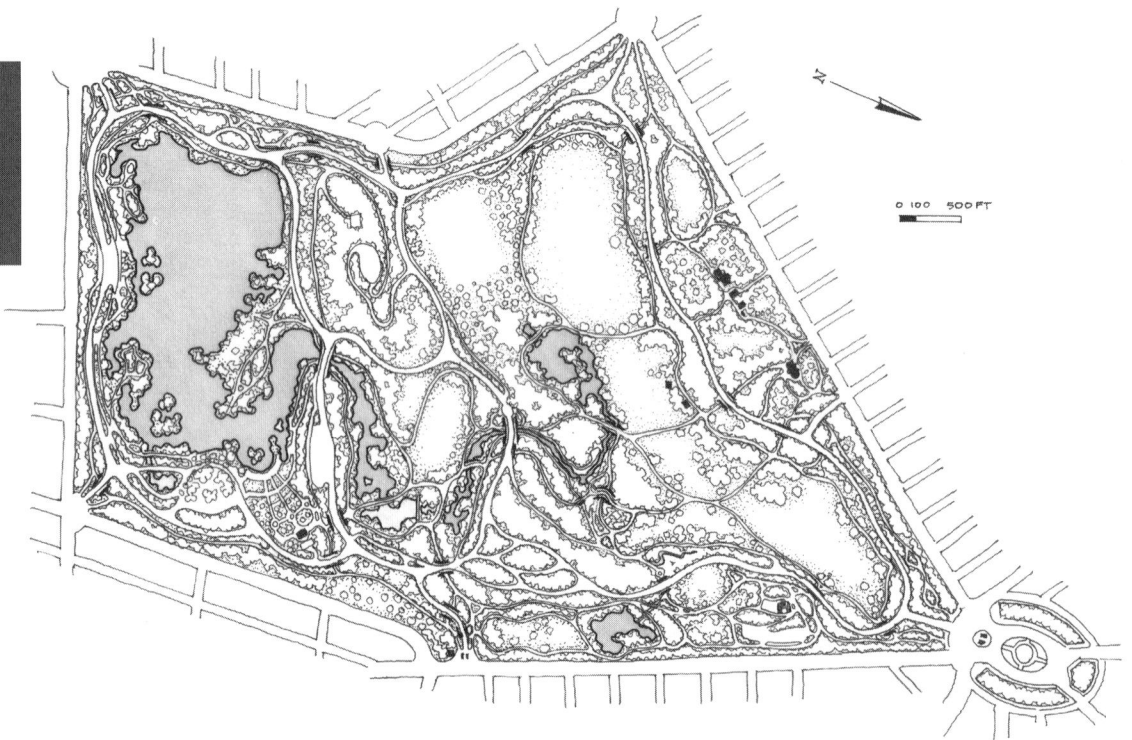

0 100   500 FT

VISUAL NARRATIVE: *Prospect Park*

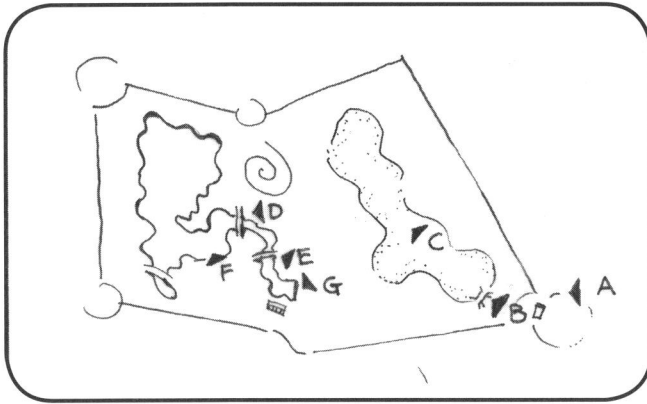

vards, 200 feet wide, connect Delaware Park, the 350-acre centerpiece, with The Front, located on Lake Erie, and The Parade, on the eastern edge of the city. Olmsted began planning Boston's "Emerald Necklace" in 1875, initially as a drainage and flood control project along the Back Bay Fens. He went on to develop a linear greenway that linked the Boston Common with Jamaica Pond, the Arnold Arboretum and Franklin Park, the 500-acre "jewel."

BILTMORE ESTATE

The Biltmore estate, in Asheville, North Carolina, was Olmsted's last private commission. Richard Morris Hunt designed the French-style chateau for George Vanderbilt. Olmsted began to develop the site plan in 1888. A 3-mile-long approach road winds through the 250-acre estate, terminating in a formal entry court. The contrast of the picturesque experience with the sudden presentation of formal geometries heightened the drama of the visitor's arrival. The esplanade is defined by two *allées* that continue the lines of the mansion. Parallel to the esplanade is the lower parterre known as the Italian Garden. Further down the slope are the walled flower and vegetable gardens and the Conservatory. A woodland vernal garden borders a low-lying stream. Olmsted collaborated with Gifford Pinchot in 1898 to develop a school for scientific forestry on the grounds, the extents of which reached over 120,000 acres.

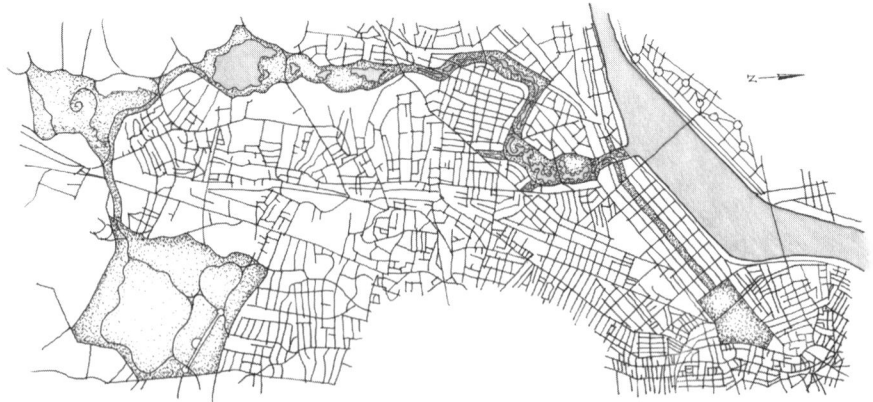

EMERALD NECKLACE: A network of parks and greenways ring the city.

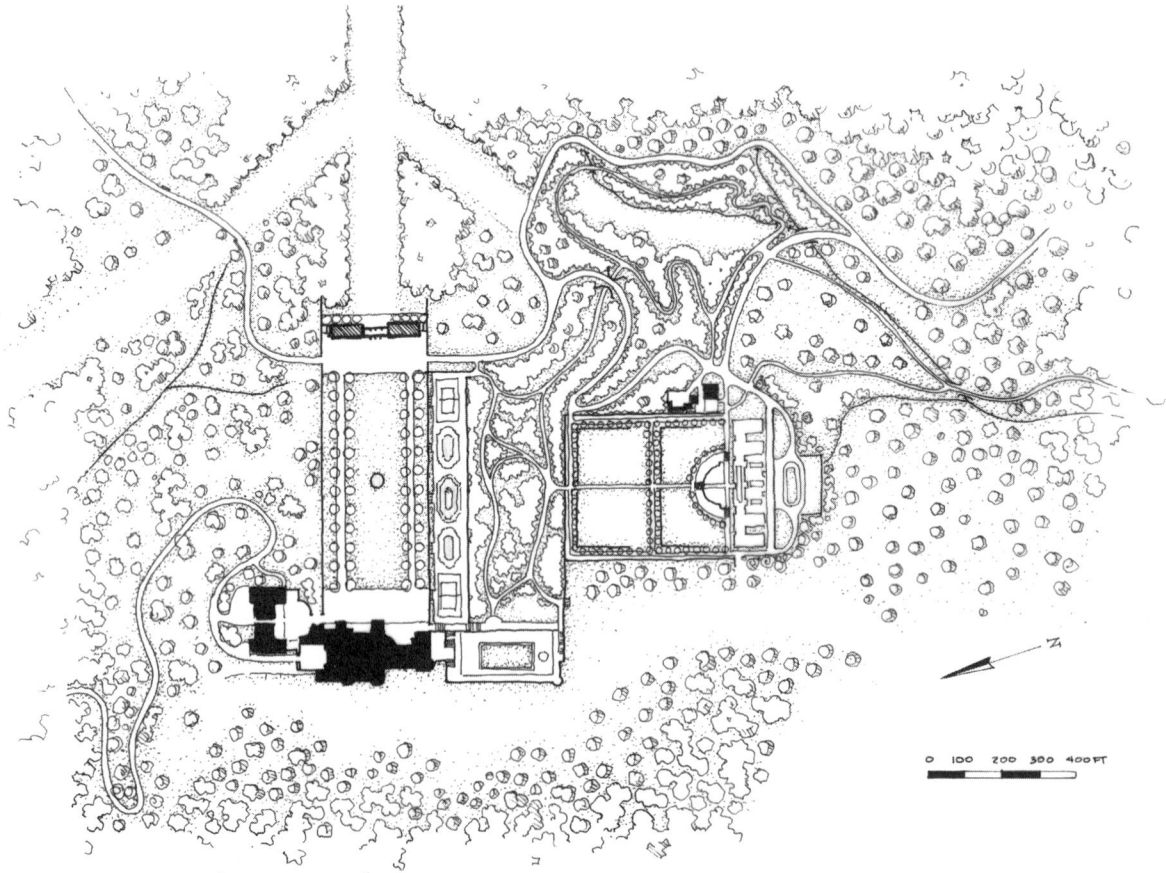

0 100 200 300 400 FT

BILTMORE ESTATE: In addition to an eclectic mix of gardens, the estate contained a school of scientific forestry.

VISUAL NARRATIVE: *Biltmore*

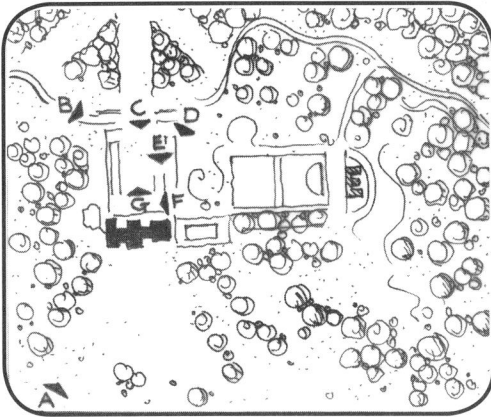

ROMANTIC IDEALS OF NATURE

The social reform movement and the cause for wilderness preservation can both be understood as Romantic efforts to counter the negative consequences of the Industrial Revolution. Artists and writers came to appreciate nature as an aesthetic object in the 19th century. They celebrated in their work the awe-inspiring phenomena and natural scenery that they believed was capable of transforming one's soul. Transcendentalists like Henry David Thoreau, Ralph Waldo Emerson, and Walt Whitman saw in untamed nature the hand of God. The Hudson River School painters were the first to treat the landscape as a legitimate genre in itself, devoid of any classical imagery. They were instrumental in developing a sense of pride and value in the unique American landscape.

NATIONAL PARKS

The idea of a "nation's park" is deeply rooted in the American character. The breathtaking landscape of the American West, first known only to Native Americans, was astonishing to early explorers. Yosemite Valley, in California, and the Wyoming territory called Yellowstone captivated the young republic's Romantic imagination.

John Colter, a member of the Lewis and Clark Expedition, along with other explorers and trappers, spoke of the astounding scenic wonders and frightful natural phenomena in the West.[16] Decades later, in the 1870s, the government sponsored expeditions to the Montana and Wyoming territories. Thomas Moran was one of the artists who accompanied the 1871 expedition. He captured the overwhelming majesty of the landscape and helped inspire the public's recognition of the landscape as a unique treasure. The expedition returned with the suggestion that the magnificent natural scenery be preserved as a public park. Under the provisions of the Yellowstone Act of 1872, the area was established as the

TWILIGHT IN THE WILDERNESS, 1860: Frederick Edwin Church and the Hudson River School painters helped define a distinct American art form.

first national park, "for the benefit and enjoyment of the people."

The landscape of Yosemite Valley was equally valued as an icon of American identity. During a sabbatical from his work on Central Park, Olmsted accepted a post with the Mariposa Mining Company to oversee operations in the Sierra Nevada. From 1863–1865 Olmsted undertook a series of commissions in northern California. Most significant was his appointment by the governor to develop a management plan for Yosemite Valley, which was designated a state park in 1864.

YOSEMITE

The public's first glimpse of Yosemite Valley was through the photographs of Carleton Watkins, the drawings of Thomas Ayres, and the large-format paintings of Albert Bierstadt. Many artists depicted the same view, creating iconographic images of humans dwarfed by the great mountains, trees, and waterfalls. American character came to be defined by the idea of rugged individualism—by wilderness unlike any other in the world.

The 1890 census declared the frontier officially closed.[17] Suddenly, Americans sought to retain the wilderness areas that had become critical to their national identity. The Romantic sentiment of the 19th century planted the seeds of a conservation and wilderness ethic.

Opinions differed on how the landscape should be preserved. John Muir, a naturalist, environmental observer, and founder of the Sierra Club, advocated a preservation ethic and concluded that nature should be left alone. He supported public ownership of wilderness areas. Gifford Pinchot, a forester, advocated a conservation ethic based on the wise use and management of resources through scientific principles such as sustained yield of forests.

THE GRAND CANYON OF THE YELLOWSTONE RIVER, 1871: Thomas Moran's paintings introduced the majesty of the American West to the public.

VALLEY OF THE YOSEMITE, 1864: Albert Bierstadt's paintings were known for their luminous atmospheric effects.

Muir's relationship with President Theodore Roosevelt was key to the setting aside of public lands to be established as national parks. Early 20th-century environmental legislation created the National Forest Service, in 1905, and the National Park Service, in 1916. Stephen Mather, the first chief of the Park Service, determined criteria for designating park land (scenic value, scientific value, or historic value) and developed master plans for the management of each site.

WORLD'S COLUMBIAN EXPOSITION OF 1893

The conceptualization and representation of America's unique wilderness helped the nation compete culturally with Europe. In addition to artistic production, countries sought to showcase on the world stage their industrial and technological advancements. International expositions and world's fairs were popular 19th-century attractions.

America had emerged as an agricultural and economic leader, and by the second half of the 19th century, a political and industrial power. The World's Columbian Exposition was held in 1893 to showcase American progress since Columbus's arrival 400 years earlier. The City of Chicago beat out St. Louis, New York City, and Washington, DC, to host the event. It became known as the Chicago World's Fair.

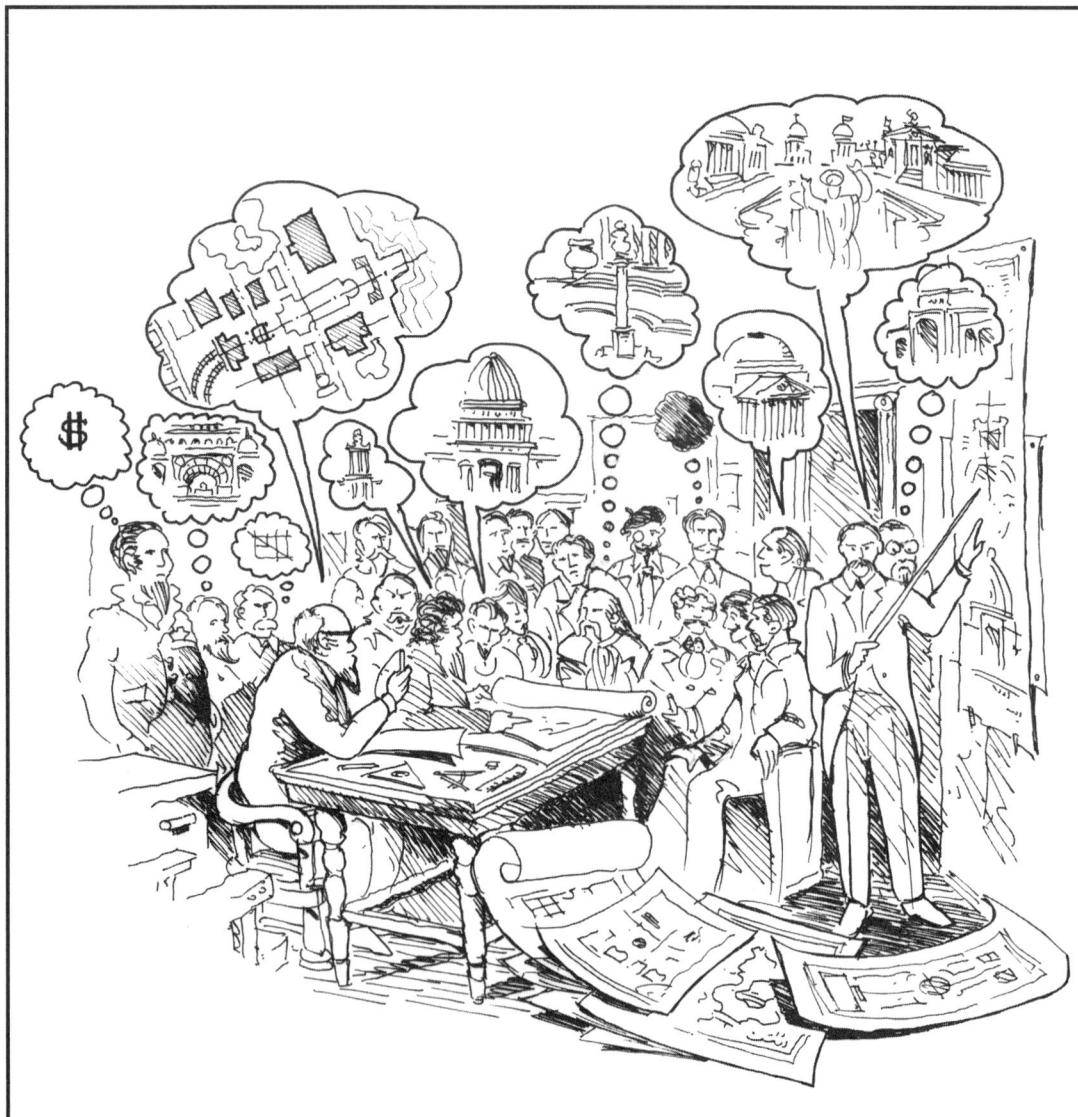

MEETING OF THE MINDS: The World's Columbian Exposition brought together artists, sculptors, architects, and landscape designers, initiating a collaborative approach to design.

CASE STUDY: *Chicago World's Fair*

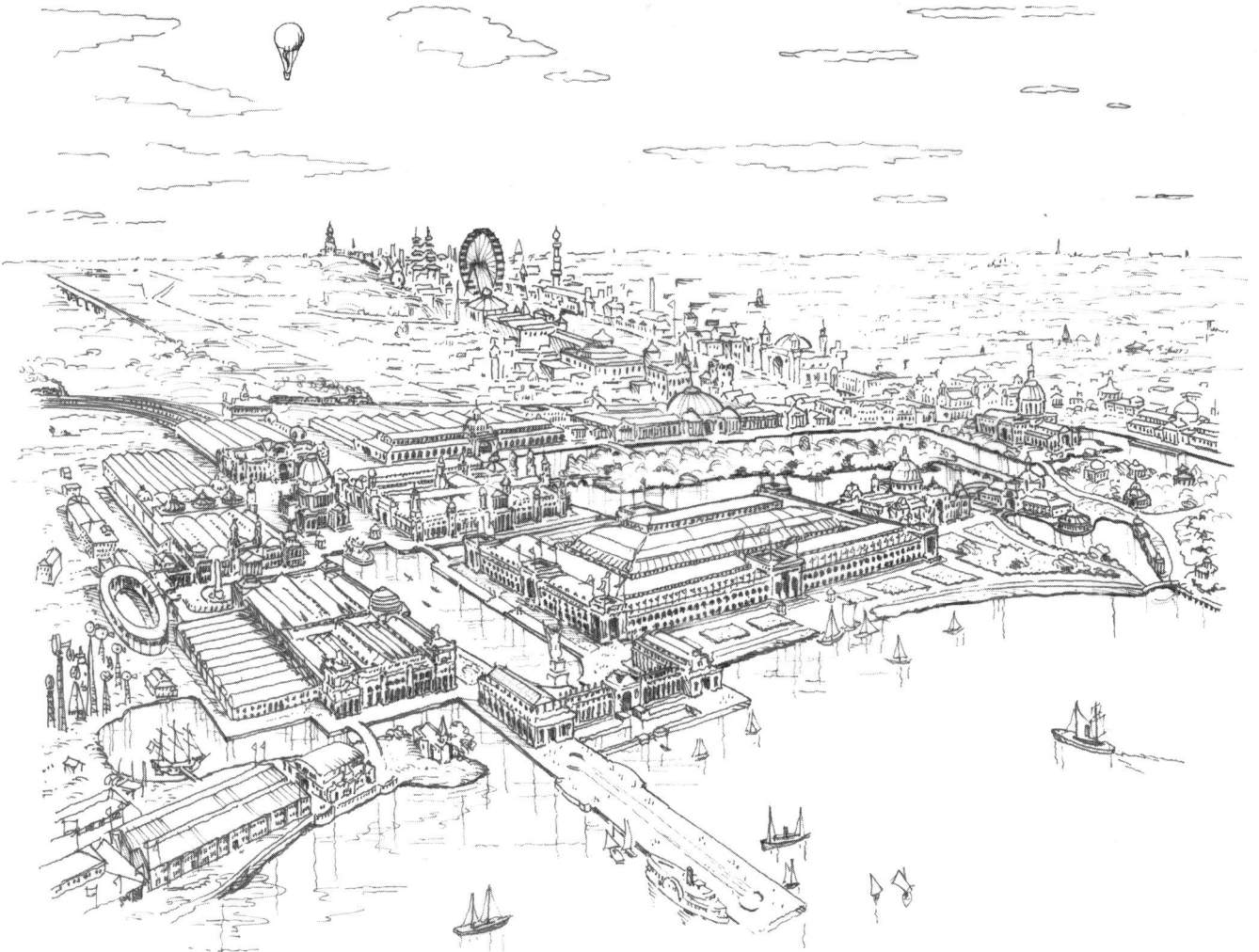

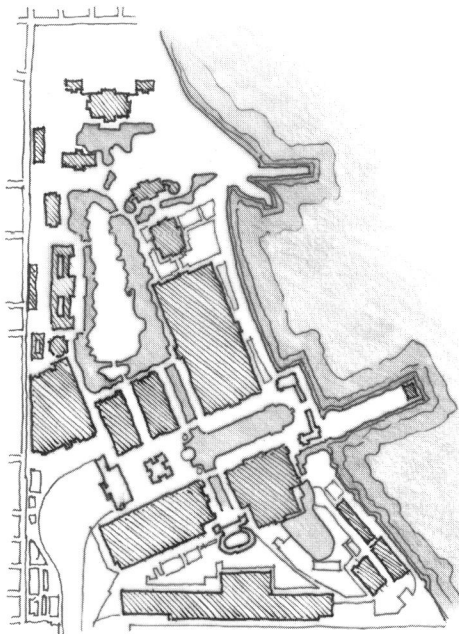

Olmsted's site plan for the fairgrounds helped establish a new language of urban design.

A DAY AT THE FAIR: Spectators could purchase blue-tinted glasses to cut down on the glare from the White City.

BEAUX-ARTS IDEALS

Olmsted collaborated with Beaux-Arts-trained designer Daniel Burnham (1846–1912) to create the master plan for the fairgrounds. A neoclassical design vocabulary was adhered to by most of the architects invited to design the temporary structures. The pavilions were all 60 feet high and made out of nondurable materials; the plaster and stucco finishes created a uniform complex known as the White City. Olmsted showed the monumental buildings located around a central basin of water called the Court of Honor. The buildings framed a powerful rectangular void; open space organized architecture. Although Gilded Age grandeur was antithetical to Olmsted's ideal of pastoral urban open space, he did offer a naturalistic escape—he created a tree-lined island with curvilinear pathways in the free-form lagoon north of the Court of Honor.

The Chicago World's Fair was a great success and very well attended. Its lasting impact was the new spirit of multidisciplinary collaboration and the growing sense of civic pride that inspired the City Beautiful movement in the early 20th century. Many civic beautification projects adopted the same neoclassical idiom. Modern conceptions of urban planning emerged from this influential exposition of art and technology.

SUMMARY

The Industrial Revolution brought widespread change to the landscape and to society. The shift from an agricultural to an industrial economy created a new class of low-wage workers in European and American cities. Social reformers lobbied to improve the living conditions of the urban poor by providing public parks. The aesthetic language of the English landscape garden was adopted as a model for the parks, and persists in the Western imagination as an icon of nature. The physical and social structures that have come to define city life took shape in the 19th century.

The Romantic sentiment of the 19th century contributed to a conception of nature as being restorative. People understood the political, economic and social value of the landscape, and campaigned to access its benefits. By the end of the century, landscape architecture was established as a profession in America.

DESIGN PRINCIPLES

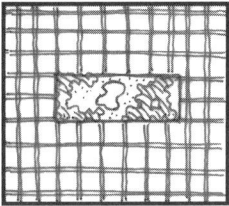

ACCESSIBILITY
An awareness of social factors is critical to a successful design. The first public parks opened in the 19th century.

IDENTITY
Space becomes place when it has identifiable character. Alphand's design vocabulary defined Second Empire Paris.

TRANSFORMATION
Landscapes, both built and natural, are capable of altering emotional states. Transcendental philosophers helped create a wilderness myth about the American West.

OBSERVATION
Urban environments create opportunities for social exchange. Parisian boulevards accommodated a variety of interactions.

COLLABORATION
Design is a collaborative and iterative process. A multi-disciplinary team of experts assembled to design the Chicago World's Fair.

DESIGN VOCABULARY

ENGLAND
Beds and Borders

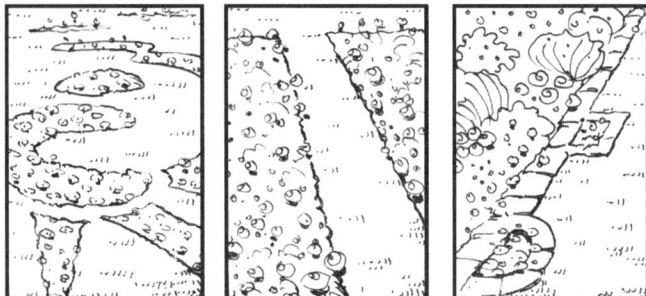

FRANCE
Place and Promenade

AMERICA
Mountains and Monuments

For further exploration

BOOKS
COLD MOUNTAIN, by Charles Frazier
THE DEVIL AND THE WHITE CITY, by Erik Larson
GREAT EXPECTATIONS, by Charles Dickens
THE LAST OF THE MOHICANS, by James Fennimore Cooper
LITTLE WOMEN, by Louisa May Alcott
MY ANTONIA, by Willa Cather
MOBY DICK, by Herman Melville
NATURE, by Ralph Waldo Emerson
PASSAGE TO INDIA, by E.M. Forster
THE RAVEN, by Edgar Allan Poe
WALDEN, by Henry David Thoreau
WUTHERING HEIGHTS, by Emily Bronte

FILMS
AMISTAD (1997)
ANGELS AND INSECTS (1995)
DAISY MILLER (1974)
THE GANGS OF NEW YORK (2002)
AN IDEAL HUSBAND (1999)
JANE EYRE (1996)
OSCAR AND LUCINDA (1997)
THE SWAN (1956)
SWEENEY TODD (2007)

PAINTINGS AND SCULPTURE
THE THIRD OF MAY, by Francisco Goya (1804)
THE HAYWAIN, by John Constable (1821)
SCHROON MOUNTAIN, ADIRONDACKS, by Thomas Cole (1838)
FUR TRADERS DESCENDING THE MISSOURI, by George Caleb Bingham (1845)
NOCTURNE IN BLACK AND GOLD, by James McNeil Whistler (1874)
LE MOULIN DE LA GALETTE, by Auguste Renoir (1876)
THE THINKER, by Auguste Rodin (1879)
WHEAT FIELD AND CYPRESS TREES, by Vincent Van Gogh (1889)

20th CENTURY

Over the course of a century, the world saw the biggest wars ever fought, the fastest speeds ever achieved, an enormous growth in population and migration, a revolution in manufacturing, the greatest economic catastrophe and recovery, the formation of "superpowers," and massive devastation to the Earth in terms of species extinction and climate change. The magnitude of change is almost incomprehensible. The institutions and foundations that structured and supported human life advanced, but not without consequence. While communication and transportation systems seemingly shrunk the world, the distance between industrialized societies and developing nations remained great.

Western culture reached new heights of complexity in the 20th century. Influences on the built landscape were tremendously diverse. No single style or approach represents the age. The development of the profession of landscape architecture accelerated in the early 20th century, particularly in America. Significant movements that affected American landscape design include the Country Place Era, the City Beautiful Movement, Modernism, Land Art, Environmentalism, Postmodernism and Ecological Design. The following chapter is organized according to these themes, through a discussion of key people and representative projects.

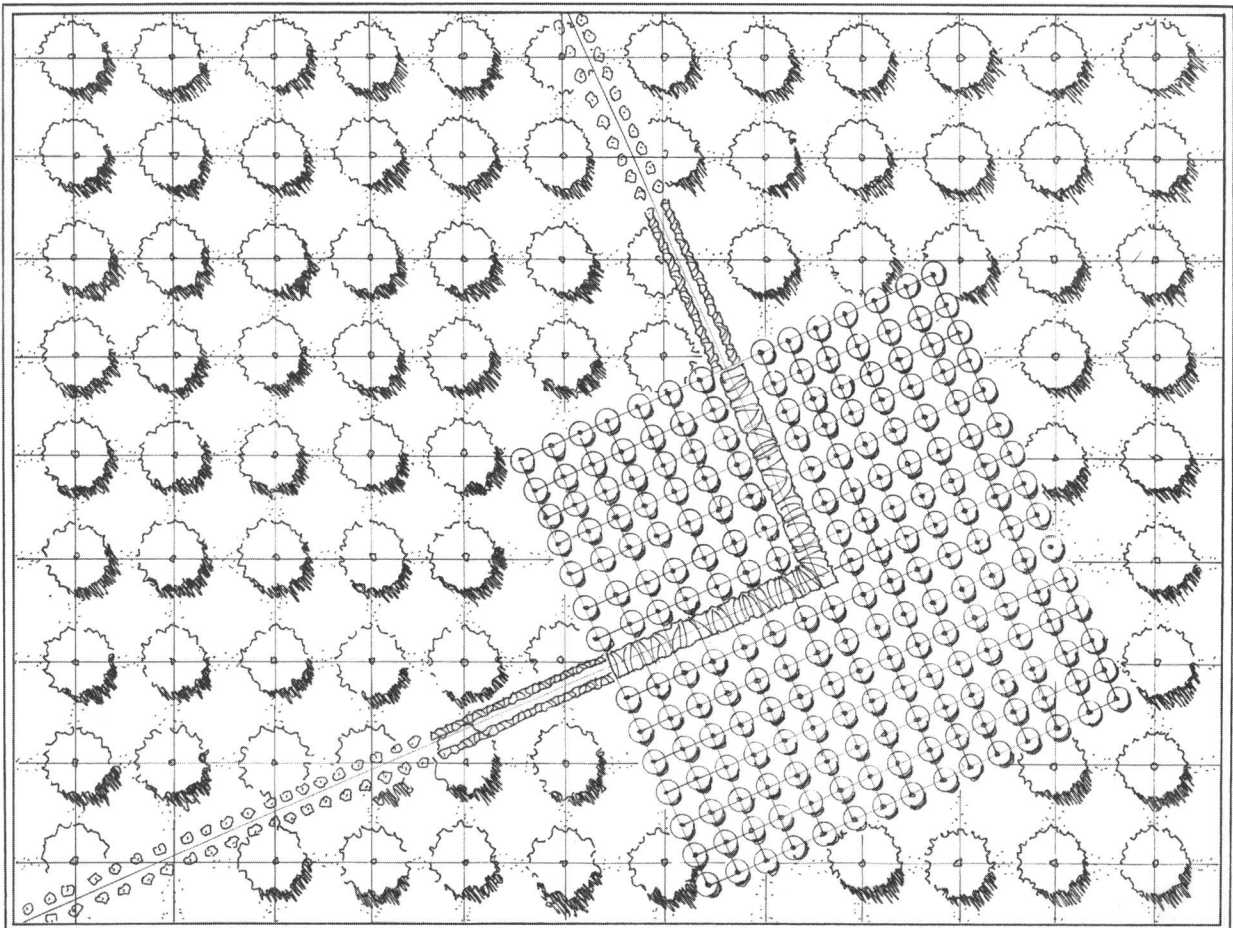

1911
HOLLYWOOD

1913
CARS

1900

1910

1914–1918
WORLD WAR I

1914
PANAMA CANAL

1935–1943
NEW DEAL

1935
BLUE RIDGE PARKWAY

1930

1940

1950

1939–1945
WORLD WAR II

1939
WORLD OF TOMORROW

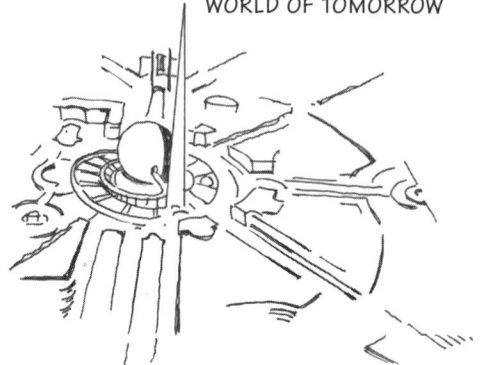

$$E = Mc^2$$

1915
SPACE / TIME

1920
SUFFRAGE

1920

1922
RADIO

1928
TELEVISION

1915
GANDHI

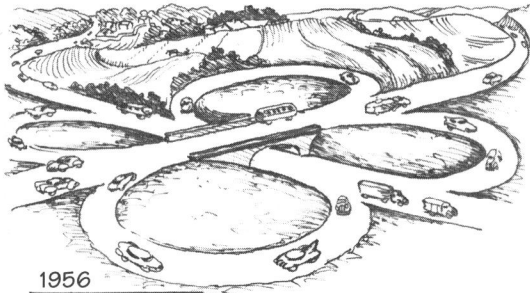

1956
HIGHWAY ACT

1973
OIL CRISIS

1994
END OF APARTHEID

1960 **1970** **1980** **1990** **2000**

1969
MOON LANDING

1970
EARTH DAY

1989
FALL OF THE BERLIN WALL

1911   HOLLYWOOD
Nestor Company opened the first movie studio on the corner of Sunset Boulevard and Gower Avenue. Film became a major industry in southern California. In the second half of the 20th century, consumerism and popular entertainment became the industries that changed the face of the landscape.

1913   CARS
Henry Ford invented an assembly-line process for the mass production of automobiles. Cars became the dominant form of transportation and had the greatest single effect on the landscape.

1914–1918   WORLD WAR I
The assassination of the heir to the Austro-Hungarian Empire led to war in Europe, which grew to involve countries on all continents. The redrawn map of Europe and the subsequent shift of power set the stage for the next world war. Resources were scarce at the end of the war; food crops were planted in homeowner's front yards as "victory gardens."

1914   PANAMA CANAL
The Atlantic and Pacific Oceans were now connected.

1915   SPACE/TIME
Albert Einstein published his general theory of relativity.

1915   MAHATMA GANDHI
Mohandas Gandhi became known as "mahatma," or great soul, because of his efforts to eradicate poverty and help India gain independence from Britain. He returned to India from South Africa in 1915 and led nonviolent protests and other acts of civil disobedience.

1920   SUFFRAGE
The Nineteenth Amendment to the U.S. Constitution gave women the right to vote.

1922   RADIO
KDKA in Pittsburg, Pennsylvania, was the first radio station to broadcast to the public. At the time, radio had a more widespread influence on culture than the Internet has today.

1928   TELEVISION
Milo T. Farnsworth invented the first working television in 1928. The technology evolved over the next decade. The first commercial television transmission was in 1941. Cultural trends were initiated and spread through mass media, feeding a consumerist society.

1935–1943   NEW DEAL
U.S. President Franklin Delano Roosevelt initiated the Works Progress Administration (WPA), employing millions of workers and artists in the repair and adornment of public properties. The Civilian Conservation Corps (CCC) maintained forests, beaches, and parks.

1935   BLUE RIDGE PARKWAY
Landscape architect Stanley W. Abbott planned the 500-mile scenic byway between North Carolina and Virginia, linking the Great Smoky Mountains National Park and Shenandoah National Park. The CCC constructed the project.

1939–1945   WORLD WAR II
Germany's attempt to reorganize Europe according to Fascist doctrine resulted in a war of unprecedented dimensions. More than 55 million people died, including millions who perished in Nazi concentration camps. The first atomic bomb was dropped by the U.S. on Japan. The United States and the Soviet Union emerged as world superpowers. Ideological differences led to the Cold War and the establishment of Eastern and Western blocs.

1939   THE WORLD OF TOMORROW
The 1939 World's Fair held in Queens, New York, presented a vision of America in the future. One of the attractions was Futurama, where people rode above a model of "Democracity"—an urban environment consisting of residential, commercial, and industrial regions separated by a superhighway.

1956   HIGHWAY ACT
To facilitate rapid evacuation of cities during the Cold War, the U.S. government funded the construction of an Interstate Highway system. The superhighways and expressways facilitated suburban growth and led to dependence on the automobile.

1969   MOON LANDING
Americans Neil Armstrong and Buzz Aldrin walked on the moon. The Apollo VIII mission (1968) transmitted the first images of the Earth seen from space.

1970   EARTH DAY
The efforts of U.S. Senator Gaylord Nelson to raise the environmental consciousness of the country led to the declaration of the first Earth Day, which is now celebrated worldwide.

1973   OIL CRISIS
America's dependency on foreign oil was brought to the attention of the public when the Organization of Petroleum Exporting Countries (OPEC) oil embargo ended shipment of oil to America, in protest of the country's support of Israel.

1989   FALL OF THE BERLIN WALL
East and West Germany were reunited. The dissolution of the Eastern Bloc in 1991 ended the Cold War. Globalization had begun.

1994   END OF APARTHEID
In 1990, political activist Nelson Mandela was released from prison in South Africa, after 27 years. The first democratic elections, open to all races, were held in the country in 1994. Mandela was elected president.

EXTREMES OF WEALTH AND POVERTY

America experienced tremendous growth in industry and a great wave of immigration in the period between Reconstruction (1877) and the country's entry into World War I (1917). Fortunes were made for investors in steel, oil, and railroads. The very rich indulged themselves in Roaring Twenties speakeasies, while the very poor struggled to survive in overcrowded tenements. In 1873, Mark Twain collaborated with the author Charles Dudley Warner on a book entitled *The Gilded Age: A Tale of Tomorrow*—a satire about the polished surface disguising the underlying greed and corruption in society. The term came to characterize the era. The dramatic changes of the 20th century were written on the landscape and completely shifted the priorities of design.

THE COUNTRY PLACE ERA

From the 1880s to the 1920s, wealthy American industrialists and bankers expressed their power by building estates in the countryside, much like ancient emperors and Renaissance princes did. European-styled houses and gardens—manors, villas, castles, and chateaux—dotted the landscape outside major cities. The period is contemporary to that of the Lutyens/ Jekyll partnership (1893–1912) and is characterized by a similar focus on high-quality materials and clearly structured space. Typical of the era is an enhanced relationship between house and garden, a balance of naturalistic and formal areas, and a hierarchical ordering of space. The stock market crash of 1929 and the new income tax laws enacted in 1933 put an end to the Country Place Era.

Beatrix Jones Farrand (1872–1959) was a founding member of the American Society of Landscape Architects (ASLA) and a pioneering woman designer. Her privileged background put

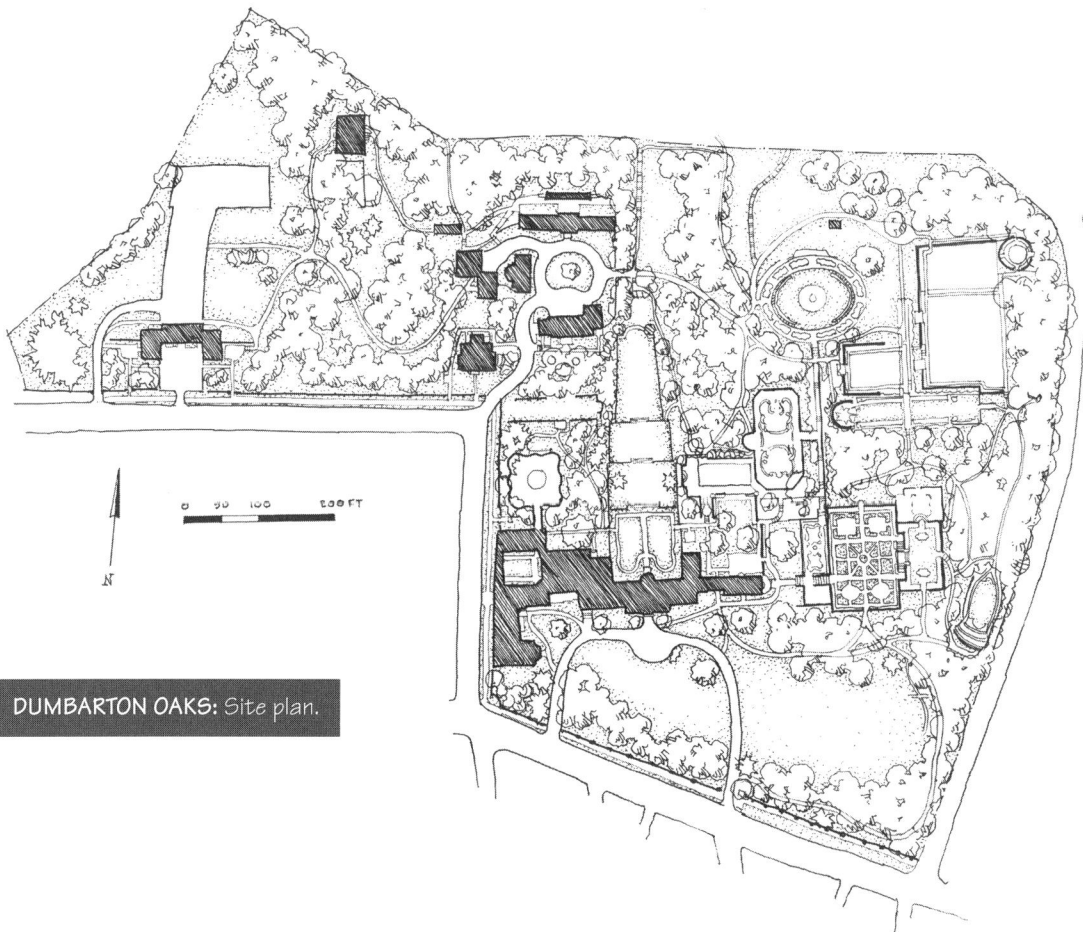

DUMBARTON OAKS: Site plan.

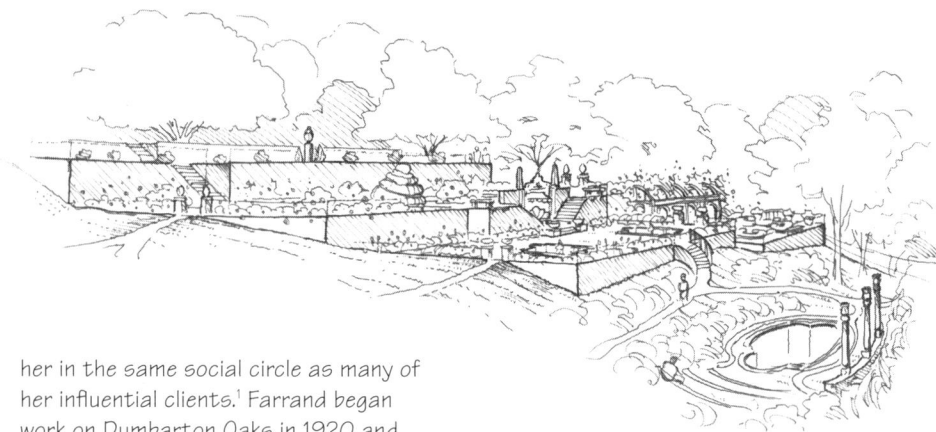

TERRACE GARDEN: Farrand created a wonderful harmony of planting, paving, and architectural elements.

her in the same social circle as many of her influential clients.[1] Farrand began work on Dumbarton Oaks in 1920 and remained engaged in the project for 27 years. Located in Georgetown, near Washington, DC, Dumbarton Oaks was the home of Mildred Barnes Bliss and Robert Woods Bliss. Architectural elements structure the terraces that descend the woodland slope. Outdoor rooms, like the rose garden, north vista, and pebble garden are distinguished by their Arts and Crafts detailing.

Charles A. Platt (1861–1933) was an architect whose work was informed by a sense of spatial order and visual coherence reminiscent of Italian Renaissance gardens. His book, Italian Gardens (1894), was influential in introducing architectonic spatial relationships to residential design in America. He conceived

of the house and garden as a single composition, connecting interior and exterior spaces through proportional relationships and sight lines. His work at Gwinn, the Cleveland estate of William G. Mather, began in 1906. Warren Manning laid out the 27-acre estate for which Platt designed the house and its 5-acre

PLATT RESIDENCE: Charles Platt's own house in Cornish, New Hampshire, exemplifies the balancing of space through the use of lateral axes.

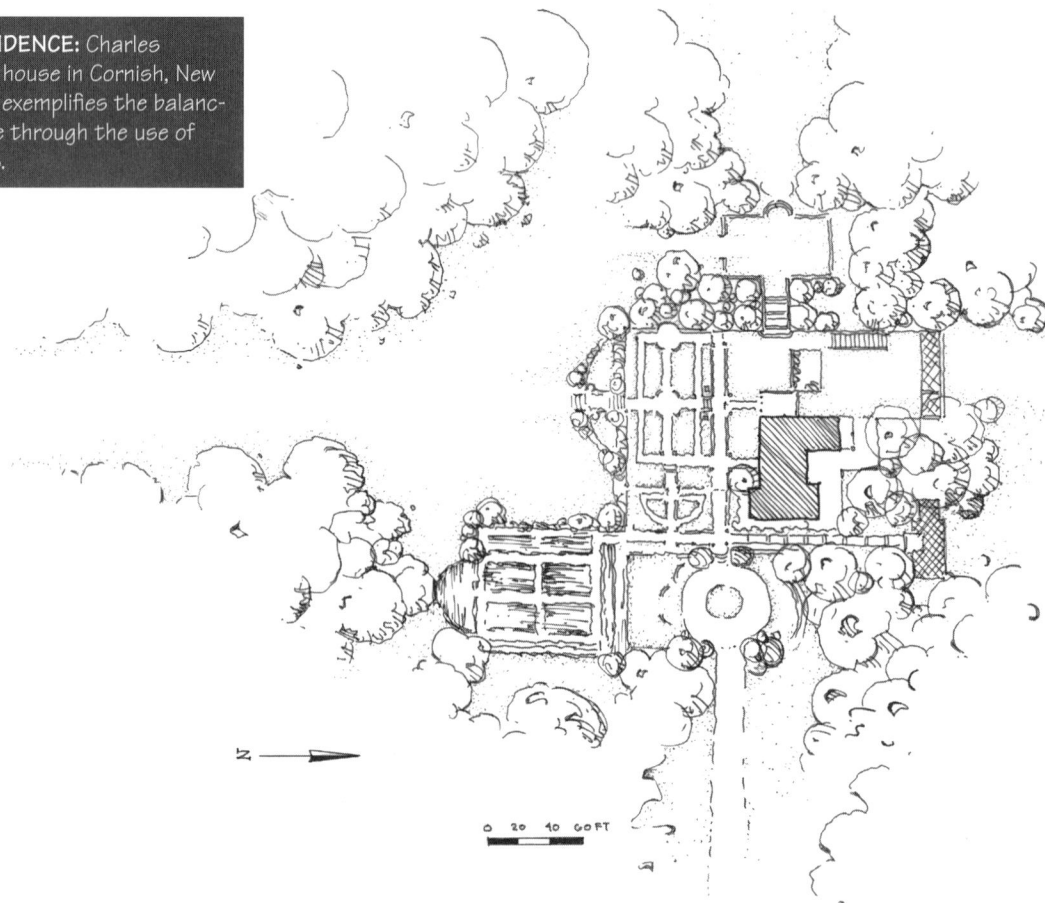

garden. Platt structured the formal and informal spaces through sight lines. In 1935 Mather hired Ellen Shipman to redesign Platt's formal gardens.

Other notable country place estates include Filoli, the Bourn family estate in Woodside, California; Winterthur, home of the du Ponts, in Delaware; the Mount, Edith Wharton's house in Lenox, Massachusetts; John Deering's Villa Vizcaya in Miami, Florida; and Biltmore in Asheville, North Carolina (discussed in the previous chapter). In the second half of the 20th century, the focus of professional practice shifted away from residential design. Landscape architects adopted corporate business models to undertake large-scale projects for corporate clients and municipalities.

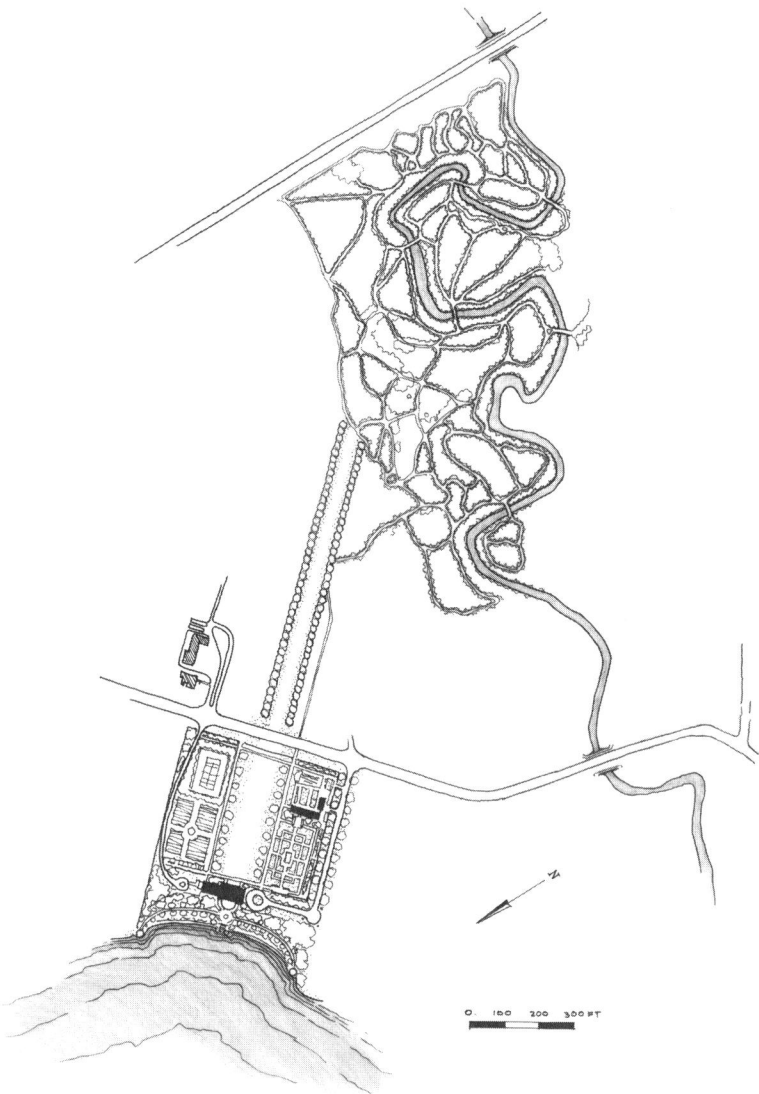

GWINN MASTER PLAN: Platt and Manning juxtaposed naturalistic and formal geometries.

GWINN SITE PLAN: A curving terrace formed an elegant seawall on the shores of Lake Erie.

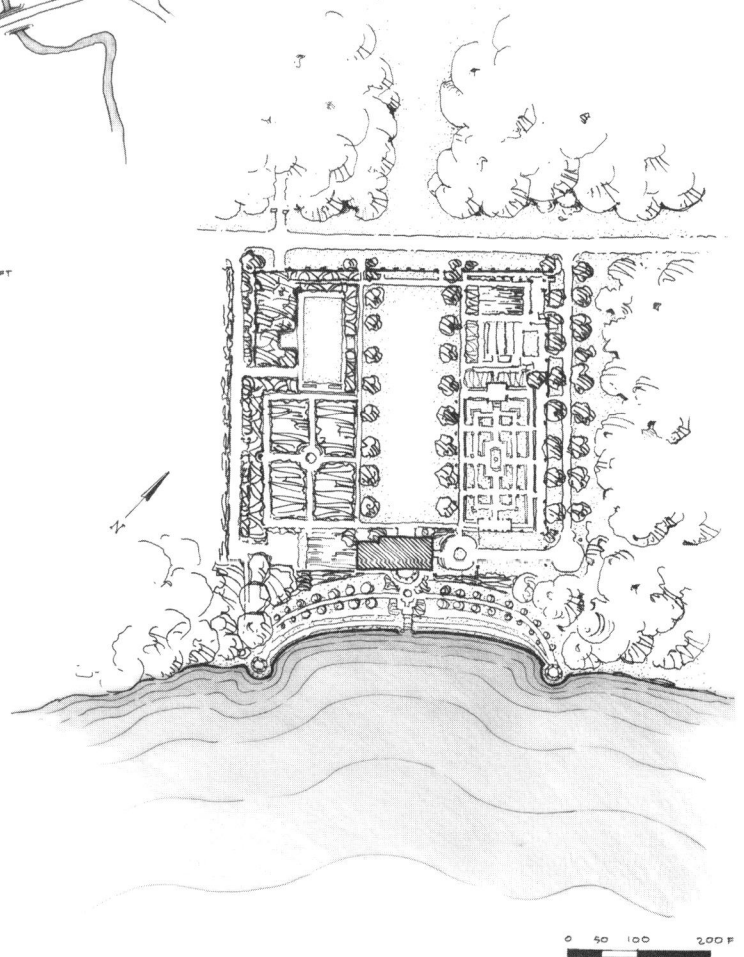

THE CITY MADE BEAUTIFUL

The veneer of grandeur that characterized Gilded Age estates was also applied to cities by reformists who perceived the advantages of representing a city as a single, unified vision. The success of the Chicago World's Fair brought the idea of city planning to the forefront of public consciousness. Journalist and author Charles Mulford Robinson (1869–1917) reviewed the fair in the press and subsequently developed theories of "civic aesthetics," which were enthusiastically received by the public. His book, *Modern Civic Art, or the City Made Beautiful* (1903) helped make the commitment to civic improvement a fashionable cause.[2]

The City Beautiful movement resulted in the piecemeal addition of monuments and sculptures to urban spaces, and the construction of public institutions like libraries and post offices. Architects, conforming to Beaux-Arts ideals, proposed comprehensive urban plans for cities, but for a variety of reasons, none were realized.[3] Daniel Burnham's formal plan for the redesign of Chicago included radial and diagonal street systems, wide boulevards, and a monumental civic center. His approach was criticized for its emphasis on appearance rather than social responsibility, and for many additional reasons, the plan was never actualized.[4]

BEAUX-ARTS CHICAGO: Burnham's plan for the redesign of Chicago was not realized.

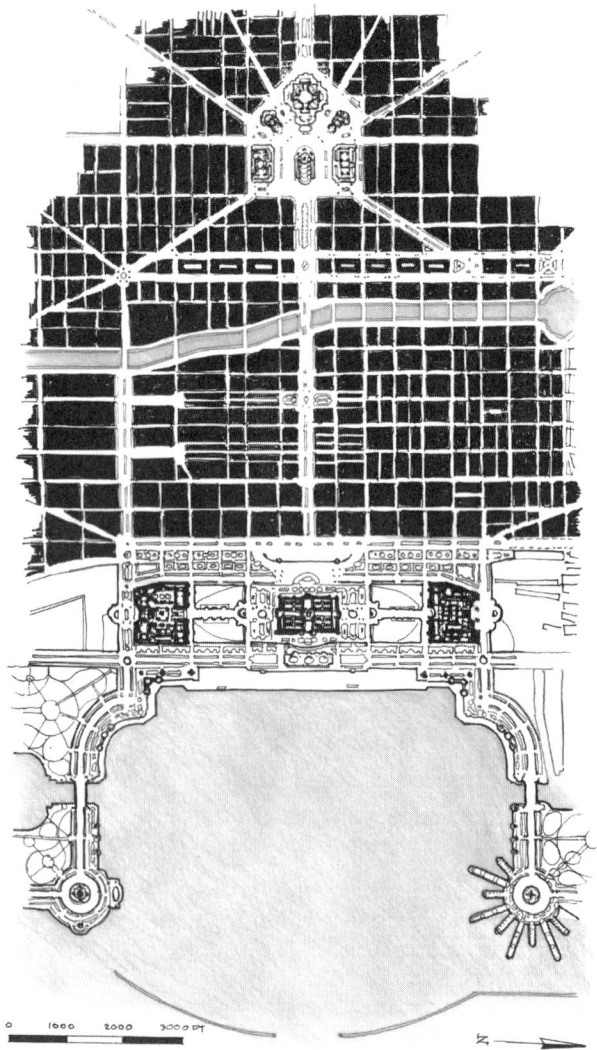

McMILLAN PLAN: The McMillan Plan of 1901 gave the nation's capital a Beaux-Arts facelift.

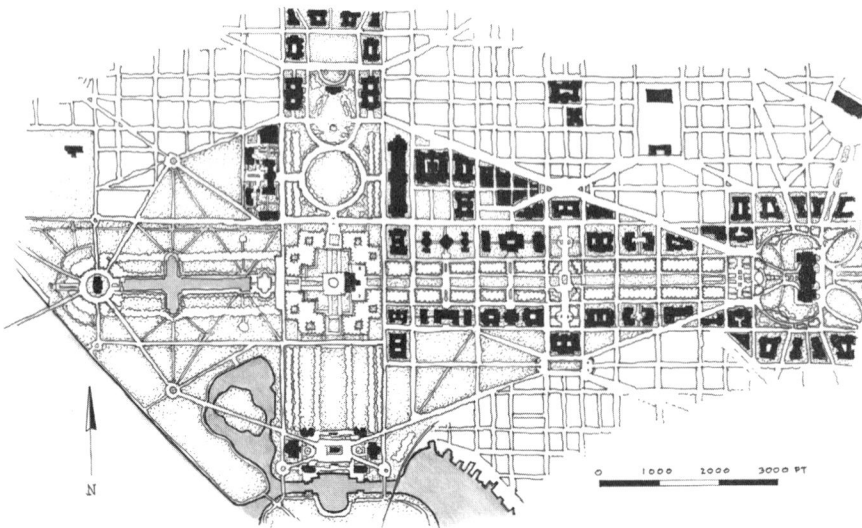

Burnham, however, did get an opportunity to remake an entire city in the neoclassical manner. Burnham, along with landscape architect Frederick Law Olmsted Jr., sculptor Augustus Saint-Gaudens, and architect Charles McKim, was appointed by the McMillan Commission to enact Pierre L'Enfant's 1791 plan for the redesign of Washington, DC. Known as the McMillan Plan, the capital was given a Beaux-Arts facelift.

The City Beautiful movement helped city planning evolve as a discipline separate from landscape architecture in the late 1920s. The first professional city planning curriculum was established at Harvard University in 1929.

THE NEW AESTHETIC OF MODERNISM

Modernism in landscape architecture refers to the rejection of traditional styles and approaches and the embrace of functionalism. The new aesthetic of modernism overcame the eclectic mix of historical styles that was prevalent at the turn of the century. Modern designers articulated in their work values that were democratic, accessible, and reflective of a new more casual lifestyle. Landscape designs were antiaxial and omnidirectional, and incorporated nontraditional materials, abstract shapes, and sculpture. Designers employed plants and sculptures purely for aesthetic impact, not their associative meanings.

THE INTERNATIONAL STYLE

Designers in the first half of the 20th century were optimistic about the role of machine-age technology, and saw its potential to encourage healthy and leisurely lifestyles. Architectural theorists promoted a single International Style that expressed industrial materials and processes and that was free of any trace of authority, hierarchy, social class, or vernacular flavor.[5] Modernist objects and spaces expressed utilitarian functions. Ornamentation was

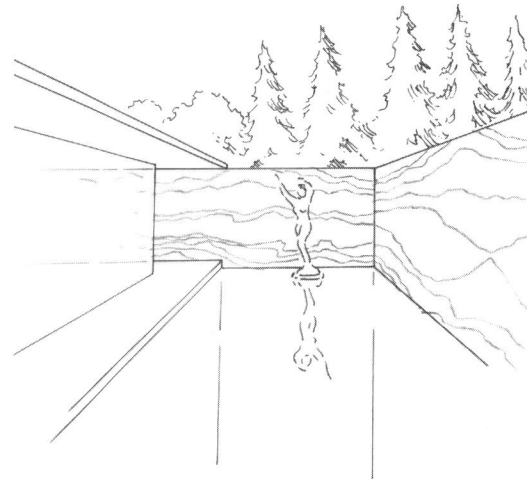

ALBA (DAWN), by GEORG KOLBE: Sculptures created dynamic focal points in modern gardens.

unnecessary; design elements had to be purposeful.

"Form follows function" was the slogan that summarized modernist intentions.[6] The interdisciplinary art and design school called the Bauhaus, in Dessau, Germany, stressed the unity of art, industry, and nature. Students explored the use of industrial materials and technologies, which were less expensive and therefore indicative of a more egalitarian aesthetic. Walter Gropius (1883–1969) founded the Bauhaus and was its director from 1925 to 1933. He became the head of the Graduate School of Design at Harvard, in 1933, and brought the International Style to America.

Ludwig Mies van der Rohe's German Pavilion, designed for the Barcelona Exposition in 1929, became the archetype of modern spatial composition. Its open floor plan and modular system of support created a new sense of space, defined by interpenetrating vertical and horizontal planes. Charles-Edouard Jeanneret

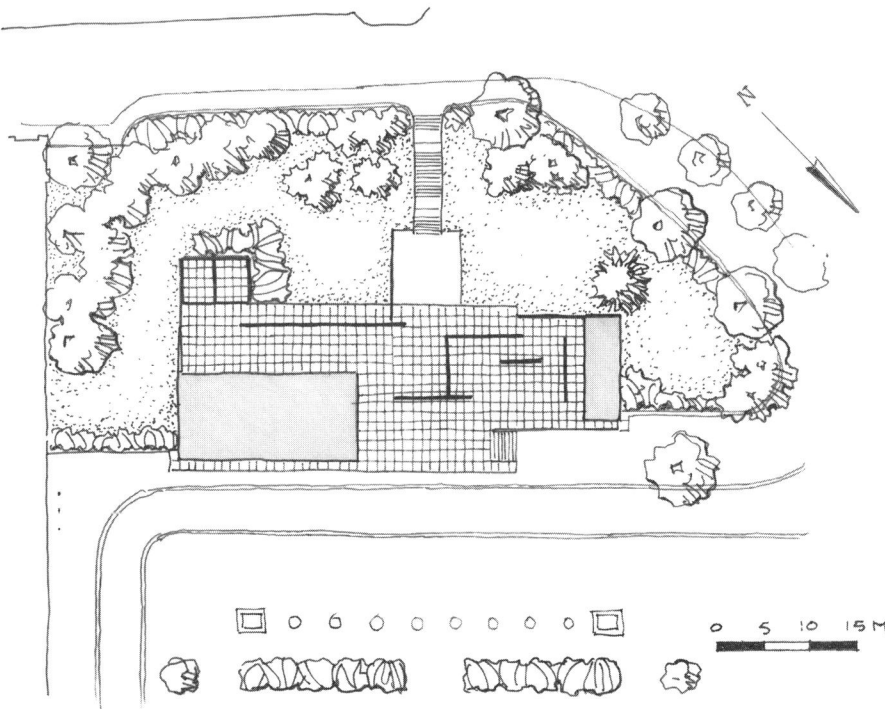

BARCELONA PAVILION: The lack of load-bearing walls created an open floor plan.

(Le Corbusier, 1887–1965) applied the International Style to residential design. He considered the house a "machine for living."[7] His Villa Savoye of 1929, at Poissy, outside Paris, was raised up on *pilotis* (columns) and disconnected from the landscape. Nature functioned as a romantic backdrop for architecture, an attitude that lingered in the minds of many architects.

EARLY INFLUENCES ON MODERNIST GARDENS

MACHINE FOR LIVING: The landscape continued uninterrupted beneath the elevated structure of Villa Savoye.

The 1925 *Exposition Internationale des Arts Decoratifs et Industriels Modernes* in Paris helped establish a new vocabulary of design, known as Art Deco. The temporary "viewing" gardens that were on display at the expo had an enormous influence on early 20th-century landscape design. A new concept of space was explored in the work of Gabriel Guevrekian (1900–1970), who was asked by J. C. N. Forestier, the site designer for the exposition, to design a modern Persian garden.[8] His solution, called the Garden of Water and Light, was based on the use of triangular forms and reflective surfaces, as well as on optical color theories that created the illusion of a three-dimensional painting.[9] The plan formed a large triangle, broken up by triangular planting beds and triangular pools of water. The surrounding "fence" was composed of tinted glass triangles. A rotating spherical sculpture, illuminated from within, was made of faceted reflective glass.

Guevrekian's work positioned the garden as a conceptual artistic statement, where plants functioned as abstract masses of color. He explored many of the same ideas in his later work at Villa Noailles (1927). His gardens were often referred to in the press as "cubist" gardens because they created the illusion of representing multiple points of view all at once, as did cubist still-lifes. However, scholars point out that it is impossible to replicate the visual effects of two-dimensional cubist paintings in physical space.[10] While it was difficult to apply the rigid modernist aesthetic to the landscape—which is shaped by dynamic processes—several individuals became key figures in promoting a new style of landscape design.

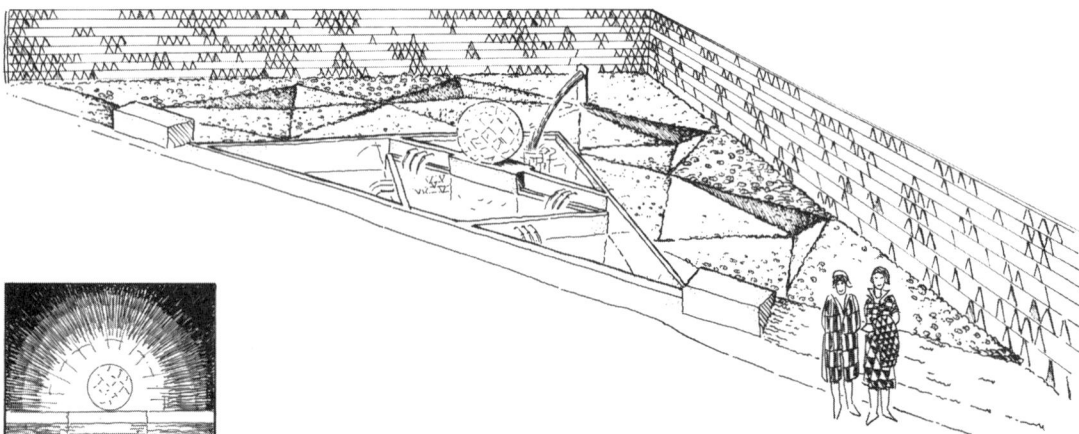

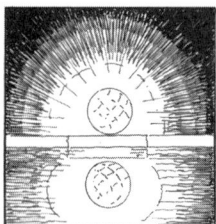

GARDEN OF WATER AND LIGHT: Repetitive forms defined the space.

CASE STUDY: *Villa Noailles*

AVANT-GARDEN: Plan and sequence of space at the Villa Noailles in Hyeres, France. Raised planters and a revolving sculpture created a surreal experience of landscape space.

NAUMKEAG: Fletcher Steele's design of the Rose Garden at Naumkeag reveals Art Deco influences.

Fletcher Steele (1885–1971) was a Boston writer, critic, and landscape designer whose work can be seen as a link between Beaux-Arts formality and modernism. He received his practical training in the office of Warren Manning (1860–1938). He attended the 1925 Paris Expo and was influenced by the abstract concepts represented in the demonstration gardens.[11] His purity of line, fluid geometric forms, and use of color typify the Art Deco style.

The series of gardens Steele created at Naumkeag, a private estate for Mabel Choate in Stockbridge, Massachusetts, illustrated a new conception of the landscape as a setting for outdoor living. Starting in 1938, and continuing over a 30-year period, he composed a series of garden rooms including the Rose Garden, the Afternoon Garden, and the iconic Blue Steps. Curving white tubular steel handrails draw attention to the stand of white birch trees, and contrast

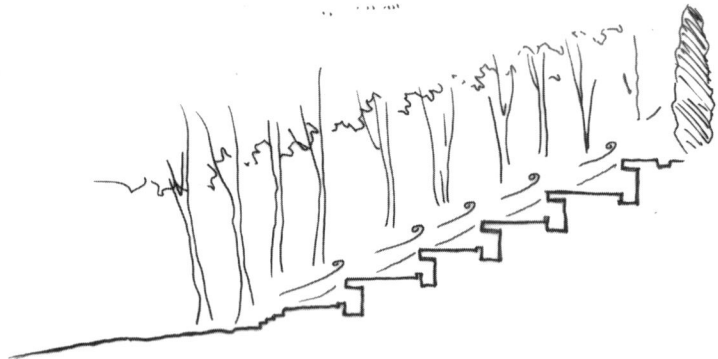

BLUE STEPS: Terraced stairs and landings are symmetrical about a vertical stack of blue arched grottoes.

with the surrounding green woodland and blue recesses at the stair landings.

In 1938, Christopher Tunnard (1910–1979) wrote a book entitled *Gardens in the Modern Landscape* that pre-sented the garden as a social concept, where functional requirements dictated form. Inspired by Japanese gardens and their emphasis on line, Tunnard advocated asymmetrical balance and a harmony of indoor and outdoor spaces.[12]

MIDCENTURY MODERNISTS IN AMERICA

The Mediterranean-type climate in California is conducive to outdoor living. The patios of Spain and the loggias of Italy served as design precedents for Californians who increasingly sought outdoor living and recreational areas in their gardens. Sunset Magazine (originally established in 1898) published landscape architects' plans, and was influential in promoting the low-maintenance, laid-back lifestyle of the West Coast. In response to this new way of using outdoor space, a group of influential designers created functional, user-driven, modernist landscapes that have come to define the "California garden style."

Thomas Church (1902–1978) was a Beaux-Arts trained landscape architect based in California whose practice primarily focused on residential design. His influential book of 1955, Gardens Are for People, advised designers to consider foremost the needs of the client in designing landscape spaces. He provided practical advice to homeowners about how to exploit unique aspects of a site. Church abandoned the central axis and organized space functionally. He employed line, texture, and form in asymmetrical compositions that were both pragmatic and artistic settings for family life and casual entertaining. His hallmark was the patterning of the ground plane, with emphasis on the structure of space rather than the planting. He often juxtaposed curvilinear and biomorphic forms against orthogonal shapes. The Donnell Garden, completed between 1947 and 1949, in Sonoma, California, is perhaps his most recognizable work.

Similarly, Garrett Eckbo (1910–2000) was dedicated to providing affordable, functional, and dynamic landscapes for middle-class families. His books Landscape for Living (1950) and The Art of Home Landscaping (1956) provided guidance appropriate for the design of

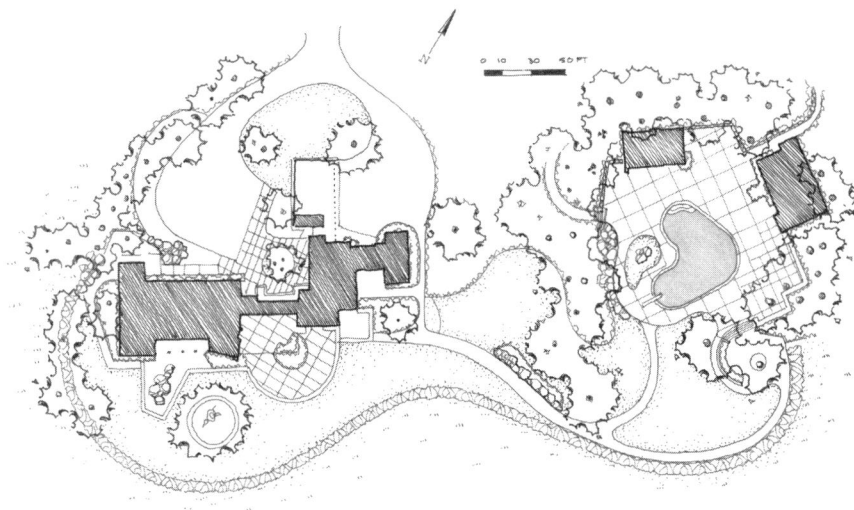

DONNELL GARDEN SITE PLAN: The California garden style accommodated the informality of midcentury lifestyles.

small-scale spaces. He believed that the organization and composition of space itself should be the focus of the garden, and developed plans based on user needs and functional spatial relationships. Eckbo was one of the first landscape designers to rebel against the Beaux-Arts formalism that was still being taught in professional schools.[13] Gropius was at Harvard while Eckbo and Daniel Urban Kiley (introduced below) studied there, but the landscape architecture program was slow in adopting the modernist curriculum.

Eckbo sought a more relevant design response to the larger issues facing contemporary society. He was inspired by contemporary cultural trends and let his interests in jazz, fashion, film, and art influence his work. Eckbo was also concerned with progressive causes and socially conscious design. He worked for the Farm Security Administration, designing migrant-worker housing and community centers. The Alcoa Forecast Garden (1959), in Laurel Canyon, California, was financed by the Aluminum Company of America to demonstrate how the new material could be used in residential applications. Eckbo used his own backyard to showcase his innovative design solutions, which included screens, trellises, and a fountain, all made from aluminum.

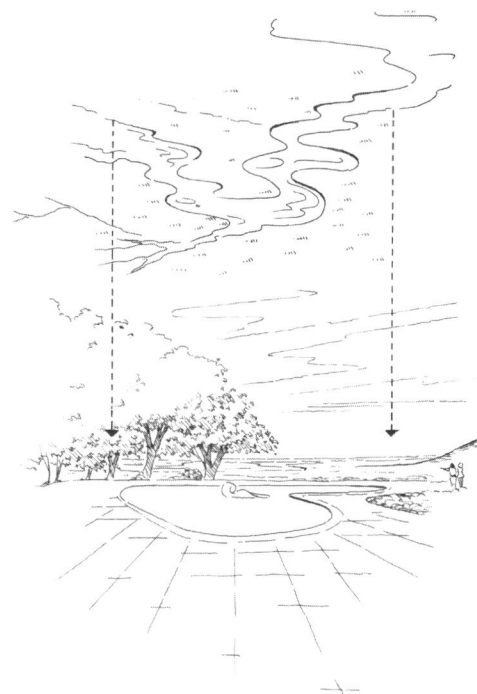

ARC-AND-TANGENT: The kidney-shaped pool became the ultimate icon of the modernist garden. The marshlands of Sonoma, visible from the Donnell garden, mimic the pool's curves.

COMPOSITION (1923) by WASSILY KANDINSKY: Walking through an Eckbo garden is like walking through an abstract painting.

FORECAST BROADCASTED: The Aluminum Company of America commissioned designers to explore the lightweight material through their "Forecast" program. Eckbo's garden received national acclaim when it was featured during the Company's *Alcoa Presents...One Step Beyond* television series in 1960.

the FORECAST GARDEN
ON
TELEVISION
be sure to watch ALCOA
on PRESENTS
ABC-TV TUESDAY—JUNE 21

Dan Kiley (1912–2004) worked for both Warren Manning and the architect Louis Kahn. His work demonstrated a concern with form and spatial hierarchy. He used strong geometries to order the landscape, and like the French formalists of the 17th century, was able to achieve a sense of directionality. Kiley worked closely with many of the great modernist architects. He developed a style characterized by the use of overlapping planes and repeated modules to create a dynamic interpenetration of landscape space. The offset axes, long *allées*, and rectilinear forms that define the Miller Garden (1955), in Columbus, Indiana, work with the geometry of the house designed by Eero Saarinen. Kiley's practice also included corporate work; he designed many well-known plazas for banks and private businesses.

MODERN MAVERICK

The work of Lawrence Halprin (1916–2009) serves as a bridge between the modernist and environmental design movements. Halprin started his career in the office of Thomas Church. His interest in "process" was consistent. His book, *RSVP Cycles: Creative Processes in the Human Environment*, published in 1969, outlined his ideas about the relationship between humans and nature, and his belief that a holistic site analysis was integral to the development of a successful design. He developed an original technique for "scoring" the landscape that maps natural, social, and cultural patterns.

Halprin's work and his approach were innovative. He found inspiration in many different sources, and encouraged collaboration. Halprin was also one of the first advocates for citizen participation in the design process.[14]

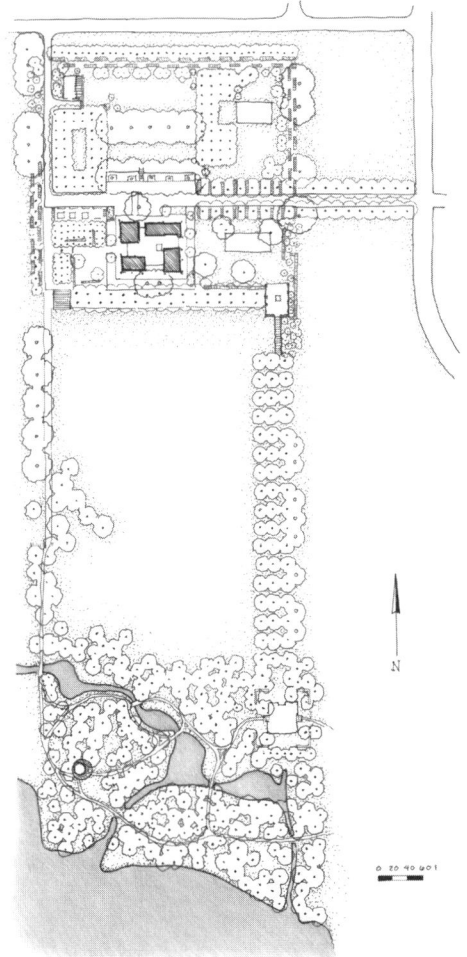

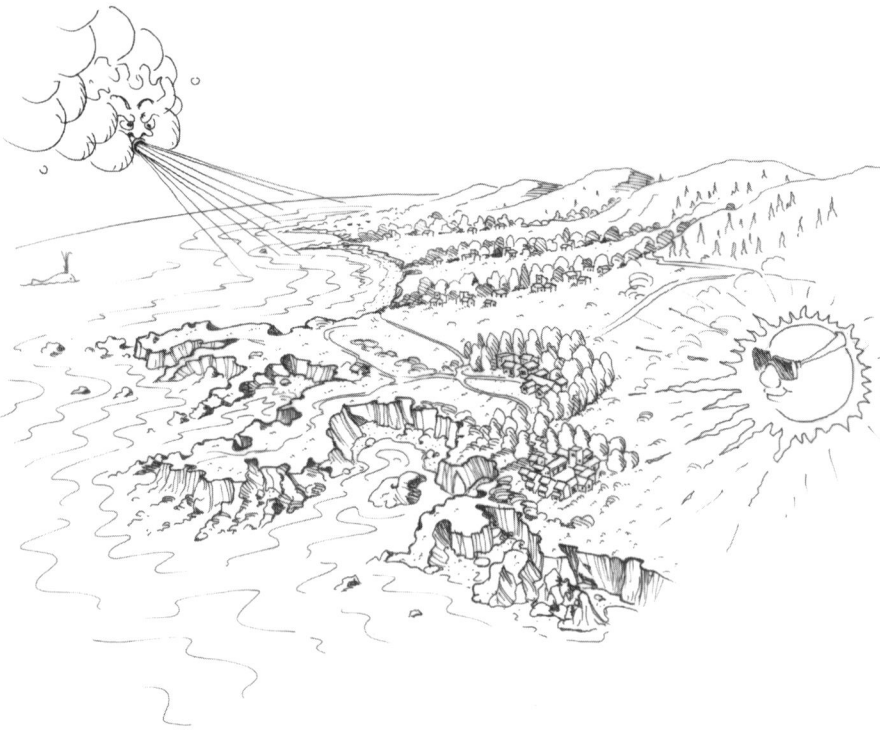

Sea Ranch, a housing development in Gualala, California, completed in 1965, is an excellent example of Halprin's commitment to working collaboratively with other professionals and with the forces of nature.

Halprin also valued urban life, and promoted the revitalization and greening of cities. His 1962 renovation of the old Ghirardelli chocolate factory into a public plaza in San Francisco was one of the first examples of successful adaptive reuse. Other well-known Halprin designs include the Ira Keller fountain in Portland, Oregon; Freeway Park in Seattle, Washington; Levi Strauss Plaza in San Francisco, California; and the FDR Memorial in Washington, DC.

SEA RANCH: Halprin clustered the houses and tucked them into slopes to preserve open space, maintain view corridors, and provide shelter from the wind.

FOUNTAIN PLAZA: People can climb on and participate with the water feature that occupies an entire city block.

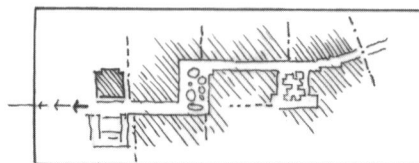

NATURE AS MEDIUM

People have understood the landscape as an expressive medium since prehistoric times. As landscape architects became more focused on corporate culture in the 1960s, artists began to find opportunities for creative expression in the landscape. Environmental artists work with the earth itself as their medium. Their engagement with the landscape can be understood as a reaction to large-scale cultural and environmental changes in the second half of the 20th century.

Environmental artists challenged the idea of art as a marketable product isolated in galleries. Their frame of reference shifted from commodity to concept. Earthworks were large-scale landscape interventions that required heavy machinery to realize. Often in remote locations, distance and solitude became part of the experience. Documentation of the work, particularly through the use of photography, was critical. Robert Smithson (1938–1973) constructed the Spiral Jetty in Great Salt Lake, Utah, in 1970. It remains a powerful icon of the land art movement.

Other environmental artists seek to express the ephemeral or unseen processes of nature. Andy Goldsworthy (b. 1956) works with nature and time to construct temporary sculptures. He uses natural materials—ice, leaves, stones, wood—found on a particular site to create patterns and forms in the landscape. The works remain as photographic images after the effects of wind, water, and weather reclaim the form.

The environmental art and land art movements gave visual expression to ecological processes and brought the idea of the landscape as an expressive medium back into the focus of landscape architects.[15]

SPIRAL JETTY: Earthworks often contain cosmological references.

TEMPORARY SPHERE: Goldsworthy's art pieces are formed from nature and eventually return to nature.

ARTISTIC TRENDS IN LANDSCAPE DESIGN

The work of two international designers, Roberto Burle Marx and Luis Barragan, set modern precedents for approaching the landscape as a work of art. Common to both was a focus on form-giving through the manipulation of color, texture, and line.

Burle Marx (1909–1994) was a Brazilian landscape designer whose work reflected his interests in botany and painting. He treated the ground plane as a canvas on which he painted abstract compositions with colorful masses of typically native plants. His

1948 plan for the Monteiro garden (now the Fernandes garden) treats the space as a purely visual experience. The landscape asserted its identity independent of the architecture; Burle Marx did not extend the geometry of the house into the garden.

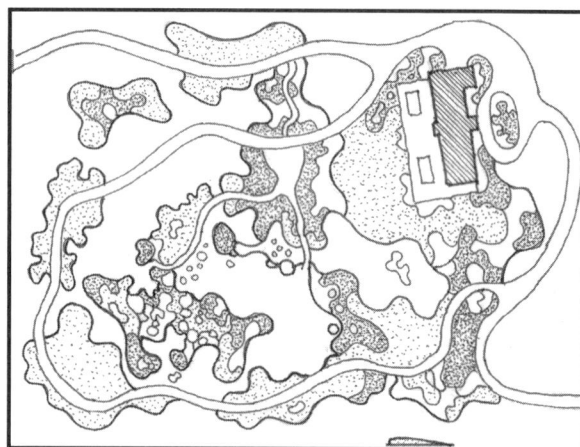

PLANT PAINTER: Burle Marx's biomorphic shapes at the Monteiro Garden resemble paintings by Jean Arp.

LANDSCAPE AS CANVAS: Burle Marx painted in his garden. His abstract compositions influenced his landscape designs. Shown to the right is his design for the plaza at Banco Safra, in Sao Paulo, Brazil (1983).

HORSE FARM, SAN CRISTOBAL:
Barragan created lively volumes of
space with painted stucco walls and
water features.

Barragan (1902–1988) was a Mexican architect who was known for his
colorful, minimalist spatial compositions. He used walls to subdivide
landscape space in a way that recalled
the courtyards of the Alhambra in
Spain, which he visited. His interior and
exterior spaces were artfully fused in a
vocabulary of form that was influenced
by vernacular Mexican traditions. Rural
ideals can be seen in his design for the
San Cristobal horse farm near Mexico
City, completed in 1969. The composition of house, pools (for horses and
for people), and stable still inspires
contemporary architects, designers,
and landscape architects.

The work of more recent landscape
designers such as Kathryn Gustafson,
Patricia Johanson, and Spanish landscape architect Fernando Caruncho
speaks to the legacy of Burle Marx
and Luis Barragán. Gustafson folds
and pleats the ground plane like fabric;
Johanson translates organic forms
into built elements; and Caruncho
structures the landscape with agrarian geometry, combining plants, water,
and mineral elements.

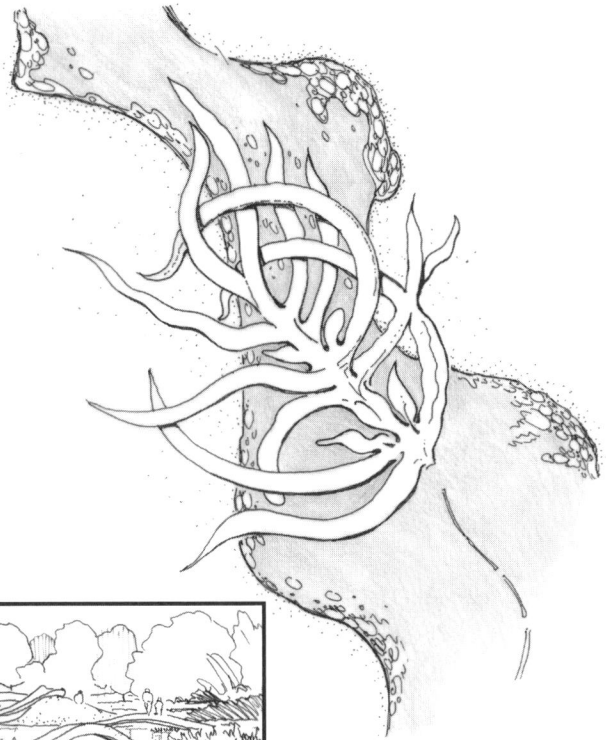

LEONHARDT LAGOON: Patricia Johanson translated the
form of an aquatic plant into
a path system at Fair Park, in
Dallas, Texas.

WHEAT PARTERRES: Fernando Caruncho reinterpreted
the ferme ornée at Mas de
les Voltes, Spain.

PIONEERING NEW DIRECTIONS

Homeowners and groundskeepers battled with the landscape in the first half of the 20th century—huge amounts of weed killers, fertilizers, and pesticides were dumped on the earth. The dangers of degraded environmental conditions were brought to the attention of the American public in 1962 with the publication of the book *Silent Spring* by Rachel Carson. The first Earth Day celebration, in 1970, also advanced the foundation of ecological awareness.

Citizens called the government to action. Key environmental legislation included the Clean Air Act (1970), the Clean Water Act (1972), and the National Environmental Protection Act (1970), which required that an Environmental Impact Statement be prepared for all projects receiving government funding. The design team was required to evaluate the natural, social, and economic impact of a project and make the plans available for review by the community.

Ecological designers continued the pioneering work of 18th-century botanists and 19th-century conservationists. Jens Jensen (1860–1951) was conscious of environmental themes early in his professional career. Jensen was born in Denmark, immigrated to the States in his early twenties, and established a landscape design practice in Chicago. He worked in the naturalistic style and believed in the social benefit of public parks and recreational facilities. Jensen was a transitional figure, influenced by 19th-century reformist ideals and 20th-century Prairie Style design, as exemplified by the work of Frank Lloyd Wright. His sphere of influence was centered around the Midwest, and his practice consisted of large-scale residential projects and smaller urban parks. Jensen's palette was distinguished by his use of native plants and local stone, inspired

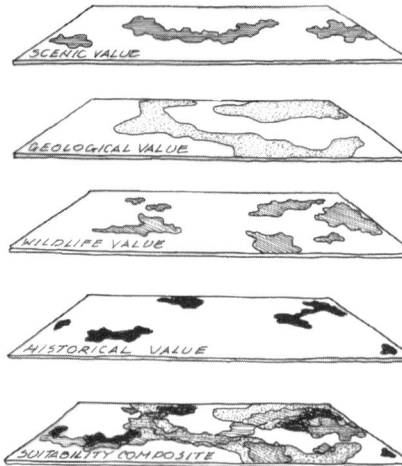

OPPORTUNITIES AND CONSTRAINTS: McHarg developed the overlay analysis process used in GIS.

by the natural meadows and woodland plantings he treasured. His book *Siftings*, from 1933, presented his ideology of environmental design. He established a "folk" school of horticulture and the arts in Wisconsin, called the Clearing, in 1935.

An ecological ideology also drove Ian McHarg (1920–2001) to advocate a holistic approach to design. In his book, *Design with Nature* (1969), he championed site analysis techniques based on the carrying capacity of the land and its fitness to intended use. McHarg developed a methodology based on coordinated overlays of maps, which became the foundation of geographic information systems (GIS) technologies. He pioneered the analysis of opportunities and constraints to assess the many social and environmental costs of a project.

PRAIRIE STYLE: Jens Jensen's work fostered an ecological aesthetic.

Current trends in the participatory design process and the development of healing gardens and community gardens all stem from this conception of land stewardship and the idea of a partnership between humans and the Earth. Randolph T. Hester, in his book *Design for Ecological Democracy* (2006), presents a poetic vision of this kinship that empowers people toward positive environmental change.

Ecological designers seek creative solutions to environmental problems, and include in their approach the science of biological systems. Their goal is to develop solutions that are beautiful, functional, and sustainable. Project types include the bioremediation and rehabilitation of brownfield sites, landfill reclamation, and wetland restoration.

One of the first landscape reclamation projects was Gas Works Park in Seattle, Washington. The park was designed in 1975 by Richard Haag (b. 1923) on the 19-acre site of an abandoned gas plant. Industrial remains were repurposed as picnic and play structures. A more recent example, Duisburg-Nord Park, in Germany, was completed by Peter Latz

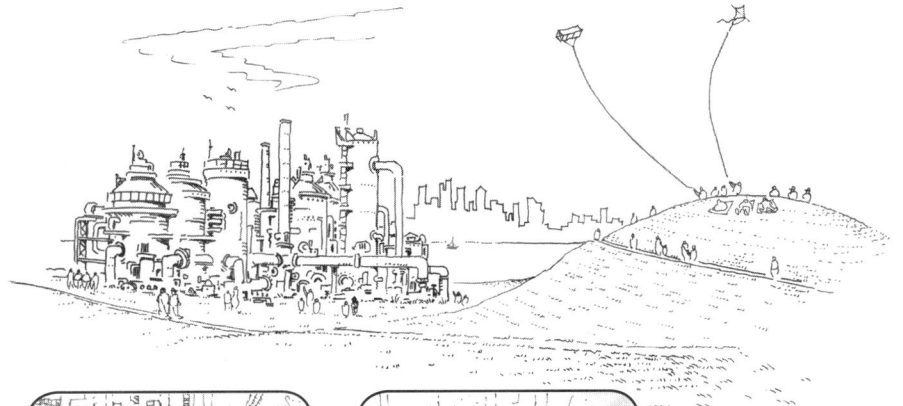

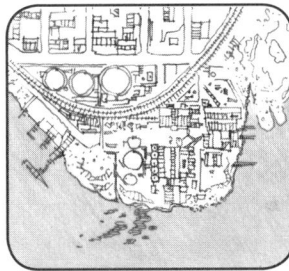
BEFORE

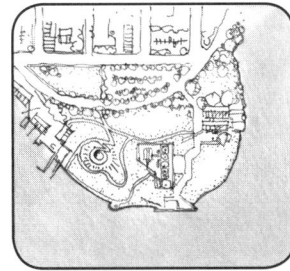
AFTER

GAS WORKS PARK: An abandoned gas plant was transformed into a public park.

(b. 1939) in 1994. He transformed a 500-acre abandoned steel and coal production facility in the Ruhr River valley into public open space as part of the Emscher Park regional redevelopment plan. Ore bunkers, smokestacks, and a blast furnace became climbing walls, garden rooms, and sculptural features.

POSTMODERN LANDSCAPES

Postmodernism implies skepticism about the assumptions of modernism. In the latter half of the 20th century, philosophers, artists, and writers began to challenge the idea of a privileged or dominant point of view. They thought of contemporary culture like a collage, subject to many different influences and interpretations. In the arts, postmodernism was characterized by ambiguity and simultaneity. Meaning could not be embedded in a work of art; it was relative to the viewer. Space, too, was considered "neutral."[16] As a reaction to modernist sterility, artists and designers reintroduced playful ornament, color, and historic motifs into their work.

TANNER FOUNTAIN: Peter Walker blurred the line between landscape design and environmental art.

223

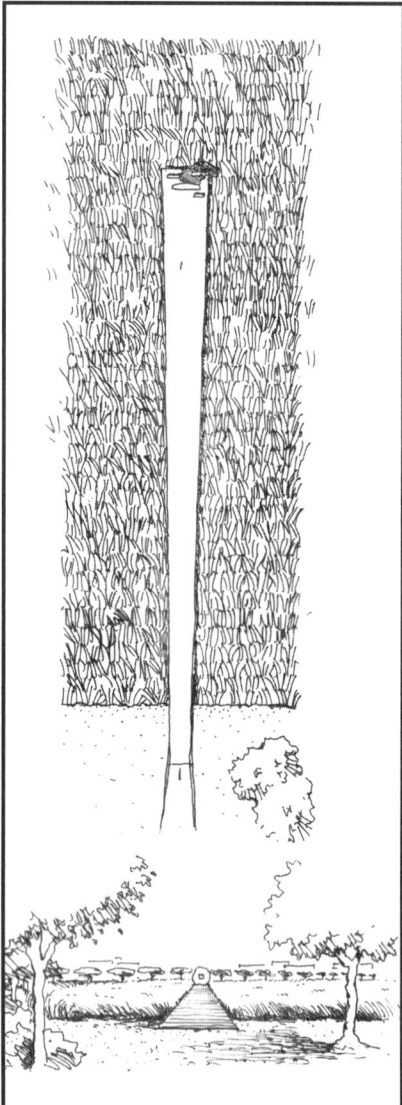

WHEAT WALK: Ron Wigginton was one of the first landscape architects to approach the design of a landscape as a conceptual work of art. His award-winning proposal for the arboretum at the University of California, Davis (1988) poetically conveyed his belief in the landscape as a place of collective memory.

FRACTAL LAKE: Quantum theories were explored in Charles Jencks's garden.

LIMELIGHT: Landscape architects David Meyer and Ramsey Silberberg celebrated one of Britain's "champion" trees in their installation at the 2003 Westonbrit International Festival of the Garden. Set within a constructed earth mound that imitates an amphitheater, the tree occupies center stage.

A renewed interest in metaphor was also evident in postmodern gardens. Landscape design became increasingly conceptual. Ideas of framing nature, using the landscape itself as a material, and making natural processes explicit were common themes explored by landscape designers.[17] Michael Van Valkenburgh's Krakow Ice Garden (1990) on Martha's Vineyard, Massachusetts, and Peter Walker's Tanner Fountain (1984), at Harvard University, exemplified this trend. Conceptual projects included Martha Schwartz's Splice Garden (1986) at the Whitehead Institute in Cambridge, Massachusetts; Ron Wigginton/Land Studio's Wheat Walk (1988) proposed for Davis, California; and Charles Jencks and Maggie Keswick's Garden of Cosmic Speculation (1990) at their home in Dumfriesshire, Scotland.

Postmodernist designers employed allegory like 18th-century Whig landowners did. Ian Hamilton Finlay constructed a poet's garden at his home in Lanarkshire, Scotland. He is known for his "concrete poetry"—words carved into stones and set into provocative pictorial compositions. His garden, Little Sparta, came to reflect his fascination with the French Revolution and his disappointment in contemporary society.[18]

At the end of the 20th century, international garden expositions and festivals resurfaced as popular cultural phenomena. The Chaumont Garden Festival in Chaumont-sur-Loire, France, initiated the trend in 1992, showcasing the work of renowned landscape designers as well as emerging talents. Annual festivals in England, Germany, Canada, and the Netherlands feature temporary, themed gardens, and help shape the public's idea of what a garden can be.

Sequence of space in the postmodern picturesque stroll garden.

DECONSTRUCTION AND RECONSTRUCTION

Trends in architecture and literary theory also influenced the postmodernists. The architect Bernard Tschumi won the design competition for the construction of a new public park on the grounds of an old slaughterhouse on the outskirts of Paris. His design for Parc de la Villette (1985) was based on deconstructivist theories that questioned the boundaries and definitions of architecture and space. The park provides 85 acres of open space as part of a large-scale redevelopment project that includes a science and technology museum and a music center.

PARC DE LA VILLETTE: People make their own connections in deconstructed space.

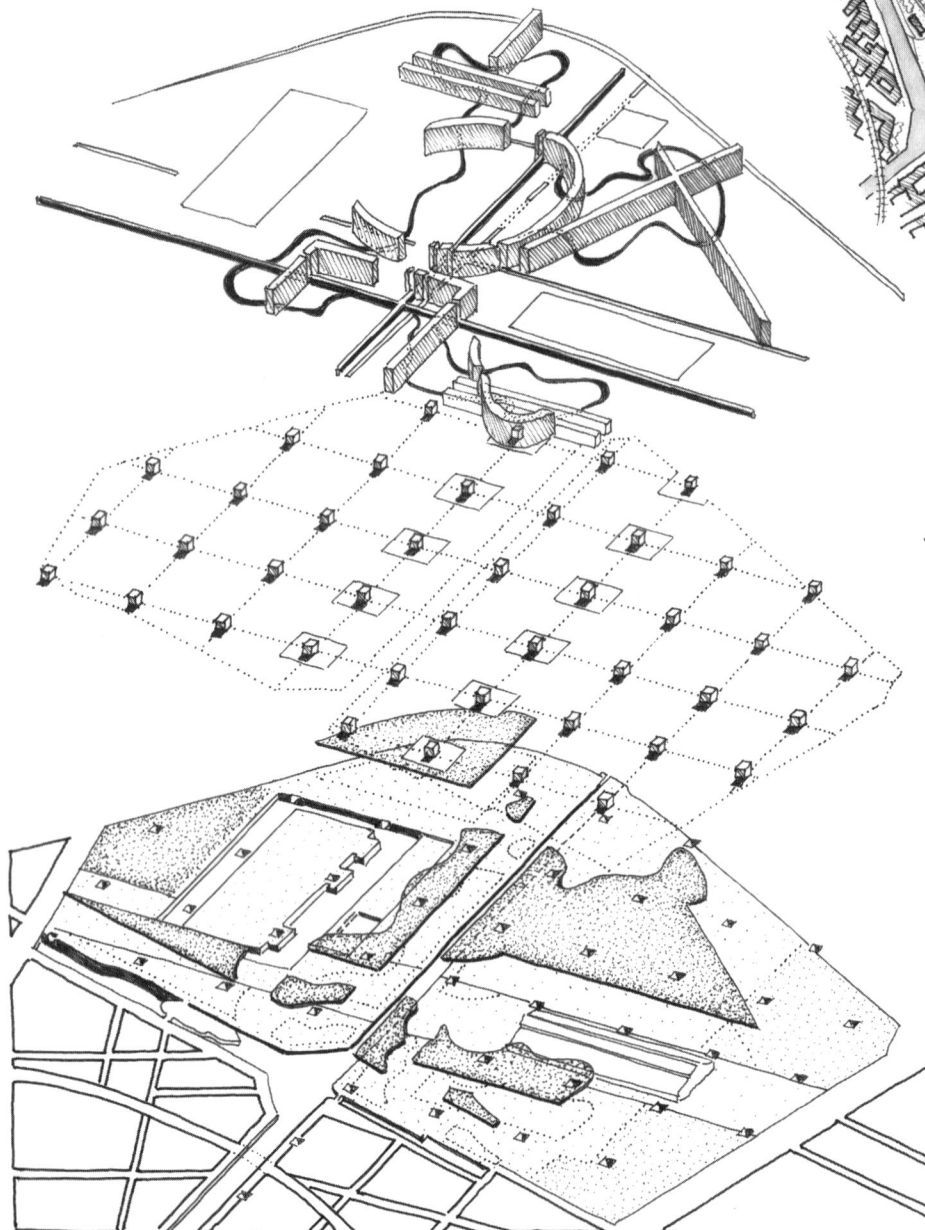

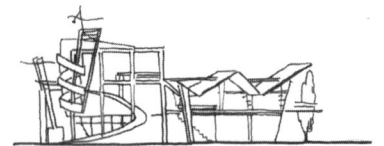

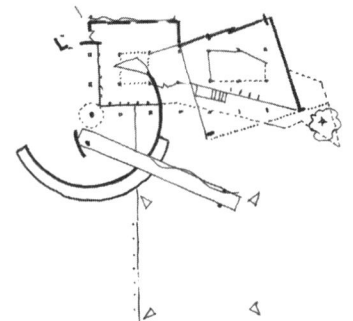

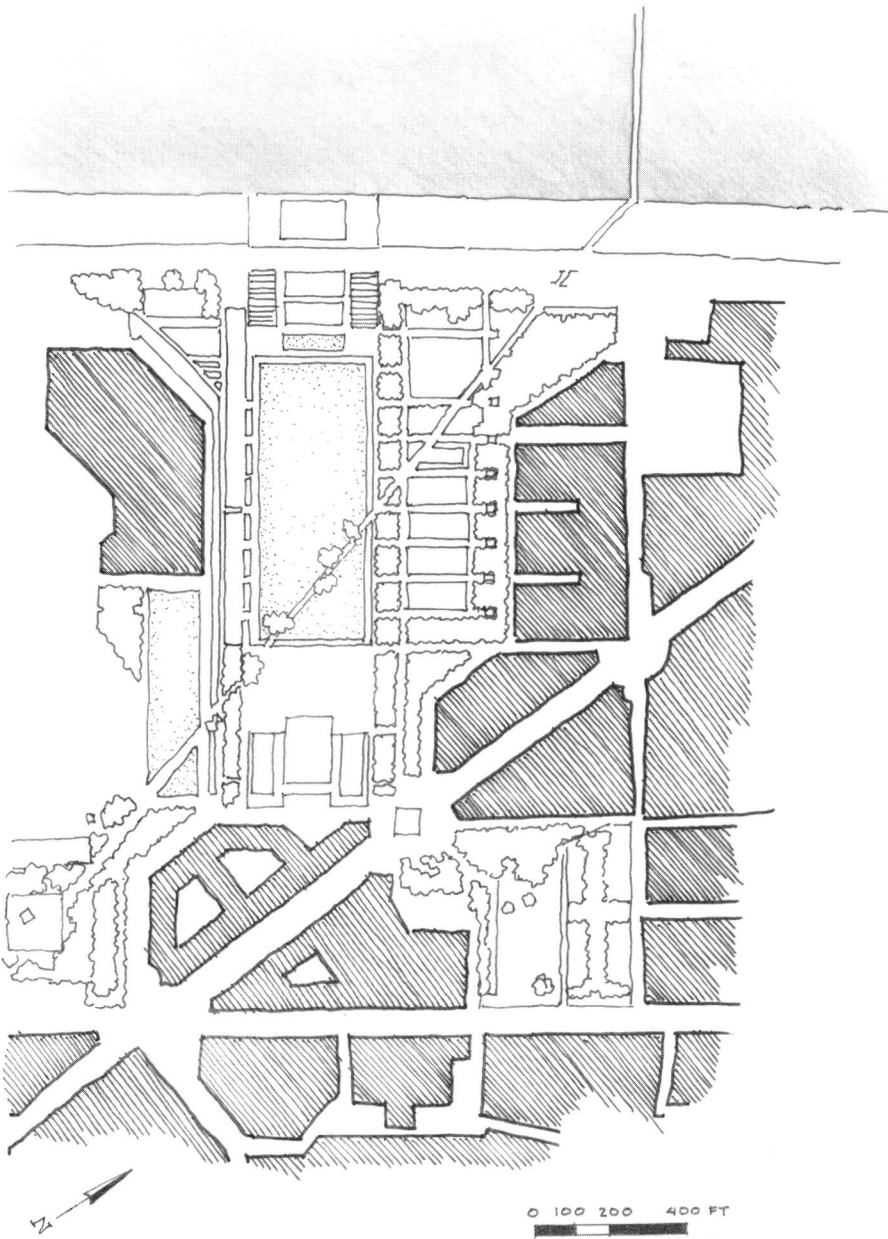

Landscape architects Alain Provost and Gilles Clement took a different approach to their design of Parc André Citroën (1992), built on the site of a former car plant on the outskirts of Paris. Organized by precise geometry, the 35-acre park might be understood as a bold, minimalist interpretation of a 17th-century French formal garden. A large central lawn (a *tapis vert*) forms an axis perpendicular to the Seine, as did historic riverfront gardens in the city center. Six themed gardens on the north side of the open lawn all have an alchemical symbology: each is associated with a metal, a planet, a day of the week, a state of water, and a sense (the sixth sense being intuition).[19] Water channels subdivide the spaces. Two glasshouses on the eastern end of the park are separated by a plaza with dancing jets of water. An elevated walkway on the south side of the lawn parallels a reflecting pool. A long diagonal path cuts across the park and creates a variety of dynamic spatial experiences.

These two urban parks represent a new idiom of park design, one vastly different from the 19th-century conception of a picturesque ideal. Whereas Parc de la Villette presents a purposely unresolved space in which a variety of activities and paths can be determined by the visitor, Parc André Citroën, nestled within the urban fabric, provides a sense of place determined by the landscape. Its enclosed gardens return us to the idea of the *hortus conclusus*, a place of peace, pleasure, and joy.

BLUE GARDEN — VENUS — COPPER — SMELL

GREEN GARDEN — JUPITER — TIN — HEARING

ORANGE GARDEN — MERCURY — MERCURY — TOUCH

RED GARDEN — MARS — IRON — TASTE

SILVER GARDEN — MOON — SILVER — SIGHT

GOLDEN GARDEN — SUN — GOLD — 6th. SENSE

ALCHEMY IN THE GARDEN: The six intimate garden rooms at Parc André Citroën all represent a different theme.

SUMMARY

New resources, technologies, modes of transportation, and communication systems transformed the way people interacted with each other and with the natural world in the 20th century. The ideals expressed in the landscape reflected these changing values.

Landscape design in the 20th century was subject to a variety of influences. Space became very architectonic. Trends in the art world were interpreted by landscape architects. Analyses of site conditions and user needs determined the form and function of the modernist landscape. Postmodernist designers searched to rebuild a traditional sense of community. The so-called green revolution focused the profession on ecological design.

DESIGN PRINCIPLES

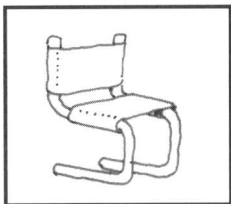

UTILITY
Form determined by functionality makes users' needs a priority.

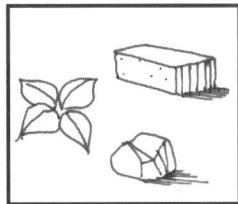

TRUTH
Honest design expresses the inherent quality of a material or a site.

CORRESPONDENCE
Beauty results from an awareness of the synchronicity of time, place, and idea.

ORIGINALITY
Innovation results from rejecting preconceived ideas and being open to all possibilities.

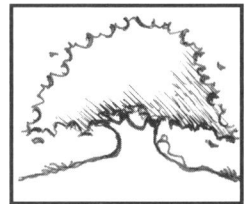

INTEGRITY
A design is complete in itself when it acknowledges the moral component of beauty.

DESIGN VOCABULARY

Grids

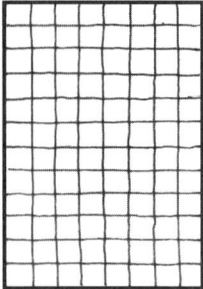

Shifted axes

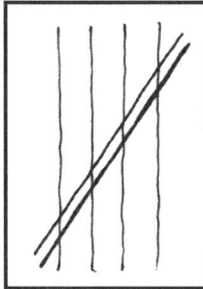

Arcs and tangents

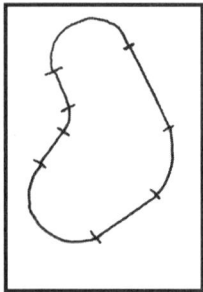

Biomorphic shapes

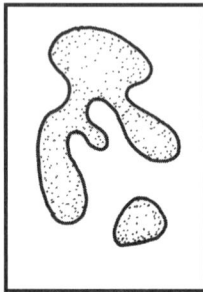

Synthetic material

Landform

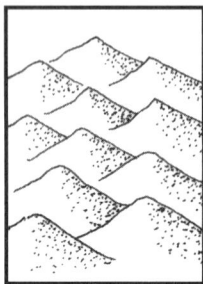

Collage

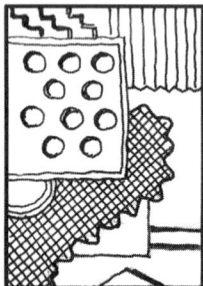

Color

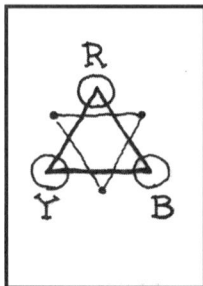

For further exploration

BOOKS

1984, by George Orwell
THE AGE OF INNOCENCE, by Edith Wharton
BRAVE NEW WORLD, by Aldous Huxley
THE FOUNTAINHEAD, by Ayn Rand
THE GRAPES OF WRATH, by John Steinbeck
THE GREAT GATSBY, by F. Scott Fitzgerald
THE JUNGLE, by Upton Sinclair
ON THE ROAD, by Jack Kerouac
OVERLAY, by Lucy Lippard
SAND COUNTY ALMANAC, by Aldo Leopold
SILENT SPRING, by Rachel Carson

FILMS

ALL'S FAIR AT THE FAIR (1938)
APOCALYPSE NOW (1979)
THE CABINET OF DR. CALIGARI (1920)
CASABLANCA (1942)
CITIZEN KANE (1941)
DR. STRANGELOVE (1964)
GONE WITH THE WIND (1939)
HOTEL RWANDA (2004)
THE LAST EMPEROR (1987)
METROPOLIS (1927)
MON ONCLE, by Jacques Tati (1958)
SCHINDLER'S LIST (1993)
THE TRUMAN SHOW (1998)

PAINTINGS AND SCULPTURE

LES MADEMOISELLES D'AVIGNON, by Pablo Picasso (1907)
NUDE DESCENDING A STAIRCASE, by Marcel Duchamp (1912)
SUPREMATIST COMPOSITION: WHITE ON WHITE, by Kazimir Malevich (1918)
BIRD IN SPACE, by Constantin Brancusi (1928)
COMPOSITION WITH RED, BLUE AND YELLOW, by Piet Mondrian (1930)
RECUMBENT FIGURE, by Henry Moore (1938)
LOBSTER TRAP AND FISH TAIL, by Alexander Calder (1939)
AN AMERICAN EXODUS, photographic series by Dorothea Lange (1939)
AUTUMN RHYTHM (NUMBER 30), by Jackson Pollock (1950)
LIGHTNING FIELD, by Walter de Maria (1977)
SURROUNDED ISLANDS, by Christo and Jean-Claude (1983)
BOHEMIA LIES BY THE SEA (1996), by Anselm Kiefer

21st CENTURY

Everything depends on an unforeseeable historic continuity. But if we succeed in developing our culture while continuing to respect our past, we have a chance of preserving it.

—Stephen Jay Gould (2000)

Cultural trends have become linked to the marketplace; 21st-century culture is mobile, networked, and instantly available. The fashionable trend at the moment is "green"; what started as a countercultural movement has now become mainstream. Everything is green. Sustainability is a buzzword. One hopes that this trend will be permanently instilled into the global consciousness and become the origin of all design.

The early modernists were optimistic about the potential for industrial materials and methods to offer promise for the future. Designers are again hopeful that technology can help reestablish a harmonic balance with nature. The projects described in this chapter demonstrate that art and science can combine to create beautiful and ecologically responsible design.

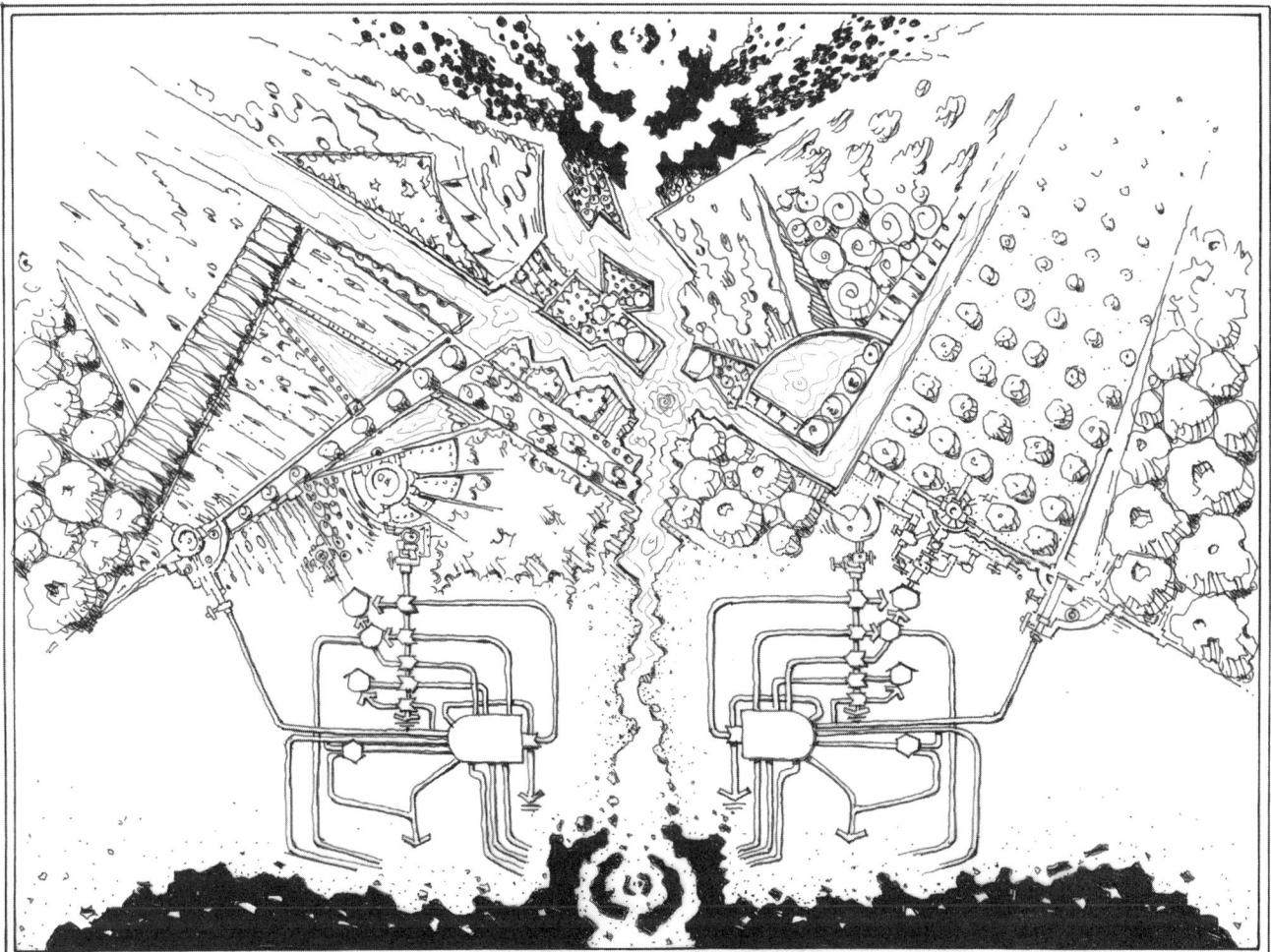

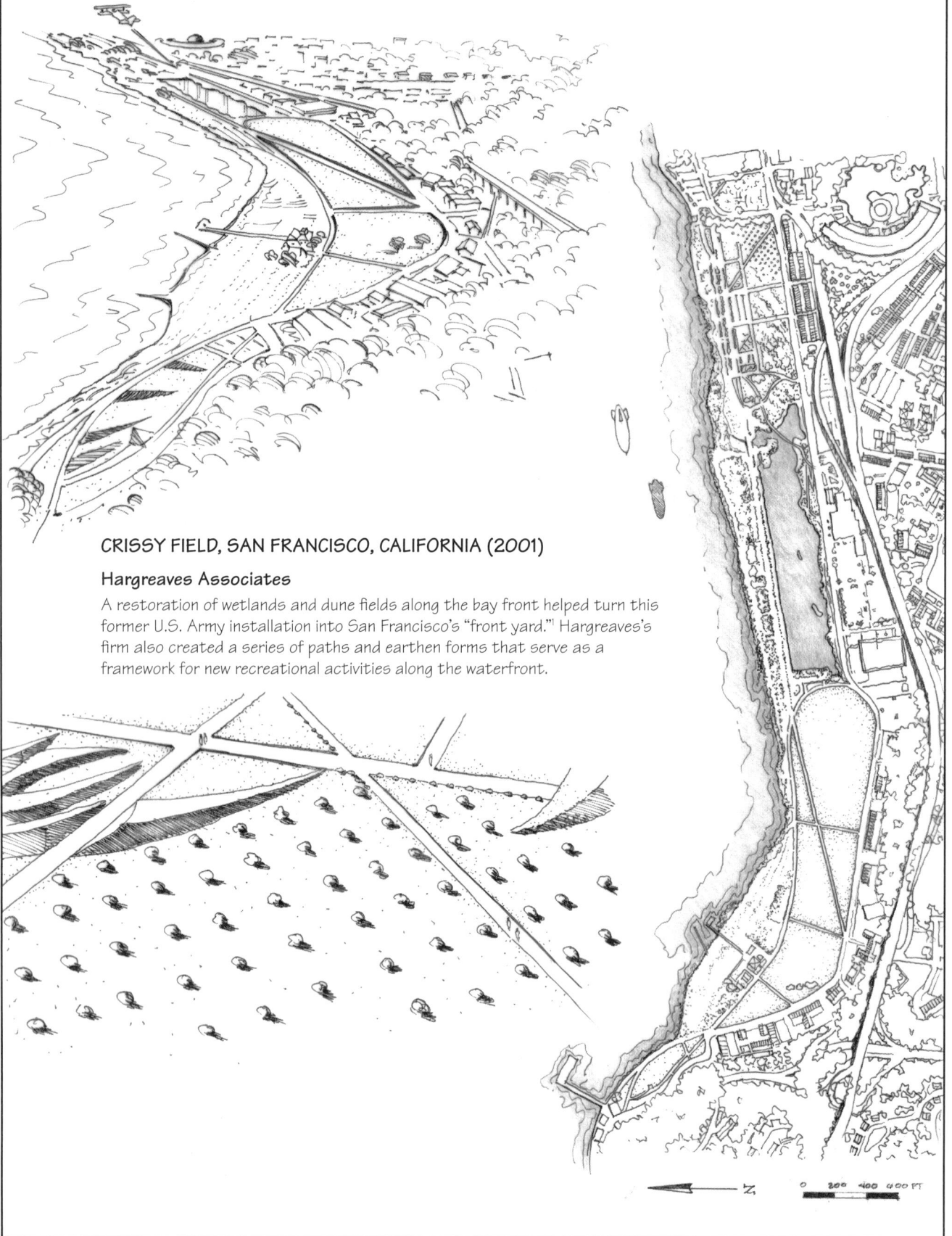

CRISSY FIELD, SAN FRANCISCO, CALIFORNIA (2001)

Hargreaves Associates

A restoration of wetlands and dune fields along the bay front helped turn this former U.S. Army installation into San Francisco's "front yard."[1] Hargreaves's firm also created a series of paths and earthen forms that serve as a framework for new recreational activities along the waterfront.

HERMAN MILLER FACTORY LANDSCAPE, CHEROKEE COUNTY, GEORGIA (2001)

Michael Van Valkenburgh Associates, Inc.

The design for this rural factory was driven largely by hydrologic management. The entire 22-acre building site is graded at a 5 percent slope, allowing for runoff from the built surfaces to sheet into wetlands without the use of pipes or curbs. When the wetland system is dry, it functions as a meadow, with trees creating thickets along the edges of the floodplain.

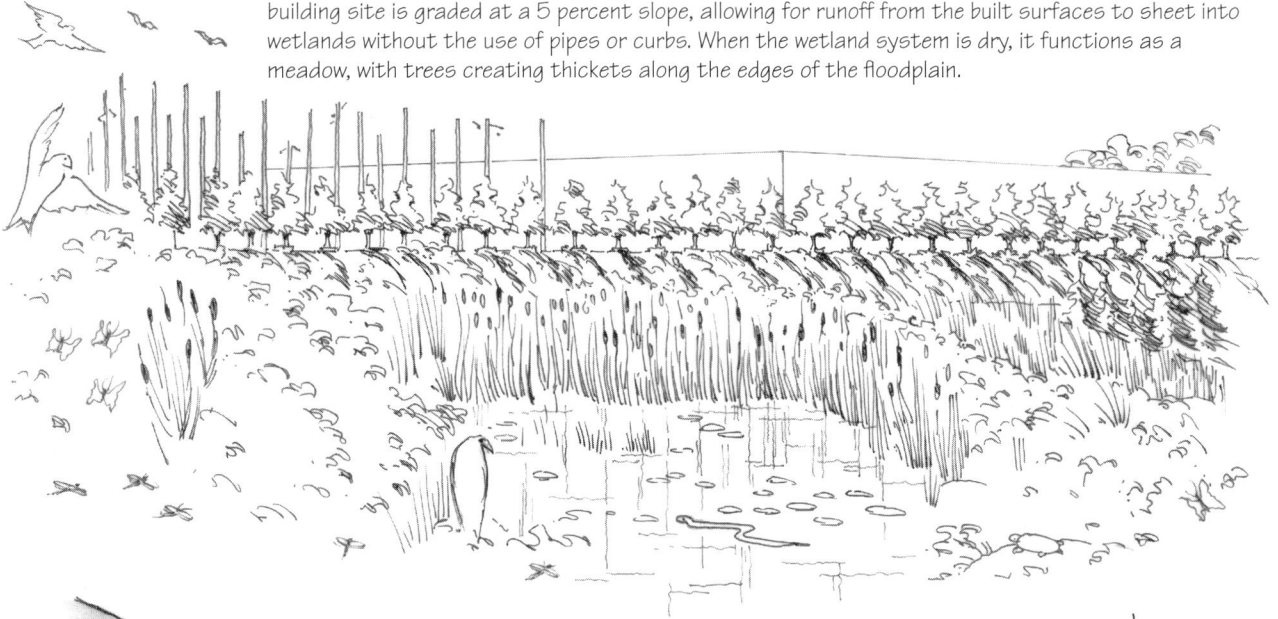

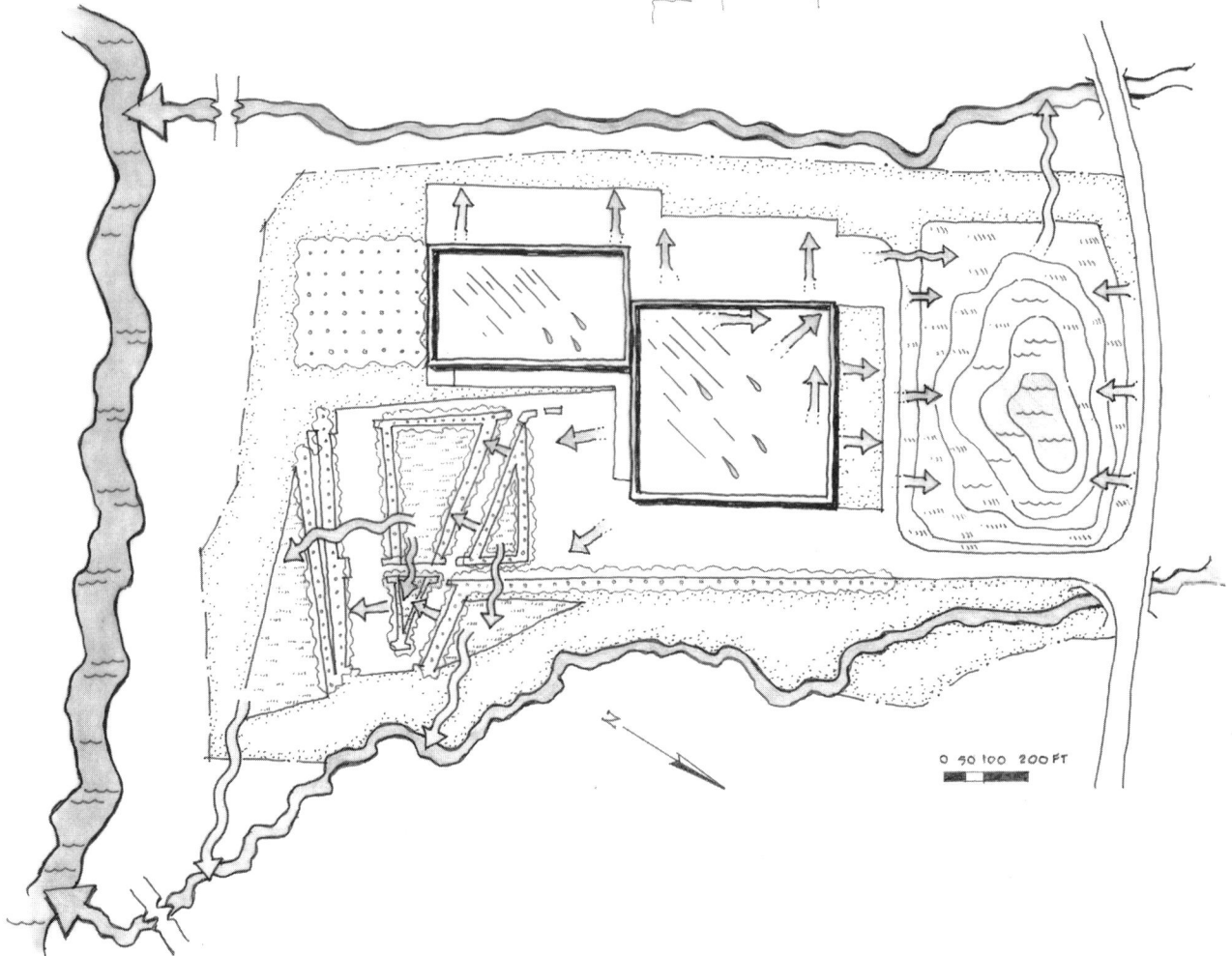

BLUR BUILDING AND ARTEPLAGE, YVERDON-LES-BAINS, SWITZERLAND (2002)

**Diller + Scofidio (architects),
West 8 (landscape architects)**

Built as the Exposition Pavilion for the Swiss Expo, this space takes the line between architecture and landscape, structure and atmosphere, and erases it completely. The site is consistently engulfed in fog, thanks to water pumped from Lake Neuchatel and shot as a fine mist through 35,000 nozzles. The resulting whiteout effect leaves the visitor in a space that is both formless and scaleless. It is a 21st-century rumination on the limits of physical spatial design.

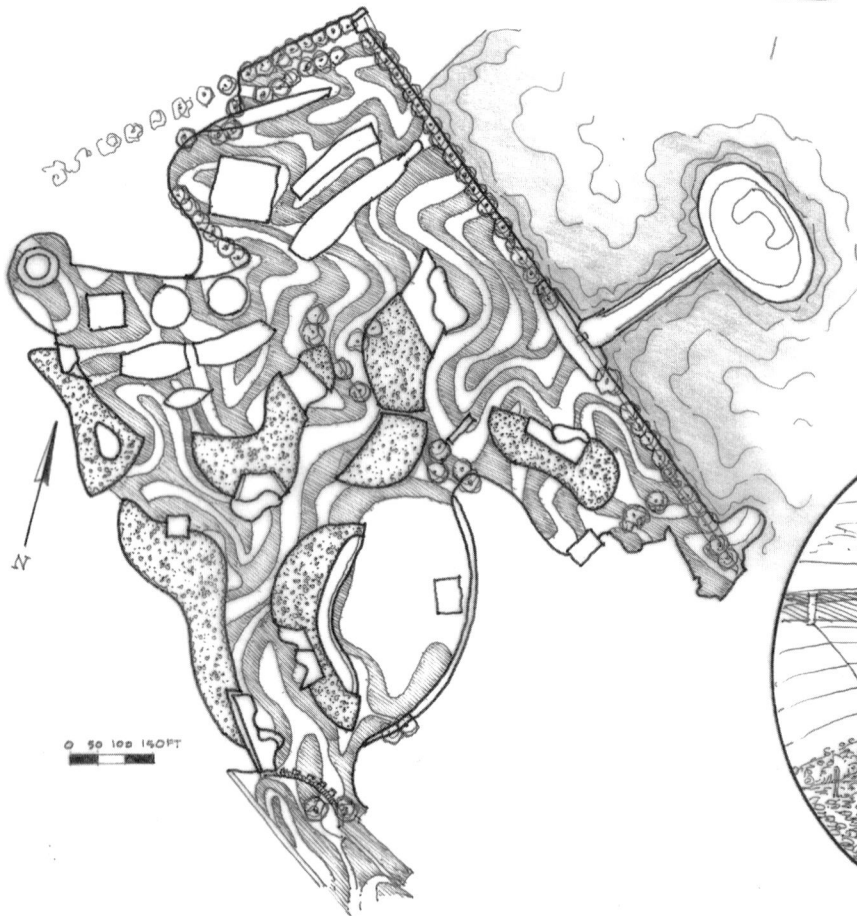

Access to the pavilion was across a plaza constructed entirely with recyclable materials. Eighteen-foot-high artificial dunes collided with rough timber structures and biomorphic patterns of fragrant, colorful flowers, adding to the visitor's sense of disorientation.

0 50 100 150FT

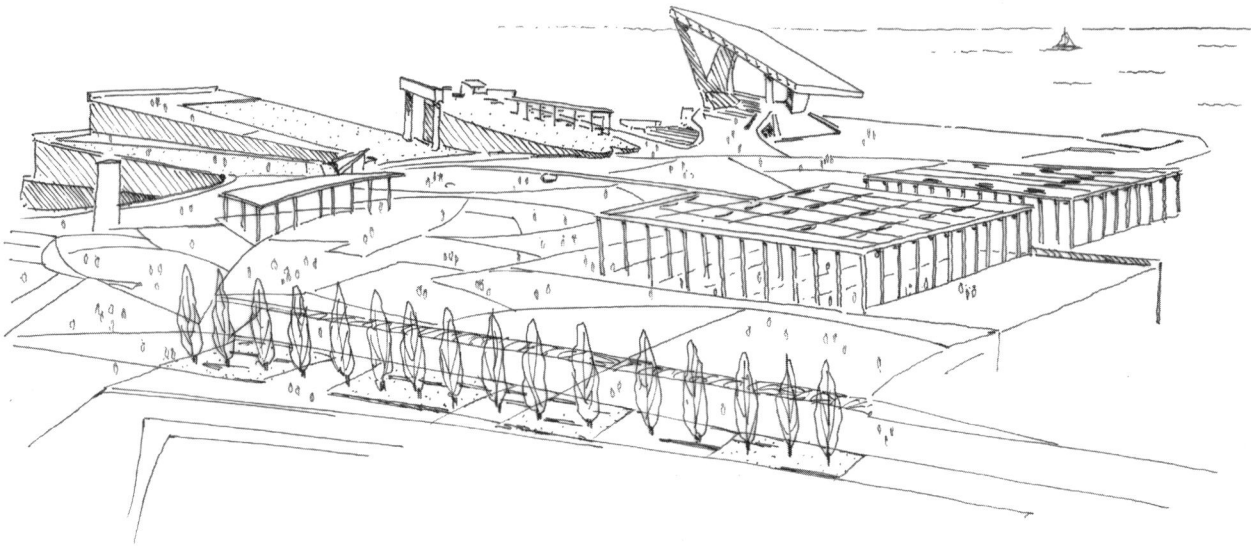

FORUM ESPLANADE BARCELONA, SPAIN (2004)

Torres & Lapena

When designers began employing renewable energy technologies in their designs in the latter part of the 20th century, the electricity-generating infrastructure often served merely as a skin applied to a design. However, the photovoltaic "pergola" at the Forum Esplanade Barcelona employs solar energy production as an integral space-making device. The grand scale and skewed plane of the pergola's canopy provides crucial shade, 4,500 square meters of photovoltaic panels, and a clear terminus for the waterfront esplanade.

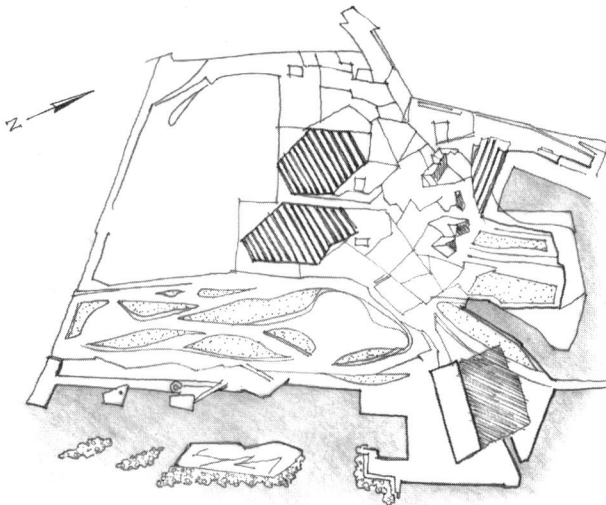

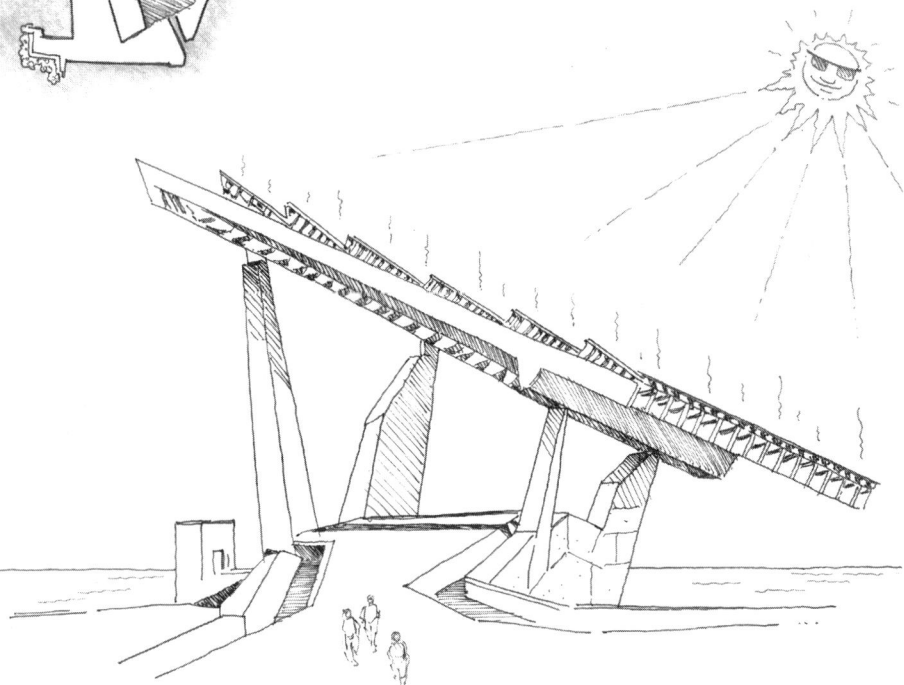

LURIE GARDEN, CHICAGO, ILLINOIS (2004)

Gustafson Guthrie Nichol Ltd., Piet Oudolf and Robert Israel

Built atop an underground parking structure and former rail line in Chicago, the Lurie Garden is the focal point of Millennium Park, the open space that connects the city's downtown to Lake Michigan. Gustafson tapped into Chicago's ecological history, using native plants and local stones to reference the Midwestern prairie in a grouping of geometric gardens. A boardwalk runs beside a stylized stream where pedestrians can sit with their feet in the water—a new promenade for the tourists and businesspeople, who crowd into the park during the humid summer months.

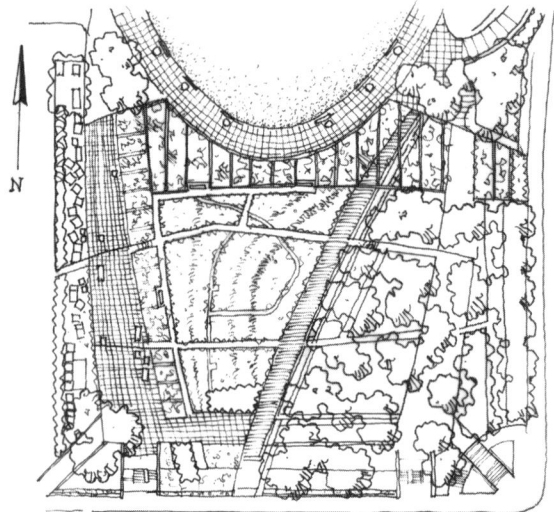

0 30 60 90FT

SHENYANG ARCHITECTURAL UNIVERSITY CAMPUS, SHENYANG CITY, LIAONING PROVINCE, CHINA (2004)

Kongjian Yu and Lin Shihong

With China's stunningly quick turn toward urbanization in the 20th century, food-production landscapes in the country have come under increasing pressure. In response, landscape architect Kongjian Yu combined rice fields and native vegetation to frame spaces for outdoor education, helping make clear the connection between productive agriculture and urban existence.

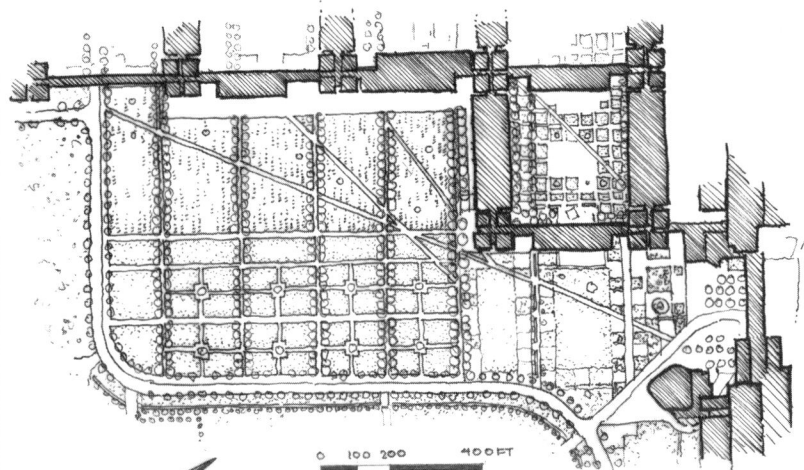

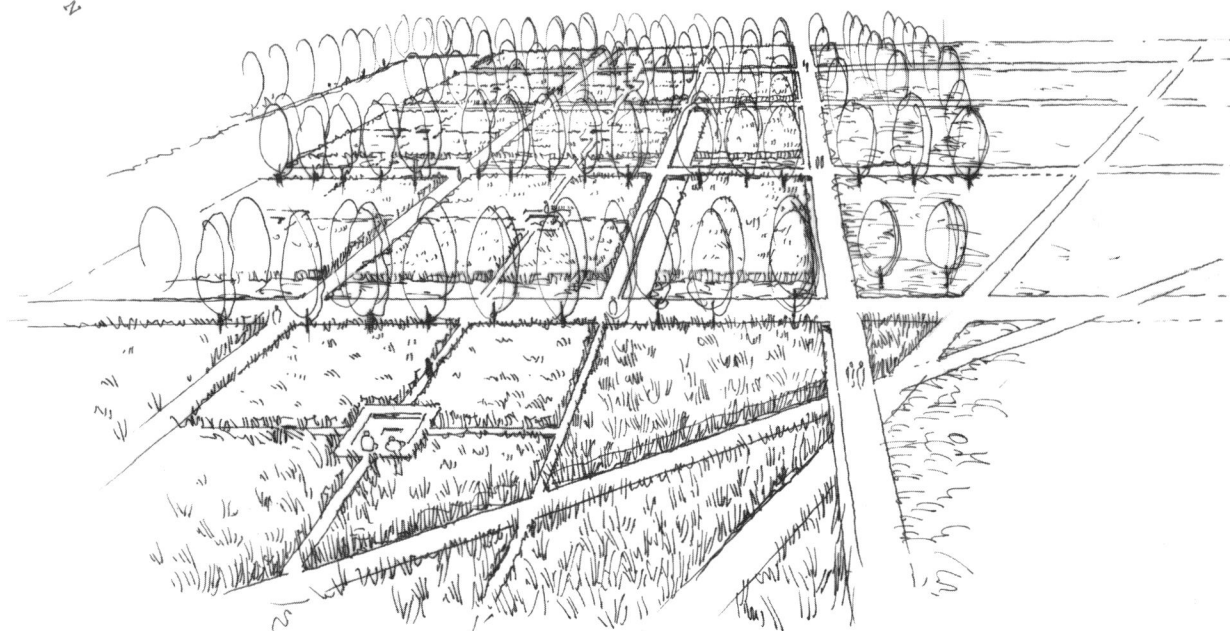

0 10 20   40 FT

TANNER SPRINGS PARK, PORTLAND, OREGON (2005)

Atelier Dreiseitl

In a city widely noted for its sustainable water practices, Tanner Springs Park stands out for its combination of smart hydrology and thoughtful aesthetics. Rainwater is collected and purified through a wetland system. An orthogonal boardwalk floats over the wetlands, bringing urban dwellers in close contact with these natural hydrological processes.

FOUNTAIN PROMENADE AT CHAPULTEPEC PARK, MEXICO CITY, MEXICO (2006)

Grupo de Diseno (Mario Schjetnan)

One of several phases of redesigns for Chapultepec Park by Schjetnan and company, this piece sought to attract families to a previously underused area of the city's central park. A promenade, stone-and-steel pergolas, and a children's play area are integrated with the green infrastructure of the park, which includes new canals for water quality improvement and reforestation programs.

THE LIVING ROOF: CALIFORNIA ACADEMY OF SCIENCES, SAN FRANCISCO, CALIFORNIA (2008)

Renzo Piano

The architect employed a series of seven undulating landforms atop the roof of the Academy of Sciences to reference San Francisco's iconic hills. The design allows Golden Gate Park to climb up and over the new building. The slopes draw cool air into the open piazza in the middle of the building, while the rooftop's weather stations regulate its passive ventilation system.

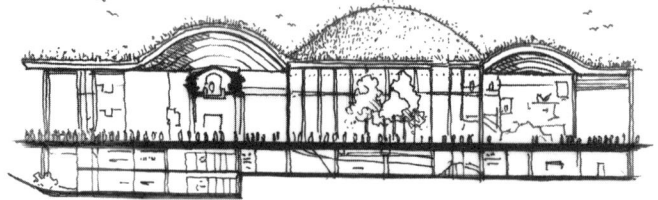

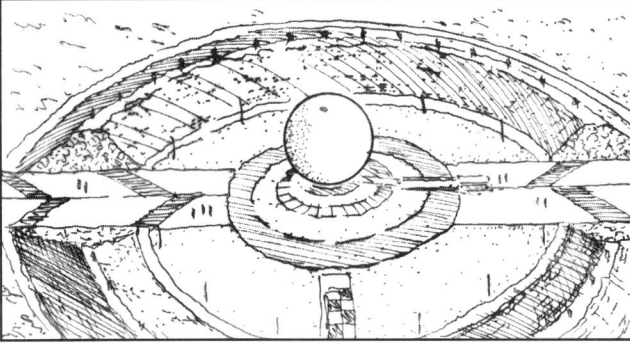

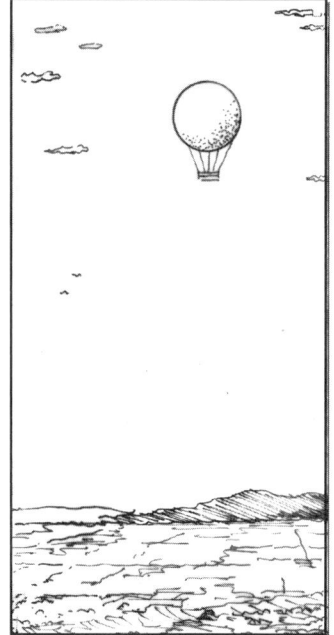

ORANGE COUNTY GREAT PARK, IRVINE, CALIFORNIA (2010)

Ken Smith Workshop, with Mia Lehrer + Associates

The competition to design a park on the former El Toro Marine Base resulted in the greatest urban park commission since Olmsted's Central Park. The project involves the restoration and transformation of more than 1,300 acres of land. The designers envision the park as three distinct conceptual areas: habitat, fields, and canyon. Features include a sports park and recreational fields; a Veterans Memorial; a Botanic Garden; cultural facilities, including a Library, Museum, and café; and a wildlife corridor contiguous to a State Park and National Forest. Goals of sustainability will be met through habitat restoration, natural water treatment systems, and the use of photovoltaics.

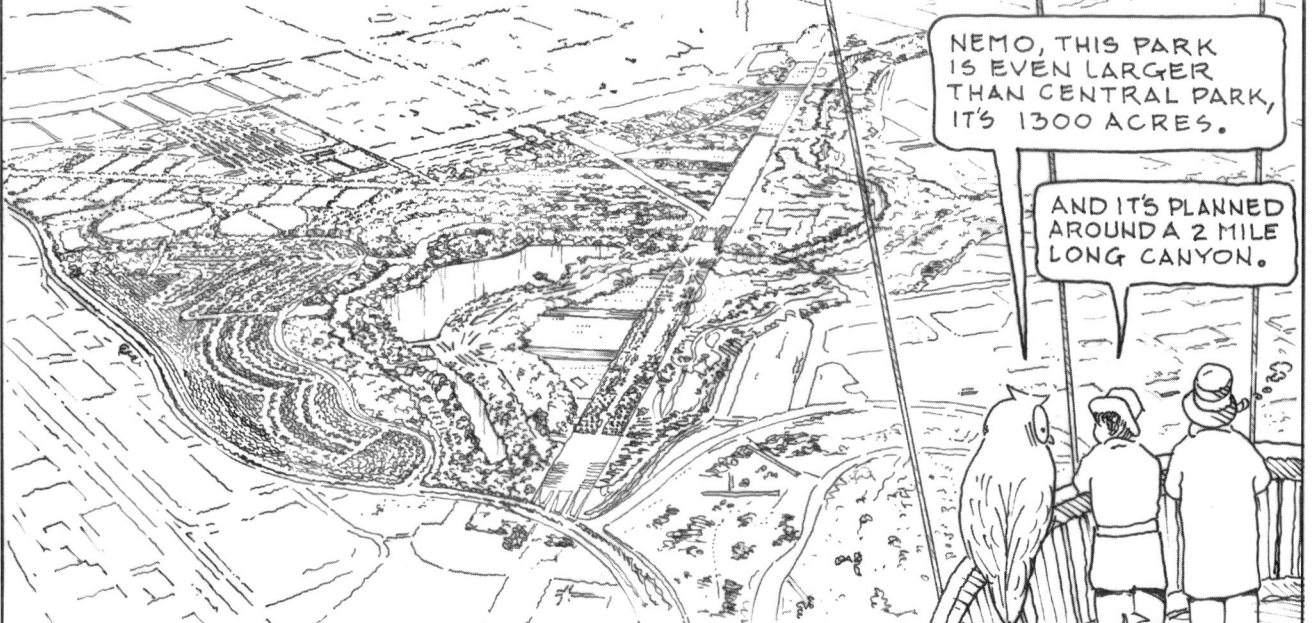

NEMO, THIS PARK IS EVEN LARGER THAN CENTRAL PARK, IT'S 1300 ACRES.

AND IT'S PLANNED AROUND A 2 MILE LONG CANYON.

SUMMARY

Thus our visual romp through landscape design history comes to a rest, as a whole new set of challenges faces the 21st century designer. In the first decade of this century, it is difficult to judge which of the more recent projects will survive the test of time. Go forth and plant the future.

> *Whatever befalls the Earth,*
> *befalls the children of the Earth.*
>
> CHIEF SEATTLE

DESIGN PRINCIPLES

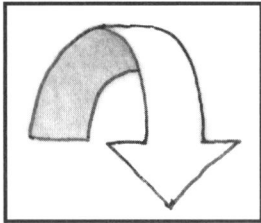   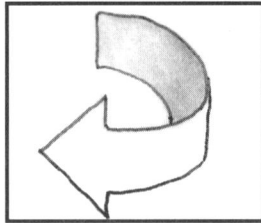   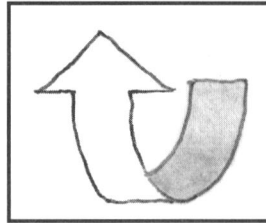

REDUCE   REUSE   RECYCLE

GARDEN FOR THE 21st CENTURY: Chip Sullivan's proposal for an energy-conserving garden.

DESIGN VOCABULARY

EARTH

WIND

SUN

WATER

For further exploration

BOOKS

CRADLE TO CRADLE: REMAKING THE WAY WE MAKE THINGS, by William McDonough and Michael Braungart

DESIGN FOR ECOLOGICAL DEMOCRACY, by Randolph T. Hester

THE DIAMOND AGE, by Neal Stephenson

DUNE, by Frank Herbert

THE END OF OIL: ON THE EDGE OF A PERILOUS NEW WORLD, by Paul Roberts

GARDEN AND CLIMATE, by Chip Sullivan

THE MEMOIRS OF A SURVIVOR, by Doris Lessing

THE OMNIVORE'S DILEMMA, by Michael Pollan

ORYX AND CRAKE, by Margaret Atwood

RECLAIMING THE AMERICAN WEST, by Alan Berger

FILMS

2001: A SPACE ODYSSEY (1968)

AN INCONVENIENT TRUTH (2006)

BLADERUNNER (1982)

LOST IN TRANSLATION (2003)

THE MARCH OF THE PENGUINS (2005)

THE MATRIX (1999)

RIVERS AND TIDES (2001)

SLUMDOG MILLIONAIRE (2008)

SUPER SIZE ME (2004)

WALL-E (2006)

ARTWORKS

RODEN CRATER (earthwork), by James Turrell (2000)

EVERY SHOT, EVERY EPISODE (installation), by Jennifer and Kevin McCoy (2001)

SETO INLAND SEA, YASHIMA (photography), by Hiroshi Sugimoto (2001)

THE WEATHER PROJECT (installation), by Olafur Eliasson (2003)

CLOUD GATE, by Anish Kapoor (2004)

FOR NEW YORK CITY (light projection), by Jenny Holzer (2004)

Notes

PREHISTORY–6TH CENTURY CE

1. Archeologist Alfred Kroeber and Peruvian scholar Toribio Mejia first documented the lines in their travel diaries in 1926. German mathematician Maria Reiche began studying the geoglyphs at Nazca in 1946. She dedicated her life to the documentation and preservation of the enigmatic lines and figures. Reiche published her photographs and influential theories on the astronomical orientation of the Nazca lines in her pamphlet *Mystery on the Desert* (1949). Reiche acknowledged the work of historian Paul Kosok, who first noted the alignment of one of the traces with sunset on the summer solstice, and who referred to the markings as a "gigantic calendar."

2. The tale of adventure known as the Epic of Gilgamesh dates from the 7th century BCE and was written in cuneiform on a series of clay tablets. In the story, the walled city of Uruk enclosed "one league city, one league palm gardens, one league lowlands." See *The Epic of Gilgamesh*, translated by Maureen Gallery Kovacs (Stanford, CA: Stanford University Press, 1989), p. 3.

3. This drawing is based on the plan reconstructed by Elisabeth B. Moynihan in *Paradise as a Garden in Persia and Mughal India* (New York: George Braziller, 1979), p. 17. See also Ralph Pinder-Wilson, "The Persian Garden: Bagh and Chahar Bagh," in *The Islamic Garden*, Dumbarton Oaks Colloquium on the History of Landscape Architecture IV, Elisabeth B. MacDougall and Richard Ettinghausen, eds. (Washington, DC: Dumbarton Oaks, Trustees for Harvard University, 1976), pp. 71–72.

4. The total area of Hadrian's villa is estimated at 300 acres. See William L. MacDonald and John A. Pinto, *Hadrian's Villa and Its Legacy* (New Haven: Yale University Press, 1995), p. 29.

5. Hobhouse, Penelope. *The Story of Gardening* (London: Dorling Kindersley Ltd., 2002), p. 27.

6. The classical "orders" refer to specific compositions of column, capital, and base, and include the Doric, Ionic, and Corinthian orders. The Doric order is the simplest in design, and the oldest. The Ionic order is taller and more slender, its capital distinguished by scrolling volutes. The Corinthian capital is more ornate, with carved acanthus leaves. Vitruvius cataloged the orders in the 1st century. Serlio elaborated on the proportioning system during the Renaissance.

7. In his book *Design of Cities* (1974), Edmund Bacon described the development of the agora over time, particularly noting the relationship between architecture and open space, and its effect on movement systems (see pp. 64–71). The open space of the agora was most clearly articulated during the Hellenistic era. In the Roman period, the addition of fountains, sculptures, and temples affected the clarity of the space. The agora was destroyed in 267 CE.

8. Emperor Qin Shi Huangdi unified all of China. Great advancements took place during his reign; weights, measures, currency, and writing were standardized. He initiated a canal-building project to connect northern and southern river systems, and expanded existing border fortifications to form the Great Wall. The imperial system stayed in place until the 20th century.

   Qin Shi Huangdi commissioned a new royal palace and great hunting park, Shanglin, built along the Wei River near the capital of Chang-an, on the slopes of Li Shan mountain. Written accounts describe a miniature universe of rare plants and animals and a network of secret passageways and corridors that connected the opulent palace complex. He also ordered the construction of an enormous mausoleum that included an army of life-size terracotta soldiers. His lavish extravagances led to the downfall of his dynasty, but established a prototype for imperial gardens.

9. The Neolithic Revolution refers to the important societal shift from hunting and gathering to settled agriculture. Glaciers began to recede at the end of the Paleolithic Era, or Old Stone Age (500,000 BCE–8,000 BCE). The cave paintings in southern France date from this period. During the Neolithic Era, or New Stone Age (8,000 BCE–4,000 BCE), belief in celestial gods replaced notions of an earth goddess. The first urban civilizations developed in the fertile crescent during the Bronze Age (4,000 BCE–2,000 BCE), when writing and metallurgy advanced.

   Jane Jacobs disputed the theory that settled agriculture was a prerequisite for the development of cities in her book *The Economy of Cities* (1969), stating that agriculture and the domestication of animals emerged from urban centers.

6TH–15TH CENTURIES CE

1. "A garden enclosed is my sister, my spouse; a spring shut up, a fountain sealed." Song of Solomon 4:12.

2. See Ferguson, George. *Signs and Symbols in Christian Art* (London: Oxford University Press, 1961).

3. From *The Romance of the Rose*, Guillaume de Lorris and Jean de Meun; translated and edited by Frances Horgan (New York: Oxford University Press, 1999).

4. King, Roland. *The Quest for Paradise* (New York: Mayflower Books, 1979), p. 70.

5. Illustration after M. Gomez-Moreno, in Marianne Barrucand and Achim Bednorz, *Moorish Architecture in Andalusia* (Cologne: Taschen, 2007), p. 69. See also Hobhouse, Penelope. *The Story of Gardening* (London, Dorling Kindersley Limited, 2002), pp. 66–67.

6. Wright, Richardson. *The Story of Gardening: From the Hanging Gardens of Babylon to the Hanging Gardens of New York* (New York: Garden City Publishing Co. Inc., 1938), p. 30.

7. James Dickie, "The Islamic Garden in Spain," in *The Islamic Garden*, Dumbarton Oaks Colloquium on the History of Landscape Architecture IV, Elisabeth B. MacDougall and Richard Ettinghausen, eds. (Washington, DC: Dumbarton Oaks, Trustees for Harvard University, 1976), p. 99.

8. Casa Valdes, Marquesa de. *Spanish Gardens*. Translated by Edward Tanner (Woodbridge, Suffolk, UK: Antique Collectors' Club Ltd., [1973] 1987), p. 41.

9. Keswick, Maggie. *The Chinese Garden: History, Art & Architecture* (New York: Rizzoli, 1978), pp. 48–49.

10. Kostoff, Spiro. *The City Shaped: Urban Patterns and Meanings Through History* (Boston: Bulfinch Press/Little Brown and Co., 1991), p. 33.

11. See Tuan, Yi-Fu. *Topophilia: A Study of Environmental Perception, Attitudes, and Values* (New York: Columbia University Press, 1990), pp. 164–166. Also, Tuan, Yi-Fu. *Space and Place: The Perspective of Experience* (Minneapolis: University of Minnesota Press, 2001), p. 134.

12. Wang Wei (701–761), poems from the Wang River sequence, in *The Anchor Book of Chinese Poetry*, Tony Barnstone and Chou Ping, eds. (New York: Anchor Books/Random House, 2005), pp. 106–107.

13. Jellicoe, Sir Geoffrey, Susan Jellicoe, Patrick Goode, and Michael Lancaster, eds. *The Oxford Companion to Gardens* (Oxford, UK: Oxford University Press, 1986), p. 541.

14. Keswick, *The Chinese Garden*, p. 56.

15. See Cahill, James. *Chinese Painting* (New York: Rizzoli, 1977).

16. Thacker, Christopher. *The History of Gardens* (Berkeley, CA: University of California Press, 1979), p. 55.

17. Image and poem adapted from the work of Chen Congzhou (1956) as presented by Stanislaus Fung in "Longing and Belonging in Chinese Garden History," in *Perspectives on Garden Histories*, Dumbarton Oaks Colloquium on the History of Landscape Architecture, vol. 21, Michel Conan, ed. (Washington, DC: Dumbarton Oaks, Trustees for Harvard University, 1999), pp. 209–210.

18. *The Travels of Marco Polo*, Art Type edition, The World's Popular Classics (New York Books, Inc., undated).

19. Flower-viewing festivals remain popular in Japan. Springtime celebrations include the plum blossom festival in February, the peach blossom festival in March, and the cherry blossom festival in April. See also Thacker, *The History of Gardens*, pp. 63–66.

20. Yuniwa refers to the purified space of Shinto shrines. A discussion of the evolution of the term can be found in Camelia Nakagawara, "The Japanese Garden for the Mind: The 'Bliss' of Paradise Transcended," in *Stanford Journal of East Asian Affairs*, vol. 4, no. 2, Summer 2004, pp. 84–85, 88–89. Retr. 3.1.09 from http://www.stanford.edu/group/sjeaa/journal42/japan2.pdf.

    Irmtraud Schaarschmidt-Richter discusses the function of the "sandy parterre" in *Japanese Gardens* (New York: William Morrow & Co. Inc., 1979), pp. 95–98. The changing use of the yuniwa at Kyoto Imperial Palace is described by Marc Treib and Ron Herman in *A Guide to the Gardens of Kyoto* (New York: Kodansha America Inc., 2003 revised edition), pp. 6, 72.

21. Schaarschmidt-Richter, *Japanese Gardens*, p. 50.

22. See Morris, A. E. J. *History of Urban Form: Before the Industrial Revolution* (New York: John Wiley & Sons, Inc., 1982), pp. 292–295.

23. See Nitschke, Gunter. *Japanese Gardens: Right Angle and Natural Form* (Cologne: Taschen, 1999), pp. 34–35.

24. Shikibu, Murasaki. *The Tale of Genji*. Translated by Edward G. Seidensticker (New York: Alfred A. Knopf, 1987), p. 386.

25. See Keane, Marc. *Japanese Garden Design* (Rutland, VT: Charles E. Tuttle Inc., 1996), p. 50.

26. Nitschke, *Japanese Gardens*, pp. 76–77.

15th CENTURY

1. For a discussion of how changing architectural styles affected the perception and use of gardens, see Camelia Nakagawara, "The Japanese Garden for the Mind: The 'Bliss' of Paradise Transcended," in *Stanford Journal of East Asian Affairs*, vol. 4, no. 2, Summer 2004, p. 93. Retr. 3.1.09 from http://www.stanford.edu/group/sjeaa/journal42/japan2.pdf.

2. See the section on "The Rise of the Working Garden Master" by Irmtraud Schaarschmidt-Richter in *Japanese Gardens* (New York: William Morrow & Co. Inc., 1979), p. 257.

3. Kuck, Loraine. *The World of the Japanese Garden: From Chinese Origins to Modern Landscape Art* (New York: Weatherhill, 1968), p. 142.

4. Ibid., p. 139.

5. Gunter Nitschke discusses the symbolism of the garden in *Japanese Gardens: Right Angle and Natural Form* (Cologne: Taschen, 1999), p. 93.

6. Schaarschmidt-Richter, *Japanese Gardens*, p. 75.

7. Keswick, Maggie. *The Chinese Garden: History, Art & Architecture* (New York: Rizzoli, 1978), p. 59.

8. Yi-Fu Tuan explains how the form of the city is based on traditional symbolism in *Topophilia: A Study of Environmental Perception, Attitudes, and Values* (New York: Columbia University Press, 1990), pp. 164–166. Also, Tuan, Yi-Fu, *Space and Place: The Perspective of Experience* (Minneapolis: University of Minnesota Press, 2001), p. 165.

9. See Ruy Gonzalez de Clavijo, *Embassy to Tamerlane 1403–1406*, translated by Guy LeStrange (London: George Routledge & Sons, 1928).

10. Wilber, Donald Newton. *Persian Gardens and Garden Pavilions* (Washington, DC: Dumbarton Oaks, Trustees for Harvard University, 1979), p. 32.

11. Ralph Pinder-Wilson, "The Persian Garden: Bagh and Chahar Bagh," in *The Islamic Garden*, Dumbarton Oaks Colloquium on the History of Landscape Architecture IV, Elisabeth B. MacDougall and Richard Ettinghausen, eds. (Washington, DC: Dumbarton Oaks, Trustees for Harvard University, 1976), p. 80.

12. de Clavijo, *Embassy to Tamerlane 1403–1406*, p. 206.

13. Ibid., p. 227.

14. Masson, Georgina. *Italian Gardens* (Woodbridge, England: Antique Collectors' Club, 1987), p. 57.

15. Van der Ree, Paul, Gerrit Smienk, and Clemens Steenbergen. *Italian Villas and Gardens*. (Munich: Presel-Verlag, 1993), p. 24.

16. Cicero, in the 1st century BCE, coined the phrase "second nature" to denote a landscape shaped by use; the conceptual framework was expanded upon during the Renaissance to include a third state of nature shaped by art. See John Dixon Hunt, *Gardens and the Picturesque* (Cambridge: MIT Press, 1992), pp. 3–4. Claudia Lazzaro discusses the categorization of plantings in chapters two and five of *The Italian Renaissance Garden* (New Haven, CT: Yale University Press, 1990); her explanation of the origin of the concept of second and third nature occurs on page 9.

17. Ackerman, James S. *The Villa: Form and Ideology of Country Houses* (Princeton, NJ: Princeton University Press, 1990), p. 73.

18. Sica, Grazia Gobbi. *The Florentine Villa* (Oxford: Routledge, 2007), p. 47.

NOTES

16th CENTURY

1. Painters, sculptors, and architects working in the Mannerist style exploited classical prototypes, applying classical motifs and conventions in a manner removed from and often contradictory to historical contexts.

2. Masson, Georgina. *Italian Gardens* (Woodbridge, England: Antique Collectors' Club, 1987), p. 122.

3. Lazzaro, Claudia. *The Italian Renaissance Garden*, (New Haven, CT: Yale University Press, 1990), p. 236.

4. Ibid., pp. 246–247.

5. Pliny described a table in the garden at his Tuscan villa that contained a basin of water where dishes could be floated during a meal. See Masson, *Italian Gardens*, p. 25.

6. See the section on "The Concept of Stage Management," in *Italian Villas and Gardens* by Paul Van der Ree, Gerrit Smienk, and Clemens Steenbergen (Munich: Prestel-Verlag, 1993), pp. 25–27. Also Lazzaro, *The Italian Renaissance Garden*, pp. 110–111.

7. Van der Ree, *Italian Villas and Gardens*, pp. 191–195.

8. Ackerman, James S. *Palladio* (New York: Penguin Books, 1991), p. 25.

9. Woodbridge, Kenneth. *Princely Gardens: The Origins and Development of the French Formal Style* (London: Thames and Hudson, 1986), p. 44.

10. Ibid., pp. 81–82.

11. Newton, Norman T. *Design on the Land: The Development of Landscape Architecture* (Cambridge, MA: Belknap Press/Harvard University, 1974), p. 183.

12. The forthright is described by G. B. Tobey in *A History of Landscape Architecture: The Relationship of People to Environment* (New York: American Elsevier Publishing Company, Inc., 1973), p. 123.

13. The design of the pond and privy gardens, including the summerhouse, is described by Julia S. Berrall in *The Garden: An Illustrated History* (New York: Penguin Books, 1978), p. 237.

14. Lazzaro, *The Italian Renaissance Garden*, p. 11.

15. See Prest, John. *The Garden of Eden: The Botanic Garden and the Recreation of Paradise* (New Haven, CT: Yale University Press), 1988.

16. Babur's gardens served social and political ends, and were symbolic of the subjugation of conquered lands. For a discussion of the political expediency of royal encampments, see Thomas W. Lentz, "Memory and Ideology in the Timurid Garden," in *Mughal Gardens: Sources, Places, Representations and Prospects*, James L. Wescoat, Jr. and Joachim Wolschke-Bulmann, eds. (Washington, DC: Dumbarton Oaks Research Library and Collection, 1996), p. 56.

17. Moynihan, Elizabeth. *Paradise as a Garden in Persia and Mughal India* (New York: George Braziller, 1979), p. 83.

18. Wybe Kuitert explains the relationship between "Tea and Politics," particularly the role of Nobunaga's advisors, in *Themes in the History of Japanese Garden Art* (Honolulu: University of Hawaii Press, 2002), p. 152.

19. Ibid., p. 142.

20. Ibid., pp. 143–146.

21. Ibid., p. 147. The author discusses how nature was romanticized by urban dwellers, and relates the story of an aristocrat's visit to Soshu's tea hut.

17th CENTURY

1. See Penelope Hobhouse's description of the Hortus Palatinus in *The Story of Gardening* (London: Dorling Kindersley Ltd., 2004), pp. 144–145.

2. Wright, Richardson. *The Story of Gardening: From the Hanging Gardens of Babylon to the Hanging Gardens of New York* (Garden City, NY: Garden City Publishing Co. Inc., 1938), p. 301.

3. Keswick, Maggie. *The Chinese Garden* (New York: Rizzoli, 1980), p. 123.

4. Ibid., p. 158.

5. Gunter Nitschke explains aspects of neo-Confucianism in *Japanese Gardens: Right Angle and Natural Form* (Cologne: Taschen, 1999), p. 172.

6. Keane, Marc. P. *Japanese Garden Design* (Rutland, VT: Charles E. Tuttle, 1996), p. 103.

7. Kuitert, Wybe. *Themes in the History of Japanese Garden Art* (Honolulu: University of Hawaii Press, 2002), p. 172–173.

8. See ibid., the section on the discovery of the romantic countryside by the imperial court and their enjoyment of the "idle landscape," pp. 173–176.

9. Keane, *Japanese Garden Design*, p. 104.

10. Kobori Enshu was a tea master and flower arranger and a disciple of Furuta Oribe, who in turn was student of Sen no Rikyu. Enshu was appointed Commissioner of Public Works in Hideyoshi's bureaucracy, where he managed construction projects for the shogun. His design aesthetic included the introduction of right-angle geometries to garden form. The use of clipped shrubs to function as rocks in a garden also originates with Enshu.

11. Keane, *Japanese Garden Design*, p. 86.

12. Nitschke, *Japanese Gardens*, p. 158.

13. Crowe, Sylvia, Sheila Haywood, Susan Jellicoe, and Gordon Patterson, *The Gardens of Mughal India: A History and a Guide* (London: Thames and Hudson, 1972), p. 132.

14. Moore, Charles, William J. Mitchell, and William Turnbull Jr., *The Poetics of Gardens* (Cambridge, MA: MIT Press, 1988), p. 171.

15. Brookes, John. *Gardens of Paradise: The History and Design of Great Islamic Gardens* (New York: New Amsterdam, 1987), p. 154.

16. Crowe, et al., *The Gardens of Mughal India: A History and a Guide*, p. 168, contains an image of the layout plan prepared in 1828 by the surveyor-general of India, Colonel Hodgson. Each quadrant is subdivided three times, for a total of 256 beds.

17. Wilber, Donald Newton. *Persian Gardens and Garden Pavilions* (Washington, DC: Dumbarton Oaks, Trustees for Harvard University, 1979), p. 39.

18. Ferrier, Ronald W. *A Journey to Persia: Jean Chardin's Portrait of a Seventeenth-Century Empire* (London: I.B. Tauris, 1996), p. 149.

19. Wilber. *Persian Gardens*, pp. 89–90.

20. Brookes describes the collection and distribution of water in detail in *Gardens of Paradise*, pp. 112–113.

21. Franck, C. L. *The Villas of Frascati* (London: Alec Tiranti, 1966), p. 26.

22. Ibid., pp. 20–33.

23. Kluckert, Ehrenfried. *European Garden Design* (Cologne: Konemann, 2000), p. 155.

24. Lazzaro, Claudia. *The Italian Renaissance Garden* (New Haven, CT: Yale University Press, 1990), p. 191.

25. Clifford, Derek. *A History of Garden Design* (New York: Frederick A. Praeger, 1966), pp. 44–45.

26. Ibid., pp. 103–104.

27. In France and Holland, Renaissance garden "compartments" became elaborate parterres (literally, "on the ground") styled with a wide variety of imaginative motifs, including the *parterre de broderie*, meant to imitate the scrolls and swags of brocade.

28. During the 17th century, the adventuresome Tradescant family made important contributions to the field of horticulture, particularly in their introduction of North American plants to England. They also collected curiosities from around the world and displayed them to the public in their London garden, called the Ark. Their collection formed the core of the natural history exhibits at the Ashmolean Museum at Oxford.

29. Andre Mollet was the son of Claude Mollet, and grandson of Jacques Mollet, patriarch of the renowned Mollet family of royal gardeners. Jacques Mollet was the head gardener at Anet. Claude Mollet designed many of Henry IV's gardens, and credited himself with developing the first *parterre de broderie* in his influential book, *Theatre des plans et jardinages* (1652). Andre Mollet worked in France, Sweden, the Netherlands, and England; his book, *Le Jardin de plaisir*, applied theories of perspective to planting design. Gabriel Mollet is thought to be Andre's nephew.

30. Weiss, Allen S. *Mirrors of Infinity: The French Formal Garden and 17th-Century Metaphysics* (New York: Princeton Architectural Press, 1995), pp. 61–62.

31. Verin, Helene. "Technology in the Park: Engineers and Gardeners in Seventeenth-Century France," in *The History of Garden Design: The Western Tradition from the Renaissance to the Present Day*, Monique Mosser and Georges Teyssot, eds. (New York: Thames and Hudson, 1991), p. 135.

32. Referred to as "the politics of the gaze" in Weiss, *Mirrors of Infinity*, pp. 25–26.

33. Verin, "Technology in the Park," pp. 136–137.

34. The Grotto of Thetis was the first sculpture completed in the heliocentric program. In the myth, Apollo retires to sleep in the home of the sea goddess Thetis after completing his circuit of the Earth—just as Louis retires to sleep in his apartments directly above the grotto. Other key sculptures with Apollo themes include the Fountain of Latona and the Fountain of Apollo. The Fountain of Latona marked the beginning of the axis within the Petit Parc. Latona was the mother of Apollo. When fleeing with her children, Apollo and Diana, from the wrath of Hera, she attempted to draw water from a pond and was thwarted by shepherds. She turned them into frogs. The myth referenced Louis and his mother escaping the Paris mobs during the fronde. See Kenneth Woodbridge, *Princely Gardens: The Origins and Development of the French Formal Style* (London: Thames and Hudson, 1986), p. 203. At the opposite end of the *allée*, Apollo rises from the water in his horse-drawn chariot, indicating the dawn of a new day.

35. Berrall, Julia S. *The Garden: An Illustrated History* (New York: Penguin Books, 1978), p. 203.

36. *The Way to Present the Gardens of Versailles*, by Louis XIV, translated by John F. Stewart (Paris: Editions de la Réunion des Musées Nationaux, 1992), p. 28.

18th CENTURY

1. The "naturalistic" style characteristic of the English landscape garden has its roots in the 17th century. In the late 1600s, Timo-thy Nourse wrote a book about the design of country houses that suggested one part of the garden should be a "natural-artificial" wilderness. See S. Lang, "Genesis of the Landscape Garden," in *The Picturesque Garden and Its Influence Outside the British Isles* (Washington, DC: Dumbarton Oaks, 1974), p. 8.

2. The Epistle was written before Kent reworked Bridgeman's design. See *Descriptions of Lord Cobham's Gardens at Stowe 1700–1750*, G. B. Clarke, ed., Buckinghamshire Record Society, 1990, p. 31.

3. "All gardening is landscape painting. (Spoken on the round of Inigo Jones and the view through it at the Physic Garden at Oxford.) Just like a painting hung up." From Joseph Spence, *Observations, Anecdotes and Characters of Books and Men*, James M. Osborn, ed., Volume I (Oxford, England: Oxford University Press, 1966), p. 252 (anecdote 606).

4. By the 18th century, many Italian Renaissance villas were in a state of disrepair. The gardens that the English visited were tempered by time and neglect, and mellowed with overgrown vegetation, contributing to a Romantic conception of the landscape.

5. Derek Clifford describes the history and theory of the ferme ornée in *A History of Garden Design* (New York: Frederick A. Praeger, 1966), pp. 139–140.

6. "At that moment appeared Kent, painter enough to taste the charms of landscape, bold and opinionative enough to dare and to dictate, and born with a genius to strike out a great system from the twilight of imperfect essays. He leaped the fence, and saw that all nature was a garden." From *On Modern Gardening, An Essay by Horace Walpole*, (New York: Young Books Inc., 1931), pp. 43–44. Walpole's book was first published in 1785.

7. From a letter by Sir Thomas Robinson to Lord Carlisle; as quoted in Richard Bisgrove, *The National Trust Book of the English Garden* (London: Viking, 1990), p. 86.

8. Wright, Richardson. *The Story of Gardening: From the Hanging Gardens of Babylon to the Hanging Gardens of New York* (Garden City, NY: Garden City Publishing Co. Inc., 1938), p. 308.

9. See Elisabetta Cereghini, "The Italian Origins of Rousham," in *The History of Garden Design: The Western Tradition from the Renaissance to the Present Day*, Monique Mosser and Georges Teyssot, eds. (New York: Thames and Hudson, 1991), p. 320.

10. John Dixon Hunt points out that in the early 18th century, the term "picturesque" referred specifically to the subject matter of paintings, their themes, and meanings; it was not a quality of gardens. In the later 18th century, the word took on a different connotation. A picturesque landscape was not one that represented a specific iconography, but one that had scenic attributes. See John Dixon Hunt, *Gardens and the Picturesque: Studies in the History of Landscape Architecture* (Cambridge, MA: MIT Press, 1992), pp. 105–136.

11. Wright comments on the dedication to agricultural improvement in France during the second half of the 18th century in *The Story of Gardening*, p. 368.

12. Morris, Edwin T. *The Gardens of China: History, Art and Meanings* (New York: Charles Scribner's Sons, 1983), p. 23.

13. Keswick, Maggie. *The Chinese Garden* (New York: Rizzoli, 1980), p. 15.

14. Chen, Lifang, and Yu Sianglin. *The Garden Art of China* (Portland, OR: Timber Press, 1986), p. 63.

15. Morris, *The Gardens of China*, p. 99.

16. See Peter Martin, *The Pleasure Gardens of Virginia: from Jamestown to Jefferson* (Princeton, NJ: Princeton University Press, 1991), pp. 145–148.

NOTES

19th CENTURY

1. Thacker, Christopher. *The History of Gardens* (Berkeley, CA: University of California Press, 1979), p. 237.

2. Wheelchair-bound for the last seven years of his life, Repton became concerned with accessible garden elements and the close-up view of the landscape. See Richard Bisgrove, *The National Trust Book of the English Garden* (London: Viking, 1990), pp. 138–139.

3. See Renzo Dubbini, "Glasshouses and Winter Gardens," in *The History of Garden Design: The Western Tradition from the Renaissance to the Present Day*, Monique Mosser and Georges Teyssot, eds. (New York: Thames and Hudson, 1991), p. 428.

4. See Kate Colquhoun, *"The Busiest Man in England": A Life of Joseph Paxton, Gardener, Architect and Victorian Visionary* (Boston, MA: David R. Godine, 2006), p. 110. An illustration of Paxton's "Plan for Forming Subscription Gardens" (1834) appears in Alessandra Ponte, "Public Parks in Great Britain and the United States," in *The History of Garden Design: The Western Tradition from the Renaissance to the Present Day*, Monique Mosser and Georges Teyssot, eds. (New York: Thames and Hudson, 1991), p. 376.

5. Bisgrove, *The National Trust Book of the English Garden*, p. 174.

6. Robinson, William. *The English Flower Garden: Design, Arrangement, and Plans*, Fourth Edition (London: John Murray, 1895), p. 30. Retreived July 3, 2009 from www.books.google.com.

7. Bisgrove, *The National Trust Book of the English Garden*, p. 189. See also Ponte, "Public Parks in Great Britain and the United States," p. 373.

8. Thomas von Joest describes improvements made to the Champs-Elysées by architect Jacques-Ignace Hittorff, in "Haussmann's Paris: A Green Metropolis?" in *The History of Garden Design: The Western Tradition from the Renaissance to the Present Day*, Monique Mosser and Georges Teyssot, eds. (New York: Thames and Hudson, 1991), p. 388.

9. Alphand's book is titled *Les Promenades de Paris (1867–1873)*, and was reprinted by Princeton Architectural Press, Princeton, NJ, in 1984.

10. von Joest, "Hausmann's Paris," p. 392.

11. Ibid., p. 397.

12. Schuyler, David. *Apostle of Taste: Andrew Jackson Downing 1815–1852* (Baltimore: The Johns Hopkins University Press, 1996), p. 92.

13. See Roy Rosenzweig and Elizabeth Blackmar, *The Park and the People* (Ithaca, NY: Cornell University Press, 1996), pp. 65–77.

14. Olmsted's publications include: *Walks and Talks of an American Farmer in England* (1852), *The Seaboard Slave States* (1856), *A Journey in Texas* (1857), *A Journey in the Back Country* (1860), and two volumes of previously published essays titled *Journeys and Explorations in the Cotton Kingdom* (1861).

15. "It is one great purpose of the Park to supply to the hundreds of thousands of tired workers, who have no opportunity to spend their summers in the country, a specimen of God's handiwork that shall be to them, inexpensively, what a month or two in the White Mountains or the Adirondacks is, at great cost, to those in easier circumstances." Olmsted quoted in Norman T. Newton, *Design on the Land: The Development of Landscape Architecture* (Cambridge MA: Belknap Press/Harvard University Press, 1974), p. 289.

16. See Warren Angus Ferris, *Life in the Rocky Mountains: A Diary of Wanderings on the Sources of the Rivers Missouri, Columbia, and Colorado, 1830–1835*, Leroy R. Hafen, ed., new revised edition (Denver, CO: Fred A. Rosenstock/The Old West Publishing Company, 1983). Ferris's descriptions of Yellowstone appear on pp. 326–329. See also Burton Harris, *John Colter: His Years in the Rockies* (New York: Charles Scribner's Sons, 1952). Accounts of "Colter's Hell" are described on pp. 91–96.

17. A section of the 1890 census noted that settlement had expanded so rapidly across the West that there was no longer a clear line demarcating populated areas from wilderness areas. Frederick Jackson Turner developed an influential 'frontier thesis' in his essay "The Significance of the Frontier in American History." See *Rereading Frederick Jackson Turner: "The Significance of the Frontier in American History" and other essays*, with commentary by John Mack Faragher (New York: Henry Holt and Company, 1994), pp. 31–60.

20th CENTURY

1. See Robin Karson, *A Genius for Place: American Landscapes of the Country Place Era* (Amherst, MA: University of Massachusetts Press, 2007), pp. 133–147. Farrand's papers are archived at the College of Environmental Design, University of California, Berkeley.

2. Emily Talen discusses the rise in civic improvement associations and examines the idea of 'urban plan-making' as an instrument of social control in *New Urbanism and American Planning: The Conflict of Cultures* (New York: Routledge, 2005), pp. 114–125. See also Norman T. Newton, *Design on the Land: The Development of Landscape Architecture* (Cambridge MA: Belknap Press/Harvard University Press, 1974), pp. 414–416, for his description of the popularity of Robinson's articles.

3. Spiro Kostof attributes the failure of monumental urban planning in America to the lack of a centralized local authority in *The City Shaped: Urban Patterns and Meanings through History* (Boston, MA: Bulfinch Press/Little, Brown and Co., 1991), p. 217. Burnham created monumental plans for the cities of Chicago, Cleveland, San Francisco, Washington, DC, and the cities of Manila and Baguio in the Philippines. Although only the plan of Washington, DC was implemented (as an extension of the federal government's power), the idea of comprehensive urban planning endured and helped develop a conception of urbanism in America.

4. Talen, *New Urbanism and American Planning* p. 114. See also Newton, *Design on the Land*, pp. 421–423, and Lewis Mumford, *The City in History* (New York: Harcourt, Brace and World, Inc., 1961), p. 401.

5. In 1925 Walter Gropius published a volume entitled *Internationale Architektur* that showcased some of the work exhibited at the Bauhaus in 1923. Gropius believed that functionalism could express the values of a unified society. See Harry Francis Mallgrave, *Modern Architectural Theory* (Cambridge, UK: Cambridge University Press, 2005), p. 252.

In 1932, the Museum of Modern Art in New York mounted a show titled "Modern Architecture: International Exhibition." The accompanying book *The International Style*, written by Henry-Russell Hitchcock and Philip Johnson, introduced the 'new style' to America. The book and the exhibit highlighted the work of European architects who were working in avant-garde, not historical, styles. The avant-garde represented a progressive ideology that sought to express commonalities rather than differences. See Terence Riley, *The International Style: Exhibition 15 and the Museum of Modern Art* (New York: Rizzoli/Columbia Books of Architecture, 1992), pp. 9–64.

6. In his 1896 essay, "The Tall Office Building Artistically Re-considered," American architect Louis Sullivan (1856–1924) wrote "all things in Nature have a shape…a form…that tells us what they are…Whether it be the sweeping eagle in his flight or the open apple-blossom…form ever follows function, and this is the law." The phrase expressed his belief that the ornamentation of skyscrapers (a totally new form of building) should be inspired from organic nature and not classical motifs. See *Louis Sullivan: The Public Papers*, Robert Twombly, ed. (Chicago, IL: University of Chicago Press, 1988), p. 111.

7. Le Corbusier, *Toward an Architecture*, introduction by Jean-Louis Cohen; translation by John Goodman (Los Angeles, CA: Getty Research Institute/Texts and Documents, 2007), p. 87.

8. Imbert, Dorothee. *The Modernist Garden in France* (New Haven, CT: Yale University Press, 1993), p. 128. George Dodds makes a case that Guevrekian's triangular garden was "half of a Paradise garden" bisected by a diagonal cut line that symmetrically reflected the rest of the garden. See George Dodds, "Freedom from the Garden: Gabriel Guevrekian and a New Territory of Experience," in *Tradition and Innovation in French Garden Art: Chapters of a New History*, John Dixon Hunt and Michel Conan, eds. (Philadelphia, PA: University of Pennsylvania Press, 2002), pp. 192–193.

9. Imbert, *The Modernist Garden in France*, p. 128.

10. Ibid, p. 65. See also Dodds, "Freedom from the Garden," p. 185.

11. Karson, Robin. *Fletcher Steele, Landscape Architect* (A Ngaere Macray Book/New York: Harry N. Abrams, Inc., 1989), p. 108.

12. Neckar, Lance M. "Christopher Tunnard: The Garden in the Modern Landscape," in *Modern Landscape Architecture: A Critical Review*, Marc Treib, ed. (Cambridge, MA: MIT Press, 1994), p. 146.

13. See Marc Treib and Dorothee Imbert, *Garrett Eckbo: Modern Landscapes for Living*, (Berkeley, CA: University of California Press, 1997), pp. 16–20.

14. Halprin was involved in "Take Part" workshops in the 1960s. See Jim Burns, "The How of Creativity: Scores & Scoring" in *Lawrence Halprin: Changing Places* (San Francisco, CA: The San Francisco Museum of Modern Art, 1986), p. 57.

15. For discussions of the land art movement and its impact on architecture and landscape architecture, see John Beardsley, *Earthworks and Beyond* (New York: Abbeville Press, 1984), p. 122; also Michael McDonough, "Architecture's Unnoticed Avant-Garde" in *Art in the Land*, Alan Sonfist, ed. (New York: E.P. Dutton Inc., 1983), pp. 233–252; and Catherine M. Howett, "Landscape Architecture: Making a Place for Art," in *Places*, vol. 2, no. 4 (1985).

16. The idea of value-neutral space and open-ended meaning stems from the philosophical discourse of post structuralism and the linguistic theory of deconstruction. Jacques Derrida (b. 1930) is a philosopher whose writing on 'value-laden hierarchies' and 'slippery meanings' has influenced architects. Derrida collaborated with Peter Eisenman and Bernard Tschumi on the conceptual design of Parc de La Villette. The park was featured in a 1988 exhibition titled *Deconstructivist Architecture* at the Museum of Modern Art in New York. Excerpts from Derrida's works are included in *Rethinking Architecture: A reader in cultural theory*, Neil Leach, ed. (London: Routledge, 1997), pp. 317–336. See also the exhibition catalog, *Deconstructivist Architecture*, Philip Johnson and Mark Wigley/The Museum of Modern Art, New York (Boston, MA: Little Brown and Co., 1988).

17. In 1986 Harvard University Graduate School of Design mounted an exhibit titled *Transforming the American Garden: 12 New Landscape Designs*. The goal of the show was to examine the garden as an expressive and conceptual medium representative of the age. For critical commentary on the exhibit, see *Places*, vol. 3, no. 3 (1986). The July 1989 issue of *Progressive Architecture* magazine was also dedicated to the 'New American Landscape' and examined the "new emphasis on landscape as art." The issue highlighted the work of many of the same landscape architects who contributed to the 1986 exhibit.

   (Interestingly, in 2005 a new set of circumstances affecting professional design practice was examined in the exhibition titled *Groundswell: Constructing the Contemporary Landscape* held at the Museum of Modern Art in New York. The show featured creative responses to the design of public urban open space in a postindustrial landscape, and included projects on reclaimed and formerly degraded sites.)

18. McIntosh, Christopher. *Gardens of the Gods* (London: I.B. Tauris, 2005), p. 116.

19. Clement, Gilles. *Le jardin en mouvement de la Vallée au champ via le parc André-Citroën*, 3rd edition ([Paris]: Sens and Tonka, 1999), pp. 172–175. See also Alan Tate, *Great City Parks* (London: Spon Press, 2001), p. 45.

21st CENTURY

1. The project as described by its designer, George Hargreaves, in Jim Doyle's article, "The City's Front Yard," *San Francisco Chronicle*, 23 September 2001: CM-10.

Bibliography

Ackerman, James S. *Palladio.* New York: Penguin Books, 1991.

———.*The Villa: Form and Ideology of Country Houses.* Princeton, NJ: Princeton University Press, 1990.

Arden, Heather M. *The Romance of the Rose.* Boston: Twayne Publishers, a division of GK Hall & Co., 1987.

Bacon, Edmund. *Design of Cities.* New York: Penguin Books, 1985.

Barnstone, Tony, and Chou Ping, eds. *The Anchor Book of Chinese Poetry.* New York: Anchor Books/Random House, 2005.

Barrucand, Marianne, and Achim Bednorz. *Moorish Architecture in Andalusia.* Cologne: Taschen, 2007.

Beardsley, John. *Earthworks and Beyond.* New York: Abbeville Press, 1984.

Berrall, Julia S. *The Garden: An Illustrated History.* New York: Penguin Books, 1978.

Bisgrove, Richard. *The National Trust Book of the English Garden.* London: Viking, 1990.

Blomfield, Reginald, and F. Inigo Thomas. *The Formal Garden in England.* London: Waterstone, 1985. First published in 1892.

Brookes, John. *Gardens of Paradise: The History and Design of the Great Islamic Gardens.* New York: New Amsterdam Books, 1987.

Byne, Mildred Stapley, and Arthur Byne. *Spanish Gardens and Patios.* Philadelphia: J.B. Lippincott Co., 1924.

Cahill, James. *Chinese Painting.* New York: Rizzoli, 1977.

Caplow, Theodore, Louis Hicks, and Ben J. Wattenberg. *The First Measured Century.* Washington, DC: The American Enterprise Institute Press, 2001.

Carroll, Maureen. *Earthly Paradises: Ancient Gardens in History and Archaeology.* Los Angeles: The J. Paul Getty Museum, 2003.

Casa Valdes, Teresa Ozores y Saavedra, marquesa de. *Spanish Gardens.* Woodbridge, England: Antique Collectors' Club, 1987.

Chen, Lifang, and Yu Sianglin. *The Garden Art of China.* Portland, OR: Timber Press, 1986.

Chittenden, Hiram Martin. *The Yellowstone National Park.* Norman, OK: University of Oklahoma Press, 1964.

Clarke, G. B., ed. *Descriptions of Lord Cobham's Gardens at Stowe 1700–1750.* Buckinghamshire Record Society, 1990.

Clary, David A. *"The Place Where Hell Bubbled Up": A History of the First National Park.* Washington, DC: Office of Publications, National Park Service, U.S. Department of the Interior, 1972.

Clement, Gilles. *Le jardin en mouvement de la Vallée au champ via le parc André-Citroën,* 3rd edition. [Paris]: Sens and Tonka, 1999.

Clifford, Derek. *A History of Garden Design.* New York: Frederick A. Praeger, 1966.

Colquhoun, Kate. *"The Busiest Man in England": A Life of Joseph Paxton, Gardener, Architect and Victorian Visionary.* Boston, MA: David R. Godine, 2006.

Conan, Michel, ed. *Perspectives on Garden Histories.* Washington, DC: Dumbarton Oaks, Trustees for Harvard University, 1999.

Conder, Josiah. *Landscape Gardening in Japan.* Tokyo: Kodansha International, 2002.

Crandell, Gina. *Nature Pictorialized.* Baltimore: Johns Hopkins University Press, 1993.

Crisp, Sir Frank. *Mediaeval Gardens,* Volumes 1 and 2. London: John Lane the Bodley Head Ltd., 1924.

Crowe, Sylvia, Sheila Haywood, Susan Jellicoe, and Gordon Patterson. *The Gardens of Mughal India: A History and a Guide.* London: Thames and Hudson, 1972.

de Clavijo, Ruy Gonzalez. *Embassy to Tamerlane 1403–1406,* translated from the Spanish by Guy Le Strange. London: George Routledge & Sons, 1928.

de Lorris, Guillaume and Jean de Meun. *The Romance of the Rose,* translated and edited by Frances Horgan. New York: Oxford University Press Inc., 1994.

Engel, David H. *Japanese Gardens for Today.* Rutland, VT: Charles E. Tuttle Co., 1982.

Fairbairn, Neil. *A Brief History of Gardening.* Emmaus, PA: Rodale Inc., 2001.

Ferguson, George. *Signs and Symbols in Christian Art.* London: Oxford University Press, 1961.

Ferris, Warren Angus. *Life in the Rocky Mountains: A Diary of Wanderings on the Sources of the Rivers Missouri, Columbia, and Colorado, 1830–1835,* Leroy R. Hafen, ed., new revised edition (Denver, CO: Fred A. Rosenstock/The Old West Publishing Company, 1983.

Fleming, Laurence and Alan Gore. *The English Garden.* London: Michael Joseph Ltd., 1979.

Franck, C. L. *The Villas of Frascati*. London: Alec Tiranti, 1966.

Geddes-Brown, Leslie. *The Walled Garden*. London: Merrell Publishers Ltd., 2007.

Gothein, Marie Luise. *A History of Garden Art*. New York: Hacker Art Books, 1979.

Gould, Stephen Jay, Umberto Eco, Jean-Claude Carriere, and Jean Delomeau. *Conversations About the End of Time*. New York: Fromm International, 2000.

Gromort, Georges. *Jardins d'Espagne*. Paris: A. Vincent, 1926.

Haines, Aubrey L. *The Yellowstone Story: A History of Our First National Park*. Yellowstone National Park, Wyoming: Yellowstone Library and Museum Association, 1977.

Hales, Mick. *Monastic Gardens*. New York: Stewart, Tabori & Chang, 2000.

Halprin, Lawrence. *Lawrence Halprin: Changing Places*. San Francisco CA: The San Francisco Museum of Modern Art, 1986.

Harris, Burton. *John Colter: His Years in the Rockies*. New York: Charles Scribner's Sons, 1952.

Hazelhurst, F. Hamilton. *Gardens of Illusion: The Genius of Andre Le Nostre*. Nashville, TN: Vanderbilt University Press, 1980.

Hobhouse, Penelope. *The Story of Gardening*. London: Dorling Kindersley Ltd., 2002.

Holborn, Mark. *The Ocean in the Sand*. Boulder, CO: Shambhala, 1978.

Hunt, John Dixon. *Garden and Grove: The Italian Renaissance Garden in the English Imagination, 1600–1750*. London: J.M. Dent & Sons Ltd., 1986.

————. *Gardens and the Picturesque: Studies in the History of Landscape Architecture*. Cambridge, MA: MIT Press, 1992.

Hunt, John Dixon, and Michel Conan, eds. *Tradition and Innovation in French Garden Art: Chapters of a New History*. Philadelphia: University of Pennsylvania Press, 2002.

Hunt, John Dixon and Peter Willis, eds. *The Genius of the Place: The English Landscape Garden 1620–1820*. Cambridge, MA: MIT Press, 1988.

Imbert, Dorothee. *The Modernist Garden in France*. New Haven, CT: Yale University Press, 1993.

Itoh, Teiji. *The Gardens of Japan*. New York: Kodansha America Inc., 1998.

Jacobs, Jane. *The Economy of Cities*. New York: Random House, 1969.

Jellicoe, Sir Geoffrey, Susan Jellicoe, Patrick Goode, and Michael Lancaster, eds. *The Oxford Companion to Gardens*. Oxford, UK: Oxford University Press, 1986.

Karson, Robin. *A Genius for Place: American Landscapes of the Country Place Era*. Amherst, MA: University of Massachusetts Press, 2007.

————. *Fletcher Steele, Landscape Architect*. A Ngaere Macray Book/New York: Harry N. Abrams, Inc., 1989.

Keane, Marc P. *Japanese Garden Design*. Rutland, VT: Charles E. Tuttle, 1996.

Kenna, Michael. *Le Notre's Gardens*. San Marino, CA: Ram Publications/Huntington Library, Art Collections and Botanical Gardens, 1997.

Keswick, Maggie. *The Chinese Garden*. New York: Rizzoli, 1980.

King, Ronald. *The Quest for Paradise: A History of the World's Gardens*. New York: Mayflower Books, 1979.

Kluckert, Ehrenfried. *European Garden Design*. Cologne: Konemann, 2000.

Knight, Richard Payne. *The Landscape, A Didactic Poem: in 3 books: addressed to Uvedale Price, Esquire*. Westmead, Farnborough: Gregg International Publishers Limited, 1972. Reprint of the 1795 edition published by W. Bulmer, London.

Kostoff, Spiro. *The City Shaped: Urban Patterns and Meanings through History*. Boston: Bulfinch Press/Little Brown & Co., 1991.

Kovacs, Maureen Gallery, trans. *The Epic of Gilgamesh*. Stanford, CA: Stanford University Press, 1989.

Kuck, Loraine. *The World of the Japanese Garden*. New York: Walker/Weatherhill, 1968.

Kuitert, Wybe. *Themes in the History of Japanese Garden Art*. Honolulu: University of Hawaii Press, 2002.

Landsberg, Sylvia. *The Medieval Garden*. London: Thames and Hudson, 1996.

Lang, S. "The Genesis of the English Landscape Garden," in Nikolaus Pevsner, ed. Dumbarton Oaks Colloquium on the History of Landscape Architecture II. Washington, DC: Dumbarton Oaks, Trustees for Harvard University, 1974.

Lazzaro, Claudia. *The Italian Renaissance Garden*. New Haven, CT: Yale University Press, 1990.

Le Corbusier. *Toward an Architecture*, introduction by Jean-Louis Cohen; translation by John Goodman. Los Angeles, CA: Getty Research Institute/Texts and Documents, 2007.

Leach, Neil, ed. *Rethinking Architecture: A reader in cultural theory*. London: Routledge, 1997.

Lehrman, Jonas. *Earthly Paradise: Garden and Courtyard in Islam*. Berkeley, CA: University of California Press, 1980.

MacDonald, William L., and John A. Pinto. *Hadrian's Villa and Its Legacy*. New Haven: Yale University Press, 1995.

MacDougall, Elisabeth B. *Medieval Gardens*. Washington, DC: Dumbarton Oaks, Trustees for Harvard University, 1986.

MacDougall, Elisabeth B., and Richard Ettinghausen, eds. *The Islamic Garden*. Washington, DC: Dumbarton Oaks, Trustees for Harvard University, 1976.

Macy, Christine, and Sarah Bonnemaison. *Architecture and Nature: Creating the American Landscape*. London: Routledge, 2003.

Mallgrave, Harry Francis. *Modern Architectural Theory*. Cambridge, England: Cambridge University Press, 2005.

Martin, Peter. *The Pleasure Gardens of Virginia: From Jamestown to Jefferson.* Princeton, NJ: Princeton University Press, 1991.

Masson, Georgina. *Italian Gardens.* Woodbridge, England: The Antique Collectors' Club, 1987.

McIntosh, Christopher. *Gardens of the Gods: Myth, Magic and Meaning.* London: I.B. Tauris & Co., 2005.

Moore, Charles, William J. Mitchell, and William Turnbull, Jr. *The Poetics of Gardens.* Cambridge, MA: MIT Press, 1988.

Morris, Edwin T. *The Gardens of China: History, Art and Meanings.* New York: Charles Scribner's Sons, 1983.

Morrison, Tony. *The Mystery of the Nasca Lines.* Woodbridge, Suffolk, England: Nonesuch Expeditions Ltd., 1987.

Mosser, Monique, and Georges Teyssot, eds. *The History of Garden Design: The Western Tradition from the Renaissance to the Present Day.* New York: Thames and Hudson, 1991.

Moynihan, Elizabeth. *Paradise as a Garden in Persia and Mughal India.* New York: George Braziller, 1979.

Murray, Peter. *The Architecture of the Italian Renaissance.* New York: Schocken Books, 1986.

Nakagawara, Camelia. "The Japanese Garden for the Mind: The 'Bliss' of Paradise Transcended," in *Stanford Journal of East Asian Affairs,* vol. 4, no. 2, Summer 2004, pp. 83–102.

Newton, Norman T. *Design on the Land: The Development of Landscape Architecture.* Cambridge, MA: Belknap Press/Harvard University Press, 1974.

Nichols, Rose Standish. *Spanish & Portuguese Gardens.* Boston: Houghton Mifflin Company, 1924.

Nitschke, Gunter. *Japanese Gardens.* Cologne: Taschen, 1999.

Pevsner, Nikolaus, ed. *The Picturesque Garden and Its Influence Outside the British Isles.* Washington, DC: Dumbarton Oaks, Trustees for Harvard University, 1974.

Pizzoni, Filippo. *The Garden: A History in Landscape and Art.* New York: Rizzoli, 1999.

Prest, John. *The Garden of Eden: The Botanic Garden and the Recreation of Paradise.* New Haven, CT: Yale University Press, 1988.

Reed, Peter. *Groundswell: Constructing the Contemporary Landscape.* New York: The Museum of Modern Art, 2005.

Reiche, Maria. *Mystery on the Desert.* Lima, Peru, 1949.

Riley, Terence. *The International Style: Exhibition 15 and the Museum of Modern Art.* New York: Rizzoli/Columbia Books of Architecture, 1992.

Robinson, William. *The English Flower Garden, and Home Grounds of Hardy Trees and Flowers.* Roy Hay, ed. sixteenth edition. [London: John Murray] Fair Lawn, NJ: Essential Books, 1956.

_____. *The Parks and Gardens of Paris.* London: Macmillan and Co., 1878.

_____. *The Wild Garden.* Portland, OR: Sagapress, 1994.

Rogers, Elizabeth Barlow. *Landscape Design: A Cultural and Architectural History.* New York: Harry N. Abrams Inc., 2001.

Rosenzweig, Roy, and Elizabeth Blackmar. *The Park and the People.* Ithaca, NY: Cornell University Press, 1996

Schaarschmidt-Richter, Irmtraud. *Japanese Gardens.* New York: William Morrow & Co., 1979.

Schama, Simon. *Landscape and Memory.* Toronto: Random House/Vintage Canada edition, 1996.

Schuyler, David. *Apostle of Taste: Andrew Jackson Downing 1815–1852.* Baltimore: The Johns Hopkins University Press, 1996.

Scully, Vincent. *The Earth, the Temple, and the Gods: Greek Sacred Architecture.* New Haven, CT: Yale University Press, 1979.

Shepherd, J. C., and G. A. Jellico. *Italian Gardens of the Renaissance.* New York: Princeton Architectural Press, 1993.

Shikibu, Murasaki. *The Tale of Genji,* translated by Edward G. Seidensticker. New York: Alfred A. Knopf, 1987.

Sica, Grazia Gobbi. *The Florentine Villa.* Oxford, UK: Routledge, 2007.

Siren, Osvald. *Gardens of China.* New York: Ronald Press Company, 1949.

Sonfist, Alan, ed. *Art in the Land.* New York: E.P. Dutton Inc., 1983.

Spence, Joseph. *Observations, Anecdotes and Characters of Books and Men,* Volume I, James M. Osborn, ed. Oxford, UK: Oxford University Press, 1966.

Stewart, John F., trans. *The Way to Present the Gardens of Versailles,* by Louis XIV. Paris: Editions de la Réunion des Musées Nationaux, 1992.

Sullivan, Louis. *Louis Sullivan: The Public Papers,* Robert Twombly, ed. Chicago, IL: University of Chicago Press, 1988.

Swaffield, Simon. *Theory in Landscape Architecture.* Philadelphia: University of Pennsylvania Press, 2002.

Talen, Emily. *New Urbanism and American Planning: The Conflict of Cultures.* New York: Routledge, 2005.

Tate, Alan. *Great City Parks.* London: Spon Press, 2001.

Tatum, George B., and Elisabeth Blair MacDougall, eds. *Prophet with Honor: The Career of Andrew Jackson Downing 1815–1852.* Washington, DC: Dumbarton Oaks, The Trustees for Harvard University, 1989.

Thacker, Christopher. *The History of Gardens.* Berkeley, CA: University of California Press, 1979.

Thompson, George F., and Frederick R. Steiner. *Ecological Design and Planning.* New York: John Wiley and Sons, Inc., 1997.

Thompson, Ian. *The Sun King's Garden: Louis XIV, Andre Le Notre and the Creation of the Gardens of Versailles*. London: Bloomsbury, 2006.

Tobey, G. B. *A History of Landscape Architecture: The Relationship of People to Environment*. New York: American Elsevier Publishing Company, Inc., 1973.

Toman, Rolf, ed. *European Garden Design: From Classical Antiquity to the Present Day*. Cologne: Konemann Verlagsgesellschaft mbH, 2000.

The Travels of Marco Polo, Art Type edition, The World's Popular Classics, New York Books, Inc., undated.

Treib, Marc, ed. *Modern Landscape Architecture: A Critical Review*. Cambridge, MA: MIT Press, 1994.

Treib, Marc, and Ron Herman. *The Gardens of Kyoto*. Tokyo: Kodansha International, 2003.

Treib, Marc, and Dorothee Imbert, *Garrett Eckbo: Modern Landscapes for Living*. Berkeley, CA: University of California Press, 1997.

Tuan, Yi-Fu. *Topophilia: A Study of Environmental Perception, Attitudes, and Values*. New York: Columbia University Press, 1990.

———. *Space and Place: The Perspective of Experience*. Minneapolis: University of Minnesota Press, 2001.

Turner, Frederick Jackson. *Rereading Frederick Jackson Turner: "The Significance of the Frontier in American History" and other essays, with commentary by John Mack Faragher*. New York: Henry Holt and Company, 1994.

Valery, Marie-Francoise. *Jardins du Moyen Age*. Tournai (Belgique): La Renaissance du Livre, 2001.

Van der Ree, Paul, Gerrit Smienk, and Clemens Steenbergen. *Italian Villas and Gardens*. Munich: Prestel-Verlag, 1993.

Villiers-Stuart, C. M. *Spanish Gardens*. London: B.T. Batsford Ltd., 1929.

Walpole, Horace. *On Modern Gardening*. New York: Young Books Inc., 1931.

Weiss, Allen S. *Mirrors of Infinity: The French Formal Garden and 17th-Century Metaphysics*. New York: Princeton Architectural Press, 1995.

Wescoat, Jr., James L., and Joachim Wolschke-Buhlmahn, eds. *Mughal Gardens: Sources, Places, Representations, and Prospects*. Washington, DC: Dumbarton Oaks, Trustees for Harvard University, 1996.

Wilber, Donald Newton. *Persian Gardens and Garden Pavilions*. Washington, DC: Dumbarton Oaks Trustees for Harvard University, 1979.

Williams, Dorothy Hunt. *Historic Virginia Gardens: Preservations by the Garden Club of Virginia*. Charlottesville, VA: University Press of Virginia, 1975.

Wines, James. *Green Architecture*. Cologne: Taschen, 2000.

Woodbridge, Kenneth. *Princely Gardens: The Origins and Development of the French Formal Style*. London: Thames and Hudson, 1986.

Wright, Richardson. *The Story of Gardening: From the Hanging Gardens of Babylon to the Hanging Gardens of New York*. Garden City, NY: Garden City Publishing Co. Inc., 1938.

Yoshida, Tetsuro. *Gardens of Japan*. New York: Frederick A. Praeger, 1957.

Yourcenar, Marguerite. *Memoirs of Hadrian*. New York: Farrar, Straus and Giroux, [1951] 1983.

Index

A

Abbott, Stanley W., 206
Absolute monarchy, 93, 137
Acropolis, 6
Adaptive re-use, 218
Addison, Joseph, 151, 154
Age of Reason, 107
agora, 6
Akbar's tomb (Agra), 120
Alberti, Leon Battista, 60, 68–69, 72
Albertus Magnus, 18
Alcazar (Seville), 34–35
Alcoa Forecast garden (Laurel Canyon),
    215–217
Alhambra (Granada), 30, 32–33, 221
Ali Qapu (Esfahan), 124–125
allées, 136
Allegory:
    allegorical iconographies in Renaissance
        gardens, 79, 96
    allegorical symbolism in medieval gardens,
        21
    in Daisen-in, 62
    of control of nature, 83
    of Hercules, 81
Alphand, Jean-Charles-Adolphe, 186–188,
    201
Alternate attendance, 111
Amboise, 94–95
American gardens and parks:
    18th century, 171–174
    19th century, 189–200
    20th century:
        Gilded Age, 207–210
        Modern, 214–218
        Postmodern, 223–224
    design vocabulary, 176, 202, 230
American Society of Landscape Architects,
    180, 207
Ammannati, Bartolomeo, 88, 130
Analysis of Beauty, the, 161
Anasazi, 18
ancien régime, 147, 150
Ancient gardens, 4–5
    Hadrian's Villa (Italy), 5
    House of the Vettii (Pompeii, Italy), 4
    Mesopotamian hunting parks, 4
    Pasargadae (Persia), 4
    Pliny's Seaside Villa (Italy), 5
    Tomb of Nebamun (Thebes, Egypt), 4
Anet, 96
Angkor Wat (Cambodia), 18
Apse, 13
Aqueduct(s), 29, 60, 128
Arcadia (idyll), 151

Arp, Jean, 220
Art Deco, 212, 214
Arts and Crafts Movement, 185, 208
asymmetry, 62
Atelier Dreiseitl (designers), 238
Athens (Greece), 6
Attiret, Jean-Denis, 152, 164, 168
automata, 82
axis mundi, 12, 18, 128
Aztec civilization, 7

B

Babur, 66, 100, 119
Baghdad (Iraq), 18
Bagh-e Fin (Kashan), 126
Bagh-e Vafa, 100
Bagnaia (Italy), 82–83
Bananas, 110
Banco Safra (Sao Paulo), 220
Banqueting house(s), 98
baradari, 120
Barcelona Pavilion. See German pavilion
barchetto, 82, 86–87
barco, 83, 88
Baroque style(s), 87, 107, 110, 127–132, 136,
    150, 153, 168, 187
Barragan, Luis, 220–221
Bauhaus, 211
Bayeux tapestry, 18
Beaux-Arts ideals, 200, 210, 214–215
Bedding out, 184
Beijing, 42, 65
berceaux, 133
Bernini, Gian Lorenzo, 110
Bierstadt, Albert, 197
Biltmore Estate (Asheville), 194–195, 209
Birkenhead Park (Liverpool), 183, 189, 191
Black Death. See plague
Blenheim (Oxfordshire), 158
Blois, 95
Blomfield, Reginald T., 185
Blue Ridge Parkway, 206
Blue Steps (Naumkeag), 214
Blur Building and Arteplage (Yverdon-les-
    Bains), 234
Boboli gardens (Florence), 130
Bodhi tree (India), 9
Bois de Boulogne, 186–187
Bois de Vincennes, 186–187
bonsai, 61
bonseki, 61
bosco, 127
bosquet(s), 138, 141–143, 146
Boston (Massachusetts), 194
Botanic gardens, 99, 133

Boyceau, Jacques, 137, 140
Bramante, Donato, 79–80
Bridgeman, Charles, 153–154, 156, 158
Brown, Lancelot "Capability", 153–156, 158,
    161, 163, 165, 184
Brunelleschi, Filippo, 7, 60
Budding's lawn mower, 181
Buffalo, New York, 192
Burke, Edmund, 161
Burle Marx, Roberto, 220–221
Burnham, Daniel, 200, 210
Buxus sempervirens 'Suffruticosa', 78
Byodo-in (Kyoto), 50

C

California Academy of Sciences, Living Roof
    (San Francisco), 240
California garden style, 215
campidoglio (Rome), 78
Caravaggio, 79
Cardinal directions, orientation to, 7, 99
Carpet bedding, 184
Cartesian logic, 137
Cartesian space, 140
Caruncho, Fernando, 221
Caryatid(s), 10, 86
Castle Howard, 152
Cathay (China), 44
Cathedrals, 18, 20
Catholic Church, role of, 20, 79, 97
Cemetery(s), rural, 185, 190–191
Census of 1890, 197
Central Park (New York), 189, 191–192, 197,
    241
ceques, 60
Certosa di Pavia, 23
cha niwa, 102
cha no yu, 102
chabutra(s), 105, 120, 122, 146
chadar(s), 120, 122, 146
Chahar Bagh Avenue, 124, 126
chahar bagh, 57, 66, 72, 100, 119, 145–146
Chambers, William, 152, 161–163, 165
Chang-an (Xian), 39–40, 47, 49
Chantilly, 143–144
Chapman, John, 180
Chapultepec Park, Fountain Promenade
    (Mexico City), 239
char bagh, 100, 120, 123
Chardin, John, 124
Charlemagne, 20, 21
Chehel Sotoon, (Esfahan), 125
Cheng, Ji, 110
Chenonceaux, 96
Chicago (Illinois), 199, 210

Chicago World's Fair. *See* World's Columbian Exposition
Chinese gardens:
  6th–15th centuries (medieval), 37–44
  18th century, 165–170
  design vocabulary, 56, 176
chini-kana(s), 120–121, 146
chinoiserie, 153, 162
Church, Frederick Edwin, 196
Church, Thomas, 215, 217
City Beautiful movement, 200, 203, 210
City-states (Italian), 68
ciudadela, 7
Civic aesthetics, 210
Civilian Conservation Corps, 206
civitas, 60
Classical ideology, 153
Climatic design:
  Pasargadae (Persia), 4
  Persian gardens, 124
  Pliny's Seaside Villa (Italy), 5
Cloister garden, 23
Collaborative approach, 198, 200–201, 218
Colter, John, 196
Compartment garden(s), 94–96, 98–99, 133
Conceptual frameworks:
  first nature, 69
  second nature, 69
  third nature, 69, 75
Concrete poetry, 224–225
Conservation ethic, 197
Constantinople (Turkey), 18
Contemplative-style gardens, 53–54, 61
Cordoba (Spain), 28–29
Cortile del Belvedere (Rome), 80–81
Cosmological landscapes, 2–3, 219
  Nazca lines (Peru), 3
  New Grange (Ireland), 2
  Stonehenge (England), 2
Cosmology(s) expressed in the landscape:
  Buddhism, 39, 41, 47, 102, 111
    Zen, 51–52, 54, 61, 102
    Amida, 50
  Confucianism, 39
  Daoism, 39, 41, 111
  Hinduism, 18
  Islamic, 123
  Neo-Confucianism, 111, 165
  Shintoism, 46–47
Cottage garden, 185, 190
coulisse, 138
Counter-Reformation, 75, 79, 136
Country Place Era, 203, 207–209
Court etiquette, 137
Court of the Lions (Alhambra), 30, 33
Court of the Myrtles (Alhambra), 30, 32
Court of the Oranges (Cordoba), 29, 36
Court of the Oranges (Seville), 36
Courtyards:
  at Isola Bella, 131
  at Wangshi Yuan, 170
  Cortile del Belvedere, 80
  Forbidden City, 65
  medieval cloisters, 22–23, 26, 55–56,
  Moorish, 28–31, 34, 36, 55, 221

Shinden-style, 47, 50, 116
sunken, at Pitti Palace, 130
telescoping, at Villa Giulia, 88
tsuboniwa, 111
Crete, 8
Crissy Field (San Francisco), 232
Crusades, 18, 22, 68
Crystal Palace (London), 183
Cubist garden(s), 212
Cult of the melancholy, 164
Curtilage, 174
Cuzco (Peru), 60

D

d'Argenville, Antoine-Joseph Dezallier, 137
da Vignola, Jacopo Barozzi, 79, 82, 86, 88, 95
da Vinci, Leonardo, 95
Daimyo(s), 101, 118
Daisen-in, 62, 64
de Caus, Salomon, 110, 134
de Clavijo, Ruy Gonzalez, 66–67
de Girardin, Rene-Louis, 164
de l'Orme, Philibert, 96
de' Crescenzi, Piero, 18
Deconstruction (theory), 226
Decorative use of water:
  at Fontainebleau, 95
  at Pasargadae (Persia), 4
  in Italian Renaissance gardens, 81–85
  in Mughal gardens, 100, 120–123
del Duca, Giacomo, 82, 86
della Porta, Giacomo, 127
Delhi (India), 119
Delphi (Greece), 8
Derby Arboretum, 182
Descartes, Rene, 110, 136, 138
Design principles:
  abstraction, 63–64, 72, 118
  accessibility, 191, 201
  allusion, 38, 52, 152, 157, 165, 175
  appropriation, 50, 55, 112, 127, 132, 155, 215
  asymmetry, 214–215
  axial symmetry, 6, 80, 82–83, 86, 105, 121
  balance, 38, 55
  borrowed scenery, 116, 145
  boundary, 94, 96, 105
  collaboration, 198, 201
  contrast, 23, 55, 81, 83
  correspondence, 29, 215
  extension, 134, 137, 140, 145
  framing, 41, 51, 61, 122, 170, 175
  harmony, 92, 105, 214
  hide and reveal, 112–113, 115, 145
  hierarchy, 23, 39, 65, 72, 91, 101
  identity, 8–9, 187, 199–201
  illusion, 52, 128, 130, 138, 145, 212
  integrity, 221, 229
  narrative, 64, 82–85, 90, 155, 157, 159, 166, 175
  observation, 163, 175, 186, 201
  occupying space, 100, 105
  originality, 79, 216–219, 229

proportion, 71–72, 91, 137
reduction, 61, 72, 102, 242
scale, 32–33, 55, 61, 208
subdivision of space, 4, 67, 125–126, 145
symmetry, 66, 72, 83, 92, 96, 119–120, 123, 133, 172
transformation, 197, 201
transition, 32–33, 102, 105
truth, 211, 223, 229
utility, 26, 55, 172, 211, 229
variety, 152, 175, 184
di Bartolommeo, Michelozzo, 70–71
Diller + Scofidio (architects), 234
Dioscorides, 99
District of Columbia, 174
Dolmen, 13
domus, 23
Donnell garden (Sonoma), 215
Doric order, 6
Downing, Andrew Jackson, 189, 191
Dragon gate waterfall, 52–54
Dream of the Red Chamber, 165–166
du Cerceau, Jacques Androuet, 93
Duisborg-Nord Park (Ruhr valley), 223
Dumbarton Oaks (Georgetown), 207–208
Dutch gardens, 17th century, 133
Dutch styles, 97, 134–135, 151

E

Earl of Shaftesbury (Anthony Ashley Cooper), 151
Earth Day, 206, 222
Earth Goddess, 8
Earth(en) bridge, 104, 118
Earthworks, 136, 219
Eckbo, Garrett, 215–216
École des Beaux-Arts, 180
Ecological design, 222–223, 231–242
Edo (Tokyo), 51, 111
Effects of Good and Bad Government on the City and Countryside, 21
Eiffel Tower (Paris), 188
Eleusis (Greece), 8
Elysian fields (Stowe), 156–157
Emerald Necklace (Boston), 194
Enclosure Acts of Parliament, 151, 154
English garden style, 137, 173, 187
English gardens:
  16th century (Tudor and Elizabethan), 97–98
    common elements, 97
  17th century, 134–135
  18th century (landscape gardens), 151–163
    design elements, 153
    influential garden designers, 153
  19th century (Victorian), 181–185
  20th century, 224–225
  Chinese influence, 147, 152, 161
  design vocabulary, 106, 176, 202
English landscape garden, 110, 147, 151, 165, 172, 181, 190, 191, 201
Enlightenment, the, 99, 147, 150, 174–175, 177
Enshu, Kobori, 113, 118
Environmental art, 219
Epic of Gilgamesh, 4

INDEX

Equinox, 12
Ermenonville, 164, 190
Esfahan (Iran), 124–126
Exedra, 13, 80, 86, 127, 132
Expositions, International, 188, 198, 211–212, 234
Eyecatcher, 154

F
fabriques, 154, 164
Famous sights of Japan, 111
Farrand, Beatrix Jones, 207–208
Federal District. See District of Columbia
feng shui, 41
ferme ornée, 153, 172, 221
Feudalism:
    feudal system in England, 18
    feudal system in Western Europe, 21, 93
Finlay, Ian Hamilton, 224
Florence (Italy), 69, 79
Florilegium, 180
Flowery mead, 18, 22
Fontainebleau, 95, 137
Forbidden City, 65, 72, 165, 167
Form follows function, 211
Forthright, 97
Forty best views of the Yuanming Yuan, 167–168
Forum Esplanade (Barcelona), 235
Fountain Plaza (Portland), 218
Fouquet, Nicolas, 138
Four-square patterns:
    Pasargadae (Persia), 4
    Taj Mahal (Agra), 123
    See also chahar bagh and char bagh
Framed views:
    Amboise, 94
    as characteristic of Renaissance gardens, 79
    from the shoin, 54, 61, 103
    Gilpin's picturesque tours, 162–163
    orientation of Frascati villas, 127
    Shih Tzu Lin, 41
    Tenryu-ji, 51
    Villa Giulia, 88
    Wangshi Yuan, 170
Frascati villas, 127–129
French gardens and parks:
    16th century (Renaissance), 93–96
    17th century (classical), 136–144, 174, 217
    18th century, 164
    19th century (Second Empire), 186
    20th century, 226–227
    design vocabulary, 106, 146, 202
fronde, 137
Functionalism, 210, 229

G
Ganges River, 9
Garden festivals, 224
Garden of Cosmic Speculation (Dumfriesshire), 224
Garden of Eden, 99
Garden of Harmonious Interest (Yihe Yuan), 169
Garden of Harmony and Ease. See Yihe Yuan

Garden of Perfect Brightness. See Yuanming Yuan
Garden of the Master of the Fishing Nets. See Wangshi Yuan
Garden of Water and Light (Paris), 212
Garden suburb, 185
Garden theater(s), 127
Garden writing (literature), 181–182
Garden(s) of the simples, 99
Gardenesque, 163, 182, 184
Gas Works Park (Seattle), 223
Gen Yue, 41
Generalife (Granada), 30–31
Genius loci:
    Bodhi tree (India), 9
    cave at Eleusis (Greece), 8
    Crete, 8
    definition of, 12
    Delphi (Greece), 8
    Ganges River, 9
    islands of the Immortals (China), 9
    Mt. Fuji (Japan), 8
    Siwa oasis (Egypt), 9
Genius of the place, 151
Geoglyph(s), 3, 13
Geomantic principles, 39, 41, 47, 49
Geometric division of space:
    at Pasargadae (Persia), 4
    at the Alcazar (Seville), 35
    four-square gardens, 66–67, 145
    See also chahar-bagh
German Pavilion (Barcelona), 211
ghats, 9
giardino segreto, 71, 86
Gilded Age, 207–210
Gilpin, William, 162–163
Ginkaku-ji, 62, 102
Giverny (France), 180
Glasshouse(s), 181, 183, 227
glorieta, 28
Goethe, Johann Wolfgang von, 150
Goldsworthy, Andy, 219
Gomizuno-o, emperor, 116, 118
Gothic style, 18, 20
Granada (Spain), 28, 30
Grand tour(s), 151, 161
Gravity, 110
Great Stove (Chatsworth), 183
Greensward plan, 191
Gropius, Walter, 211, 215
Guevrekian, Gabriel, 212
Gustafson, Kathryn, 221, 236
Gwinn (Cleveland), 208–209

H
Haag, Richard, 223
Haddon Hall (Derbyshire), 97
Hadrian, emperor, 5, 7, 10
Hadrian's Villa (Tivoli), 5, 10–11, 81
Hagia Sophia (Constantinople), 18
Ha-ha, 153, 176
Halprin, Lawrence, 217–218
hameau, 164
Hampton Court (Middlesex), 98, 134–135
Han dynasty, 9
Hangzhou (China), 41–42, 118, 169

Hargreaves Associates, 232
Hatfield House (Hertfordshire), 134
Haussmann, Georges-Eugene, 186
Haussmann's plan of Paris, 186, 188
Heian period gardens, 48–50, 52
Heian-kyo. See Kyoto
Heliocentric iconography at Versailles, 141
Hellenistic principles of movement, 7
Henge, 2
Henry VIII, 97–98, 135
Herat (Afghanistan), 66–67, 100
Herbals, 99
herbarium, 23
Herman Miller Factory (Georgia), 233
Het Loo (Apeldoorn), 133
Hezar Jarib (Esfahan), 124
Hideyoshi, Toyotomi, general, 101–104, 111, 113
Hierarchy of space, examples of:
    Certosa di Pavia (Italy), 23
    Forbidden City (Beijing), 65
    Gilded Age estates, 207
    Momoyama castle towns, 101
    Palladian villas, 91
    Shalamar Bagh (Kashmir), 121
Highway Act of 1956, 206
Hogarth, William, 161
Hohokam canals, 18
Horns of consecration, 8
Horse Farm (San Cristobal), 221
hortus conclusus, 22, 71, 227
Hortus Palatinus (Heidelberg), 110
House of the Vettii (Pompeii), 4
Hudson River School, 196
Humanism, 15, 20, 68
    humanist allegories, 60
    humanist ideals, 20, 68–69
    humanist ideologies, 15, 70
Hunting parks:
    imperial Chinese, 28, 42
    Mesopotamian, 4
    Persian, 124
Hypnerotomachia Poliphili, 60, 69, 90

I
Ieyasu, Tokugawa, general, 111
Ile des Peupliers (Ermenonville), 164
Industrial Revolution, 177, 185, 196, 201
Informal style(s), 184
International Style, 211–212
Irrigation systems:
    Court of the Oranges (Cordoba), 29
    evidence at Samarra (Iraq), 18
    Hohokam canals (Native American), 18
    qanats, 124
Islands of the Immortals, 9, 39, 50, 52
Isola Bella (Lago Maggiore), 131–132
Isolotto (Boboli Gardens), 130–131
Istanbul (Turkey), 60
Italian gardens:
    15th century, 68–71
    16th century (Renaissance), 79–92, 154, 208
        characteristics of, 79
    17th century (Baroque), 127–132
    design vocabulary, 73, 106, 127, 146
Italian villa (concept of), 57, 69–71

J

Jahangir, 119, 121–122
Japanese gardens:
  Chinese influences, 47, 51–52, 118
  design vocabulary, 56, 73, 106
  6th–15th centuries:
    medieval, 45–54
    Nara period, 47
    Heian period, 48–50, 111
    Kamakura period, 51–54, 101
  15th century (Muromachi period), 61–64, 101
  16th century (Momoyama period), 101–104
    tea gardens, 102–103, 105, 111–112
    characteristics of, 104
  17th century (Edo period), 103, 111–118
    stroll gardens, 111–115, 145
jardin anglo-chinois, 161, 164
Jeanneret, Charles-Edouard. See Le Corbusier
Jefferson, Thomas, 150, 173–174, 180
Jekyll, Gertrude, 185, 207
Jensen, Jens, 222
Jesuit missionary(s), 152, 165, 168
Johanson, Patricia, 221

K

Kabul (Afghanistan), 100
Kaifeng (China), 41
Kamakura period gardens, 51–54
kami, 46
Kandinsky, Wassily, 216
kare sansui, 53–54, 57, 61–62, 72
Kashmir, 119–120
Katsura imperial villa (Katsura-rikyu), 107, 113–115
kawaramono, 61
Kent, William, 153–156, 158
Kew, royal gardens at, 162, 180
Khan, Kublai, 42, 44, 65
Kiley, Daniel Urban, 215, 217
Kinkaku-ji (Kyoto), 54, 62
kiva, 13
Knight, Richard Payne, 161–163
Knossos (Crete), palace at, 8
Knot gardens, 97–98
Korakuen (Koishikawa Korakuen, Tokyo), 118
Kunming Lake (Yihe Yuan), 169
Kyoto (Japan), 47, 49, 51, 54, 61, 101, 111–112

L

L'Enfant, Pierre Charles, 174, 210
Lake-and-island garden(s):
  Heian period, 50
  Kamakura period, 53
  medieval Chinese, 39
  Muromachi period, 62
  Nara period, 47
  prototypes, 9
Lake Dal (Kashmir), 119, 121–122
Land art, 219
Land Ordinance of 1785, 150
Landscape architect(s), 192, 209, 219, 221
Landscape architecture, 201, 203
Landscape gardener, 153
Landscape gardening, 153

Landscape painting:
  influence of
    on medieval Chinese gardens, 39–42,
    on medieval Japanese gardens, 51–52, 54
    on 15th century Japanese gardens, 61–62
    on 18th century English gardens, 151,
  Kano school, 101
  Neo-Romantic, 145
  Song dynasty, 41–42, 51–53, 61, 64
Le Corbusier, 212
Leasowes, the, (Warwickshire), 153–154, 164
LeBrun, Charles, 137–138, 140
LeNotre, Andre, 137–138, 140, 143, 151
Leonhardt Lagoon (Dallas), 221
LeVau, Louis, 137–138, 140
Levens Hall (Cumbria), 135
Ley lines, 2
Ligorio, Pirro, 79, 81
Limelight (Westonbrit), 224
Linear perspective, 68
Linnaeus, Carl, 150
Little Sparta (Lanarkshire), 224–225
locus amoenus, 22, 55
Loire Valley, 93
London (England), 110
Lorenzetti, Ambrogio, 21
Lorrain, Claude, 137, 151–152, 154
Loudon, Jane, 182
Loudon, John Claudius, 163, 181–182, 184
Louis XIV, 136–138, 140–143, 150, 157, 167
Louisiana Purchase, 189
Loyang palace garden, 38
Lurie Garden (Chicago), 236
Lutyens, Edwin, 185, 207

M

Machine de Marly, 141–142
Machine for living, 212
Maderno, Carlo, 127
Madinat al-Zahra (Cordoba), 29
maidan, 124, 126
Mannerist style, 79, 89–90, 110, 127
Manning, Warren, 208, 214, 217
Maritime theater, 10, 130
Marly, 141–142, 173
Mas de les Voltes (Spain), 221
Masaccio, 60
Masanobu, Kano, 101
Mathematics of infinity, 136, 140
Matsumoto castle (Kyoto), 101
Mattioli, Andrea, 99
McHarg, Ian, 222
McMillan Plan, 210
Medici family, 69
  Cosimo I, 130
  Cosimo the Elder, 69–71
  Lorenzo the Magnificent, 71
Medieval city(s), 18
Medieval gardens in Western Europe, 15–56
  common attributes, 22
  design vocabulary, 56
  sources of form, 21, 24–25
  See also Moorish gardens
Medieval mind-set, 18

menhir, 13
Mesa Verde, Colorado, 18
Meyer, David and Ramsey Silberberg, 224
Michelangelo, 88
Middleton Place (South Carolina), 150
miegakure, 112
Military engineering, influence on French gardens, 136
Millennium Park (Chicago), 236
Miller garden (Columbus, Indiana), 217
Ming dynasty, 40, 42, 60, 65, 170
Miniatures, 119
mirador, 28, 31, 32
Missions, 78
Modernism, 203, 211–218, 223
Mollet, Claude, 137
Mollet, Gabriel and Andre, 135
Monasteries, 20, 23
Montacute (Somerset), 98
Monteiro garden (Fernandes garden), 220
Monticello (Virginia), 173
Moorish gardens, 27–36
  attributes of, 28
  decorative patterns, 28
  design vocabulary, 56
  typical courtyard form, 28
  water management, 29
Moran, Thomas, 197
Morris, William, 185
Mount Auburn Cemetery (Cambridge, Massachusetts), 190
Mount Vernon (Virginia), 172
Mt. Fuji (Japan), 8, 111–112, 180
Mt. Vesuvius (Italy), 4
mudejar style, 34
Mughal empire, 119
Mughal gardens:
  16th century, 100, 105
  17th century, 119–123, 145
  design vocabulary, 146
Muir, John, 197
Muromachi period gardens, 53–54, 61–64
Muso Soseki (Muso Kokushi), 52–53

N

Naming, 154, 165, 170, 175
Napoleon III, 186
Nara period gardens, 47
Nara (Japan), 18, 47, 49
Narrative circuit, 154, 159
Narrative expression, 155
National Environmental Protection Act (1970), 222
National Forest Service, 197
National Park Service, 197
Naturalistic style, 153, 153, 158, 161, 173, 189, 222
Naumkeag (Stockbridge), 214
Nazca lines (Peru), 3
negotium, 69
New Grange (Ireland), 2
New York City, 191
Nicotinia, 110
Nishat Bagh (Kashmir), 121–122
Nobunaga, Oda, 101, 104, 111
nymphaeum, 10, 88, 127

O

Oblique perspective, 154
oculus, 7
Oil Crisis, 206
Olmsted, Frederick Law, 183, 187, 189–192, 197, 199–200, 241
omphalos, 8
Optical illusions, 128, 130, 145
Optics, laws of, 136, 138
Oracle of Amun (Egypt), 9
Orange County Great Park (Irvine), 241
orangerie, 95
Orto Botanico (Padua), 99
otium, 12
otium, 69
Outdoor living, 214–215
Overlay analysis, 222

P

pairidaeza, 67
palissades, 136
Palladian villas, 91, 173
Palladio, Andrea, 91
Panathenaic Way, 6
Pantheon (Rome), 7, 92, 173
paradeisos, 67
Paradise garden(s):
    depiction of, 5
    Islamic, 67, 119, 124–126, 145
    Japanese, 53, 103
    Pasargadae (Persia), 4
Parc André Citroën (Paris), 227–228
Parc de la Villette (Paris), 226
Parc des Buttes-Chaumont (Paris), 186–188
Paris (France), 186, 188
Park systems, 192, 194
Parterre(s), 79, 94, 168
parterres de broderie, 133, 135–136, 146
parterres de pieces coupées, 133
Participatory design, 223
Pasargadae (Persia), 4
Patio de la Acequia (Generalife), 31
patte d'oie, 135
Pavilion of the Arriving Moon and Wind (Wangshi Yuan), 170
Paxton, Joseph, 181, 183
Perception of nature, 15
Pere Lachaise Cemetery (Paris), 190
Peristyle, 4, 13
Peristyle garden(s):
    House of the Vettii (Pompeii, Italy), 5
    prototype for medieval cloister, 23
Persian gardens:
    17th century, 124–126
    design vocabulary, 146
Petrodvorets, 150
Philosophical retreats, 69
Physic garden(s), 23
piano nobile, 91, 97, 127, 130
Piano, Renzo, 240
Pictorial composition of space, 112, 154
Picturesque (style), 156, 162–163, 184, 190, 227
    movement, 151, 156
Pienza (Italy), 60
Pinchot, Gifford, 194

Pitti Palace (Florence), 130
place(s), 186
Plague, 18, 20
Platonic Academy, 70–71
Platt Residence (Cornish), 208
Platt, Charles A., 208–209
Pleasance, 22–23, 55
Pleasure gardens, 21, 66, 134
Pliny the Younger, 5, 68
Pliny's Seaside Villa (Italy), 5
Poetry, influence of:
    on English gardens, 151, 162
    on Japanese gardens, 46, 49, 101, 118
    on medieval Chinese gardens, 39–41, 43
polis, 12
Polo, Marco, 42, 44
Pond-and-island garden(s). See lake-and-island garden(s)
Pope, Alexander, 151
Poplar Forest (Virginia), 174
Postmodernism, 203, 223–228
Poussin, Nicolas, 110, 151, 154
Prairie style, 222
Preservation ethic, 197
presidios, 78
Processional axis, 6
Professional garden design(ers), 112, 153
Proportioning systems:
    Classical orders, 6
    Palladian, 91, 105
    Renaissance, 60
    Thomas Jefferson's, 174
    Vitruvian man, 60
Prospect Park (Brooklyn), 192–193
Provost, Alain and Gilles Clement, 227
Public park(s), 183, 186–187, 189, 201, 222
Public space, ideas of shaping, 6
pueblos, 78
Pyramids, 12

Q

qanat(s), 124, 126
Qianlong, emperor, 165, 167–169
Qin Shi Huangdi, emperor, 9
Qing dynasty, 42, 165, 167, 170

R

Ram Bagh (Agra), 100
Red books, 154
Redouté, Pierre-Joseph, 180
Reformation, '75, '79
Renaissance designers:
    inspired by ancient sources, 5, 7
    inspired by medieval sources, 18
Renaissance scholarship, 18
Repton, Humphry, 153, 156, 162–163, 181, 184
Revolution of taste, 147
Rikyu, Sen no, 101–102
Robinson, Charles Mulford, 210
Robinson, William, 184
Rock collecting, 41, 165
Rococo, 150, 161
roji, 102–103
Roman arch technology, 7
Roman de la Rose, 24–25
Roman design vocabulary, 10

Romanesque style, 20
Romantic views of nature, 110, 112, 185, 196–197, 201
Romanticism, 150, 164, 177
Rome (Italy), 12, 18, 75, 79
rond-points, 186
Roosevelt, Theodore, 197
Rousham (Oxfordshire), 154–155, 159
Rousseau, Jean-Jacques, 164, 190
Ruskin, John, 185
Ryoan-ji (Kyoto), 62–63

S

Sacred space. See *genius loci*
Sacro Bosco (Bomarzo), 90
Saiho-ji, 52–53, 62
Sakuteiki, 49, 53–54
Samarkand (Uzbekistan), 66–67, 100
Samarra (Iraq), 16, 18
Sambo-in (Kyoto), 103–104
samurai aesthetics, 51, 54
Scale, 31, 55, 137
Scenographic effects, 151
Schjetnan, Mario, 239
Scholar gardens, 40, 170
Scientific forestry, 194
Scoring the landscape, 217
Sea Ranch (Gualala), 218
Second Empire, 186, 201
Secret garden. See *giardino segreto*
Sento Gosho (Kyoto), 113, 118
Sequence of space:
    Bagh-e Vafa, 100
    Biltmore Estate, 195
    Boboli gardens, 131
    Chantilly, 144
    Chicago World's Fair, 200
    Court of the Oranges (Cordoba), 29
    Delphi, 8
    Dream of the Red Chamber, 166
    Hampton Court, 134
    Little Sparta, 225
    Nishat Bagh, 122
    Prospect Park, 193
    Roman de la Rose, 24–25
    Ryoan-ji, 63
    Saiho-ji, 52
    Stourhead, 160
    tea garden, 102
    Villa Aldobrandini, 129
    Villa Farnese, 87
    Villa Lante, 84–85
    Villa Noailles, 213
Serlio, Sebastiano, 79, 91, 95
Serpent Mound (Ohio), 18
Serpentine line of beauty, 154, 161, 175
Sesshu, 61
Seville (Spain), 28, 34
Shah Abbas I, 124, 126
Shah Abbas II, 126
Shah Jahan, 119–121, 123
shakkei, 54–55, 112, 116, 145
Shalamar Bagh (Kashmir), 120
Shambles, the, 18
shan shui, 39
Shenstone, William, 153–154

Shenyang Architectural University Campus
  (Liaoning Province), 237
Shih Tzu Lin (Suzhou), 38, 41
shimenawa, 46
shinden-zukuri, 48, 50, 54, 116
Shinto shrines, 46
Shipman, Ellen, 209
shoin, 61, 103
shoin-zukuri, 54, 113
Shugaku-in (Kyoto), 113, 116–117
Shurcliff, Arthur, 171
Sight lines, 95, 105, 127, 145, 173–174,
  208–209
Silk Route, 66
Site planning principles:
  14th century treatise of Ibn Luyun, 31
  Palladio's, 91
  Pliny the Younger's, 68
Siwa oasis (Egypt), 9
Smith, Ken, 241
Smithson, Robert, 219
Soami, 62
Social reform, 189, 196, 201
Solstice, 2, 12
Song dynasty, 41–43, 54
Song of Solomon, 22
Songlines, 2
Spatial illusions. *See* optical illusions
Spiral Jetty (Salt Lake), 219
Spontaneous beauty, 165
Spring of Khosrow carpet, 5
St. Gall, plan of, 21
Steele, Fletcher, 214
stoa poekile, 10
Stonehenge (England), 2
Stourhead (Wiltshire), 152, 159–160
Stowe (Buckinghamshire), 154–158
Stroll garden(s), 104
Stylistic controversy, 154, 161–163, 184–185
Sublime, the, 161–163, 165
Subscription plots, 183
Suburban villas, 181
Sui dynasty, 38
Summer Palace. *See* Yihe Yuan
Sun King, 107, 141
Sunset Magazine, 215
Sustainability, 223, 231, 241
Suzhou (China), 40, 169–170
Symbolic geometry, 67
Symbolism of plants, 43

T

Taj Mahal (Agra), 107, 120, 123
talar, 124–126, 146
Tale of Genji, 49
Tang dynasty, 39–41
Tanner fountain (Cambridge,
  Massachusetts), 223–224
Tanner Spring Park (Portland, Oregon), 238
tapis vert, 138, 227
Taste, 189

tatami, 54, 103
Tea ceremony, 101–103
temenos, 8, 12
tempietto (Rome), 79
Temple of British Worthies (Stowe), 154
Temple of Fortuna Primigenia (Palestrina), 7,
  80–81
Temple of Hatshepsut (Deir el-Bahri), 6
Tenochtitlan (Mexico), 18, 60
Tenryu-ji, 51–53
Teotihuacan (Mexico), 7
Theater, garden as, 96
tholos, 8, 13
Timur (Tamerlane), 66, 119
Timurid garden cities, 66–67
Tivoli (Italy), 81
tokonoma, 54, 103
Tomb garden(s), 119–120, 123
Tomb of Nebamun (Thebes), 4
topos, 12
torii, 46
Torres and Lapena (architects), 235
Tradescant, John, 134
Transcendentalists, 196, 201
Tray landscapes, 61, 72
Tribolo, Niccolo, 130
Tschumi, Bernard, 226
tsuboniwa, 111
Tulips, 78, 133–134
Tunnard, Christopher, 214
Turtle and crane islands, 50, 54
Turtle island(s), 52, 113, 118

U

Ukiyo-e, 180
Unicorn tapestries, 21
University of Bologna, 18
Urban planning, 200
Uruk (Iraq), 4
Utens, Giusto, 69, 130

V

Vale of Tempe, (Hadrian's Villa), 10
van der Rohe, Ludwig Mies, 211
Van Valkenburgh, Michael, 224, 233
Varanasi (India), 9
Vasari, Giorgio, 88, 130
Vaux, Calvert, 190–192
Vaux-le-Vicomte, 137–139, 143
Versailles, 107, 137–143, 157, 167, 173
Victorian garden styles, 154
Viewing gardens, 212
Villa Aldobrandini (Frascati), 127–129
Villa d'Este (Tivoli), 81
Villa Emo (Fanzolo), 91–92
Villa Farnese (Caprarola), 82, 86–87
Villa Giulia (Rome), 88–89
Villa Lante (Bagnaia), 82–83, 86–87
villa marittima, 5
Villa Medici at Careggi, 70
Villa Medici at Fiesole, 71

Villa Noailles (Hyeres), 212–213
Villa Rotonda (Vicenza), 92, 173
Villa Savoye, 212
villa suburbana, 69–70, 88
villeggiatura, 69, 127
Viottolone (Boboli gardens), 130–131
viridarium, 23
Vista, 62, 68, 134, 137, 145, 151
Visual frames, 154
von Bell, Johann Adam Schall, 165

W

Walker, Peter, 223–224
Walled gardens, 18–26
  types of medieval, 22–23
  uses and symbolism of, 22–23
  See also hortus conclusus
Walpole, Horace, 151
Wang Chuan, 40
Wangshi Yuan, (Suzhou), 170
Wardian case(s), 181
Washington, DC, 210
Washington, George, 172
Wei, Wang, 40
West 8 (landscape architects), 234
Wheat Walk (Davis), 224
White City. *See* World's Columbian Exposition
Wigginton, Ron, 224
Wilderness aesthetic, 189, 196–197
William and Mary, 133–135, 171
Williamsburg (Virginia), 171
Woodhenge, 2
Works Progress Administration, 206
World of Tomorrow, 206
World's Columbian Exposition, 198–201, 210
Wren, Christopher, 110, 135
Wudi, emperor, 9

X

Xueqin, Cao, 165

Y

Yangdi, 38, 47
Yellowstone Act of 1872, 196
Yihe Yuan (Beijing), 169
yin and yang, 39
Yosemite, 196–197
Yu, Kongjian and Lin Shihong (landscape
  architects), 237
Yuan dynasty, 42, 65
Yuan Yeh, 110
Yuanming Yuan (Beijing), 167–168, 180

Z

zazenseki, 52
Zen gardens, 62, 73
Zen-ami, 61
zenana, 121–122
Zhao Ji, emperor, 41
Ziggurat, 13